ADVICE to the SEALORN

BY THE SAME AUTHOR

Blown Away
You Can't Blow Home Again

For Dean
S/V The Wanderin' Star

ADVICE to the

SEALORN

HERB PAYSON

Herb Payson 1999

S

SHERIDAN HOUSE

*To our sons and daughters, who continue to lead me
as best they can toward enlightenment;
and to our grandchildren,
who are almost ready to receive the baton.*

First published 1997 by
Sheridan House Inc.
145 Palisade Street
Dobbs Ferry, NY 10522

Library of Congress Cataloging-in-Publication Data

Payson, Herb.
    Advice to the sealorn / Herb Payson.
        p.   cm.
    Includes bibliographical references (p. 337–338) and index.
    ISBN 1-57409-002-X
    1. Sailing.   I. Title.
GV811.P345   1997
797.1' 24—dc21   97-28086
                                              CIP

Project editor: Janine Simon
Designer: Jeremiah B. Lighter

Printed in the United States of America

ISBN 1-57409-002-X

ACKNOWLEDGMENT

I want to thank Dan Spurr and Tom Linskey for their invaluable suggestions; Lothar and Janine Simon for patient and perceptive editing; and the many others who provided input on a smaller scale. I'm especially grateful to my wife Nancy, both for her many contributions, and for the equanimity with which she dealt with my preoccupation.

I have a daughter who used to be a potter, and who, when the glazing went wrong, would call her creations fah-cups. ('Fah' is the ancient Morondian word for a mistake—my grandkids call them boo-boos.) There may be an overlooked fah-cup or two in the following pages. If so, they are mine. However, inasmuch as one of the secrets of satori is forgiveness, I'm hoping that you, the reader, will forgive my fah-cups as I forgive those who have fah-cupped against me.

Contents

CHAPTER 1

Everyone Was a Beginner Once

Dear Herb: Why yet another book on cruising—aren't there dozens of them already on the bookstore shelves?

Sleepy in Seattle

Dear Sleepy: Well you might ask. We have talked about this before, and in the end the answer is always the same. Just as there is always room for another cookbook, there is always room for another book about long distance cruising. Not only is it a matter of updating information on equipment, but each writer has a different point of view on a lot of critical topics.

I remember when Nancy and I were conspiring to defect from suburbia and go cruising. We sought inspiration in every article, every book on the subject that we could get our hands on. Sure, we were searching for information, but we were also looking for soul mates. Contemplating casting off one deeply ingrained life style for another, we needed nourishment and encouragement. Not only does the process get more complex as the years go by, but hosts of friends make it their personal business to tell you how crazy you are.

Don't you remember, Sleepy, how confused and alone you felt when you first started dreaming about sailing to far away shores? I sure do. And I remember being grateful for anything that reminded me that I was not alone in my quest. Together, Nancy and I soaked up gallons of information. Sure, after we had been out cruising for awhile we came up with our own techniques, and even though these often were different from and even preferable to what we'd read about in the books by experts, those books were crucial in getting us started.

There are only a few cruising theorems, if you will. Immutable dicta, such as "reduce sail when the wind pipes up to where the wife can't stop screaming," could all be contained in a pamphlet which might be called "The Straight Scoop." Most so-called rules, however, are subject to discussion. An example might be: In this age of GPS, is learning celestial navigation necessary? The ideas generated by this question involve more

1

than tales of cases when both the principal and the backup GPS units failed on the same passage. More important to me are matters of aesthetics, and the fulfillment and, yes, even revelation that come with getting acquainted with the heavens.

So, sure, we'll talk about roller furling, Stoway masts, GPS, multihulls, and other controversial subjects. And what we hope to come up with are intriguing notions, varied opinions, ideas, assuming that if you're motivated enough to read and imaginative enough to dream, all you need is the raw material for making your own decisions.

Not all of the ideas will be mine. Some come from other cruisers we've interviewed. Our objective is a symposium, not a soap box.

Recently at a national sailboat show a member of the marine industry threw a party. The theme was, come for wine and food with cruising gurus Lin and Larry Pardey (okay so far), Donald Street (still okay), a couple named Jessie (of whom I'd never heard but who might very well be the guruest), and Nancy and Herb Payson (I felt they were really reaching here). People paid to come, eat, drink wine, and pick our brains—for five minutes at the most, we were instructed. Then we must move on.

Strangely enough, it worked, although touching base at as many tables as possible forced us to keep the chats too short. It was exhausting trying to compress our thoughts into at least one worthwhile idea that people could take with them and mull over, while at the same time responding to their input.

In retrospect, I probably gained more from that party than the people I talked to. Reminded of what it was like to be green, I finally was able to see how far I'd come from our first faltering steps. Maybe I could pass something of value on to others.

Life finds ways to keep us humble. We were anchored at Isleta, an island just off Fajardo on the east end of Puerto Rico. We'd moved to more remote, clearer water so that I could scrub a year's accumulation of marine ecology from RED SHOES' bottom. A guy swam over, and asked if I was Herb Payson. When I told him I was, he said "You are the reason I went cruising."

"Oh?" I said, really worried. I remembered that 20 years ago, when our old wooden boat was stranded in French Polynesia, I spotted John Samson, whose book *The New Way of Life* was part of our inspiration, walking along the quay toward us. My first remark to this man whom I'd never met was, "You SOB, you got us into this, now you damn well better get us out." He roared with laughter, and a half-bottle of Scotch later we were friends.

So here was this swimmer, telling me that I was the reason he went cruising. Was I about to be thanked, blamed, sued?

"Yeah," he continued. "I read your book *Blown Away*—laughed a lot—and when I was finished, I figured 'if that asshole can do it, so can I.'"

We were all beginners once. My pledge, as we work our way through the subjects that follow, is to remember that.

As a point of departure, each chapter will begin with a paraphrase of a question that people have asked us in letters and at seminars. Many will be in a light vein, because if I stop having fun with this I'm going to quit. We get the same questions over and over, so there's no need to hang them on individuals. If you should recognize a question of your own that now strikes you as dumb, don't take it personally. It could well have been drawn from the list of questions we ourselves were asking 25 years ago, when cruising was no more than a dream, and its horizon infinitely distant.

SO YOU THINK YOU CAN'T DO IT?

I have an only brother who at age 38 was stricken with Guillain-Barré's syndrome, a paralytic disease similar to polio, except that most patients recover fully. Mike didn't, and now walks with knee braces and elbow crutches to compensate for his wasted muscles. We've had him and his wife, Barbara, on board RED SHOES several times. To get aboard from the dinghy, Mike has to stand, no mean feat. But because he can no longer crawl, he has to lay his upper body face down on the side deck, and then kind of wiggle his hips till he can roll over and sit up. I know he feels it's undignified, but he'd rather suffer it than stay home.

He can't take things for granted like we do. Our marine head has a pedal you're supposed to operate with your foot. Mike has to get down and operate it with his hand. He has significantly diminished arm strength. He exercises daily to keep what muscles he has in good shape.

Sounds like a candidate for cruising? Nope, not to me either. So what do Mike and Barbara do but buy a half interest in a Nonsuch 30, and cruise the coast of Maine each summer. He's lucky, of course, to have Barbara, a capable and adventurous woman, to crew for him. But Mike is skipper, and for the most part sails the boat. He's far from being along just for the ride.

A special place in my heart is also reserved for a certain heroine. When I met her, she was in the cockpit of her trimaran. She was totally unselfconscious about being nude in front of a stranger, and I wondered why she hadn't covered up when I arrived, as did the other two women that were there. Then I realized she was blind. She had had normal sight when she and her significant other began building the trimaran that would take them on their dream cruise. Then her vision became impaired, and the doctors told her the deterioration was irreversible. As she gradually went blind, you can imagine the agonizing she and her man went through.

Finally she told him, "We've worked and dreamed, let's go ahead. It'll be different, but it'll be our dream, and not one we've merely read about."

They were in the Cook Islands of the South Pacific when we met them. They'd sailed there from Hawaii. One day we went out on the reef together. While we walked carefully, wearing protective shoes, she felt ahead with her bare hands as she crawled. We would 'show' her a shell, place it in her hands, and she would memorize it with touch. Occasionally her hand would find a spiny sea urchin before we could warn her. No pain, no gain, she'd say, and continue crawling the reef.

Remembering her, I have to think of what fellow cruiser Mary Richards said: "Life is a series of adventures for those with the courage to explore."

It's easy to think that such people are special, that we could never be like them. But I'll bet my life that before their disability, they never thought they could do it, either. One thing's for sure, they aren't looking for praise or pity. They're having adventures, and in so doing, they're inspiring the rest of us to transcend our excuses.

And now we'll talk about how.

GETTING STARTED

Recently we got a letter from a prospective cruiser who lived in one of those desert states like Nevada. Both he and his partner were professionals, earning good incomes. Neither knew much about sailing, let alone ocean cruising. But cruising to exotic and distant ports was something they wanted to do. The letter ended with a kind of plea: "If you, Herb, were just beginning to follow your dream—in our shoes, as it were—yet knowing what you know now, what would you be doing?"

This is a difficult one. My financial history could be called *The Razor's Edge*. I spend what I earn plus 10%, and dig myself out of the pits with an occasional lucky strike. Whereas most people plan for tomorrow, I assume that tomorrow may never come. My biggest enemy is boredom, and my biggest fear is that life may stop being fun. So far this hasn't happened.

To most people financial security is important. They will hang onto life insurance, investments, and other bulwarks against poverty, a tactic which, had we followed it, would have precluded our going. What we had to do was liquidate everything and spend the proceeds on a boat.

A middle class upbringing never prepared me for the feelings of loss I had after opting to fly in the face of financial common sense. We sold all the toys—cars, trailerable speed boat, water skis. We sold all the equipment from our flyer into private enterprise—the tanks and filters of our aquarium business. Rent-a-Fish, Inc. never made it big, but it was a wonderful way to pay for what had been an expensive hobby. We cashed in my life insurance policy, sold our stock. We had a garage sale that included the garage. We got a bridge loan to buy our boat, and then we sold our home!

For a while we had nightmares, but gradually the feeling of falling into a black hole disappeared, and a certain light-heartedness took over. Some fellow Californians dubbed it air-headedness. Security, we told each other, was a matter of attitude. The nightmares went away, and visions of palm trees danced in our heads.

At the end of our seven-year cruise, which I wrote about in two books, *Blown Away*, and *You Can't Blow Home Again*, we came back with only the shirts on our backs, but with a paid-for cruising boat that had doubled in value. The only trouble was, the price of California real estate had increased tenfold. So we opted for Maine, where I grew up, and where real estate prices had yet to be filled with helium. During the seven years we lived there, our little three-unit Victorian conversion more than doubled in value. We sold in October of '87, right at the height of the market—not because we were smart, or even intuitive, but because we'd acquired RED SHOES, our present boat, a Crealock 34 made by Pacific Seacraft, a California manufacturer, and we felt more secure with our money invested in mutual funds.

I said we'd acquired, not bought RED SHOES. But that's another story.

During the time we lived in Maine, SAIL Magazine, which had signed me on as a regular contributor, agreed to help us with a project: to buy a motor home and trailer a pocket cruiser (sailboat, of course) across the country, cruising all the lesser known lakes, rivers and canals along the way. Nancy and I bought the motor home and contributed our time as well as our writing and photographing abilities. SAIL provided us with the boat trailer, and arranged for several small boat manufacturers to lend us boats.

We started out with an O'Day 22, in which we cruised (and by cruising we mean more than three days, usually at least a week) in Moosehead Lake, Maine; Lake Champlain, Vermont; Lake George, Great Sacandaga, Cayuga, and Seneca Lakes, New York; Cave Run, Lake Barkley, and Kentucky Lake, Kentucky; Lake of the Ozarks, Missouri; Lake Texoma, Texas/Oklahoma; and Sam Rayburn Lake, Texas. In Los Angeles we picked up a Laguna 23 and cruised in the man-made lakes of the Colorado River (Meade, Havasu and Powell), as well as in the Gulf of California.

Approaching Bahia de Los Angeles, with a 23-foot motor home towing a 23-foot boat.

In Idaho in the Coeur d'Alène and Pend Oreille lakes we sailed a San Juan 20 and a San Juan 23. Another San Juan 23 took us through the San Juan Islands in Washington. For lakes Harrison and Quesnel in British Columbia, and Great Slave Lake in the Northwest Territories of Canada, and for Lake of the Woods, we had the use of a 22-foot S-2. One of the results of the exposure we gave these lucky manufacturers in feature articles in national magazines was that two of them promptly went out of business.

In the beginning it was all work and little play because we were new at stepping masts and rigging small sailboats. But as we learned, our feelings about the project improved as well. Now, looking back, we feel that the 14 months and 26,000 miles of driving and cruising in over two dozen bodies of water made for one of our greatest sailing experiences. There is no greater danger than a full gale on a big lake in a small boat. There is no greater fright than weathering 70-knot winds at anchor off a deserted island in Baja California. There is no greater adventure than exploring a 300-mile, only partially charted lake, such as Great Slave Lake, in a wilderness just 200 miles south of the Arctic Circle. And there is no greater satisfaction than surviving, in our 22-foot mobile home towing a 25-foot boat trailer, rush hour traffic in Montreal.

About sailing in small boats: Nancy loved it. The immediate feedback from luffing, from too much sail, from wandering attention, taught her more about sailing in a year than she'd learned in seven years of ocean cruising in the South Pacific on our 36-foot, 27,000-pound wooden ketch. SEA FOAM was a grand old lady, but her responses made the sprint of a tortoise seem like the flight of a scared rabbit. Sailing a small boat is the best and quickest way to acquire the 'feel' of wind and wave.

In spite of our trailer-sailer trip, of many generous charter assignments for the magazine, and of the use of friends' sailboats during the Maine summer, we became restless with land living. Here is how we managed, for the second time in our lives, to move from land to the cruising life.

And after all, wasn't that the question?

HOW WE GOT STARTED WITH *RED SHOES*

After we sold SEA FOAM, our seven years on land were for the most part no more profitable financially than our earlier ventures had been. At a Long Beach boat show, Nancy met Henry Morschladt and Mike Howarth, the young owners of a Southern California boat manufacturing company called Pacific Seacraft. After Nancy told them about our trailer-sailer trip, they said, "Next time you have a project in mind, please let us know. We'd like to be part of it." (Part of it? Huh. They didn't know Nancy.)

Back in Maine, Nancy went on to become a florist. I was writing articles and rehabbing our three-unit Victorian. There came a time when Nancy and I looked at each other and said, "This is all very well, but wouldn't we rather be cruising?" The answer was yes.

But in what? Our prospects for buying a decent cruising boat ranged from nil to zip. Then we remembered Pacific Seacraft. We called Henry and Mike, a team that was already the twentieth century's answer to

Unstepping the mast of *Bittersweet*. Our first effort took us a half day, but within weeks we had it down to 30 minutes.

Nancy sailing the S-2. The feedback in a small sailboat is the best sailing teacher there is.

Horatio Alger. From a bankrupt backyard operation turning out one model, the Flicka, their company had paid off every debt and was now building seven or eight different models. I reminded them of their request—that if we should embark on another project, would we please include them? They remembered.

"We're thinking of exploring the coast, sailing up and down U.S. rivers, maybe daring the Bahamas." Fine with them. "We're thinking in terms of two to three years." Dandy. They were thinking of something of about 20 feet. We were thinking more along the lines of 37 feet. After a trip to California and some unrealistic projections by us, we ended up with RED SHOES, a Crealock 34, now Pacific Seacraft's most popular model.

We've never sailed RED SHOES up even one U.S. river, and we've had the use of her for nine years. Pacific Seacraft has received invaluable exposure. We live like kings on a nothing budget. Pacific Seacraft gets the benefit of our small talents. We do work that we enjoy.

On the subject of work: a Maine woman who worked with Nancy in the flower shop heard that we were being sent by *SAIL* to the Virgin Islands on an all-expense paid two-week charter in order to write a feature for the magazine. "That's double dippin'," she said vehemently. Angrily. Accusingly. And in spite of Nancy's explanations—that this was the way I earned what the census has determined to be a below-the-poverty-level income—she insisted that because it was fun and we enjoyed it, it was double dippin'. In Maine you're not supposed to enjoy your work. If you find something that's fun and that you also get paid to do, you should either quit or tear up your paycheck.

After that, Nancy never dared tell Ms. DoubleDip how much she loved being a florist.

WHAT OTHER PEOPLE HAVE DONE

We know a guy who built his own ferro-cement cruising yacht. He worked in a building materials yard and stole every bit of the stuff that went into his boat. He and his family were Catholic, and each Sunday, in any port with a Catholic church, his wife and three daughters would march off to mass. How she managed starched pinafores and huge broad-brimmed hats on a 30-foot boat crewed by two adults and three children is more than I can figure.

A good friend of mine recently gave NUNKI, his 40-foot ferro-cement sloop to a young couple who wanted to go cruising. He explained his generosity thus: "Home-built ferro-cement boats sell for a fraction of the price of boats of similar size in fiberglass. Even older, well-maintained wooden boats bring far higher prices." The reason for this is that ferro-cement boats are almost impossible to survey for hull integrity. In spite of the depressed prices of ferro-cement boats, a fact which is common knowledge in the business, the state of Washington wanted to tax my

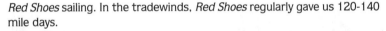

Red Shoes sailing. In the tradewinds, *Red Shoes* regularly gave us 120-140 mile days.

friend a flat fee for a 40-foot sloop based on length—and a value of $100,000.

The amount my friend would have had to pay was roughly equal to the boat's full market value, so he balked. He'd met two young people who were enthusiastic about ocean cruising and offered them the boat for free. This included the equipment, the charts—everything but the tools.

Naturally the couple was ecstatic. Inexperienced sailors, they asked my friend to sail with them from Washington to San Francisco. During the trip they were hit by a freighter in the fog. The freighter never slowed, let alone stopped, and failed to answer my friend's repeated calls on VHF Channel 16. Monitoring Channel 16 while at sea is the law. The damage to my friend's boat was serious but not disabling, and he was able to make it into port safely. The shipping company finally paid an amount far greater than the cost of repairs, so that the lucky couple not only received a free boat and invaluable experience, but they ended up with a substantial cruising kitty as well.

A hippie-crewed schooner, a hogged, rotted out, communally owned wooden hulk cruised the South Pacific on a nothing budget. Each person paid so much per week, and each took a turn being skipper. With continual crew changes to a degree that made the immigration authorities' heads spin, the schooner made it to New Zealand. Its main claim to fame was an abundance of nude bodies and an ambiance of Hawaiian gold.

A fellow took 'think small' to its limits, and attempted to sail around the world in a 9-foot boat. He made it to the Cook Islands, but after leaving Aitutaki he was never heard from again.

There are others: The Canadian who built his own hard-chine steel boat in Tahiti. . . The adventurer who earned the money for his first boat by hunting alligators in Malaysia. . . The fellow who was buying his boat on time payments. When things got rough for him financially, he just sailed away. His boat was repossessed in mid-dream.

Literally legions bought boats and cruised with a payment book stapled to the cover of the ship's log, and consequently struggled to meet the exorbitant premiums of yacht insurance for world cruisers. For them, cruising was hardly the laid-back experience we all dream about.

There are many different ways to get started. Some are more effective than others. If I remember rightly, you asked me, if I were in your shoes, knowing what I know now, what would I do? Not an easy question, but we'll give it a shot. Read on for some customized suggestions.

CHAPTER 2

Really Getting Started

Dear Herb: We've been sailing BUFFALO CHIP, our MacGregor 26, in Lake Roosevelt, Arizona, but we long for wider horizons. I'm fifty-eight years old. My wife is fifty. What are the pitfalls? What should we be doing to get ready?

George and Georgine

Dear George and Georgine: I love to answer letters like yours, and I always wonder what happens later. Did they act on their dream?

I often hear "It's too good to leave," when the job you hold and the income you make are more than you care to walk away from. This usually comes up when the couple is split in their goals—he wants to cruise now, she doesn't want to quit her job, or vice versa.

Once past that, the two biggest enemies are procrastination (we're getting ready, we're not ready yet, oh dear we'll never be ready) and money. You, George, are 13 years older than I was when Nancy and I sold everything and bought an old wooden sailboat. Advancing age, it seems, makes it more difficult to cash in one's chips (financial, not buffalo). You realize that your earning years are growing short, and if this expensive dream is all a terrible mistake, what do you do next? Right now, at age 69, I'm supporting cruising by writing, but it took 20 years to get to that point.

It would all be easier for you if you had enough money to keep a pied-à-terre—a condo, a car, and your precious insurance. If not, the only thing to do is hold your nose and jump.

I spent a lot of my youth on the water, although most of it on power boats rather than sail. I acquired seamanship, and more confidence than good sense. Nancy had no experience whatsoever, so we chartered a Mariner 32 in Newport Beach, California, and sailed to Mexico for two weeks. I partied with her enough that she decided she liked the life, and over 20 years later we are still at it. She learned photography and I learned to write. She learned sailing and I learned patience (although not perfectly).

Here are some suggestions:

Get in touch with the head of one of the blue water sailing schools. Tell him where you're headed, and take one or more of the courses he suggests. I can recommend Steve Colgate, who runs the Offshore Sailing School in Florida.

Join the SSCA. For a nominal fee you become an associate member of a group of liveaboard sailors for whom cruising is paramount. The SSCA Bulletin is published monthly and contains priceless, up-to-date information, letters from cruisers who are out there living your dream.

To keep your interest up while negotiating the potholes of dream realization, read, saturation mode, books about the places you want to visit. Read books of voyages—those by Joshua Slocum, Miles Smeeton, the Hiscocks, Tristan Jones, Lin and Larry Pardey, Hal and Margaret Roth among others. Be sure to read Hiscock's *Cruising Under Sail*, and *Heavy Weather Sailing* by K. Adlard Coles. Study *Ocean Passages of the World* for advice on seasonal passagemaking. Buy for your library what is still the best book bargain, *Bowditch American Practical Navigator*, where you'll learn all about hurricanes and other stuff. The book is kept up to date by the U.S. Navy. Steve Dashew has written a couple of books—lots of good info, and good to read after this book for different opinions on many topics (he's into big boats); a more recent valuable addition is Jim Howard's *The Handbook of Offshore Cruising*. See if you can dredge up a copy of a book that fueled our fires, an out-of-print jewel called *The New Way of Life* by John Samson of ferro-cement boat fame. The book is fun, with a lot of helpful suggestions. And read my two earlier books, which recount the troubles of a learn-as-you-go cruising family.

Learn celestial navigation, even though electronics have made it obsolete. It's humbling to become familiar with the sky. Use a nav calculator—no need to give priceless space to multiple volumes of sight reduction tables.

Get a ham radio license. We've found that with many cruising couples the woman has taken to the radio like great grandma took to the old rural telephone party line. Regular electronic klatches called 'nets' provide not only up-to-date info but also the gossip we call "keeping up with our friends." I heartily recommend that the mate makes it her job to get a ham license, as a typical distaff objection to cruising is being out of touch.

Your MacGregor 26 has served you well by getting you out on the water, but you need to graduate to a stronger and perhaps larger vessel for ocean voyaging. Our boat is a Pacific Seacraft designed by William B. Crealock. Other great cruising boats include but aren't limited to the Hans Christian; Valiant (but don't buy one that was made during their bad blister years); Cabo Rico; Shannon. Keep an eye on sailing magazines, because they sometimes run articles on good buys in older, used cruising boats. For example, a Columbia 50 would be super, if you can find one. A more modest choice would be an Alberg 35 or 37. For a motor sailer consider the Cal 2-46.

There are boats not to buy—talk to a yacht surveyor and learn what they are, and then get a second opinion. Depending on where you want to cruise, some boats are use-specific: if you'll mostly cruise the East Coast and the Bahamas, you might consider a shallow draft boat such as a Pacific Seacraft, Island Packet, or perhaps a larger medium draft boat such as the Whitby 42. Another shallow draft choice might be one of the many multihulls. However, crossing oceans suggests having the strongest and best boat you can afford, and that still means to me a well-designed monohull. Nancy wants to know, "Why do they build trimarans with trap doors in the bottom?" And what prompted a trimaran skipper in the Sea of Cortez to name his boat THIS SIDE UP, complete with arrows?

By all means, network—talk your dream, take notes, and act.

Are you a do-it-yourselfer? You'd best think about becoming one. The biggest reason people learn to maintain and repair their own yachts is money. An even more important reason, however, is that most things break when you're miles from skilled help.

Large men should be particularly careful that the boat they choose offers sufficient access to all quarters. For engine and system repairs on smaller boats, you're better off if you're a gnome with rubber joints. Recently, aboard RED SHOES, curled up in the engine compartment, I looked aft and saw a broken hose clamp. It was one of three that secure the hose that holds the gland for the rudder post, and it had rusted till it had simply come apart. And if one fails, can the others be far behind? Time to replace.

Try as I would, however, I could not get my 5'8", 190 pounds in position to do the job. Whom did the manufacturers hire to install the clamps in the first place—dwarves? Or did they unfairly assemble the rudder post gland before putting the deck in place?

I told my story to an acquaintance, asking if he knew anyone small enough that I might hire to do the job. He was small, he admitted, and offered to do it. I watched him work, passed him clamps, screwdrivers, encouragement. Even for him, a slender man of less than average height, it was difficult and uncomfortable to get into position. But he managed, lying between two through-hull fittings, to get three new clamps in place and tighten them. Had I hired a large man to do the job, we would have ended by taking a Sawzall to our afterdeck.

One of the advantages in servicing and maintaining your own boat is that you get around and see things. Had I not been maintaining my engine, my first discovery of the failed hose clamps on the rudder shaft gland might have been at sea—on it or under it.

You'll hear people complaining about how hard it is to maintain a boat. We'll talk more about maintenance in later chapters. All I wish to say here is that maintaining a boat, to me, is at least as satisfying as maintaining a house or garden; and that anyone who is even moderately skillful with his or her hands can learn to do most repair and maintenance tasks on his own yacht.

The mystique about cruising is nonsense—it's a lot easier than most Old Salts would have you believe. But you do need to learn the basics so that they become second nature. After that you need inventiveness and common sense.

Still want to sail into the sunset? Find your own little bay in some exotic tropical island? Snorkel among coral castles with brilliantly colored fish? Be caressed by gentle trade winds? Enjoy a tall, cool one while relaxing in the cockpit of your boat-home, anchored behind an atoll's coral reef?

If so, let's continue.

CHAPTER 3

Destinations

Dear Herb: There are so many wonderful places to voyage to on a yacht. How did you pick your destinations? And how did reality measure up to your expectations? My husband's all for cruising, and I'm all for him, but I'm worried that after all the work and investment he'll be disappointed.

Concerned And Loving Mate

Dear CALM: We sailed RED SHOES to the Amazon, and cruised there for three months. We cruised mostly in the huge ganglion of streams that lace the delta between the Para River and the Amazon.

We had been in Antigua enjoying Race Week when a friend who makes normally aggressive folks seem like they're on valium brought up the Amazon. There was a boat in Antigua that had just crossed the Atlantic and had all the charts. We're going, she said, and you might as well have copies of the charts just in case you decide to go, too.

I consider myself a weathervane, as I usually feel that going with the flow is easier than making decisions. But where waterfalls and rapids exist, going with the flow is far from tranquil. Cruising the Amazon, and getting there, were both highly stressful.

"I want to go," said Nancy.

"You have no idea what you're letting yourself in for," I told her.

"It's only 600 miles," said our proselytizing friend. She was only off by 1300 miles—at least the way we sailed.

"It's all to weather," I pointed out.

"I've always wanted to see the Amazon," said Nancy, who, when she fastens onto an idea, will brook no objections, real (they exist) or imagined (usually mine).

We paid for copies of the charts, and I put the whole ridiculous idea out of my mind. Don Street, when he heard about our plans, said the only smart way to do it was to sail to the Azores, south to the Canaries, and then west with the trades. I thought the best way to do it was not at all, and bought Nancy a National Geographic in hopes it would be enough. All it did was fertilize the beanstalk of her determination.

From Antigua we sailed south to St. Lucia, where we both caught dengue fever. Our friends set off for the Amazon without us, but had to put into Kourou, French Guiana, because of a sick pet.

"They're too far ahead of us," I said.

"If we go now, we can catch them," said Nancy, "depending on how soon their cat recovers."

I agreed to sail as far as Barbados, and there we'd reconsider. Our radio wasn't working, but I'd heard there was a competent Icom man on the island. Wrong. Unfortunately for my campaign of caution, we had an easy crossing. My next excuse was we had no short wave radio telephone, and I refused to go without one. However the guy in Barbados offered to take my radio in trade and give me for $400 one just like it, except that it was working. So now we had a radio and I had no more excuses.

From Barbados to Brazil, our only problems were avoiding hurricanes, staying out of the Guiana current, and finding usable wind in the doldrums. We had a number of questions: What were the boundaries of the Guiana Current? Where was the counter-current? At what latitude did the northern trades stop? How far south did the Inter Tropical Convergence Zone (a big name for the doldrums) extend?

Our friends had stopped in French Guiana, and were saying daily on the radio that their time was running out. They had to be back in Martinique by the end of September, and had best get on with it. So they left Devil's Island for Brazil just about the time we left Barbados.

Misty, our Siamese cat, stopped throwing up after three days, and soon was staggering around trying to get used to having her home constantly at a 15- to 20-degree heel. Her face took on a 'Why-are-you-doing-this-to-me?' look that lasted the whole passage.

At the end of our first week we'd made 600 miles and had logged 650. We were far enough south to feel secure from the path of hurricanes. So far, there had not been enough current to complain about. And for the first time in a lifetime of sunsets, I had seen the sun dive into the horizon with a green splash. An omen, sure enough.

Then a fix showed us practically stopped. We had found the northern edge of the Guiana Current. There was nothing for it but to tack east northeast, even though it meant giving up some latitude. Misty, who had finally gotten used to the port tack, once more had her bearings screwed up. Shedding hair like a wheat combine sheds chaff, she moved resignedly to the lee side.

Twelve hours later we tacked back south. Misty by now had learned 'ready about' and had changed sides even before 'hard a-lee'.

Fourteen hours later we again hit the edge of the current and tacked east northeast, except that now the best we could make good was northeast. Every mile east put us a mile further north of Brazil. We'd already been out 12 days, and I was no longer having fun.

To add to our gloom, our friends had turned back. Having made two unsuccessful attempts to motor sail around Cabo Orange against a three- to four-knot current, they'd decided their time had run out.

I began to lose faith in our own tactics. In a referendum over turning back I knew I had Misty's vote. But Nancy pointed out that we were making progress, however slow, so why not continue on a 24-hour reassessment basis?

For three more days we tacked every 12 hours. At one point a tropical depression formed just to the north. With the rain the depression brought, we re-filled our half-depleted water tanks. Omens were piling up.

Motor sailing southeast through squalls, calms, and chaotic seas, we came into clear skies and a 15-knot easterly. I couldn't bear the thought of sailing back up into the doldrums. It was time to head for Brazil.

"Let's go for it," I said.

We sailed south full and by, logging every SatNav fix, counting each decreasing minute of latitude that brought us a mile nearer our goal. We crossed our fingers that the east wind would continue, and were thankful that so far the current was less strong than we'd dared hope.

A couple of days later, during my night watch, we passed a group of local fishing boats. Fishermen like to cluster on the current edge: we'd made it across the Guiana! Turning westward toward the Rio Para, RED SHOES scudded along happily. With eased sheets I felt a delicious easing of inner tension. Enter the god with the long middle finger.

A SatNav fix showed that the minutes of latitude were increasing. Correcting, I added a little more south to our course. Next fix showed an even greater increase in latitude. We were obviously losing ground.

Nancy woke up, and I shared the bad news.

"Somehow we're back in the current," I said. I told her about the fishing boats. "So we must be in some freaky eddy," I concluded. "We're being pushed further and further north. We've got to do something."

The winds were gusty, blowing 15 to 25 knots. In spite of this, we added reefed main and altered course another 20 degrees to the south.

Our next fix showed five more minutes of latitude.

Frustrated to the point of fury, we stared at each other. After all our determined efforts, were we to be swept past the river? Were we to have to face all the "I told you so's?" No way. Braving the heaving foredeck, I added the staysail and hardened up. RED SHOES was crashing into 12-foot seas, rail plunging deep during the gusts, green water everywhere. The punishment was brutal, but we were making better than five knots. This was our best shot. If we didn't score, we'd blown it.

We smashed south for another hour. Finally a good fix showed that our latitude had increased another five minutes.

I stared hopelessly at the read-out. Suddenly I saw it, the little 'S' on the SatNav display. We had crossed the equator. Minutes of latitude now measured miles south, not north. I collapsed, laughing. Nancy wasn't so amused.

My only excuse was that for sixteen days, degrees of latitude had meant miles north. Twenty fixes a day had conditioned an automatic response. Habit had had me.

Heading west before the wind, we weaved and slalomed down giant sea slopes. The pitching motion of weatherly sailing had not prepared Misty for exaggerated downwind rolling, and she spent most of her time spread-pawed on the sole, trying to stay vertical. I asked myself if she might have preferred to remain a skinny, sick stray, winter-wandering the alleys of Portland, Maine. My answer was far from comforting.

Our troubles with current weren't over. Approaching the maze of shoals which make up the entrance to the Rio Para, we were looking in vain for the mast of a charted wreck. Had it been washed off the shoal? A nervous hour later we sighted it, attributing its tardiness to the last of a strong ebb. But where was the 33-foot tower that was supposed to mark the south-westerly edge of the shoal? Nowhere. In rivers, reality changes faster than charts.

Now I was disoriented. How much current? What effect? According to the tables, the tide should have turned. Had it? Where was the end of the shoal? Were we in the channel? The shore was too far, too hazy, too low and undistinguished for bearings. It would be hours before our next SatNav fix.

Uncertain, we nevertheless turned and headed up river. Every couple of minutes Nancy would announce the depth—around 80 feet. Neither of us were concerned when it dropped to 60. But then it dropped to 20, and continued to drop.

"Aren't those breakers ahead?" I asked her.

"Breakers? Omigod!"

We panic-jibed to starboard. Had we overshot or undershot the main channel? I had a 50-50 chance, a hunch being the only thing tipping the scales. Gradually the depths increased, till once more we were in 60 feet or better. We jibed back onto our up-river course. Sighting a charted beacon, we knew at last that we were in the channel and clear of the entrance shoals.

Our destination was Foro Da Laura, a little creek 40 miles from the river mouth where a friend, Frank, had anchored three years ago. The tide had turned fair, and with a stiff breeze we hoped to reach Frank's anchorage by last light.

There was no other good shelter that I could see—possible little stream mouths, but they would take time to investigate, and the chart's comment "unexplored" at the mouth of each creek was no help. So we went for Foro Da Laura. In the event we couldn't get in, we'd simply drop the hook in the main river and suffer a bouncy night.

As we rounded the final point of land, the sun dropped into the horizon's pocket. We could see the lights of fishing boats anchored in the calm of the creek. So close. But where the chart showed eight feet at mean low water, we were seeing six feet at high water. Eight feet at low water plus a 10-foot tide equals 18 feet. Subtracting the six feet we actually had gave a difference of twelve—twelve feet of shoaling in three years! But that's the way it often was with river charts.

"Five feet," said Nancy. (We draw 4'2".) Lip-chewing, she slowed RED SHOES to a crawl.

But gradually the depths increased, and as dusk ripened, we motored into welcome shelter, dropped anchor, and retired below to the solace of a rum and tonic.

Local sailboat in the Amazon Delta. In the dense, boggy jungles, boats are the sole means of transportation.

At Trinidad's Carnival, it's almost impossible to remain an onlooker.

Unable to deal with a stable cabin sole, Misty lurched about with her paws determinedly braced abeam. I too felt giddy, elation and inner ear memory skewing equilibrium. But it was time to celebrate. In eighteen days we'd made good 1,100 miles, having logged 1,900 miles to do it. We were exhausted but elated. We had, as the song promised, overcome.

Why did we go to the Amazon?

Because.

Our reasons for going to each of our many destinations varied widely. A few follow:

Venezuela: It's cheap.

Antigua: Race week.

Guadeloupe: It's on the way.

St. Lucia: Borrow charts of Brazil from a ham friend.

Martinique: Eat well.

Dominica: Visit Trafalgar Falls.

Devil's Island: Visit the site of *Papillon*, a book and movie about an incredible escape from prison.

Maroni River: See animals disappointingly absent from Amazon.

Tobago: Join up with friends.

Trinidad: Celebrate Carnival.

U.S. Virgin Islands: Recoup.

Bermuda: Herb wanted to.

Maine: Herb wanted to.

Grenada: Spend Christmas with friends.

Bonaire: Spend Christmas without friends.

Honduras' Bay Islands: Nancy wanted to.

Rio Dulce of Guatemala: Nancy wanted to.

San Blas Islands of Panama: On the way.

Colón, Panama: Necessary evil.

Providencia, Colombia: Undiscovered jewel.

Vivorillo Cays: Beautiful way stop.

From time to time we'll refer to one of the above, and elaborate. For now, let's move on to what you might expect an ocean passage to be like.

CHAPTER 4

What's It *Really* Like Out There?

Dear Herb: What's it *really* like out there at sea? We hear so many conflicting accounts.

Worried in Wichita

Dear Worried: The answer to your question depends on so many variables we can only offer the following scenarios. Anyone who has cruised for a year or more can usually find himself in all three.

1. BEST CASE: You're with someone you love; the wind is moderate and fair; the sky is clear; the boat doesn't leak; everything's working; no fresh food has gone bad yet; you think you know where you are; you've only been out a week, and you have only one more day (you hope) before landfall.

2. HALF ROTTEN: You're with the one you love; the wind is fair; but the sky is cloudy and you haven't had a sight for three days; you aren't sure where you are but you reckon your landfall to be the middle of the night; the boat leaks, but the pump keeps up with it; your loving partner is seasick, and tends to hiccup during intercourse.

3. ROTTEN: Your wife/husband/lover/friend has come to hate you; the wind is 25 knots on the nose; it's cold and rainy; the boat is leaking so badly you have to pump every half hour; there are deck leaks over all berths; the cat has impregnated your mattress with a full catalog of body fluids: all the fresh food has spoiled or been eaten, and you're down to rancid peanut butter and rusty cans with no labels; salt water has gotten into your water tanks through the vents, so the water supply is brackish and your coffee undrinkable; the alternator has packed up (the fan belt failed and you haven't a spare) and the batteries are dead, so nothing (running lights, radios, cabin lights, instruments, GPS, electric bilge pump, autopilot, solenoid for propane stove) works; the head is clogged and overflowing with pre-cloggery; you've been out 39 days, and the prospect of making a landfall before

next week is dim. Lastly, you have just spotted an iceberg and you thought you were approaching the Bahamas.

Fortunately it's almost never as bad as 3), and there are enough 1)s to erase your memories of 2)s, otherwise none of us would ever go out there again.

CHAPTER 5

Building Your Own Boat:
A Fateful Decision

Dear Herb: Should I consider building my own boat?

Ginga Dunne, Singapore

Dear Ginga: In a word, no!

Do you want to be a cruiser or a boat builder? If you're already determined to build your own boat, you'll no doubt disagree. But if you're not, here's how I feel about it.

If you're not particularly wealthy, you'll probably have to keep working while you build. Maybe you'll even moonlight on weekends, in order to afford the bronze keel bolts or lead ballast that are required for the next step. Besides your job, there's the time you spend working on the boat. If you don't make a marathon out of it, it will make an old man out of you. In other words, work at your fastest, or the project will drag on forever.

Maybe you're lucky, and your wife or partner is an experienced boat builder. You would indeed be even luckier if her enthusiasm was as high and deep as yours. In most cases, the wife is merely tagging along with her husband's dream, and soon loses patience with indentured servitude. Maybe she'll take up bridge, or adultery, but who cares? At least she's no longer nagging at you for spending so much time in the yard.

Time passes. So now, if you're a family man, don't worry about it, because they've forgotten what you look like. For this project to succeed, obsession is the only way to go, and obsession means tunnel vision, blindness to whatever unrelated stuff is going on around you.

At last you've finished, and now all you have to do is learn to live, not only without your family, but with all your boat-building mistakes. Because if you, who never built a boat before in your life, get it all right the first, or even the second time, you're a better man than I am, Ginga Dunne.

There is one exception to which I'll admit. For a rare few, the whole process of readying and doing comprises one philosophical entity. "I am going to build a boat and sail it around the world" is a whole different thing from "I want to go cruising—should I build my own boat?" I have a deep regard for the dedication of the former, and pity for the confused state of mind of the latter.

The first guy is after enlightenment and self-realization. For him, wholeness of experience is an issue. He's maybe a Thoreauvian, or perhaps a Hessean, a modern Siddhartha looking for meaning and relatedness. He wants to build his boat because that's part of it. If, because of technical limitations, his yacht turns out to be a raft with a tent for a cabin, he couldn't care less. Furthest from his mind is the need to impress anyone.

The second guy is trying to save money. Nothing wrong with that, except he won't. Mistakes are costly, and time is worth more than we know, until we see its end approaching. A far better way to go is to buy a neglected boat, or perhaps an impounded one, and having surveyed it so that there'll be no surprises, to fix it up. Why? Because the lines are already there, designed and built by experts. The money saver has only to fill in the blanks.

One other exception would be the experienced boat builder. Larry Pardey is one, and Lin and Larry are dedicated cruisers. But inasmuch as few boat builders ever really want to go cruising, the occurrence is so rare as to be hardly worth elaborating on.

CHAPTER 6

Naming the Ark

Dear Herb: We are in the process of buying a Pacific Seacraft 44, thus realizing a dream we've had for years. Strange that during all that time we haven't been thinking of a name—prospective parents do, but we didn't. So what should we be thinking of? Haven't all the good names been used?

Perplexed

(This letter came from a retired gynecologist from Plymouth, Mass-achusetts. I wish all questions were as much fun to respond to.)

Dear Perplexed: You show great insight with your deep concern for your boat's name, and very little has been written about this. For one thing, you'll live with it forever—there's a real superstition about changing a boat's name, and one should never risk bad karma when heading into the mysterious kingdom of Neptune.

On the other hand, a boat bought at a drug boat auction should definitely have its name changed. Otherwise, you'll always be prey to Coast Guard boardings, as the name may not be taken off their list for months or even years.

So let's make some suggestions. The name should be relevant—appropriate to you, your life, or your feelings about adventures on the sea. Or it can express a non-marine passion. Two of my cousins have owned several cruising sailboats, and although neither is a musician, they both love classical music. Their last two boats were COUNTERPOINT and CADENZA. (Now if you were buying a used Columbia 45, I might suggest SCHERZO, which means joke.) Beware of the karma of CODA or FINALE. And never, never name your boat HURRICANE, or OVERBOARD, or, horror of horrors, SHARK BAIT.

We've seen song titles, great as long as they're short. We would never use, for example, ON THE ACHESON, TOPEKA AND THE SANTA FE. We met SEPTEMBER SONG in Guatemala; MARGARITAVILLE in the Bahamas; MOONGLOW and BLUE MOON in Trinidad; and SATIN DOLL in Tahiti. I'd avoid using PERDIDO, THE PARTY'S OVER, or THAT'S ALL.

When we named RED SHOES, we were thinking of the Hans Christian Andersen fairy tale, on which the movie with Moira Shearer was loosely based, and the shoes that made the young woman a marvelous dancer. We hadn't forgotten, but chose to ignore, that when she tired, she was unable to remove the shoes, and ultimately they danced her to death. Now, after nine years aboard, we're grateful that we still love cruising, as we're faced with the fact that we can no longer afford to live ashore in the U.S. We may someday wish we'd chosen our boat's name with more foresight.

Although you feel now that your Crealock 44 will be your ultimate boat, you may be surprised. 'Still love cruising' and 'Satisfied with boat' are not synonymous. You may, down the line, want something smaller, or a multihull, or a World War II submarine (for all those batteries), or you found that having three to four hundred thousand dollars tied up in a boat prevented you from undertaking other ventures. Keep in mind that you may change boats someday, and heed the words of the Pardeys when asked why they didn't name their second boat SERAFFYN II. Said Lin, "Would you name your three sons George, George II, and George III?" Each vessel deserves the distinction of its own name. Their second boat was named TALEISIN, a name chosen for them by Tristan Jones.

Some eventualities you can't prepare for. Back in the 50's, a black man who loved all Bogart movies named his vessel AFRICAN QUEEN. He has lately had to parry numerous improper advances. An old Noel Coward

Nancy vinylized the name and port on *Red Shoes'* stern.

fan named his boat GAY ADVENTURE, and regrets his choice for the same reason.

And what's politically correct today may be anathema tomorrow. A women's group has begun a class action suit against the sailor who named his pretty little ketch GIRL FRIEND. And there's decided antipathy toward the Marlboro Man, complete with eye patch, who named his boat TONTO. His wife has even stopped him from saying "Geronimo" when he makes landfall.

Names of constellations and stars can inspire philosophical musings on the cosmos. We've known NUNKI, ANTARES, SCHEDAR, SAGITTARIUS, CYGNE, PISCES, and others. Stars' names inspiring more earthly thoughts and to my knowledge not yet taken are MADONNA, CHER, and LINDA LOVELACE (could be LINDA L, if you insist on a plain, brown wrapper).

Nancy reminds me to mention "think radio." It was pure luck, not careful planning, that RED SHOES turned out to be so easily understood on the air. At the other end of the scale, we have a friend who can spell HUKULEIA phonetically in his sleep. On DIASTOLE, at least until the skipper became a Caribbean radio fixture, the name of the boat had to be repeated three times for every new radio contact.

Beware also of foreign names, like AUDACIEUSE and ATHABASCA, unless you want to spend your life repeating explanations and spellings. A guy whose boat is named BEVI-ANNIE finally gave up, and now uses 'Home Base' as his radio call. And imagine putting out a Mayday on Channel 16 from the boat TO BOLDLY GO.

It's a New England tradition to name a boat after an ancestral female. Usually this applies to commercial fishing boats and ferryboats, but an occasional cruiser transfers the practice to his beloved yacht. We've known TRUDY M and MELINDA B. But dearest to my heart is the name chosen by our good friends, Scott and Mary Beth Teas, whose first boat was named after Scott's grandmother, HARRIET B. HAYMAKER. You can bet that the Teas either hated to get on the radio from square one, or soon learned to. (In fact, for radio purposes their boat's name became simply HAYMAKER.)

And beware of naming a boat after a beloved woman, unless you know the boat. My father named one of his boats EILEEN after my mother. Unfortunately it leaked like a sieve, eventually revealed acres of hidden rot, and finally sank. My mother outlived my father by nearly three decades, however, which proves that karma is not always predictable.

With these ideas in mind—that it's a serious choice; that it's appropriate to have the name mean something special to you and yours; that you should consider how it will be understood on the radio; that an off-color joke will not wear well; and that karma should be considered—let's look at just a few of the hundreds of names we've met during our years of live-aboard cruising.

ADL: Stands for Anti-Destination League.

AKA: Also Known As. Dinghy was ALIAS.

BALLERINA: RED SHOES should be cruising with them.

BLUE CHIP: One wonders, Vegas or Wall Street?

BOW STRING: Owned by a cellist.

BYPASS: Heart surgeon. Likes to talk to DIASTOLE.

CABLE BABY: Cable network owner.

CARPE DIEM: Good advice for cruisers of any age, but especially for us retirees.

CHUCKLYN: Combination of couple, Chuck and Lyn.

CLIMAX: Subtler than, well, a lot of things.

C.O. JONES: How's your Spanish?

CONCUBINE: The way some women feel about their husband's boat.

COURTSHIP: Subtler than 'foreplay'.

DADDY'S DREAM: What do you bet the kids named it, tongue in cheek?

DAYLIGHT ROBBERY: He'll take the fifth. Or two.

DIASTOLE: Owned by a heart surgeon.

DUET: Simple, sharing, couply name.

EGRESS: Haven't heard of another one of these.

ENTROPY: Existentialist humor.

FREELANCE: Independent video producers.

FREUDIAN SLOOP: I like it, I like it!

FUNSEACA: Ingenious combo of fun, sea, and California.

GOOD NEWS: Well, would you name it bad news? (In the Bahamas, calling on VHF, it was "Shoes? News.")

GRAND FINALE II: Funniest name of all time.

HELLS BELLS: 'Fire and Damnation' hasn't been used.

HI C: A family of musicians. Logo was a treble staff.

HONEY TOO: First boat was HONEY, after his wife. This is their second boat. Or his second wife. Coming up: THIRD HONEY?

HOT CHOCOLATE: Owned by a black Hollywood stuntman.

HOT FLASH: Wife's boat.

JACARDE: Jack and Carly.

JALAN JALAN: A favorite name of ours—an Asian term that I'm told means walkabout.

JUNK BOND: Yuck—has all the charm of a runny nose.

KEEP ON DANCING: RED SHOES should have met.

KISSES: Another yuck—and for a Columbia 45, yet already.

LI'L SUGAR: How about 'Li'l Darlin'; or better, 'Li'l Pest'?

LITTLE HASTE: A laid back, restful name.

LOOK FAR: Hand over eyes, staring at western horizon.

MARGIN CALL: A lot of boat names recall how the price was met. See MONOPOLY.

MIDLIFE CRISIS: Wife usually waves goodbye from dock.

MILELOWER: From Denver.

MOLAR MECHANIC: Traveling dentist.

MONOPOLY: Never learned whether this guy formed a successful one in the business world, or invented the game.

NOMAER: *No Money After Early Retirement.*

PASSING WIND: About as subtle as SLEDGEHAMMER.

PERFECT CRIME: Never turns back for man (or woman) overboard.

PERIWINKLE: This is okay, whereas 'Mussel', 'Clam', or 'Barnacle' doesn't make it.

PUTTY TAT: Name chosen by adult male for his catamaran.

QUARTER DECK: Owner made his money from a vending machine route, for which quarters were the coins that decked him.

QUANDARY: Describes the skipper, not the boat.

QUO VADIMUS: If they don't know, they might as well name it 'Lost'.

REBOUND: Bought after recovery from serious illness.

SALLY ON: Should be 'Sally Forth'?

SEA LATION: Perhaps an overstatement, but nice.

SEA LEVEL: Neat name for a catamaran.

SLEDGEHAMMER: Not with a whimper, but with a bang.

SLO LANE: Escaping from the fast lane?

SLOW SHOES: Nice pace.

SQUARE PEG: You don't forget it, but what round hole? I guess I don't want to know.

TA TA: Beyond midlife crisis and into second childhood?

THAR Y'ARE: Whar? and Why?

THIS SIDE UP: Hopeful or prayerful? A Neptunal reminder? He ships his boat to major ports?

TIME OUT: More original than 'Sabbatical' with the same suggested meaning.

TO BOLDLY GO: Ta-da-da dum-dee-dum!

TOLAKI: Sounds like exotic term, means TOny, LAddy, and the KIds.

TRANSITION: Journey from one lifestyle into another. See MIDLIFE CRISIS.

TWINSUM: A catamaran.

WELUVIT: As opposed to a wife's IHATEIT.

WET DREAM: Implies disappointment or loneliness.

WET SNEAKERS: A salute to the discomfort of weatherly sailing.

WHITE KNUCKLES: Heard on VHF in one of Maine's thicker fogs.

WHY NOT?: Going with the flow.

WILD CARD: Can be anything you want it to be.

WILD OATS: Sow 'em while you have 'em to sow—nothing lasts forever.

X-PENSE: What better name for a boat?

YARNSPINNER: Sheep farmers from Alaska, plus sea stories.

ZIVIO (My favorite): Said to be Croatian for "all the love you can endure."

I've suggested names for a couple of boats, one in particular for Katy Burke and Taz Waller, DUCHESS, for their beautiful, stately river boat that Taz built to the quality of fine furniture. Regarding your question, I thought of MOLAR MECHANIC, hoping to find an equivalent for gynecology, but came up with nothing a gentleman could live with. My choice would be GYN pronounced like that alcoholic beverage without which the world would be far poorer. In the card game it means you've won the hand. It would work wonderfully on the radio, it has personal significance. And who knows, GYN on the transom might even stir up a little business.

CHAPTER 7

What Should I Look For
in a Cruising Boat?

Dear Herb: We own a Catalina 25, but we realize it may not be adequate for serious cruising. What kind of boats should we be looking at, and why?

Confused in Medicine Hat

Dear Confused: Because of where you live, I'm tempted to suggest you get a dirt boat and a tent. (A dirt boat is like an iceboat with wheels, and a real thrill to sail on the salt flats in the desert.) However, I'm assuming that you do mean ocean and not local cruising.

I've already named a few boats, a list that is by no means complete. At this point, it might be more helpful to give you some guidelines.

MATERIALS

These days, most boats are made of fiberglass. We used to think that hulls made of fiberglass and resin were a yacht owner's panacea, but time has shown that even fiberglass has its drawbacks. Blisters remain a problem, although one that is being dealt with more effectively each year. Crazing and cracking with age will happen. But basically, fiberglass remains a wonder material for both manufacturers and owners.

Before fiberglass, most cruisers started with a wooden boat. A surprising number then switched to steel. Steel is strong and will forgive more mistakes than any other material. However, it requires constant maintenance. With a steel boat, you'll spend a lot of time chipping and painting.

Aluminum is becoming more popular as aluminum welding technique has improved. Aluminum boats are strong, lighter than steel, and therefore can be fast. I've asked cruising friends Scott and Mary Beth Teas who've owned two aluminum boats over a period of eight years to comment:

Scott: "Aluminum provides an exceptionally strong and lightweight hull. There are literally hundreds of aluminum alloys. ASIA [the Teas' 50-foot ketch] is constructed of 5052, which is exceptionally resistant to salt-water corrosion.

"As for electrolysis, it is always a concern. The use of zincs goes a long way to protect the hull from stray currents. Paint seems to adhere well when properly prepared and not in contact with stainless steel fittings. Stainless steel fittings passing through aluminum must be kept dry. We embed all fastenings with an anti-corrosive substance; set fittings in Sikaflex urethane sealant. In short, we do whatever is required to keep salt water from fueling the electrical action between the two dissimilar materials."

Mary Beth: "Wherever the aluminum comes in contact with other metals we get corrosion, which means patches of blistering, flaking paint. We commonly get blisters around the edges of ports, hatches, and occasionally under deck fittings. This makes our spring-in-the-boatyard routine a little longer than it might be with other materials.

"So why did we choose a second aluminum boat? Probably as a result of my having read three or four survival-in-a-liferaft stories. I have a recurring image of a collision with a whale. With an aluminum hull, both the sailboat and the whale, dented but intact, wallow on into the sunset. The aluminum hull just makes me feel better!"

Wood is still the material of choice for the purist. Good boat-building woods are available, but they're becoming more and more scarce, as are good builders in wood. An older wooden boat with a thorough and proper survey could well be your least expensive selection.

For seven years we cruised in SEA FOAM, an Angleman/Davies design called a Sea Witch, a wooden ketch with masts of almost equal height, with deadeyes and lanyards in place of turnbuckles. I cursed her 11-foot bowsprit and gaff-headed mainsail many times, but when we sailed into a harbor with varnish gleaming, her classic lines made the true sailor's heart skip a beat.

Some people complain that after a while cruising gets boring, there is so little to do. Owning and maintaining a wooden boat will solve that problem.

Maintaining such a boat properly requires some specialized knowledge. Many wonderful, fun-to-read books on the subject are available. If you love wood, enjoy working with it, finishing it, making it glow with inner beauty; if you can shoulder the greater burden of wooden boat maintenance; and if you want a boat with soul (wooden boat souls come

Sea Foam sailing. *Sea Foam* was fast on a reach, but downwind she was under-canvassed, and to weather we relied on the auxiliary.

in loving-and-giving and malicious), choose wood. If you want to learn something of the down side of wood, read Farley Mowat's *The Boat Who Wouldn't Float*. Read it anyway, because it will make you feel smug as a fiberglass or steel or aluminum boat owner. And read it for pleasure, because it's one of boating's funniest yarns.

Last but not least in the list of hull materials is ferro-cement. Building in ferro-cement is a lot like building a swimming pool whose purpose is to keep the water *out*. One of our best friends built his own ferro-cement 40-foot sloop and sailed it thousands of Pacific, Atlantic and Mediterranean miles. I've seen ferro-cement yachts that were so fair and beautifully made that any owner would be proud to sail them. Some of the worst monstrosities afloat are ferro-cement. Ferro-cement earned a bad name back in the sixties because so many people were persuaded to build in it, and so few had the persistence to finish. The material must hold the all-time record for abandoned boat-building projects.

Building in ferro-cement takes the least skill, although fiberglass is becoming a close second. Many people chose ferro-cement to save money. If you're counting every penny, fine, but on a percentage basis, what you save is small indeed. The hull is not where the bulk of your money goes—it goes into the rig, sails, interior finish, hardware, and electronics.

A well-built ferro-cement hull will last a lifetime. It will stand up to neglect better than any other material. It is lowest of all materials on impact strength (don't hit a reef) but is second only to steel for torsion (flexing in storms) and is eminently repairable. The dark side is that its resale value will in most cases be very low. And if you're the buyer, you should know that a reliable survey of ferro-cement hull integrity is virtually impossible to come by. Unless you know and trust the builder personally, you'll always be buying a pig in a poke.

HULL SHAPE

Some people cruise with boats that have fin keels and spade rudders, but I feel that this configuration, while great for racing, doesn't answer a cruiser's needs. I've also known cruisers in yachts with centerboards, but I wouldn't choose that either.

The fin keel and the spade rudder will serve you well to weather. But the whole idea of cruise planning is to go to weather as seldom as possible. Experienced sailors with whom I've talked have said that the fin/spade boats are squirrely downwind—they don't "track" in a stable fashion. Now why, I ask you, given a choice, would anyone buy such a boat when his every tactic will be to choose the downwind path?

Moreover, spade rudders are extremely vulnerable. Hit anything and your rudder won't turn, your boat is crippled. Also, fin/spade configurations leave the propeller and shaft exposed and therefore vulnerable. A full keel boat with its prop in a protective cutout might well pass over a net or line that would surely disable a boat with exposed prop and spade rudder.

Centerboards are effective when they work. A hull with comparatively shallow draft will track well enough with the centerboard up sailing downwind, and will perform well to weather with the board down. But centerboards are vulnerable. Several skippers I know arrived in port with bent boards that couldn't be raised. Unless the damaged board can be removed by divers, you're looking at a haulout with crane or travel lift.

Less important, perhaps, is the vibration that a centerboard can produce in certain wind and sea conditions. This usually occurs in situations that are already making you terrified, and the hum of the vibrating centerboard drives you over the edge.

Our first boat, SEA FOAM, had deep bilges and a full ballasted keel. The Crealock 34, our present boat, has shallow bilges. Her underbody has what some call the 'Brewer Bite', which is basically a full keel with a bite or two taken out of it. It's a compromise between a fin keel and a full keel—a compromise that retains much of the full keel's tracking ability

Aground at Pine Island. Our Scheel keel allows us to go aground in shallower water.

while reducing wetted surface area. Little or none of the strength of the rudder or protection of the propeller has been sacrificed. Unlike some compromises, most designers agree that for cruising boats, this effectively combines the best qualities of each.

Pacific Seacraft, builder of RED SHOES, offers customers a choice of keel: standard, or the Scheel keel, a shallower draft configuration. A boat with the Scheel keel will lose a fraction to the standard keel on a weather leg, but the difference would only be noticed in a close race. We have a Scheel keel, which gives us a draft of four feet instead of the standard five, and on several occasions we have been most grateful for the shallower draft.

Places we have cruised where a shallow draft has mattered are rivers—any river, but notably the Amazon; the Maroni of French Guiana; the Rio Dulce of Guatemala; the Intracoastal Waterway, where we have passed many six-foot drafters waiting hopefully for a rise in tide; and of course the Bahamas, where a shallow draft probably doubles the number of anchorages available to you.

LARGE OR SMALL?

On our South Pacific cruise we sailed with our family on a 36-foot wooden ketch with deep, sloping bilges and a beam of 13'9". We called it the bowling ball. With a 55-horsepower Ford Osco diesel it went well to weather. It had a tremendous amount of room. Each settee in the main saloon made into a double berth. There was a quarter berth, a separate owner's stateroom, and in addition a forepeak with a pipe berth. The bilges held six months worth of food. We carried 150 gallons of water and 100 gallons of diesel fuel. After seven years, when we were finally just the two of us, Nancy and I decided it was too big and the rig too archaic.

Cruising yachts under 40 feet today are considered small. Couples are going to sea in yachts up to 70 feet. The reason why this has become possible is the modernization that has taken place in rigging. Furthermore, autopilots have become extremely reliable while being less demanding of current. They are often characterized as being a tireless third crewmember.

The advantage of a large boat is space. With more space you can carry a larger supply of water and fuel. You can be more independent by virtue of carrying more spares. There's plenty of room for any marine toy you can imagine. El capitán can have a desk for his computer, printer, and weatherfax. He can even have a workshop.

There's room for galley luxuries such as a large freezer and refrigerator. The larger the yacht, the more comforts of home can be included: TV, VCR, CDs, washer, and dryer help keep a reluctant partner from longing for her nest. On a larger boat you can have guests visit while giving them, and retaining for yourself, complete privacy. You can entertain a larger number of friends for cocktails or dinner. It's like having your cake and eating it too—comfort and luxury while sailing into adventure.

Sounds ideal? Ah, but disadvantages lurk in the wings. A large boat is geometrically more expensive. So is its gear. So are the haulouts, marina fees, state taxes, and all other charges based either on length or value. We can paint RED SHOES' bottom with two gallons of bottom paint, whereas a larger boat could require six gallons or more—at $100-$150 per gallon for the good stuff.

And what happens to old George with the funny heart when the electric anchor windlass fails? A 60-pound anchor, plus ⅜- or ½-inch chain at three to four pounds per foot, in 30 feet of water comes to well over 150 pounds. Well, George, you liked that anchorage anyway—might as well stay there till you can get the windlass fixed. Shipping it in for repair from the Solomons—shouldn't take much more than six months to get it back. Better to wait than to try to hand-over-hand it, no matter how much your partner would like a reason to practice CPR.

Modern gear is fine while it works, but all of it is subject to failure. Sails that roll up inside the mast, roller furling, and winches all powered with electricity—these are wonderful aids till a short circuit, or a sick alternator, or a lightning strike renders them useless. And when is it most likely to fail? When it's being put to the severest test—when you need it most—in a storm, probably at night, when you're both seasick.

What about additional crew? The only solution that I see, if you're insisting on going big, is to arrange for crew to accompany you on every passage. But unless you have strapping sons or friends who can always drop whatever they're doing to rush to your aid, you'll have to deal with strangers.

I know of one guy who took on a stranger on the basis of the fact that he was an ex-Navy seaman. During the 3,000-mile, Hawaii to California passage, they ran into a storm that brought 50-knot winds and awesome waves. The 'sailor' sat on the saloon floor keening, both arms and legs entwined around the mast. At a time when the skipper needed him most, he was catatonic and useless.

And then there was the guy who wanted company on a sail from Hawaii to Tahiti via the Marquesas. Someone he thought he knew from the Yacht Club volunteered. Once they were at sea, the 'crew' did nothing but lie on his bunk. The skipper didn't mind single-handing his boat, but he longed for someone to talk to. Silence. By the time they reached Tahiti, the skipper had learned more about himself than he'd ever wanted to—specifically, that he could seriously contemplate murder.

On arriving in Papeete, the skipper couldn't wait to get to the immigration office and remove this slug from his crew list. When he returned to his boat, however, the guy was still there. "I like it here," he said. "How about letting me stay aboard for a couple of weeks? I'll even talk to you." The skipper, remembering his do-nothing, say-nothing crewmember, shot back, "If you're not off the boat in 30 minutes, lock, stock, and duffle, I'll break your knees with a winch handle."

People who take on crewmembers they don't know very well sometimes have good experiences. But from my observation, those cases are rare.

We've been living aboard a shallow draft, shallow-bilged, narrow-beamed, short-waterlined 34-footer for nearly ten years. The quarter berth—our attic—bulges with essentials. In port, when we go to bed at night, we must remove from the V-berth to the saloon the TV, the computer, the printer, the VCR, the bowl of potatoes, the bowl of tomatoes, and assorted magazines for which we have found no home.

But I know my pack rat wife, and I know myself. As with our budget, the space we need will always be what we have plus 10 percent. So we endure, and fight over what must be discarded when something new is acquired. At anchor, we pile stuff on deck so we can live decently below, and continually burrow through overstuffed lockers to find the part/pill/ product we know is aboard somewhere. We live the way we would live on a big boat, but on a smaller, more copeable scale.

CHAPTER 8

Above Decks

Dear Herb: I have a friend who presently owns a Laguna 23 and is thinking seriously of buying a Columbia 45. I realize the 45 is roomy, but it's so ugly! My friend won't listen to me, but perhaps he'll listen to you. While you're at it, what's your opinion on aft cabins, big windows, high topsides, and center cockpits?

Disgusted in Cucamonga

Dear Disgusted: You've stumbled onto the mariner's "Want What You Don't Have" syndrome. Nowhere is the commandment not to covet thy neighbor's wife and/or his possessions broken as often as it is among cruising yachtsmen. We all suffer from the malady known as upgrade, a craving for Bigger-Better-Braver-*Yours*. I've never heard of this disease affecting someone regarding a Columbia 45, but one has to admit, beauty is in the eye of the beholder.

Rather than risk a class action suit, let's sidestep your friend's prospective purchase for a moment, and go on to your questions.

COCKPITS

The cockpit has been moved gradually forward, reaching its limit on a custom-designed catamaran I inspected recently. The cockpit was forward of the pilot house; there was nothing between it and oncoming seas. I was told that it was as ridiculously wet and uncomfortable as one would assume.

The old objection to a center cockpit was that it was wetter than an aft cockpit. This may or may not have been true. However, almost all cruising boats nowadays have some sort of dodger and some sort of bimini. The dodger wraps around. Sometimes there are even side and rear curtains, made of transparent plastic, creating a kind of Florida room out of the cockpit. In any event, spray and dampness are kept out.

So what are the possible advantages of a center cockpit? One is that it's high, and visibility is vastly better than from an aft cockpit. Two might be that its placement puts it at the fulcrum of the pitching motion, so that there is less movement in head seas than there'd be in an aft cockpit. The dark side is that you're higher up than you'd be in an aft cockpit, so that the side-to-side or rolling motion would be amplified.

Center cockpits definitely offer more useable space for entertaining, a feature that grows increasingly important as your time spent at anchor expands.

The biggest disadvantage of a center cockpit that I see is that it makes rigging a workable emergency tiller much more difficult. Hydraulic or cable-driven steering systems do fail, and as with most failures, it'll most likely occur under stress—in other words, in heavy weather. So if you do opt for a center cockpit, figure out in advance what you're going to do in a nasty situation.

A large percentage of your time on a relaxed world cruise will be spent at anchor. For this reason, the allure of a large center cockpit is attractive. On the other hand, the percentages can be misleading—the hours you spend battling a storm may be a psychological eternity, and the security of a low-centered aft cockpit then may outweigh its disadvantages.

There are other considerations as well. With center cockpit designs, the cabin is divided. Usually the aft cabin is spacious and given over to the master. At anchor in the tropics, however, ventilation of that space becomes a problem. Located aft of the cockpit, it is denied the cooling trade winds by the bimini/dodger. (We won't talk to the income bracket that affords generators and air-conditioning systems. However, we could be talked into a couple of fans. . .)

The solution to the ventilation problem is to give the aft cabin to guests—they'll think you unselfish in the extreme—while you keep the airy, cool forepeak with its funny shaped berth for yourself.

You mention big windows. In marinas, protected anchorages, and the like, big windows are wonderful—light, cheerful, homey. But at sea in a storm they are dangerous and can lead to disaster. If you choose to have them, there are two things to consider. One, you can have the windows made of Lexan, a nearly indestructible material if used in appropriate thickness, or you can have glass windows, with Lexan storm shutters.

If you select windows made of Lexan, the setting must be very strong, as the force of a huge breaking wave is almost beyond belief. Lexan scratches more readily than glass, and is subject to crazing in sunlight. If you can live with that, go for Lexan windows.

The other solution is to use thick, tempered glass for the windows, and bolt Lexan shutters over them when you set sail on a passage. The problem then is, where do you store the shutters when you're not using them? (On a hot night you could store them in the aft cabin.) The storage problem is serious enough that most of the time, when you see a boat with this arrangement, the shutters remain bolted on.

On RED SHOES we have standard bronze opening port lights for which I've made plywood shutters, which I can bolt in place quickly and easily should a wave break the glass. I'm happy with this arrangement. I don't know how happy I'd be with any other.

In discussing 'high topsides', I feel we're dealing with several elements: wetness, windage, living space and appearance. Look at the low, beautiful sheer of some Laurent Giles designs and your heart skips a beat. Go to sea, and you'll live in your foul-weather gear. As a general rule, the higher the dryer.

Also, the higher, the more living space. The space can be used either as headroom, if you're tall, or as storage space under the floorboards. Space is always desirable, and having high topsides is one way to get it.

But after a certain point, the increased windage of high topsides can be downright dangerous. Increased ballast can compensate for loss of stability, but in a storm, the boat with high topsides is going to react to the forces of the wind more than one with low topsides. The nastier the weather, the more important this factor becomes.

Finally, when we're talking about high topsides, we're talking not only comparisons (my topsides are higher than yours) but aesthetics. In extreme cases, we're talking about a yacht that looks like a container ship and presents a barn-doorish image to the world.

MORE ON TOPSIDES

Cruising on RED SHOES from Maine to Brazil, and especially in the Caribbean, we've seen all kinds—flush deck, standard trunk cabin, pilot house, and others too egregious to mention. A couple of comments follow which I confess are no more than opinion.

A flush deck is fine on a large boat. The one drawback is that flush decked boats have very dark interiors. Deck prisms and clear Lexan hatches help, but never achieve the brightness of a trunk cabin with port lights. However, if you can deal with that, a flush deck offers certain advantages. Primarily it gives you a large, flat, sail-handling platform. But as most cruisers carry a lot of stuff on deck, this advantage may be compromised.

Another advantage is greater flexibility when it comes to storing a RIB inflatable or hard dinghy. If you can afford them, a liferaft and an automatically activated EPIRB need deck space as well. Extra deck lockers make sail and line storage more convenient. And, of course, in a storm you present no glass faces to angry seas.

In thumbing through a recent issue of SAIL, I find no flush deck commercially produced yachts. I'm sure there must be some, and I know that there are used boats with flush decks. They are certainly worth considering.

Pilot houses are becoming more popular, and as sun damage continues to erode my skin, I find fewer objections to them. There are two configurations to consider: Two-station and one-station steering. Two stations allow you to choose whether to be inside or outside. Frankly, when we're sailing I want the wind blowing over my body, no matter how many telltales are strung on the stays and shrouds. With modern boats we get further and further away from the 'feel' of sailing. Steering under sail from inside a pilot house is a bit like having sex while wearing a wetsuit and two condoms.

On RED SHOES we have a bimini, no dodger, and nothing gets between the helmsperson and the apparent wind. In sailing from Maine to the Caribbean in October/November, we have longed for more protection from icy winds and even snow. Sailing to weather we occasionally are wet from spray that a dodger would deflect. But far more often, and always in the tropics, I'm glad of our obstructionless setup.

Also, I'm not happy with two-station steering for another reason. It has twice the gear, twice the propensity for failure, and the additional friction means it takes more effort to turn the rudder. Autopilots and vanes must work harder, as must the helmsperson. Furthermore, when steering from outside, visibility forward is poor, and seeing over the pilot house almost always requires you to stand up.

What if the steering is hydraulically assisted? Then it will be easy enough, but 'feel' will be virtually absent. Also, a failure in the line that results in a hydraulic fluid leak, though rare, will be messy enough to inspire wrist-slitting (your own).

And finally, a pilot house exposes large areas of glass to the elements, a disadvantage we talked about earlier. On the other hand, consider this: On a passage on RED SHOES, with the windvane steering, the person on watch is required (house rules) to come topside and have a three-to-five minute, 360-degree looksee. Below, for ten minutes, the watchkeeper can prepare and drink coffee, eat gingersnaps (great for an unsettled stomach), and read something comforting. In a pilot house, however, you could sit in comfort at the helm, read, drink, eat, and have 360-degree visibility. (I know, I know, but night vision isn't all that essential for spotting the lights of another vessel.)

For smaller boats—and these days we consider our Crealock 34 small—a trunk cabin allows you to have a lower freeboard with a nice sheer. Headroom is accomplished with a trunk cabin. If the designer of our 34 had decided on a flush deck, headroom could only be achieved by raising the topsides, and presto, you have a boxy boat.

Trunk cabins let in light through port lights, through which one can also look out without coming topside. It's a bit like living in a house with windows, as opposed to an apartment in the basement.

To go back to our seven-year cruise on SEA FOAM, we had no dodger and no bimini, and for much of the time no self-steering. My few but soul-shaping mystical experiences all happened at sea, at night, while I was sitting in the open cockpit, letting the sea and sky envelope my spirit in their loving embrace. I never tired of looking at the stars, as their distance always made whatever problems I was dealing with insignificant. I am as guilty as most in seldom considering the great scheme of things. But my memories of those several experiences on SEA FOAM are dear to me, and continue to shape my life and beliefs.

Now, aboard RED SHOES with its sun-shielding bimini, I'm cut off from the night sky. With self-steering I don't have to stay in the cockpit. Sure, I can fold back the bimini and sit there—I've done so several times. But the bimini folded back cuts off visibility aft. More importantly, mystical experiences don't come just because you prepare for them. All of mine have been unexpected, the result of hundreds of hours under the night sky. The upshot is, we've been nine years on board RED SHOES, and I've had no enlightening and uplifting experiences similar to those I had on SEA FOAM.

And I miss them.

WHEEL OR TILLER

The question comes up often. With a center cockpit you don't have a choice. On RED SHOES we have a wheel. I've sailed aboard a cruising yacht, home built with tiller steering, whose weather helm, even in a moderate breeze, would soon give you muscle cramps. This is hardly enough research on which to make an informed decision. However, even on a boat with a well-balanced rig, there is always some weather helm requiring constant tension on your steering arm. This was one of our reasons for choosing a wheel.

Wheel/binnacle arrangements use cable that leads through pulleys to a quadrant on the rudder post. The cable is subject to wear, and to stretching, sometimes enough that it can come off the quadrant. The pulleys can wear out and break. On RED SHOES, however, we've had no such problems in nearly ten years.

On SEA FOAM, our old wooden ketch, the wheel was at the rear of the cockpit. A shaft went to a worm gear which turned the rudder post via levers. The parts were all massive and bronze, and you just knew that when the boat finally went to its grave, the steering linkage would still be intact and working perfectly. However, most people, myself included, prefer to have the wheel mounted on a binnacle, thus putting the instruments and compass right before their eyes.

The biggest objection to a wheel/binnacle is that in a small cockpit they take up an inordinate amount of space. On RED SHOES they create a barrier between the cockpit's front and back areas. In port, and particularly when entertaining, we used to remove the wheel. Then one day I cast off the mooring, shouting to my brother in the cockpit to take the helm. He arrived at the helmsman's seat only to discover there was nothing to steer with but a steel shaft. I came back from the foredeck and managed, using only the shaft and proceeding at very slow speed, to thread my way through the fleet and up to the fuel dock. My brother still thinks I did it on purpose.

Most sailboat wheel steering arrangements include a brake, which allows you to leave the helm briefly. You can never take your hand off a

Herb taking off the wheel. Removing the wheel frees up cockpit space, but makes steering difficult when you forget to re-mount it.

tiller without lashing it, or, as some inventive sailors have done, fashioning some sort of adjustable tiller lock. Without such a device, letting go of the tiller will result in the boat's rounding up into the wind, thereby coming about or ending up in irons. If there's an audience, either situation can be embarrassing.

Windvanes and autopilots work equally well on either a tiller or a wheel. With a wheel, however, a windvane will require a drum, an item of considerable additional expense.

Once again, a tiller allows you more of the 'feel' of sailing. It is easier to notice bad balance, the result of poor sail trim. You'll know sooner when you're over-canvassed. And in port, a tiller can be raised so that it's completely out of the way.

Why then did we opt for a wheel? Because we had a wheel on our other boat, and that's what we're used to. Because I like a binnacle that puts the instruments, especially the compass, right in front of me. Because, when both our autopilot and windvane fail, I don't want to spend hours hand steering with a tiller. And finally, because Nancy, for all the reasons above plus a few secret ones of her own, prefers it.

CHAPTER 9

Below Decks

Dear Herb: My wife has read several articles stressing how important it is for me to keep her happy while I putter about with my dream of world cruising. She's made a list of her needs—her demands, is more accurate—which I find excessive. Could you please give me an idea of what amenities are found on cruising boats? By the way, money is not a problem, although if I accede to her wishes I envision a constant stream of repair people. We have a CSY 44, so we have plenty of space. I guess what I'm looking for is a conservative guideline to which I can point when her demands are excessive, as for instance for a washer and dryer.

What ever happened to the elemental life?

H. D. Thoreau, VII

Dear H.D.: Do I know you? Your name has a very familiar ring. Perhaps we met at the Atlantic City Boat Show? I meet so many people it's sometimes hard to keep track.

I hate to say this, but the degree of luxury to which many sailors have equipped their yachts has soared in recent years. In all fairness, the demands of the men are just as excessive as those of the women. I'll describe for you a yacht equipped to a degree equalled by more than half of all the yachts I meet, and risk contradiction by asserting that almost 100% are equipped to within 80% of this standard.

Damn, your name sounds familiar.

Although women are justly resisting being categorized as galley slaves, the galley is still what most female partners feel is their patch. If the woman does the cooking, she is *ipso facto* sheriff of the galley. As crew she may also make demands for on-deck electrical and other power assists to compensate for the difference in physical strength with the men for whom most hardware is designed.

Cooking is far more convenient if you have a stove. (Sorry, barbecue-ers, but it's a proven fact.) We have met very few skippers who still insist on alcohol or kerosene stoves because of the so-called safety factor. Once a large majority, they are now extremely rare. Propane is the standard, with most of the dangers obviated by a) an isolated, drained compartment for the propane bottles; b) a solenoid that turns off the gas at the bottle when not in use; c) a pressure gauge by which you can ascertain if there's a leak in the system; d) thermal protection devices that will not let gas escape from the burner if the flame goes out; and e) a sniffer that will detect propane in the bilge. (Propane is heavier than air, so any escaped gas will collect in the lowest part of the boat.)

According to Nancy, propane has no peer among fuels. It burns cleanly, exudes no odor—except when escaping and not burning, and then it carries a life-saving stink—and it is readily available throughout most of the world. Most importantly, Nancy adds, you don't have to prime each burner to light it! She warns that if the skipper insists on alcohol or kerosene, he must never let his wife or partner go out to dinner on a boat with a propane stove. Seeing the difference in ease and efficiency, she'll probably curtail sex until propane is installed. Or jump ship, leaving you to deal with your galley dinosaur, fighting flame-ups, lost primes, spilled lighted fuel, and the challenging task of refilling the kerosene or alcohol tank in a seaway.

We started our first cruise with an alcohol stove, which was both dangerous and expensive. When our stove rusted out from salt water having been thrown on stove fires, I bought a two-burner kerosene stove. A kerosene stove burns hotter than alcohol, but it has the drawback of requiring two kinds of fuel: alcohol to prime it, and kerosene to run it. Kerosene smells when it burns, leaves soot on pans and overhead, and imparts a real or imagined faint taste to all cooked food. After years of burned fingers and clogged burners, Nancy finally put her foot down. We were in Fiji, and a marine propane stove was not available. I installed an apartment-style propane stove on SEA FOAM. It had none of the safety measures we presently have on RED SHOES, and it was only through careful management that we avoided blowing ourselves up. But Nancy was so happy, the threat of death seemed of minor importance.

We now have a Seaward three-burner stove with oven. Nancy would like a microwave, but it would require more 110-volt power than our small inverter provides. Nancy has made toast under the stove's broiler for eight years. She would love a toaster, but the electrical demand is prohibitive. We had a blender, but used it so seldom we sold it. I have a Melitta coffee grinder without which I could not live.

We have a double sink which is appropriate for RED SHOES, as we don't have a watermaker. With a watermaker, Nancy tells me she wouldn't care, double or single. We keep dishwater for more than one meal in one sink, and we use the second to drain vegetables, etc.

Work and storage areas should be generous. Some storage compartments that look great at boat shows turn out to be an impractical use of space. RED SHOES was guilty of this, having a rounded storage area over the ice box, which I replaced with a rectangular one almost immediately.

We have a Force Ten cabin heater that has helped us survive late departures from New England. Heading south, and swearing we would never leave late again even for the fall foliage in Maine, we have had snow and ice, bitter wind and rain. Our heater runs on propane, but I would advise anyone who spends cruising time in higher latitudes to investigate diesel heaters. There are two types: a bulkhead mounted stove, and a furnace that produces hot air. My son-in-law Jerry has a Webasto forced air diesel furnace on his Nor-Sea 27, BRE ANNE MARIE. Forced air diesel heaters are available from Sure Marine in Seattle (tel. 800 562 7797), Scan Marine, also in Seattle (tel. 206 285 3675, fax 206 285 9532) and from Espar, a Canadian company (tel. from the U.S.: 800 387 4800, and from Canada: 800 668 5676). Jerry tells me it's silent, starts automatically using a glo plug, and in 30- to 40-degree weather his six-gallon fuel tank lasts about three weeks. During a cold snap with high winds it lasted a week. The Webasto produces a dry heat, as opposed to a propane space heater which, on RED SHOES, produces in short order a humid atmosphere suitable for growing orchids. For taking the chill off in weather that is not too extreme, a propane heater is convenient and performs adequately.

For most of our cruising lives we've had an ice box. When the ice ran out, we ate canned food, fresh fish if I could catch it. Most fresh veggies lasted no longer than our ice, a week at most. Potatoes, onions, carrots, beets, and cabbage will do fairly well without refrigeration.

If a propane stove brought Nancy to the first level of bliss, refrigeration brought her to the second. (She now tells me that a watermaker would bring her to level three. More on that in another chapter.) I bought an Adler Barbour Super Cold Machine (ABSCM), and after revamping the top-loading icebox, adding insulation to the interior and making it smaller, I installed the cooling unit.

The big drawback of refrigeration is the energy it requires, so anything you can do to give the box a higher 'R' value is worth doing. The insulation I added helped. Making it smaller helped. A tip from a friend prompted me to take a piece of closed cell foam and make a separate lid for the freezer compartment inside the box itself. I then added a piece of two-inch closed cell foam cut to lie over the whole top of the reefer. To get into the refrigerator you remove the two-inch foam, and open the lid. I knew that the two-inch foam on the top was a good idea when I removed it and placed my hand on the regular top-loading door and found it cold. We'd been admitting heat through the lid. Because the large piece of foam covering the top makes it more difficult to get into the fridge, we don't open it casually, thereby saving energy.

Before deciding how much you want to revamp the box, it'd be wise to fill the icebox with ice and test the outside of every interior surface that's reachable. Wherever it feels cold, consider adding insulation.

There are at least three good books on converting an icebox to a refrigerator, *Refrigeration for Pleasure Boats* by Nigel Calder, *Do-It-Yourself Boat Refrigeration* by R.R. Kollman and *The Box Book* by Mike Adler. I read them all, took something from each. As with any project I do once, I know I could do it better the second time. For the do-it-yourselfer, c'est la vie.

The ABSCM is a 12-volt system. Many people opt for an engine driven system. I have a friend whose trade was refrigeration who built a reefer using both a 12-volt ABSCM, and a cold plate whose compressor is engine driven. In a marina he uses the 12-volt system and avoids having to run his engine. At sea, if one system breaks, he can get by on the other.

The refrigerant, as it passes through the condenser, can be either air- or water-cooled. We opted for air-cooled, and have been grateful for our choice when hauled out and enjoying ice every evening. Our condenser is vented into the space under the helmsman's seat. If we ever fill the cockpit with water, there's an off chance that the unit will get wet, and subsequently suffer salt-water damage. Most air-cooled condensers are installed so that they draw air from the cabin, but we juggled precious storage space against the danger of dousing, and made our choice. A water-cooled condenser does not have to be vented, so it avoids this problem.

Frankly, we chose the ABSCM because it was the easiest to install, and by far the least expensive. I'm not sure that I wouldn't choose a 12-volt system regardless of cost or convenience. With solar panels and wind generators to augment the engine alternator, there is little or no difference in the amount of engine running time required. Engine driven systems require a compressor belted to the main engine, and often a two-belt instead of a one-belt drive. We already have so little space in our engine compartment that the mere thought of adding a compressor gives me muscle cramps. However, it's a two-sided question, with plenty of proponents on each.

I have a friend who, when he shops for a boat, first checks ease of engine access, and then galley storage to see if there's a place for a pot large enough to cook four 1¼-pound Maine lobsters. Then he looks at layout, equipment, etc.

Engine access is indeed important. When we equipped RED SHOES, we ordered the largest engine the company offered. Many times we've been grateful for its abundant power, but when I've had to work on it, I've often wished I'd chosen something smaller. No matter which engine we chose, the size of the engine room remained the same. There are certain things I must occasionally do to the engine that require using a mirror. I suffered like a Jesuit until Nancy bought me knee pads. I've had to invent methods and tools to accomplish certain space-deficient tasks. Persistence and thinking have overcome, but it would be so much better if I could get *at* everything more easily.

Just as the ideal battery bank would be modeled on a World War II submarine, so an ideal engine compartment would have full standing headroom and allow you to walk completely around the engine. The limitations of sailboats under 40 feet pretty much exclude either, so it comes down to what degree of compromise you can live with. I'm living with my cramped engine space in the hopes that one day I'll find a lamp that can summon a tiny contortionist who thrives on oil and grease.

We have a magic 34-footer that, within a week of having a guest couple on board, will gradually shrink to an overall length of something under 16 feet. We don't often have friends cruise with us, but those we invite could provide anyone with a catalog of our smells and noises. The brochure claims the Crealock 34 sleeps six. Sure. I've seen a VW bug disgorge a dozen people, too. But in our case, merely having four aboard can lay claim to being a stunt.

This is partly a small-boat, large-boat problem, and one very good reason for choosing the larger boat. Two separate cabins with separate heads are ideal for people who envision having guests aboard often. It's the word 'often' that's operative. On RED SHOES we have guests about once a year. It's not that we don't have friends or don't like company— Nancy has been known to kick and scream to persuade me to sail to where the parties are. But having guests on a small boat creates social dynamics, from frustration to suppressed aggressive tendencies, the investigation of which is beyond the scope of this book. Suffice it to say that with close friends who also cruise, we make it work.

Our head includes a toilet, wash basin, and shower. A pressure water system will use more water than a hand-pump system, so we turn off the pressure on passages. Our galley sink and head basin are plumbed for both.

Our shower drains into a pan or sump which is evacuated by a separate pump. There is a filter ahead of the pump, as humans shed hair prolifically when showering, and hair would eventually ruin the pump if allowed to reach it. Our filter originally occupied a tiny space, and the servicing operation had to be accomplished entirely by feel. Dismantling it was a test of equanimity that I continually failed. Reassembly required fitting the bowl to the filter body precisely so that a tiny screw could find its tiny receiving orifice. My longest time was 30 minutes. I felt very successful when I managed to disassemble, clean, and reassemble the filter in less than ten minutes. I have since found a filter whose bowl is threaded and twists on, and life has taken a large leap away from frustration.

Another solution is to screen the pan drain and have the shower water drain into the bilge, where it's evacuated with the bilge pump. I see nothing wrong with this as long as hairs are completely blocked from reaching the bilge. A bilge pump will *always* clog when you're terrified and need it desperately.

From our wooden boat days, experience drove me to insist on two bilge pumps, one electric and one hand-operated. The electric pump can be switched to operate automatically when the contents of the bilge reach a certain level. The problem with automatic operation is that you have no feel for how often pumping is necessary. Furthermore, ours never fails to decide to pump the bilge in embarrassing places and at inappropriate times—the tiniest traces of oil, grease, grunge and diesel fuel will surely put nearby swimmers in a bad mood.

In any boat with an engine, even the most conscientious, environmentally responsible cruiser will have trouble dealing with bilge water. Diesel engines are continually developing fuel line leaks. Bleeding air from the lines lets diesel fuel escape. When changing the oil, some always drips, particularly when changing the filters. Profligate use of absorbent material helps tremendously, but it's bulky, must be stored somewhere, and requires proper disposal, rarely found in third world countries.

Over the years we have developed methods that minimize but can't totally eliminate spillage. We clean the bilges often, using detergent to emulsify petroleum products. We're still looking for better ways.

I have little to say about storage, except that a liveaboard cruiser will want as much as possible, and it won't be enough. For areas with side access, you'll want positive closures. Our bins have friction closures, and several times when RED SHOES has been slammed by a wave we've suffered an avalanche of cans, bottles, boxes, and bags across the saloon sole. Our main food storage areas are under the saloon bunks and have both top and side access. When we go to sea I merely block off the side access from the inside, using pieces of plywood cut for the purpose.

On most yachts I've seen, the so called nav stations are a joke. Desks are usually so small a chart would have to be folded to handkerchief size. So as a postulate, we'll consider the nav station an electronics center, and plan to do all our chart work on the saloon table.

What follows is my personal preference. The nav station on RED SHOES comes close to getting it right, with a large desk that can hold 30 to 40 charts. The person using it should sit on the quarter berth but I never do, usually because it is so full there's no room to sit. I've developed the habit of standing, facing the starboard side. In any boat whose interior I design, the chart desk will be arranged thus: it will be hinged to open as I stand facing it. And it will be deeper, to hold more charts.

I manage to do some chart work on the desk, but even though the desk is comparatively large, I often move to the saloon table. I do all my log work standing up. As I face the side of the boat, I look directly at the ham radio, VHF radio, and GPS. I also look at the electrical panel and its various meters. I like it this way.

CHAPTER 10

Different Rigs

Dear Herb: I've read so much about the advantages of different kinds of rigs, I'm totally confused. I'll probably buy only one cruising sailboat in my life, and I don't want to get it wrong. If you had only one boat to buy, how would it be rigged?

Bolluxed in Biloxi

Dear B 'n B: Few people get everything right the first time. The good news is, in the long run it doesn't matter. If you're a dedicated cruiser and are flexible and inventive in your thinking, you'll make whatever rig you have work for you.

I've said that the type of boat you choose is use-specific: where are you going to sail, and how are you going to use it? Some of the same considerations can be applied to choice of rig, although proponents of each type will claim that theirs is an all-purpose choice.

Some elements to consider in choosing a rig are: How big is the boat? How many people will be sailing it? Are you going to be sailing mostly in light air? Mostly downwind?

You asked a specific question, and for what it's worth, here's my answer. If the boat I buy is a monohull of up to 36 feet LOD (length on deck), I'd choose a cutter rig with running backstays and a breakaway (detachable) inner forestay. For 40 feet LOD I'd choose a ketch rig with staysail and breakaway inner forestay (double headsail rig). The overlap (36 to 40 feet LOD) could be either cutter or ketch. I'd definitely have a roller-furling jib, but no roller-furling staysail, as this would prohibit getting rid of the staysail stay when I wanted to sail as a sloop or single-headsail ketch. And I've come to like a fully-battened mainsail with lazy jacks. The disadvantage of this arrangement is that, when you raise sail, the tips of the full battens tend to hang up in the lazy jacks. Success depends heavily on the helmsman keeping the boat directly into the wind. We generally use the engine when we raise the main.

Some folks swear by an arrangement called the Dutchman. The Dutchman depends upon literally stringing the sail on vertical monofilament lines that connect from the topping lift to the boom. The sail is supplied with cringles so that when it's dropped it falls flaked onto the boom. This arrangement is one way to eliminate the full-batten, lazy jack hangup mentioned above—a strong plus, particularly for single-handers.

A bigger boat would be more appropriately rigged as a ketch since a sloop might have sails too big to handle easily by one or two people.

This is not to say I couldn't or wouldn't sail other rigs, merely that my experience leads me to choose these. Why? Because I'm thinking neither of go-fast nor of the simplicity of the fewest sails possible. I'm thinking of heavy weather, and sailing single- or short-handed and, because I favor these rigs for dealing with heavy weather, I accept their inherent limitations.

The main drawback of most rigs is the mainsail chafe that'll occur when sailing off the wind. There are things you can do to reduce chafe: rig baggy wrinkles, or cover the offending shroud with PVC shroud cover available from marine stores. The latter is slit lengthwise, so that you don't have to undo the shroud at the turnbuckle to install it. You can also use PVC pipe, for which you would have to remove the shroud. I've even thought of using foam pipe insulation secured around the shroud with rigging tape. You need to figure out a way to prevent chafe where the sail hits the spreader. No matter what you choose to do, there'll be more wear on the sail where it rubs than where it doesn't.

On SEA FOAM, during our downwind passage from the Galápagos to the Marquesas, we set the sails and didn't change them for 16 days. We sailed under twin yankees, alternately hanked on a single headstay and held in place by twin poles. The poles were Sitka spruce and heavy, making setting the sails somewhat daunting, and even though we had strong young sons as crew, we resisted sail changes. Thus we were a tad under-canvassed in light winds, and over-canvassed in squalls. Although the wind blew consistently out of the Eastern quadrant, it varied from 20 degrees north of east to 20 degrees south of east, and we were forced to alter course with each change. Over the long haul this didn't matter much, but on shorter passages it could be a pain.

If an approaching squall looked severe enough to warrant reducing sail, we of course had to lower both poled-out jibs, as they were hanked on the same stay. An idea I came across recently suggests a neat solution: a roller-furling extrusion with two grooves. Raise twin jibs or genoas. To reduce sail, roll them both up simultaneously as much as you wish. If the wind shifts, putting you on a reach, one sail lays against the other and acts as a single sail. Only two sheets would be necessary, one for each sail. If you foresaw a prolonged leg to weather, you'd probably want to fly only one of the sails.

Some sailors have tried to rig twin headstays. However, a friend began his cruise in his 40-foot sloop with twin headstays and soon changed to a single one. He claimed that with two headstays sharing the stem-to-masthead load against a single backstay, there was an insupportable degree of jib sag when sailing to weather.

I have seen twin headstays on several boats since. With a modern rig and a properly supported aluminum mast, perhaps the necessary additional backstay tension wouldn't be a problem. But here's another thought: boats have been dismasted when sailing in relatively strong winds under jib alone. This is attributed to the fact that so much stress is concentrated at the masthead. I suppose one could make a case that the mast failed because the standing rigging wasn't tuned properly. In any case, the mainsail, reefed or not, distributes the load more evenly along the mast, and in strong winds is less likely to produce unforgivable stresses.

As our children left to pursue other goals, we found setting the twins with reduced crew more trouble than it was worth and took to sailing down-wind wing-and-wing with one poled-out jib and the mainsail prevented. Although this didn't balance as well, it did make reducing sail much easier. However, even though we'd rigged baggy wrinkles, there was always some chafe where the mainsail rubbed against the shroud.

When sailing RED SHOES downwind, we've sometimes used the mainsail for power, and have strapped the staysail (or sometimes a partially unrolled jib) hard amidships and as flat as possible, a tactic which noticeably dampens the exaggerated rolling that ocean waves can generate.

In weighing sloop versus cutter rig, consider a cutter with a detachable staysail stay. Whereas on a passage RED SHOES' staysail is always up, on a daysail both staysail and inner forestay are stowed and we sail as a sloop. Tacking is faster and smoother with no inner forestay to hang up the jib.

With either a sloop, cutter, or ketch, I would stay clear of tall masts, multiple spreaders, and high aspect ratios. We're seeking a compromise among several elements—low aspect ratio means (or should mean) less weight aloft, a shorter mast less subject to failure, and a smaller and easier-to-handle sail. For this we'll gladly give up a bit of windward performance.

One can justify the choice of almost any rig. However, for ocean cruising let's look at some reasons for rejection. Our first boat, SEA FOAM, was a gaff-headed ketch with yankee and staysail. After a passage on SEA FOAM with its gaff mainsail, I considered the calms hell, as there was no way to prevent the gaff from slamming from side to side as the boat rocked in the ocean swells. We finally rigged a kind of preventer/sheet from the top of the mizzen to the end of the gaff, and gained some control. But the overall scene—gaff plus light winds or calms— drove us all bananas.

SEA FOAM also had an 11-foot bowsprit. That's nearly one-third of the boat's on-deck length. Fortunately the bowsprit came equipped with a sturdy aluminum pulpit, which made dealing with the jib far less dangerous. Even with the pulpit, in rough seas, the crew on the bowsprit would spend half his time airborne, the up motion similar to that of a catapult, the down motion to that of an elevator with a snapped cable. Naturally, the farther forward of the center of motion you are, the more exaggerated the up and down cycle.

I've several times sailed on a Nonsuch. The 36 has so big a sail that raising it requires considerable effort, even with a winch. For us older sailors, assistance in the form of an electric halyard winch is almost a necessity. What if it doesn't work? On the other hand, reefing the sail is relatively simple. You drop the sail, tighten the luff reefing line, raise the now shortened sail, and finally tighten the leech reefing line. This is similar to a two-line, jiffy reefing system on a Bermuda mainsail.

Sandy Fowler, a cousin who cruised in his Nonsuch 36 from Nova Scotia to the Bahamas, made the following comments: "The good points of a Nonsuch rig: ease of handling, ease of reefing, minimum labor. Bad points: one large sail, sometimes not easy to handle when the wind pipes up. Also, great care is needed to avoid jibing—we always came about rather than jibed if the wind over the deck was greater than four knots. And although Nonsuchs have crossed the Atlantic, I feel that the difficulties of jury rigging a catboat in case of dismasting are a disadvantage."

Sandy also described the wishbone system for controlling sail shape. A line runs via blocks from the cockpit to the forward end of the wishbone, permitting fore-and-aft adjustment. His son is veteran sailmaker Win Fowler, a champion J-24 racer, who was loft manager for AMERICA[3] in 1992. Win said that although the wishbone acts as both boom and vang, to a sail trim fanatic this was not a satisfactory arrangement. He also said, "I don't think I'd want to try to claw off a lee shore in that boat in 50-knot winds."

On the Freedom Forty, a cat ketch with unstayed, carbon fiber masts, the sail uses no track, but is wrapped around the mast and led back on itself. This results in a double layer of sail material, so that if the sail is made of five-ounce Dacron, the weight is in fact ten ounces.

Wright Saylor, of DDRAIG, a Freedom Forty, knows of only one dismasting of a sister ship. It occurred when an owner tried to get off a grounding by pulling the masthead over using the halyard and a kedge or powerful dinghy. We have pulled the masthead over two or three times to get RED SHOES off a sandbar, and I would miss not having that option.

How about a junk rig? I once wrote: "All those heavy battens. Add to this the plethora of lines required to control each batten and you have more complication than I need. Can you think of a worse rig when it comes to slatting conditions? Imagine a mainsail with multiple gaffs. Not for me, thank you."

When I showed these remarks to a friend, Frank Schooley, who with his family has cruised the Caribbean extensively on his junk CONCUBINE, he politely pointed out that I didn't have a clue about junk rigs, and that I ought to go sailing on one before I bad-mouthed it. Here are a few of his remarks:

"A junk doesn't have a gaff, it has a yard. The big difference between the gaff and the yard is loading. The junk's yard hauls the sail up and spreads the top of the sail, and that's all." And, he pointed out, the battens aren't heavy timbers. On CONCUBINE they're aluminum pipe, and bamboo on a Chinese junk; in either case they're light.

"The real difference," Frank continued, "between a junk and Bermuda rig is, it's easier to fly a kite than a wing. The wing, the sail shape that sailors spend a lifetime learning to make happen, is difficult and expensive to achieve. The pressures on the mast and rig are incredible. On the junk sail, which is more like a kite, some of the sail is forward of the mast and acts like a balanced rudder. The loads are distributed evenly on the mast, which needs no fore- or back-stay. The sheet is so lightly loaded it never requires a winch.

"Reefing is a snap. Okay, the rig is not brilliant to weather, but then again neither am I. And due to its larger sail area and lower angle of heel, the junk will walk away from most cruising boats on a reach or run."

Recently we went sailing with him in 12 to 15 knots of wind. CONCUBINE is heavy, 30,000 pounds on a 29-foot waterline, and I was suprised at how well it performed. On a beam reach, sailing at five to six knots, the angle of heel was hardly measurable. In spite of multiple lines, sheeting was simple, and stress on both rig and crew was low.

Coming home downwind, a snaky channel required frequent jibes, but because of the absence of a boom—a heavy boom sweeping across the deck being the biggest danger in a conventional rig—they were handled with ease. And it's true, the junk sail need not be any shape in particular. In fact, the flatter the better.

I would find it hard to give up the fun of tweaking the sail shapes on RED SHOES. I don't enjoy sailing to weather at sea, but if I have to, I want to be able to do it well. And I actually enjoy sailing to weather in protected waters. Frank claims sixty degrees off the wind including leeway (my observations would put it closer to seventy), but adds that his 120-horsepower diesel engine pushes CONCUBINE to weather just fine. If you can give up some windward performance, you might look at the junk rig for its simplicity and ease of handling.

For yet another opinion on junk rigs, as well as some innovative solutions to the problems of multiple lines, read Derek Van Loan's book, *The Chinese Sailing Rig: Designing and Building Your Own.*

I've never spent much time on a schooner, either, so here are some remarks by Dodge Morgan, who briefly held the record for single-handed circumnavigation. The boat he used was a custom-designed, 60-foot cutter equipped with electric winches, autopilots, electronic navigation, and satellite communication for accessing a New England weather guru. Named AMERICAN PROMISE, the boat was as technically upscale as a schooner is traditional.

Dodge has owned two schooners: COASTER, a 36½-foot Murray Peterson design, and his present EAGLE, 30½-foot on deck, which he has owned for 28 years. EAGLE was originally designed by Alden Malibar Jr., and then redesigned by Murray Peterson. Dodge has single-handed schooners for thousands of miles, including both coasts of North America and Alaska. His first remark was, "It's better than any rig," but he then went on to qualify his statement.

"My schooners had a gaff fore. The stubby rig made it possible for me to keep up sail in rising winds. A schooner is as good as any rig on a reach. EAGLE tacked through 100-110 degrees at sea—a staysail schooner would be better on the wind. Schooners are forgiving for single-handers, and easy to balance.

The majesty of a schooner has yet to be surpassed.

"Not nice dead downwind," he concluded. But then, not many rigs are.

An interesting adaptation of the staysail schooner was George Gliksman's SYMPHONY, a 70-foot aluminum hull with three masts. Picture a roller-furling jib duplicated twice, one jib for each mast or, in schooner parlance, a jib and two staysails. The aftermost sail (the mainsail) was the only one with a boom. SYMPHONY's was by no means a tall rig; nevertheless, all except the mainsail divided the stress between two points—the tack and the masthead—making the tuning of the standing rigging critical in a blow.

Talking with only one or two people doesn't give enough information on which to base your choice for an uncommon rig. Before deciding on one I would want to sail with it several times in varying conditions. There is nothing like extensive sea trials to reveal a system's weakness. If that kind of experience isn't available, I would stick to rigs and systems that have been tried and found practical by a large number of cruisers. Which, in fact, is what we did.

Except for a brief comment here, sail trim is beyond the scope of this discussion. It's sufficient to note that almost all books on the subject deal with Bermuda mainsails and genoas. These are the rigs used in racing, and there's a good reason for this: they offer more options for better sail shape than other types of sails, and go to windward more efficiently.

I might mention that even though most sail trim discussions are focussed on how to go to weather faster, it's important to control shape even when going downwind. And the basic rule for this is to use a downhaul on the jib pole, and a vang on the main. These will keep the spars from being moved up and down by puffs or waves, thus stabilizing the sail's shape and preventing it from spilling the wind.

It's fun to play with outhauls, cunninghams, traveler settings, vangs, and jib sheet leads. Certainly on a passage that involves going to weather, increasing sail efficiency even fractionally can be encouraging. If this kind of thing fascinates you, pick up a copy of *The Best of SAIL Trim* or *The New Book of SAIL Trim*, compilations of articles that have appeared in SAIL Magazine that explain clearly and thoroughly the various aspects of dealing with Bermuda rig sails. Both are available from Sheridan House.

We could discuss rigs and optional sail combinations for pages. There's a lot of experimental stuff out there, and additional sails, such as cruising spinnakers, mizzen staysails, etc., expand your options. My suggestion would be that no matter what rig you choose, practice in benign conditions the steps you'll take in heavy weather. Find out if it's possible to heave to—a catboat can't. If standing or running rigging or sail modifications are needed, the time to find out is *before* you have to deal with winds of 40 to 60 knots. And if you're heading west to cross oceans in the trade winds, figure out what downwind sails you'll set (day and night if different) and how you'll deal with squalls.

Virtually all rigs will work in moderate conditions. The most significant differences lie in how they work when the wind is up and the chips are down. The more working sails you have, the more options you have when reducing sail or heaving-to.

Hope this helps. . .

CHAPTER 11

Roller Furling and Other Aids

Dear Herb: I'm a kinda older fella, probably shouldn't be thinkin' about goin' nowhere in a damn sailboat. But my wife just passed, and this urge I've been swallerin' for the last 40 years is about to make me plumb crazy. I been readin' a lot, but I ain't too clear on this here "roller furlin'." Is it just some new-fangled gewgaw, or can I damn well *depend* on it?

Paw Perkins

Dear Paw: Lest you tell me, given, I'm sure, the slightest chance, I'll remind you that there ain't nothin' sure exceptin' death and taxes. There are a passel of gadgets that'll make sailing easier for us old farts (let's face it, that's what the kids call us), but there isn't one of them that won't break down.

But you ask, "Can I damn well *depend* on it?" and my answer would be "yes." 'Round the world single-handers have been depending on roller furling for years. Sure, something can always go wrong, and certainly one of the principal tenets of our kind of cruising is to keep it simple. But there comes a time after something's been around for a while when you take a second look and say, yeah, that's for me. That's what's happened between me and roller furling.

When we talk about roller furling, we're talking about the gear that rotates and rolls up the jib on the headstay, a process that can be accomplished from the cockpit. When we talk about roller reefing, we're adding the concept of using the sail in a partially rolled-up state. The success of the latter depends on how the sail was made, and how much of it you've rolled up. Sailmakers will usually specify what percentage of sail you can roll up (about 30% for most) and still maintain a workable sail shape.

It has been our experience that even a sail not designed for roller reefing will work partially rolled up. The shape may not be ideal, but it works. You won't break any records for how close you sail to the wind, but fall off a tad and the sail will move the boat.

A couple of ideas for roller reefers: If, in heavy weather, you need to use a winch to roll up the sail, you may have a hard time removing the line

Roller furling drum. Note the jury rigged fairlead. The way the furling line feeds onto the drum is crucial for trouble free operation.

from the winch and securing it on its own cleat. A contributor to my column in *SAIL* "Things That Work" suggested using a block with a jam cleat. The jam cleat holds the tension on the roller reefing line while you transfer it.

The other idea is to install a piece of PVC pipe on that length of halyard that will be exposed when the jib is raised. The contributor claims that this prevents halyard wrap, which is the single biggest cause of problems in rolling or unrolling the sail. We haven't tried it, nor have we tried what another sailor suggested, which is to use a pennant at the tack long enough that the exposed length of jib halyard is as short as possible. However, this raises the center of effort.

With a sloop, in the old days you sent kids or crew up onto the foredeck to change jibs. But we're just a couple now, and we're doing what we can to avoid ever again having to change jibs in heavy weather. With roller furling we can sail with a handkerchief of a partially rolled-up jib; but the disadvantage of that is that the sail is a third of the way up the forestay, yet you want the center of effort as low as possible. It's at this point that the cutter rig becomes a blessing.

Here's what happens aboard RED SHOES when we put to sea. If it looks like we're going to be on the wind—a beam reach or closer hauled—we raise the staysail. It will most likely stay up till we reach port. Then we look at the sky and tune in to our paranoids. (Paranoids used to be removed with tonsils, but mine never were.) If they say throw a reef in the mainsail, we do. Actually, if it looks like we'll need a reef, we might decide to leave a day later.

When our boat was new, we rigged it per the rigging plan that came with it. I hadn't had much experience with modern conveniences. SEA FOAM, the boat in which we cruised the Pacific for seven years, was a gaff-headed ketch with one winch for all four working sails. The rigging plan for RED SHOES called for roller furling. For the mainsail, it called for two reefing lines leading back to the cockpit, one for the tack, and one for the clew. Putting in the first reef was simple and safe.

But guess what? Wind is up, seas are up, time to put in a second reef, and now I have to go to the mast, because there isn't enough space to lead a second set of two reefing lines back to the cockpit. This arrangement didn't make any sense to me, but we lived with it for five years before I tried something different.

My present system of *single line reefing* frees the second line for a second reef. It is far from perfect, but I've learned to work with it successfully. One line leads from the cockpit to a block at the base of the mast, up through the cringle which on reefing becomes the new tack, then through a turning block on the boom and out through a series of fairleads. It then goes through another turning block on the outer end of the boom, up through the cringle that will become the clew, and back down to tie around the boom. The second reef is rigged exactly the same way.

Don't forget that with any such system, if your sail has a bolt-rope for a foot, you'll need an extra cringle right under the reef clew and as close as possible to the boom, so that you can pass the bitter end of the reefing line around the boom. If you have cars and tracks, the extra cringle is desirable but not absolutely necessary.

When it is time to reef, we slack off the halyard till the new tack is about six inches or more higher than we want it to end up, and start winching in on the reefing line. The tension will act at the tack like a cunningham, bringing the tack down to where we want it. Further winching will pull down on the clew.

The problem is that there's too much friction where the line goes through the cringles. The fact that the sheet is loose and the sail is flogging actually helps. I'll be the first to admit that our system is far from ideal, but I've learned to make it work, and compared to the alternative of standing on the cabin top trying to tame a big sail at second reef-time, I love it.

I've seen plans for single line reefing that use lighter line and small blocks at the cringles. This would certainly cut down on friction and obviate two sites subject to line chafe. Sometimes, as on our beat to the Amazon from Barbados, or on our eight-day passage directly from the Bahamas to the Virgin Islands, a reef stays in for days. At the site of each block, a patch on the sail of extra material or even leather would be a good hedge against sail chafe.

With a tack hook, a single-hander needs the halyard at the mast instead of in the cockpit. But then he can come back to the safety of the cockpit and deal with a reefing line for the clew. Halyards coiled at the mast can come loose in a blow. It's common sense for couples to have single-hander procedures down pat. What if one person gets injured?

Some people still swear by the old style of roller reefing for the main, wherein the boom is engineered to be rotated, thereby wrapping the sail around it. I call it 'roller boom' reefing. For a while this fell out of favor, probably either because the shape of the sail suffered, or because of the unreliability of the mechanism itself.

There are signs of it coming back, however. Recently a cruising couple, Bob and Gayle on TRILITE, sailed their ultralight, Ian Farrier-designed trimaran from Florida to the Rio Dulce. They had roller boom furling and reefing and swore by it, claiming the sail shape remained perfect when reefed. The system requires that the boom be free of cleats, fairleads and other protrusions, nor can it have internal lines. The topping lift length would thus have to be controlled via the top of the mast, and the outhaul for the clew would have to be secured at the outer end of the boom. However, so far, at least until someone figures out how to electrify it, you still must go to the mast to reef.

Besides the old fashioned slab reefing, and/or jiffy reefing, there are two other systems to consider, each of which rolls up the mainsail on a vertical axis, one inside and the other behind the main mast on a separate rod, stay or extrusion. Either choice has its advantages and drawbacks. If the sail gets screwed up inside the mast, what do you do? Rolling it up outside means you'll need a sunshield (as on a roller furling jib). All that material adds bulk and windage aloft, and the cost of these systems is daunting.

The combination of fully-battened main, lazy jacks, and single line reefing has worked adequately for us.

CHAPTER 12

Water and Fuel

Dear Herb: I began this letter by remarking that asking a sailor how he feels about his boat is like asking him how he feels about his woman—a man's got to justify his choice. Then my wife jumped all over me. So I rephrase my remark: Asking him or her how he or she feels about his or her boat is like asking him or her how he or she feels about his or her mother/father. There! And the reason for *that* statement is, how much water and fuel does RED SHOES carry, and are you happy with your tankage?

Politically Corrected

Dear PC: In this world, very few of us are happy with the amount of our liquid assets. And that's what tankage comes down to. In a word, the answer to your question is: 75 gallons of water and 25 gallons of fuel. A further answer is, we carry three five-gallon jerry cans of diesel on deck. And a couple of years ago, when I realized we weren't going to bring RED SHOES back to the States in the foreseeable future, I re-plumbed our (never used) 17-gallon holding tank for a water tank. So was I happy with our tankage? No.

Am I now? Sort of.

WATER

When necessary, we carry four collapsible jerry jugs full of water on the cockpit floor. We've cruised in places where potable water was impossible, difficult, or expensive to come by: the Amazon, the San Blas Islands of Panama, and most third world countries where you're not tied up to a marina. Whenever we can we catch rain water, but in countries where there is cholera, we're extremely careful to scrub any bird droppings off the decks, as they can carry the disease. We're careful anyway, since bird droppings taste like—bird droppings. You may have guessed that we don't have a watermaker.

We have always used chlorine to purify (loose use of word), detoxify (also loose use of word), de-germ our water. Chlorine is poisonous

66

to humans, but in the dilution we use for purifying water it's thought to be harmless. There is debate on the subject, however. In general we add two ounces of Clorox (5% solution) to 40 gallons of water if we suspect minor contamination, or if the source itself is suspect. In 15 years of cruising two oceans we've never gotten sick on water from our boat tanks.

Clorox/water tank proportions:

⅓ cup per 100 gallons.

2 drops per quart if clear.

4 drops if cloudy.

1 cup per 300 gallons.

1 ounce per 40 gallons.

60 drops   = 1 teaspoon.

3 teaspoons   = 1 tablespoon.

4 tablespoons = ¼ cup or 2 fluid ounces.

There are 8 ounces per cup.

Recently a contributor to *SAIL*'s "Things That Work" suggested changing from chlorine to hydrogen peroxide, since the latter is less harmful if taken internally than chlorine. (But is it?) He recommended using ½ to 1 ounce of a 27% hydrogen peroxide solution per 10 gallons of water. Higher concentrations can be used for corrective rather than maintenance purposes.

The non-chemical solution for purifying water is to boil it. The International Association for Medical Assistance to Travelers (IAMAT) advises boiling for 10 minutes. Campers have used iodine pills, but a recent article in *Prevention* says it'll make the water taste terrible. Drop two pills into a quart of water, and 20 minutes later you can drink it. Rum might camouflage the taste, but why spoil the taste of good rum? A restaurant owner in Guatemala's Rio Dulce uses iodine-purified water to wash vegetables, leaving no discernible taste.

There are commercially available water purifiers—West Marine at this moment carries three different brands—but we have never used them. For most cruisers, chlorine is the chemical of choice, simply because it's cheap, it works, cruisers have survived minor chlorine ingestion for years, and it's available everywhere.

Tanking up is a breeze if you can do it with a hose at a marina or fuel dock. In many places there's a charge. In the U.S. and British Virgin Islands, we paid anywhere from seven to fifteen cents per gallon. In the Bahamas, we paid 50 cents a gallon for desalinated water and had to jerry jug it a half mile to the dinghy. When cruising, pulling up to a convenient dock and hosing it aboard is the exception.

In Puerto La Cruz, Venezuela, for example, there was very little rainfall, and I was always jerry jugging water out to the boat. For a while those of us at anchor were able to get it from the marina, but the management soon put an end to it. After that, we were only allowed to take water if we bought fuel, and even then only after an argument. This meant that to get water I had to dinghy in to the beach, take our four jerry jugs up to a public faucet 50 yards away, fill them, lug them or tip a boat boy to lug them back to the dinghy, brave the waves, horse the jerry jugs aboard RED SHOES, then bake in the sun while I siphoned the water from jug to tank (three minutes for each jug). As we had to make the trip four or five times to fill up, you can see why I used to embarrass Nancy by getting out on the foredeck and doing a rain dance to the accompaniment of chanted supplications.

Many people arrange their awning for catching water. One way is to make sure the middle is the lowest point, then sew in a funnel and run a hose from the funnel to the water tank. This is a great arrangement when you're at anchor, but few boats sail with their awning up.

We catch water on deck by plugging the scupper drains. At sea the decks will most likely be clean, but they'll also most likely be salty. So will sails, and anything stowed on deck, such as sail bags. We've often seen a squall coming and hove-to rather than continue sailing, thus lowering the chance of getting salt water on deck during catchment time. Of course there has to be enough rain to flush all the salt off the sails and decks before we open the filler pipe.

Monitoring use becomes important. It's necessary to work out certain procedures. Nancy is no longer willing to wash dishes in salt water, but on a long passage she would have to. We put an inch of water in the bottom of a cup or glass for brushing teeth. Baths are postponed, although sponge baths can be taken using remarkably little water. Salt-water baths require one or two cupfuls of fresh water for rinsing. If you see a squall coming, you might want to soap up. But beware! Several times in our cruising history we've seen a squall turn to disappointment, leaving one or the other of us soapy and shampooey in the sunlight.

None of our water tanks have gauges. Nor is it possible to measure with a dipstick, as the filler pipes aren't straight. I've heard of people plumbing their water tanks with a length of clear (so you can see the water level in the hose) plastic hose running from the bottom of the tank to the top, but because of the placement of most tank installations this is usually difficult. Electronic gauges tend to be unreliable.

On RED SHOES we first use up our 40-gallon aft tank, which is the easiest to fill with deck catchment. When it's empty, we can figure our daily consumption and act accordingly. Next we use the 35-gallon forward tank; when we've switched to the 17-gallon ex-holding tank, we know we're running dangerously low.

SEA FOAM had two 75-gallon tanks. On a 46-day passage (our longest) from Samoa to Kiribati (I know, I know, it's only 1,500 miles), three of us used up one tank only. Neither Nancy nor I remember if we caught rain, but chances are we did. What we do know is that we arrived in Tarawa with 75 gallons left. The point is, water use can be kept to a parsimonious minimum, and on a small boat this should be the rule for any passage of significant duration.

We delivered a boat named LISSA from Tahiti to California, and our longest leg at sea was 42 days. The problem with LISSA was that all her water (90 gallons) was stored in one tank. We carried 10 gallons in jerry jugs for emergency.

If you've read this far and haven't ordered a watermaker yet, I've failed.

FUEL

Fuel use must also be considered. Along with all your other stuff, watermakers need electricity, which on many cruising boats means running the engine to charge the batteries. In another chapter we discuss some alternative methods of replenishing batteries. Suffice it to say here that if you presently need to run your engine daily for recharging, or for driving a reefer compressor, you need to figure the hours and the fuel consumption, and decide if you have enough tankage for a long passage. On a passage on RED SHOES we burn three-quarters to a gallon of fuel a day just to keep our batteries up. Unfortunately, (or maybe fortunately,) it doesn't rain diesel fuel, so from the U.S. to the Marquesas, or crossing the Indian Ocean, we would have to be very assiduous in monitoring engine use.

Just as water should be treated, at least when suspect, so should diesel fuel. The most pernicious problem is algae, a bad infestation of which can clog your secondary fuel filter in a couple of hours. There are additives such as Biobor that will kill algae, but it must be used as directed or the additive itself can cause problems. There are other brands with which I'm not familiar. Biobor has worked well for us over the years.

Getting clean, waterless diesel fuel to the engine is priority one. The primary filter (the little one on the engine itself) cannot do the job alone, nor does it include a water separator. Therefore all marine diesel installations include a secondary fuel filter. Ours is a Racor, but other makes can also do the job.

Propane is a part of tankage. We have two aluminum 20-pound tanks in a totally isolated aft compartment that drains overboard. One tank will last us anywhere from seven to twelve weeks. With propane being heavier than air, if any should escape from the tank or the various connections, it will dissipate harmlessly. One problem, however, is that the drains, which must be at the lowest point, admit salt water when we're sailing. Aluminum does corrode and should be painted. Steel tanks must be painted periodically. Aluminum will resist corrosion better than steel, but I'm not sure the two-to-three times higher price is worth it.

RED SHOES has a wheel, and consequently a pilot's seat, under which is a well-ventilated space intended for the gas tank of the outboard motor. I installed my air-cooled Adler Barbour reefer in the very back of the quarter berth and vented it under the pilot's seat. We certainly don't want the compressor fan to suck gasoline fumes into the boat, so we now store our gas tank and gasoline jerry jugs on deck.

I was going to discuss tankage for alcohol and kerosene, but except to suggest that you monitor use on weekend or vacation cruises to find out how much you'd need for a passage, I feel that people who stubbornly insist on archaic systems should have to work out the details for themselves.

CHAPTER 13

Juice

Dear Herb: My wife and I have just finished building our dream boat, designed along the lines of a Bristol Channel cutter. We are minimalists, or at least I am; we intend not to have an engine, and although I'm leaning towards having at least one battery, we hope on our round the world voyage to get by with using as little electricity as possible. In these days of prodigality, energy-usewise, do you have any suggestions?

Bare Bones

Dear BB: I would love to have a talk with Mrs. Bare Bones—alone. She could sit on the other side of an opaque screen and speak her mind anonymously on the subject of minimalism. And if you were to eavesdrop on the conversation, you might discover that although getting back to the basics suits you, the Love Of Your (Austere) Life, LOY(A)L, thinks it's ridiculous. I hope you have a pre-nuptial agreement, or at least a pre-voyaging one, as the chance of this marriage surviving a long voyage is about one in a million. In my opinion, Mr. Bare Bones, your plan needs fleshing out.

But before talking to LOY(A)L, I would like to have a chat with you, BB. Does your minimalism spring from a need to navigate the Financial Straits, or does it satisfy a craving for romance? If the latter I can understand it, although if I were you I'd examine the idea closely before becoming too committed.

You see, I'm not immune to the siren call of romance. One of my fondest memories from childhood is of winter vacations spent in Conway, New Hampshire, where my grandfather had a 600-acre vacation home. The building was a rambling wood structure that had served earlier owners as an inn. There were probably ten bedrooms. All heat—stove, furnace, hot water—was provided by wood. The stove fire had to be started each morning, and the basement furnace had to be stoked in the wee smalls, or else it would have to be re-lit as well. The water came from five widely separated springs, each piped to its own faucet in the kitchen, each

71

having to be turned on at the source, and later turned off and the pipes drained.

As I grew older, I would bring a girl friend. By day, if there was snow, and there usually was in February, we skied. At night we played cards or read by the mellow light of kerosene lamps. Talk about romance! Even today, I can't smell a kerosene lamp or wood smoke in a house without my mind being flooded with wonderful memories.

Behind the building was a mountain with a trail to the top. When it snowed, six to ten of us would don skis or snow shoes and spend half a day packing the trail. A three-minute run required a 30-minute climb, probably the best lesson one could have on the subject of energy use. And for a treat, one of the fourteen days of our vacation would be spent at a ski area called Cranmore, where we could actually ride (Oh, the miracle of electricity!) to the top of the mountain. It wasn't cheap, but you-didn't-have-to-climb!

You may have noticed that I said our austere but wondrous, woodsy idyll lasted for fourteen days. But did I tell you how glad we all were to return to thermostatically controlled oil heat? To lights that responded to the flick of a switch, and that weren't so dim that after reading for a half hour you felt like your eyes were falling out? To our wonderful gas stove that didn't require me going out to the barn in the freezing cold to chop and fetch firewood? Did I mention the joy of hot water from a tap?

Okay, okay, I'll talk about electricity on boats, and try to sketch the spectrum of possibilities. But what I most hope is that you'll realize that romance has a short shelf life, whereas a voyage and the liveaboard life style can endure happily for years.

But only if you give it a chance.

You're 100% right about one thing: electricity on boats begins with batteries. And because 99% of all cruising sailboats of the size range we're looking at use a 12-volt system, we'll stick to discussing 12 volts.

Our seven years on SEA FOAM were more minimalist than *de luxe*. We did have electric lighting throughout, a radio telephone and later a ham radio, and an electric windlass. The windlass we used only when the engine was running, thereby allowing the alternator to carry the tremendous amperage drain. We carried a powerful spotlight for emergencies.

When RED SHOES arrived from the factory she had a fairly basic electrical setup: running and steaming lights, a masthead tricolor and anchor light, a foredeck light (usually called a spreader light, but in our case mounted on the mast, not on the spreader), and cabin lights. The lighting on RED SHOES was beautifully thought out—individual reading lights for the forepeak berth, and one for each end of the saloon settees; bright lights in the overhead; and recessed fluorescent lights. And because we had a propane stove, we were wired for the remote relay switch that shuts off propane at the tank. We had a pressure water system, and therefore an electric pressure water pump. There was a deck-washdown pump, a sump pump in the head to drain the shower pan, and an electric bilge pump with an automatic float switch. For instruments we had depth and speedo.

To get 110 volts, I installed a Heart Interface inverter. With six hundred watts, it powered my computer and printer, and more recently my electronic keyboard and amplifier. Somewhere along the line I bought one of my cherished luxuries—an electric coffee grinder. Nancy's sewing machine requires 110 volts. I carry a saber saw that is powered by 110 volts, and a battery powered drill whose battery must be recharged using 110 volts. We also had a hand-held VHF from an earlier boat, whose battery can be recharged using either 12 volts or 110 volts. For the last year or so we've had a color TV and a VCR, each requiring 110 volts. (You can get 12-volt ones, but the TV was second-hand and free, and the VCR was bought at a clearance price. After a year it no longer worked. Bargains!)

Before ever leaving the dock we added a VHF radio, Loran, autopilot, a fan for the saloon, and a cassette tape deck. I installed a chart light. After a year or so we installed a ham radio, SatNav, and three more fans. Most recently we've added GPS and refrigeration.

The boat came wired for shore power and had a Lewco automatic battery charger. Plugged in at a marina, it still operates mostly on 12 volts, but the Lewco keeps the batteries topped off. Throughout the boat there are 110-volt outlets. The water heater, which normally works off the engine, works off 110 volts when we're at the dock.

As I've been writing these words I've become more and more amazed. I've never listed all our electrical stuff before, and it's an eye-opener for me how much can be powered by a few relatively small batteries. As a minimalist you'll have laughed at a lot of it. What you have to realize is that we lived aboard SEA FOAM for seven years, and we've lived aboard RED SHOES for nearly ten years, and my wife is still with me.

What of the above list do I consider absolutely essential? Lights: in the tropics, no sane man would put up with the heat generated by kerosene lamps; the VHF radio; and the relay switch for the propane stove. I know, I know, I could go to the source and turn off the tank, but this would be so inconvenient we'd probably end up not doing it, and I consider the procedure of turning off the fuel at the tank to be absolutely essential for safety and peace of mind. As a writer I could go back to a typewriter. Heaven forbid! I could grind my coffee beans by hand. Did I hear someone suggest I buy ground coffee? Sacrilege! We have a manual bilge pump that operates from the cockpit. Our backup GPS uses flashlight batteries. We lived for years with an icebox. We have an Aries windvane that steers us flawlessly and non-electrically under sail. Our pressure water system is also plumbed for manual use, and even equipped as we are, for a passage of more than a few days we turn off the pressure system. Some short-wave receivers—for accurate time, in case the GPS quits—will operate on flashlight batteries.

At the moment I'm sitting in RED SHOES' cabin. We're at Susanna's marina in the Rio Dulce, Guatemala, and plugged into shore power. Occasionally the power goes off, which doesn't bother us, as it always comes back on long before we need to recharge our batteries. However, a bolt of lightning just reminded me how vulnerable boats are to a lightning strike—especially a boat that's as dependent on electricity as ours. Not only radios and electronic instruments, but even alternators and breaker panels can be fried.

You might think that with all the electrically powered things we have we'd need a huge bank of batteries. In fact, what we have are three size 27 Prevailers, and a smaller gel cell that can be isolated to power our ham radio. This is pretty much a minimum number of ampere hours, approximately 300, to power what we have on board.

Nigel Calder, a writer/sailor, has made quite an extensive study of batteries as they relate to a boat's electrical system. He claims that given proper charging procedures, six-volt wet cell golf cart batteries (wired in tandem to provide 12 volts) will take roughly three times as many rechargings as 12-volt gel cells. He also maintains that more ampere hours are better, because they allow you to use a smaller percentage of the battery bank's power, and to use a part of the voltage spectrum that recharges quickly. Don't hold me to the numbers, but the general rule is that it requires significantly more time and energy to bring a battery from 80% charge to 100% than it does from say 60% charge to 80%. Thus a procedure that uses the 60% to 80% charge part of the spectrum will be more efficient.

A writer has to be careful when he makes statements like this. A friend who owns an Irwin 58 read about Calder's ideas. He went out and bought 36 size twenty-seven 12-volt deep cycle batteries and arranged them in two banks of eight, two banks of six, and two banks of four. It's been a while since I've seen him, so I don't know how he feels about what he did. But talk about ample power! However, the mind boggles when I think of checking the water level in 36 times 6, or 216 cells.

The advantages of gel cells begin with the fact that if you spend any time sailing upside down, the electrolyte won't leak out. Ventilation is less of a problem than with wet cells, as they produce much less hydrogen gas when being charged. This means you have more choices as to where to store them. They are completely maintenance free. They are less likely to be damaged by deep discharge. And according to the ads, they can be charged more quickly and require less charging energy to fully recharge.

Besides being expensive, gel cells are easily damaged by improper charging procedures. Prevailers, the best-known brand of gel cells, have a guarantee. But the guarantee is void if you charge the batteries incorrectly. And even if you didn't, you might be in New Guinea when they fail. . .

Be that as it may, five years after we installed our first Prevailers we're still using them. They're showing signs of age, harder to charge, less time between recharges, but they still work. We are full-time live-aboards. A few weeks ago we came back from a six-week absence, and found that the two oldest batteries had held their charge beautifully. Two newer batteries didn't do as well. I've been told that mixing new batteries with old is poor procedure, and as that's what we did, perhaps the fault is ours. But I don't want to deal with the complication of charging three banks separately.

I just received a Boating Safety Circular from the U.S. Coast Guard saying that automatic temperature-sensing voltage regulated chargers should be used when charging gel cells. Although Prevailer type batteries are touted as 'maintenance free' and 'sealed', they will nonetheless emit a highly volatile hydrogen gas if not charged in accordance with manufacturers instructions.

Think of your battery bank as a blood donor. Having taken electricity out of your batteries you need to put it back. The most common solution is to run the main engine and let the alternator do it. There are various alternator and regulator choices.

We lived for seven years on SEA FOAM using wet cell batteries, and running the engine was the only way to recharge. We eventually bought a portable gasoline generator which powered our electric sander, drill, and saber saw, but only twice did we need it for our main batteries, having discharged them to the point where they couldn't start the main engine. I felt more secure having the portable generator as a backup, however.

On RED SHOES, until I installed refrigeration, we had only our engine's alternator for charging. After a year I figured I could shorten charging times by having a more efficient voltage regulator than the standard one that comes with the alternator.

A voltage regulator, in case you lead a sheltered life, electrical-knowledgewise, can be compared to the duenna of a properly reared virgin, as it tells the alternator how much (not) to put out. A regulator is essential for keeping the alternator from charging full bore, and either burning up or overcharging and ruining the batteries. A standard regulator does this. It also cuts back on the charging rate much sooner than is necessary for the safety of the batteries. Our answer was to install an Automac, an automatic, adjustable rate regulator. It worked fine for a year or so, at which point it broke. I called the company. When I was told the minimum charge for diagnosis and repair, I removed the device and threw it overboard.

I replaced it with a manual control, which consists of a twelve-dollar rheostat—a variable potentiometer—that feeds excitation current to the alternator's field coil. Compare excitation current to adrenaline, or testosterone, or whatever turns you on. This system requires constant monitoring to avoid overcharging. We've used it for four years without a misstep. But if you want an idiot-proof regulator that requires no attention after initial adjustment, a manual system is not for you.

Recently a profusion of automatic regulators have come on the market. They all seem to be priced around $150 to $200, compared to my twelve-dollar rheostat. However, if I had the cash and weren't already used to my manual system, I'd buy one.

Many cruisers replace the standard alternator with one that's classified as high output. For example, RED SHOES came with a 50-amp alternator, and would probably do better with one that puts out 90 to 100 amps. The theory is that by pumping more amps into the bank you shorten your charging time. This is true, but with the small bank of Prevailers we have on RED SHOES, we can only apply the high rate of amps for a few minutes before the voltage reaches 14.2, at which point we are supposed to cut back. High output alternators aren't cheap, and the amount of charging time saved wasn't justified. Furthermore, some high output alternators require two belts, or if only one is used, belt tension is critical, and increased tension can result in increased bearing wear.

Alternator alternatives. Since installing the reefer we've had a Windbugger. Wind generators require wind, and ours doesn't produce significant amps till the wind blows 12 knots. Even in the trades, I'm surprised at how often it blows less. However, when it does blow, we're the blessed beneficiaries of free juice—anything from two amps up to 15 (windy!).

There are nearly a dozen different brands of wind generators on the market. Some generators are permanently mounted on mizzen mast or pole,

Windbugger. Pole or halyard? We chose pole. For a downwind passage in the tropics we'd be better off with solar panels.

while others have to be raised on a halyard each time you anchor; some will put out in lighter winds than Windbugger, but must be turned off sooner in strong winds. Some have built-in protection against over-revving when the wind suddenly pipes up, and some don't. A little research here would be in order. Write *Practical Sailor*, Belvoir Publications, Box 2626, Greenwich, CT 06836-2626 for the back issues that compare wind generators, or for their annual Equipment Survey. If you join the SSCA (Seven Seas Cruising Association), get the issue where members rated gear. Also, while you're out cruising, talk to anyone who has a wind generator and ask how it performs. Remember that manufacturers can be overly optimistic about performance, and owners often tend to justify their choices with idealistic reports.

Wind generators aren't worth beans while sailing downwind in anything short of a gale. We tie ours off when we go to sea, as we had problems in rough seas due to the gyroscopic effect of the heavy propeller. Consider a wind generator mostly as an aid while at anchor.

Solar panels offer an excellent subsidiary (and for minimalists, a primary) source of juice replacement. They are passive, no moving parts, better made than they were ten to fifteen years ago, and many have warranties covering a decade or more.

Certain low-voltage solar panels used alone do not require regulation. However, in order to get a significant amount of help from the sun, most cruisers have several panels and install a regulator so charging doesn't have to be monitored. Solar regulators start at around $100.

Solar panels do best when oriented toward the sun. Most cruisers tire early on of hopping up several times a day to re-aim them, and opt for an installation that allows for approximate solar orientation without requiring hourly changes. For example, anchored in the northern trades in winter, you'd have your panels on the starboard side and tilted southward from the vertical. You can count on about half the rated output if you choose this middle ground. Example: a 50-watt panel should give you about 20 amp hours per day in the sub-tropics or the tropics.

Some people have a hard bimini or a flat area and just lay the panels horizontally and forget about them. They'll get significant help when the sun is directly overhead, and geometrically less as the sun hits the panels at an angle. Most people who do this take the trouble to tie off the boom so that it doesn't shade the panels, but some don't. You can almost figure a direct ratio between the help you give the panels and the help they give your batteries.

Hydro and shaft generators. Hydro generators work off propellers in the water (as opposed to in the air) that turn as the boat moves. They can be towed or mounted permanently on the transom. The only boat I know that had one is the 50-foot BOSTON LIGHT owned jointly by Kenneth and Bebe Wunderlich, Knowles Pittman, and Patience Wales. On their circumnavigation they used the Hamilton Ferris Waterpower 200, a device composed of an old-type car generator (puts out at low RPM) clamped to the taffrail and driven by a propeller that drags behind the boat on a special line. On their mostly downwind circumnavigation, they figured it slowed their speed so little it couldn't be calibrated. At six knots, the output was about six amps.

With a downwind speed that was often well over six knots, however, they had trouble with the propeller skipping out of the water. When it did this, the line would get knotted up. Eventually, with the addition of extra weights provided by the company, the skipping stopped and the performance was satisfactory.

Friends Jerry and Molly on BRITTANY, a DeLong 45, cruised with a belt-driven shaft generator. They claim they start receiving amps at four- to four-and-a-half knots, and that at five knots they get five amps, at six knots, eight amps. Jerry pointed out that if you didn't have enough room, or wanted more RPM at the alternator or generator, you could incorporate a jackshaft. Our prop on RED SHOES doesn't free wheel short of four to five knots, and with the additional drag of a belt-driven generator, who knows? My guess is that this is a better alternative for larger (40 feet and up), heavier boats, which would likely absorb the drag with less noticeable effect. In our case, we like neither the noise nor the stuffing box wear engendered by a free-wheeling propeller, so we never considered this option for RED SHOES.

Wiring. Twelve-volt systems are safer than those of higher voltages. The danger of arcing is minimal, and there is almost no possibility of electrical shock. Although it's possible to start a fire with a direct short between the battery terminals, fire-starting potential increases with voltage, making 12-volt systems safer than higher voltage systems.

The disadvantage of low-voltage systems is that given the same size wire, there's more voltage drop per unit of distance from the battery. Recommended wire size is important. The ratios of wire size to distance will be far greater than those required for house current. For example, a powerful electric windlass on RED SHOES would require two 30-foot cables of at minimum #4, and at best 1/0 at a cost for the latter of over five dollars per foot.

Breaker panels are the answer to mares' nests of unlabeled wires and line fuses of God-knows-what amperage. Each circuit is labeled. Breakers are sized to deal with circuit loads. True, there will still always be a need for some in-line fuses, but far fewer than would be needed without breakers.

Things that have fuses in addition to breakers are: VHF; ham; GPS; reefer; propane relay switch; cassette player; and autopilot.

RED SHOES has a master switch that allows me to use bank 1, bank 2, all, or 'all off'. Our radio battery has its own switch which joins it to the other batteries or, in the off position, isolates it. This battery was added because during nights at sea using autopilot, running lights, and instruments, transmitting on the radio (12 amps) brought the battery voltage too low for a decent signal. With a separate radio battery, the problem went away.

A good idea that we have yet to incorporate is a second master switch wired so we can charge the bank we're *not* using. We're told it's much quicker and more efficient and healthier to charge batteries that are not simultaneously being drained. Don't ask me why.

For gauges we have a battery voltage indicator, an ammeter for 12-volt use, an ammeter for charge rate, an ammeter for radio draw, and a separate ammeter for Windbugger charge rate. There's a voltage meter for shore power, and an ammeter for 110-volt use. A red warning light indicates the propane relay is on, and another tells us the bilge pump is running.

When anchoring in a marina, note that the breaker panel should have an indicator light that tells if the 110-volt shore power has been wired correctly as to polarity. If that light doesn't indicate "Okay," get out of there before electrolysis dissolves all underwater metal parts.

Stray currents from the dock and from other boats can do the same thing. An isolation transformer is good protection, but we don't have one. We anchor out whenever possible, and haven't given the thought to marina problems that we might have if we intended to live in one.

Devices that are miserly in amp draw: a 12-volt anchor light we made ourselves using a car ceiling light bulb and a peanut butter jar; the inverter on idle; autopilot when not turning the wheel; Hella fans. Items using more juice (* indicates a device we do not have on RED SHOES): radar*; reefer; autopilot when turning the wheel; microwave*; water-maker*. Greedy devices are the deck-washdown pump, electric windlass*, engine starter, and SSB when transmitting.

You didn't really want me to discuss minimalism, did you?

CHAPTER 14

Watts to Nurture, Already?

Dear Herb: You've convinced me. Now that I've bought the whole nine yards of electrical gear, how do I take care of it?

Anti-Minimalism Protégé

Dear AMP: Have heart. If electronics are magic, electrics are merely sleight of hand. Basic electricity is very simple. So come backstage with me and we'll watch the descendants of Franklin and Edison from the wings.

I took physics in both high school and college which gave me basic electrical knowledge. On a boat such as ours, with an elaborate but far from exceptional electrical system, this knowledge coupled with subsequent practical experience has stood me in good stead. It hasn't helped me with flashlights, however, which I buy regularly and throw away, and which, with only a few exceptions, I consider a class of gadget defying repair and exemplifying perfectly the inadequacy of 20th century technology.

Trouble shooting electrical problems requires making a few simple tests. These are done only after you've checked that the switch is on, the breaker controlling the circuit is on, any fuse in the circuit is still good, and the bulb, if the recalcitrant device is a light, is okay.

If all those checks don't reveal the problem, it's time for the VOM. I bought an inexpensive Voltage/Ohm Meter from Radio Shack a number of years ago, and it's worked flawlessly. I use it for only two tests: Is voltage getting to the problem device? And does the wire (or whatever) have continuity?

The Voltage Test: A boat's 12-volt system is a two-wire DC system, in which one wire is negative (ground) and the other positive (battery). This is in contrast to a car, also a 12-volt system, but which uses only one wire. The whole car, which is metal and connected to the ground terminal of the battery, is electrically (and sometimes attitudinally) negative.

The degree of desire that electricity has for leaping from the positive to the negative wire is called voltage, and the higher the voltage, the more the electricity wants to leap. This is the theory behind spark plugs. Twelve-volt electricity doesn't leap.

Modern theory says the electrons flow from negative to positive, but if you think that way, you're always going to put the switch in the wrong place. When you install a device, even in a low-voltage system, the switch should go on the positive or colored wire side. Thinking of amps flowing from positive to negative is a useful mental trick, a little like dealing with charts as if the earth were flat.

On the boat, if anywhere in the system you bring the ends of the positive and negative wires together, you'll kick the breaker off or burn up a fuse. If there is neither breaker nor a fuse in the system, as when you accidentally drop your wrench across both terminals of your new battery, your life can quickly get very exciting. In a circuit, the positive and negative wires are joined or bridged by the device the electricity is supposed to operate. The flow of electricity is measured in amperes (amps). It's convenient to know how many amps a given device needs to power it. Because watts equal volts times amps, you know that a 12-volt, 24-watt bulb requires two amps (24÷12). An ammeter will tell you this with fewer headaches.

I recently had an expensive lesson in electricity. The more amps flowing, the more heat is developed. If the wires are thin, they can become incandescent: this fact gives us morning toast. As an ex-professional piano player I still, on occasion, hire out to a local bistro. Recently I was running my keyboard through a 150-watt amplifier. The central power was off, so the club was using an auxiliary generator. When the freezer compressor kicked in, it drew mucho amps causing a voltage drop (watts *must* equal amps times voltage, remember?). A drop in voltage means an increase in amps. So as I was wailing away at a sophisticated improvisation on "The Whiffenpoof Song," suddenly several of the circuit boards in the amplifier became toasters. When this happens, the cost of repair is directly proportional to the stink of melting components.

Because you'll want to know which wire is negative and which positive, it's accepted practice to use black wire for the negative side, and colored wire for the positive. Let's assume this is true on your boat. You want to know if power is getting to the non-functioning device, so you set the VOM to read voltage in the 12-volt range and touch the black probe to the black wire, the red probe to the colored wire. Shazam—it reads 12 volts. Or it doesn't.

If it doesn't, you'll want to discover which wire lacks integrity. There are at least two ways to check this. Probably the simplest is to use a test wire with an alligator clip. First clip it to the positive pole at the breaker panel and test for 12 volts using the test wire for positive and the black wire at the site for negative. If it doesn't read 12 volts, the black wire is the problem. If it does, make another test by clipping the alligator clip to the negative pole at the breaker panel and testing the red wire at the site. One or the other wires should prove defective.

Do you get it? The test wire is a wire of known integrity—or is it? To be sure, we do a continuity test. Change the setting on your VOM to ohms. Test that the tester is working by touching the red and black probes together. The needle should go all the way to the right. Always test the tester first. Before I learned this, I used to waste precious hours thinking I'd found a flaw in the boat's system, when actually what I was dealing with was a bad probe wire on the test instrument. Important, but not essential for what we're doing: at this time adjust the gauge on the VOM so that the needle just barely reaches the high end of the scale when the probes are touching. There's a little knurled thingy on mine that does this. If you made a mistake and bought an expensive digital tester, you'll have to read the instructions.

Now that you know your tester is working, touch one probe to one end of the suspect wire, and the other probe to the other end. The needle should once more go all the way to the right. If it doesn't, the suspect wire has been tried and found guilty of malfunction.

Most wiring problems are caused either by a loose or corroded connection. Virtually nothing happens to the main run of a wire whose insulation is intact. On a modern boat, the electrical panel is placed in a protected area, one that is highly unlikely to get wet. Thus bad connections are most likely to occur elsewhere. A connector wetted by salt water will quickly dissolve in a welter of green goo. A loose connector may never have been properly tightened, crimped or soldered in the first place, or vibration may have loosened it.

A connector may test okay with the VOM and still be inadequate. Devices demanding a lot of amps such as the electric windlass, for example, require a high quality connection, otherwise amperage will be restricted and the device won't work. A corroded connection at the battery terminal might allow your lights to work, but not the starter; nor will the alternator charge to its full potential. Battery terminals should be clean and tight, and greased with a special grease made for this purpose, or, lacking that, with regular grease, to protect them from moisture. They should be looked at occasionally, as gremlins love battery terminals. Also check the high amperage connections (thick wires) on the engine and starter, and at the main battery switch. You never know.

I had a friend whose alternator was giving him trouble. His was the type that connects to ground through its own casing, i.e., it's bolted to the engine, which is connected to the negative battery terminal by a thick wire. The bearing surfaces, where the alternator bolts to the engine, were dirty or corroded. It took him a while to learn this, but cleaning up all the contact points solved his problem.

Twelve-volt lights can do maddening things. Usually if a light goes on and off, or won't go on unless you hit it, the problem is with the terminals on the bulb itself. The terminals develop dents over time, rendering the connections unstable.

We also have two fluorescent lights. They're recessed, and offer a soft ambiance while using few amps. One of them began to work or not work as it chose, and for a while fiddling with the slide switch was all it took to fix it. However, we've occasionally left the boat dark only to find when we return that this particular light is glowing dutifully, it having decided to work in our absence. I took it apart a dozen times, and have finally rated it flashlight quality. It understands violence and will usually work when I hit it. Maybe I'll replace it someday.

Soon after I'd installed our ABSCM (Adler Barbour Super Cold Machine), the compressor quit working. The company prides itself on the fact that their product can be user installed, and provides free technical advice, so after I thought I had checked everything I phoned them. The voice that had obviously dealt with too many Babes-in-the-Watts that day asked me tiredly if I'd checked the fuse.

"What fuse?"

"The one next to the compressor."

The voice now dripped with scorn: "Didn't you read the manual?" I don't know why he was so disdainful.

I studied the manual one more time, its pages smudged from many thumbings. There it was, the info buried in such a way that I could easily forgive myself for overlooking it, a fuse next to the compressor. It required one of those U-shaped fuses some auto maker invented to make life more complicated, and I didn't have any on board. I did have a cylinder type of the proper amperage, and an in-line fuse holder, so I bridged the factory-installed circuit with *my* fuse. The compressor worked perfectly.

There! That's the kind of thing I can fix, and I've now given you most of all I know about trouble shooting electrical systems on boats. The rest, unfortunately, I've forgotten, so you'll have to figure it out for yourself.

INSTALLING NEW DEVICES

Someone should write a book called *The Joy of Toys*. It would run the gamut of emotion from anticipation, during which time you scrimp and save; to realization, when you buy it, install it, and it works; to happiness, because most of the time it actually lives up to your expectations. Disappointment comes when you're trying to diagnose a malfunction, or you're trying to repair it, or you've sent it back to the factory and received the estimate. There is no device whose cost is limited to the purchase price, but we're eternally optimistic and remember only good things, so we continue to buy things that must be installed. And here is what is needed:

Stripping wire. I have a cheap wire stripper (a tool that removes insulation from the end of a wire), and would emphatically recommend popping for one of professional grade. Stripping wire should be simple, but with the tool I have, it's not.

My wire stripper is also a *crimping tool.* It's designed to squish end fittings onto the wire so that a) soldering is not necessary and b) the fitting is well connected and remains so. These fittings work well on multi-strand wire which is eminently squishable, but not so well on solid wire. However, as all wire recommended for boats is multi-strand, crimp fittings are useful indeed.

Connections that are properly soldered are the most reliable. Proper soldering requires technique, and it is done most easily with a workbench. I use the saloon table. You need a soldering iron, and low-heat solder. I have a little 12-volt pencil type that instead of a plug has alligator clips which I clip to the main terminals on the back of the breaker panel.

Flux cleans the wires before solder is applied and is helpful, but I've never used it. This may explain those times when I can't get the solder to stick. The down side of soldered connections is that they're difficult to do properly in the crannies where I'm doing the connecting, and if later you want to remove or replace the device, you usually have to cut the wire. If you haven't allowed extra wire in the first place, cutting out an inch or so may leave you fatally short.

There are two types of *crimp connectors* for joining the ends of two wires together. One is a tube-like device that receives the end of each wire. Like a soldered connection, it is permanent and must be cut out if you want to move or replace the device. The other type consists of a pair of male/female gadgets, the male crimped onto one of the ends to be joined, the female crimped to the other. Then the male part fits snugly into the female part. This arrangement allows for coupling and de-coupling, and may even be pleasant for the wires.

Crimp connectors come in different sizes for different size wires, and are color coded. We carry an assortment. And while we're on the subject of size, always use the proper size wire. The proper size wire is determined by the amperage requirements of the device, and its distance from the breaker panel. Usually installation instructions will give you this info. The West Marine catalog includes a wire use chart. When in doubt, choose the larger size. Also, use marine grade wire, which is higher quality than wire made for household and automobile use. Marine grade is tinned and stranded for better resistance to fatigue and corrosion.

At this point I must confess to something that will have the pros shaking their heads in denial. I use wire nuts. I use them everywhere. At the time I began doing this there were no marine grade wire nuts, so I used house construction grade. The advantages are ease of use: you just twist the wires together, and then screw on the nut; ease of disconnect, if it's not corroded; and the ability to easily join two, three, or even four wires with one connector.

The disadvantage: wire nuts are definitely more subject to corrosion than other types of connectors, particularly as you can't get them in marine grade. If I use wire nut connections outside, I seal them with a liquid sealant such as BoatLife.

A soldered connection protected with shrink wrap insulation is best for outside. Shrink wrap is a plastic tube that slides onto the wire *before* you solder it. You then slide it over the soldered connection and shrink it tight by applying heat. The trouble is, soldering outdoors, unless it's flat calm, is difficult at best, as the heat is all blown away. Here, perhaps, is where one of those gas-fired soldering irons sold by Radio Shack would come in handy.

Every older boat I know of boasts a bunch of mystery wires. These usually are the wires that feed devices installed by previous owners. Sometimes the installer lacked a piece of wire long enough, and so he joined two or more, usually of different colors. This means that a yellow wire at the device doesn't necessarily mean it's yellow at the source. And if you own the boat over a period of years, amusing stuff that *you* have done will puzzle you. All of which leads up to the admonition, *label wires* wherever possible. I have written on masking tape that's looped around the wire and stuck to itself, but with time the writing fades. Those little plastic label embossers with the wheel that contains letters, numbers, and punctuation? They're great, but the stickum is undependable. Perhaps looped around the wire, stuck to itself and stapled? Staples rust. Oh well.

And when you're all done, you'll probably want to bundle the rat's nest of wires together with wire ties, those plastic constrictors that once you put them on you have to cut them off. This will neaten up your work and help keep things in order.

Coaxial cable, sort of a wire within a wire, is used for antennas for radio, GPS, etc. I have tried to use a lower grade of coax for my ham radio, because the really good stuff is double the price per foot of the next lower grade, but there are some areas where buying cheap doesn't pay, and recently I installed RG8U grade, nearly doubling the efficiency of my antenna.

If you can't solder, and you decide to use lower grade RG8X, you can use crimp-on terminals. But if you use RG8U, you must solder the terminals. When soldering coax, there is always the danger of applying too much heat, thus melting the insulation and allowing the inner wire to touch the shield. Even if that doesn't happen, it's difficult to get a good ground connection. Be sure to make a continuity check after soldering.

Beware, however, when soldering an end fitting to RG8U. The fitting comes apart so you can do the soldering, but the removed part must be strung onto the wire *before* you solder.

CHAPTER 15

The Dinghy

Dear Herb: I'm having a terrible time figuring out what kind of a dinghy to buy. Some people say 'hard', some 'inflatable', some 'fold-up', and some, believe it or not, say 'nesting'. I don't really want to interfere in the procreation process, even of dinghies, although I heard that one cruiser took an inland trip and left his hard dinghy and soft-bottom inflatable unchaperoned. Their misbehavior wasn't apparent, but the result nevertheless was a hard/soft mutant. So I guess my question is, what is the current counsel on the optimum option?

Confused And Bewildered

Dear CAB: The bastard child of a hard and soft dinghy has turned out to offer that combination of serviceability one often finds among mongrels. Called the RIB (stands for Rigid Inflatable Boat, but etymologists are already tracing this acronym to Eve), it is an inflatable with a V-shaped fiberglass bottom—V-shaped for less pounding and less spray. The air-holding chambers provide stability, while the hard bottom weathers punishment and provides a solid platform at speed.

Times do change. It used to be that most people rowed their inflatables. Those that had engines had something like the Seagull, an ugly and ubiquitous creation, kind of the Model T of outboards. Some yachties swore by them, pointing out that they were elemental and dependable. Others swore at them, while keeping several sick Seagulls on board from which to make organ transplants in a futile effort to keep the favored one alive.

No longer. Now fellow sailors inspect your dinghy and the only thing they want to know is: "Does it plane?" The inflatable with the rigid bottom that's powered by a husky motor has taken over. Instead of easily de-motoring your dink with one hand, then deflating it and storing it in a locker, you must hoist the heavy motor to its place on the pushpit with a small tackle, and then store your RIB on deck. Ease of handling has been sacrificed to plane mania and speed.

In exchange for increased hassle, we who have defected from basic dinghying are generally happy that faster dinghies can take us farther afield in less time, giving us the long legs we need for getting to previously out-of-reach dive and snorkel sites. The sad news is that within this group, known as 'Outboard Outreach', or 'Oh!Oh!', the original objective, speed, has become a placebo to waning potency. Nor are the wives helping, as several times Nancy has remarked that there are few things more arousing than a RIB, its oversize tubes tumescent, flashing through the anchorage at 25 knots.

Earlier modes of to-and-fro transport were far more in harmony with nature. Nancy and I have explored river after river with our go-fast, chew-'em-up dink, and although we've covered more river miles than many marina mavens ever cruise, we've yet to see an animal, bird or reptile. When we were restricted to rowing we were far less decibellicose, and our rivering was a zoological encyclopedia of sightings.

We've run across cruisers with collapsible tenders, such as the Folbot. The idea is to achieve some of the space and rowing ability of a hard dinghy while retaining the stowability of a soft-bottomed inflatable. It is appealing, but I can see myself being fined for checking too late into a foreign country, having been delayed on board by a problem comparable only to assembling a Buick from parts that came in a box the size of a cigarette carton.

A nesting dinghy is a good idea if you want a hard dinghy that stores in half the space. This is a dinghy built to come apart in the middle, a kind of puntish mitosis. With the seats removed from part A, part B fits or 'nests' inside, thus making the storage space needed roughly half. This type of dinghy is popular among skippers anticipating a community property settlement.

A regular hard *sailing* dinghy would be a priority for me if I had the deck space. In Georgetown in the Bahamas, most afternoons I would watch with envy as a friend, reclining in the bottom of his sailing dinghy with a cold one, tacked happily through the anchorage. If the wind piped up dangerously, or if our friend became too drunk to navigate, someone would always go out in their RIB and tow him back to his yacht. Now that's cruising!

If you opt for a hard dink and have the deck space to store it upright in chocks specially made for the purpose, you automatically have a huge locker for sails, fenders, etc. You'll probably want to put a drain plug in the dink's transom, and you'll definitely want a rugged tarp to keep out heavy rains and Godforbid humongous breaking waves.

Sailing dinghy. We won't give up our fast RIB, but would love to add a sailing dinghy. However, that would mean a bigger yacht. . .

Stowable deflatables now come in two types: those with a plywood bottom that you—with great difficulty—install in sections, and those built using the new 'roll up' concept. The former type was difficult to assemble, and I would usually end up by insisting that someone had swapped *my* bottom panels for those of a bigger, unworkable size. We later bought a roll-up type, thinking it was a great idea, but sold it after a few weeks because its fugitive-from-a-funhouse floor provided a dangerously unstable platform from which to manhandle a heavy outboard. Another disconcerting characteristic of the floor was that its flexible sections came alive with suggestive undulations whenever we brought the dink up onto a plane.

With only Nancy and me aboard RED SHOES, one dinghy is sufficient. When we were cruising on SEA FOAM and had our son Craig as crew, a second dinghy relieved me of the role of taxi driver. We had an inflatable, and a plywood punt which rowed wonderfully. In the seven years we cruised on SEA FOAM we never had an outboard, and of course I was disdainful of those who did.

Most of my disdain drew its substance from the fact that low-horsepower outboards in those days were nowhere near as dependable as they are now. Their owners would huddle in a remote corner of the Suva Yacht Club bar and discuss outboard disease, diagnosis and treatment. And drink. The level of remedial expertise reminded me of bloodletting and leeches, and the level of drunkenness and despair among the owners reached snakepit proportions. Was this the state of mind for which we gave up concerts, libraries, and museums?

On the other hand, high-speed engine owners were steely-eyed brutes who lied about the automatic weapons they had hidden on board, and who kept a brace of killer Dobermans on deck. What sensitive retired barroom piano player could identify with them?

The group of rowers far outnumbered those with outboards, however, and our ability to exercise class distinction was honed to a fine edge. On a more practical level, oar thieves were rampant, and local oarmongers did a substantial business.

Hard dinghy versus inflatable: each has its own attributes. I hadn't thought that through when in Suva I took the hard dinghy to a friend's boat to pick up the 300 feet of ⅜-inch chain he was giving away. He'd warned me that once the chain started falling into the dink from the pile on deck, it would keep coming till it was all transferred. After only 200 feet, the waterline was within three inches of the gunwale, and in a flash I realized that the dinghy and all that chain were destined to sink in 60 feet of water. To avert certain disaster, I leapt overboard. Fortunately it was calm, and when all the chain had been transferred there was still a full inch and a half of freeboard. As I swam toward SEA FOAM, towing the overloaded little craft, I took no more care than I would have with a delivery of nitro-glycerine.

Most U.S. sailors cruising today have a RIB. Even if you don't put a megamotor on the back, you'll enjoy the stability, the drier ride produced by the big tubes, and the resistance to damage when beaching. We have a RIB which we store lashed upside down and partially inflated on the foredeck, and intend to use it as a liferaft if RED SHOES ever heads for Davy Jones' locker.

THE OUTBOARD MOTOR

It all started on our trailer-sailer trip. The pocket cruisers we towed behind our motor home had no engine, but all were equipped with an outboard bracket whose very presence required fulfillment. We tried covering it to keep it out of sight, but still the bracket nagged, a constant insistence in our otherwise tranquil lives. This sense of an obligation unmet remained until we bought a four-horsepower Evinrude which we named Evvie. Outboards for little sailboats are equipped with a long shaft, which makes the motors more useful by keeping the propeller in the water in rough weather.

Much later, our trailer-sailer trip over, we took possession of RED SHOES and bought a low-priced inflatable dinghy. We already had an outboard. The long shaft gave me no trouble, as I learned quickly how to tip up the motor, and we always carried oars for those last few feet to the beach. The problem came with getting our lightweight dinghy up on a plane. With me alone, sometimes our four-horsepower Evvie could, and sometimes she couldn't.

The Evinrude people, having read my articles on our trailer-sailer trip, offered us a free eight-horsepower short shaft if I would write about the four-horsepower long shaft for their catalog. Now, with Evvie II, we could plane at will, even with two people aboard.

In 1992, while in the British Virgin Islands giving a series of seminars for prospective offshore cruisers, we were tied up in a slip next to a boat that had a RIB for sale. Called an AB, it was made in Venezuela under license from an Italian company. Cute, fat, stumpy, it was eight feet long and had been little used. I agreed to buy it if I could try it with Evvie II. Lo and behold, even with the added weight of the fiberglass bottom, Evvie II could get the AB up on a plane with two of us aboard—most of the time. We promptly sold our nearly new roll-up and bought the AB.

Dinghying into a cave in the Bahamas. Tipping up the outboard in shallow water became routine.

By this time we had had Evvie II for four years of constant use, and she was becoming tired. (Pardon the animism, but outboards lend themselves to it.) There came a time when we could only get the dink on a plane when Nancy bounced on the bow. Then our steadfast little beauty (you see how involved one can get with an outboard?) could do it going downwind only. Finally, getting up required both those things, plus whether or not Evvie II was having a good day.

There was one other idiosyncrasy of Evvie II's that was less than endearing: she would not push El Dinko up onto a plane for a second time. Cold, right after the day's first start, was when she was perkiest. Nancy and I would slap high fives if she got us up. With unwarranted confidence we'd take off to distant destinations. On the return trip, however, no matter how long Evvie'd rested, she would never plane us again, and we could count on the fact that our homeward journey would be at displacement hull speed—i.e., slow.

Her ailments took time, energy, and money to fix, and finally persuaded us to get a new, feistier engine. And by this time (actually long before this time), I'd reached the conclusion that bigger is better. When we arrived in the Rio Dulce I bought yet another Evinrude, because a yachtie friend had the dealership and I trusted him, and because his price was significantly lower. I bought a 15-horsepower because, well, I just couldn't help myself. The highest horsepower rating for our AB is ten. I was now an outlaw.

But what fun! What fun to scare the panties off virgin riders! What fun to be airborne over the wakes of larger craft! What fun to beat everyone!

In the U.S., recreational outboards are now required to have a kill switch that will kill the motor when a lanyard is pulled. The operator wears a lanyard on a wrist, and if the boat flips or hits an obstacle, thus throwing the operator overboard, the lanyard pulls a U-shaped clip out of the switch and the engine stops.

I hated this 'protect the dummies' device. I was always losing the lanyard, and eventually defeated its safety aspect by tying the switch in 'run' position using a piece of small stuff. To stop the engine I used the choke—not a great solution. And when one day the motor refused to go, the final diagnosis was a short circuit in the kill switch, a problem that I've noticed recurs frequently among outboarders. I replaced the faulty switch with a 'push the button', non-safety type.

Evvie III, our new 15-horsepower, being a commercial model, doesn't have the safety kill switch, and I worry about it. During one year on the Rio Dulce we heard of four outboard-related accidents. One was fatal, two involved serious injury. The fourth one was actually amusing (after the fact) in that a friend, tossed from her dinghy by a freak wave, treaded water for a half hour while watching her boat make wider and wider circles around her, until finally she had to swim a mile to retrieve it from the mangroves. All the above injuries were caused by the propeller of the still-running motor, and could have been avoided, or at least reduced, if a lanyard-type safety switch had been used.

The answer to the kill switch dilemma? Leave the lanyard attached to the switch. It makes the outboard easier to steal, you say? Well, commercial outboards are just as ready to go as recreational ones with the lanyard left attached. However, I think outboard manufacturers should come up with a switch less subject to failure, one that's easy to replace, and should include a spare with the owner's tool and spares kit.

And as far as the law is concerned, I've figured out what to do about my overpowered AB. Fifteen- and ten-horsepower Evinrudes have the same basic engine. The removable cowling is where the incriminating '15' is emblazoned. I intend to seek out an owner of a ten-horsepower who wants to appear to have upgraded without undergoing the expense, and trade cowlings with him. It's nobody else's business what we each have under the hood. (See *Counterfeit Cover Equals Legal Tender*. Jailhouse pamphlet #61.352.)

POSTSCRIPT: When I told Nancy a couple of months ago that I was dying to see what a 25-horsepower would do on our AB, she persuaded me that

I needed help. Since then we've started Planers Anonymous in our river community. After turning away a few carpenters who misunderstood our purpose, we ended up with a cohesive little group. Everyone is called upon to tell his or her story, and must begin it by admitting that he or she is addicted to speed. You'd be amazed at the fine class of people that suffer from this expensive and potentially deadly affliction.

POSTPOSTSCRIPT: For those voyagers heading to the Caribbean who are thinking of stepping up to speedier times, there are still bargains to be bought in Puerto la Cruz, Venezuela, where both rigid bottom dinghies and name-brand outboards can be had at a considerable discount from prices elsewhere. For example, in 1991 an eight-foot AB like ours sold for a little over $1,000 U.S. This was less than half the stateside price for the same dink. New outboards can be bought for two-thirds the U.S. price. Outboards are also inexpensive in Dutch St. Maarten. I mean, if you own something slow and you're planning to sail there anyway. . .

CHAPTER 16

Motor Mechanics—
Beyond Kicking Your Engine

Dear Herb: I'm a lawyer, and ashore I've always felt that my time was more valuable practicing law than fixing my washing machine or servicing my car. Now, about to go cruising, I realize I've missed a great opportunity to learn basic repair skills that I'm going to need aboard. I know you're a musician and a writer by profession. Could you please give me a rundown on the things you've learned to do yourself, particularly on engines?

Inept in Indiana

Dear Inept: Thinking back, I see there were good things about growing up during World War II. For example, the school I attended gave a motor mechanic's course. We had a bunch of engines from wrecked cars which teams of four students totally disassembled and reassembled. If it ran, you passed.

I married while still in college and found that living on the GI bill didn't allow for professional mechanics' assistance. So at great detriment to my marriage I did all my own car repairs. The one I remember is the old Dodge whose engine I rebuilt. Our celebration drive was a failure, as the car had stayed so long on blocks, a family of little mice emerged from a tear in the front seat cushion and tried to escape over my wife's lap.

While I was growing up, almost all our family's boats were motorboats. I learned not to be afraid to tackle any job, an *attitude* (and I stress the word) that's essential for a do-it-yourself cruiser. Attitude, because if ignorance deters you, you'll never learn new techniques; essential, because if you hire everything out, even though you're a lawyer, you'll soon be broke, or in a place where there's no one to hire.

Here are some of the things I tackled while cruising:

The basic maintenance tasks for a diesel engine are changing the oil, the oil filter, the fuel filter; cleaning the air filter, and, if so equipped, the screen in the raw water filter.

The Racor fuel filter cartridge comes with instructions. Changing an oil filter is messy but simple. One trick to make it less messy, if you have the room, is to remove the oil first from the crankcase, punch a hole in the lower part of the oil filter using a screwdriver or an ice pick, and then use a punch to enlarge the hole. This way most of the oil trapped in the filter drips in such a way that you can deal with it. When it is through dripping, unscrew the filter and replace.

On RED SHOES, I change oil using a drill and a drill pump. The drill is a Makita battery powered drill/screwdriver, one of the handiest tools on the boat. The battery usually runs down during any operation, particularly oil changing, so I have a spare. To recharge the battery requires 110 volts, another use for our inverter. So far the pump's impeller hasn't failed, but I have a spare in case it does. I have no other way of changing oil, so if any link in the system fails, I have to find a port and either fix the system or replace it with another—a hand pump, for instance. Buy one as a backup? What a revolutionary idea!

Replacing the Racor fuel filter cartridge is easy. I also clean the bowl each time. It is a pain, but I like to see what the filter is collecting. There's a petcock at the bottom, to which I fit a short length of hose, and drain the dirty bowl into a container. Once it's empty, if I see that it needs a flush, I remove the whole valve and pour diesel through it, being careful to catch what I pour in a cup.

Now you're instructed to fill the Racor with clean diesel fuel. Where's that going to come from?

We carry spare fuel in five-gallon jerry cans on deck. Transferring fuel from jerry jug to filter bowl involves spilling, cursing, and making a mess, so we carry a two-quart container full of clean diesel just for this purpose.

One cruiser has installed in the fuel line just before the filter one of those squeeze bulbs that are standard in outboard fuel lines. This fellow's right forearm is an inch larger in circumference than his left. Another skipper installed a spare electric fuel pump on the tank side of the fuel filter. The pump has its own switch, and fills his filter bowl electrically. The advantage to this excellent idea is that if your boat normally has an electric fuel pump and it fails, you can replace it with your spare. [Note: fuel pumps that feed the engine should come *after* (on the engine side of) the secondary filter. The spare is for filling the filter bowl only. Why? Because fuel pumps last longer if they pump only clean, filtered fuel.]

Bleeding the fuel line and the injectors is very important. Vibration from continual use will eventually loosen bleeder screws, fuel line connectors, and will even wear through flexible line where the hose clamp clamps it tightly to a fitting. First you must find and repair the leak, which will require installing new copper washers, or a new flexible section, or merely tightening a loose threaded connection. Then you must evacuate all air from the system. For this, some form of pump is absolutely necessary.

Adjusting the valves is not an essential skill, but it's easy, and helps keep the performance of your engine up to specs, so why not learn? The owner's manual will tell you how. All you need is a set of feeler gauges, the proper size wrenches, and a way to turn the flywheel by hand. Be sure the fuel cutoff is in the position that stops the engine.

Adjusting belt tension is a matter of finding out which nuts or bolts to loosen. Then it's a matter of gauging the tension. Mechanics use a large screwdriver as a lever to get enough tension on the alternator/fresh water pump belt. Tension is measured by how far out of line you can depress the tightened belt. One half inch is optimum for the alternator belt on our engine. Other belts could be for the salt-water cooling pump, and the reefer compressor, if engine driven.

The engine's salt-water pump uses a neoprene impeller subject to wear and failure. We still have the original impeller in our Yanmar after 4,500 hours. However, it's wise to have a couple of spare impellers, and new gaskets for the pump cover. An interesting aside: other manufacturers make replacement impellers. I heard a fellow cruiser complaining on the radio that the replacements he'd bought only lasted a few weeks. I bought a spare impeller made by Yanmar, obviously a better investment than the cheaper choice.

Not true for the Yanmar air filters, which for some reason disintegrate into powder, even when stored in a sealed plastic bag. We now make our own, out of open cell foam, and they work and last just fine.

The cooling system for most modern engines is usually equipped with an anti-siphon loop, an upside down U of PVC pipe with a little neoprene bleeder valve on top of the loop. Its purpose is to prevent salt water from siphoning into your engine after you've shut it down. It has to be placed at the highest point in the system, well above the waterline, and the damn things always leak when the engine is running. Before we realized what was happening, ours leaked and formed a lot of rust on the forward part of our engine. I was able to clean up most of it and spray with WD-40. One injector, however, had rusted to where I ruined it in removing it.

The trick is to assume that the valve is going to leak, and control where the leaking salt water goes. On our boat I have since run a hose into the bilge—the few drips that escape the valve are insignificant as far as bilge water is concerned. Others have led a hose to a clamshell, either in the cockpit or high on the topside. What you shouldn't do is figure that if you replace the leaky devil it won't drip any more. It won't for a while, true enough, but eventually it will, and salt water on your engine can do a lot of damage before you notice it. If you're buying a new boat, you may want to insist that one of these options be installed by the manufacturer.

The technique of aligning the engine is relatively simple, or it would be, if you weren't working in a position reminiscent of a medieval torture chamber. Yanmar engine mounts are adjustable. Permanent mounts require the use of shims. Engine alignment is sometimes necessary on new boats after the tension has been applied to the standing rigging for the first time, thereby changing the shape of the boat slightly.

To align the engine, uncouple the shaft. Slide the propeller shaft out a little ways, then bring it back to join the coupling again. If the engine is out of line, the two halves of the coupling will not meet flush. If the gap is on the top, but the rims are congruent, the engine needs to be raised slightly and tilted aft slightly. Other adjustments are equally simple.

We have had a couple of esoteric and one common but nonetheless mystifying things happening to our Yanmar. Number one: We destroyed a cutless because barnacles grew *inside* it. The simple remedy is to run the engine in gear at least once every couple of weeks. The turning of the shaft will rub off incipient growth before the barnacles have time to grow their hard, destructive shells.

Number two: If you run your engine daily to charge your batteries, eventually carbon will build up in the exhaust elbow. When that happens, the free flow of exhaust is diminished, power is diminished, and as in our case, when it becomes extreme, the engine won't even run. Some people claim to have cleaned out carbon from the elbow by using acid. This is risky, as there's a little baffle in the elbow that must remain intact, otherwise you'll get salt water coming back into your engine. The first time ours clogged I tried cleaning it with a hammer and cold chisel, but in short order realized that I had let it go too long. (Carbon can be hard—it's on its way to becoming a diamond.) Cleaning the exhaust elbow is a regular maintenance task, and I've found that if I get to it before it's too impacted, it's not too difficult.

Finally, if the engine suddenly starts to overheat, look for an obstruction in the raw water intake. A plastic bag is often the culprit. After a time of disuse, barnacles, fish, grass, and all kinds of stuff can clog the intake. Check salt-water flow before trying other, more drastic remedies.

I've rattled on under the assumption that you intend to buy a sailboat with a diesel auxiliary. It's certainly possible to cruise successfully in an engineless craft—the Pardeys have done it for years. It's even possible, on an engineless boat, to have a respectable battery bank, using for recharge an array of solar panels and one or even two wind generators. This system would also require a backup portable generator for when the wind doesn't blow and the sun doesn't shine. How much electricity you can use will of course depend on how much you can make.

But I'm guessing that you will fall into the norm, the 99% who intend to have a diesel engine. Most people have come to see it as a necessity. And because you're going to live with and depend upon your diesel engine, and probably travel to places where competent mechanics aren't available, some basic skills are necessary.

A few final reminders then: if you buy a Yanmar or other foreign made engine, you'll no doubt need metric tools. Study your owner's manual thoroughly, and buy a shop manual, which tends to be thorough and more technical. Owner's manuals so often say, "If such and such happens, run to your dependable dealer." All very well, but does he make boat calls in Phuket?

There are diesel engine maintenance courses given by various manufacturers. For Yanmar owners, write to Mack Boring Co., 2365 Route 22, Union, NJ 07083. During the winter months they sponsor classes in New York, New Jersey, and Massachusetts. For other areas or engine makes, call your local distributor.

The problem with the modern *outboard motor* is that it's too good. Because it runs well with little attention, people think it will run forever with *no* attention. Such an attitude invites trouble.

I won't list here the chores you'll find described in your owner's manual. I merely suggest that you read it and do them. However, here are some notes from our experience with outboards:

With the exception of a visible loose or broken wire, there are only two electrical problems that I can fix. I can clean or replace spark plugs (replace is better, except in emergencies); and I have bypassed the kill switch when it was shorting out and causing the engine not to run (see Chapter 15 for a discussion of kill switches).

Outboard design has been 'improved' by the introduction of the black box, a sealed, plastic box wherein electronic magic occurs. You can't get into the box, and even if you could, you couldn't repair a problem without specialized electronic knowledge. So if the problem is electrical and the cause is neither faulty spark plugs nor the kill switch, nor a visible loose or broken wire, that's when I run for a professional.

The do-it-yourselfer has a better chance when the problem is in the fuel system. Carburetion hasn't changed much over the years, and rebuilder kits are available. Boiling out a dirty carburetor is no more difficult than boiling an egg. There are also inexpensive rebuild kits for the fuel pump. Carry both, as they're not always available in foreign countries, although I did with much difficulty find a carburetor kit in Puerto La Cruz, Venezuela, and a fuel pump kit in the Bay Islands of Honduras.

It's unlikely you'll have to get into the fuel system if you keep the fuel clean. Adding a fuel filter is excellent insurance. Adding a gasoline conditioner to the fuel tank when the outboard isn't going to be used for a few weeks will keep fuel from becoming gummy.

Closing the gas tank vent when not in use will help keep water out. The problem is that water sometimes comes with the gas you buy. This is another reason for a fuel filter with a transparent bowl. The bowl traps water, and its transparency allows you to see it.

A reminder: Use an anti-seize product (see Chapter 18) to periodically lube the bolts that clamp the outboard to the transom, as on most motors the bolt is stainless steel, but it passes through an aluminum casting.

Happy outboarding!

By the way, don't feel that you're in this mechanical maze alone. With SSB or ham radio, or even VHF, you have a world of experience at your earlobe. I have heard engine problems analyzed more times on the radio than I can count. You'll have to bolt the bolts and screw the screws, but there'll always be someone out there who has the knowledge and experience that you may lack. And for all you sailors hung up on self-sufficiency, as far as I'm concerned there's no shame in asking another cruiser for help, only in not giving it when *you're* asked.

CHAPTER 17

More Handy Skills

Dear Herb: How about sharing with us some of the skills you were glad you had or that you developed while cruising?

Brain Picker

Dear BP: The following must of necessity be a kind of mishmash. What I consider essential, or at least important, varies from day to day, or from problem to problem. There are things I *always* wish I knew more about, such as cosmetics. How, for instance, to match gelcoat color when making fiberglass repair—this in order to avoid having to paint the whole boat after filling a screw hole. My solution: learn to love the cute little white spot. And there are days when I wish I knew more about electronics, although I haven't been moved yet to actually *do* something about it. But when I gaze at the mystifying electronic assemblages called circuit boards that have multiplied on RED SHOES, I wish, I wish, I wish.

We'll talk about A) skills you really should have, and B) those that it would be nice to have. The first item in class A is:

KNOTS

If you want to fill your life with Turk's heads, or make attractive doormats, buy *Ashley's Book of Knots*. It's encyclopedic. As with all sets of encyclopedia, you're buying more material than you'll ever use. On a small boat, the storage space for big books should be carefully rationed. Buy a small knot book—it's all you'll ever need. Trust me.

However, be sure it deals at least with the following:

BOWLINE (for loops). Learn to tie this one in the dark, while chewing gum and having sex. Speed and automatic reflex with this all-purpose knot may save your life.

SHEET BEND (for joining the ends of two lines). Better than two bowlines, and if you use the reef or square knot, kiss goodbye to whatever you're trying to secure. The sheet bend can also be used to secure a bitter end to an eye splice.

ROLLING HITCH. Used to tie a line to a rope or chain not at the end, as when you attach a nylon spring line to your all-chain anchor rode.

TRUCKER'S HITCH. Used for tight lashings.

SQUARE KNOT. Better called a reef knot, because that's one of the few places you should use it. To put its vulnerability in perspective, remember that it's called a reef knot because one yank undoes it when you're unreefing.

CLOVE HITCH for tying up to bollards or trees.

TWO ROUND TURNS AND TWO HALF HITCHES for the same purpose. Under extreme stress, it is even more secure and less likely to chafe than the clove hitch. During Hurricane Hugo, this knot held RED SHOES securely and showed no appreciable chafe.

ANCHOR KNOT. I love this knot. Use it to tie a line to any rigid piece: to a shackle; to secure a lanyard to a bucket. I've even used it sometimes in place of a rolling hitch because in certain situations it holds better. If you're afraid of the bitter end working its way out from under the hitch, put a stop knot in it. I just love this knot.

FIGURE EIGHT to use as a stop knot.

The proper way to tie a line to a cleat.

Eye splice. An eye splice in a three-strand line is simple, if the approach is carefully prepared. After separating enough of the strands for the splice, seize the line so that further separation won't occur. Then tape the ends of the three strands so they don't unlay. After that, it's a matter of choosing how big you want the eye, then feeding a separated strand under one strand of the standing part; the next separated strand under the next strand of the standing part, etc. One cycle will have all three single strands tucked under a different strand in the standing part.

Continue by taking strand #1 and going over one and under one strand of the standing part. Then take each strand in rotation, etc., till the splice is done. If this seems difficult, get someone to show you how to do it, or buy a knot book with lots of illustrations.

I used to think that tapering a splice was a cosmetic device, but it's not, it's a strength enhancer. After three tucks, cut off and remove half of each of the remaining exposed separated strands. Do three more tucks with each of the partial strands that remain. This will keep the first three tucks, where most of the holding power lies, from untucking, and it will make a tapered and more graceful splice into the bargain.

Eye splices in braided line are more complicated, and are analogous to two snakes each eating the other's tail. I bought the special fid put out by New England Ropes because it came with instructions and illustrations. I worked for hours on my first splice, unsuccessfully, because the writer of the instructions had left one important step out. When I finally realized this, I did fine.

The theory behind the fid is to push one snake into and completely through the other. A friend of mine used another technique, a wire that's inserted into the receiving snake first, which then *pulls* the other snake through. This is easier by far, but I go for long enough between splices that I forget the process, and each time I must learn all over again.

The ends of Dacron and nylon lines can be kept from unraveling by burning, but a more reliable method is to whip them as well. All this requires is a special waxed string (waxed dental floss will work perfectly), and wrapping it around and around the bitter end of the rope. The trick is to secure the ends of the whipping stuff so that they won't unwhip. There are many satisfactory methods for doing this. If you don't have a knot book, invent your own method. Or if your wife sews, she can show you one.

SAIL REPAIRS

Sail repairs become necessary whether you like it or not. We carry a sail repair kit that contains needles, a leather palm, thread, and sail cloth. For jury rig repairs of tears, we have *sail repair tape*—wide, white, very sticky stuff that I have used by itself and at other times strengthened with stitches, just as I would with sail cloth. Nancy has a sewing machine, but it is not very good with heavy duty repairs. However, we are self-sufficient, at least until we run into a professional sail repair person.

Working with Sunbrella. We had our bimini made by a professional. In these days of ozone depletion, sun protection is essential. We don't have a dodger, but we have only missed it in northern climes when we occasionally stayed too late in the year.

The bimini cloth used to wear at the stainless supports (called 'bows', and pronounced 'bose') where the boom brushed across it, so Nancy added strips of vinyl across where the bows are. She also made what I call flies, a cloth flap which fills the open space at the front and rear of the bimini, and which rolls up and is secured with snaps when not in use. The front one keeps out rain when we're at anchor—i.e., when the boat is weathervaning, keeping the wind from the bow. The rear one is mostly used to block the afternoon sun—afternoon, because if we're anchored in the trades, as we usually are, RED SHOES is facing east.

Nancy also made awnings for both Bomar hatches in the cabin roof. We carry grommets and grommet setting tools. They're somewhere on this boat, but I haven't been able to find them for months, so maybe we don't really have them any more. We also carry snap hardware, the tool for snap assembly, and the little part that screws into the boat that you snap to. Our awnings are snapped around the hatch, and secured forward by bungee cords tied or hooked into grommets. We had enough space that we could make the forward awning over the forepeak berth—where we sleep—long enough that we can leave that hatch open in the rain. Ventilation, especially where you sleep, is a blessing.

I've replaced our forestay myself, and can assure you that applying Sta-Lok fittings is easy if you follow carefully the instructions that come with them. We carry a complete set of Sta-Loks and one day I'll put them on every stay. However, after eight and a half years it's getting time to replace the wire, so I'll probably replace that also. You can re-use Sta-Lok fittings, but you need to carry extra little bits called wedges and wire formers in case you need to remove and re-attach a fitting, or replace a wire using your old fittings. In an emergency I imagine the old wedges and wire formers would get you home, but they're not that expensive, so why not have some spares?

CHANGING PROPANE TANKS

There is a knack to changing propane tanks—an empty for a full one—and because a propane leak, even in the sealed, self-draining tank compartment, is to be avoided, you should take extra care. We carry a ⅞-inch wrench solely for that purpose—except in an emergency and used with special care, a crescent wrench is *not* satisfactory. We tighten the fitting to the full tank until it's tight. (Remember, the threads are backward, and tighten when turned *counter*-clockwise). We back off the nut *slightly* and turn the other part back and forth so that the tapered fitting seats itself; then we gradually tighten the nut while twisting the other part back and forth until we can't turn it any more. Finally we tighten the nut forcefully. (I don't believe a man of average strength using a nine-inch wrench could ever strip those threads, so don't go out now and prove me wrong.)

I didn't believe a friend when he told me *never to use any lubricant on propane fittings*, and sprayed mine with WD-40. The truth is, something like that always introduces foreign vapors into the line. Our stove burners snapped, crackled and popped like lethal Rice Crispies for days. You can, if necessary, clean the threads with a wire brush, and even use soap and detergent if you rinse and let dry before assembling.

For detecting leaks, a pressure gauge is the only way other than sniffing to check the whole system. Make sure the relay switch is on so that the whole system is in the loop, turn on the gas till the pressure builds, then turn it off. If the pressure decreases, you have a leak.

We used the soapy water technique at first to detect leaks, but I now have enough experience seating the fittings by the method explained above that I no longer bother.

OTHER SKILLS THAT MIGHT COME IN HANDY

Working with fiberglass is not all that difficult, and once you've made the mistakes that most of us make in the beginning, it can be one of your most valuable skills. I've used fiberglass and either epoxy or polyester resin to rebuild a cupboard; build a battery box for our dedicated radio battery; convert our icebox to a refrigerator; and make a new windvane paddle (the part that hangs in the water).

None of these projects became a journeyman's pride, but all are serviceable. The windvane paddle was actually never finished, but that's another story.

In order to do work with fiberglass, you'll need fiberglass, both polyester and epoxy resins and catalysts, acetone for cleanup and perhaps preparation, mixing cups, plastic squeegees, and some throwaway paint brushes. The way I learned was to read the mixing instructions on the resin can, and then just have a go at it. Initial results were what you might expect, but I gained experience.

When you have a choice of resins, polyester has the advantage that it goes off quickly. The disadvantages are that it goes off too quickly, or not at all. Gauging the proper amount of catalyst is the trick, so now I always do a test mix. Catalyst weakens with age; different batches of resin react differently; and the heat and humidity where you're working have an effect on reaction time.

Epoxy resin comes as a fast setting-up or a slow setting-up brew. The longer setting-up type allows you more time to go over the work, make it smoother, improve it in whatever way. The disadvantage, however, is that you spend a lot of time waiting for it to set up so you can take the next step—a second layer, paint, whatever.

Acetone cleans up both you and the work, but it's hard on the hands. White vinegar works—sort of. My present policy is to clean my hands with a mechanics hand cleaner that is loaded with lanolin first, and use acetone for cleanup. So far the residue of lanolin has kept my skin from dissolving.

Incidentally, you can't buy acetone in Venezuela and some other countries because it's a product used in the refining of cocaine. I used lacquer thinner. If you need to earn money while you cruise, you might consider smuggling acetone.

Working with wood will always come in handy. On board I carry an electric saber saw powered by the inverter, a hand saw, a battery powered drill, chisels, a little block plane, hole saws, a plug cutter, measuring tape, an inexpensive plastic caliper, plus an assortment of glues and stainless steel screws. I'm by no means a furniture maker, but I'm able to do serviceable work.

Working with metal is a constant requirement on RED SHOES. After all, the spars are metal, the stanchions and pulpits are stainless steel, etc. I carry a small tap and die set so that I can drill and tap for machine screws. And a hacksaw, of course, as well as a husky set of cable cutters (*not* bolt cutters).

The dies are mostly used to clean up damaged bolts, but I have actually *made* bolts in a time of no longer remembered need. We also have a pop riveter and aluminum rivets, which can be used when strength doesn't require stainless machine screws. We carry an assortment of machine screws as well. Machine screws are used to attach most hardware to mast or boom, and hold much better than self-tapping screws. When I installed our Windbugger on its stainless steel pole, I had to drill and tap for machine screws for the diagonal supports. The nut that holds our wheel on the shaft used to come loose, so I drilled and tapped for a set screw. Working with metal is far from difficult if you have the tools. (Instructions for drill sizes to use for taps came with our Craftsman tap and die set.)

Most skippers nowadays must work with products designed to *caulk, seal* or *glue*. Although clear silicon seal comes close to being all-purpose, most jobs are better done using a specific product. The West Marine master catalog is the best all-in-one-place source of product info. One thing they don't tell you is that all these sealants have a limited shelf life once the container/tube/cartridge is opened. 3M 5200 is the worst offender, and will go off in the container sooner than the others. For small jobs buy tubes, even though the cost per ounce is considerably more than for cartridges. Be sure the tube is kept properly capped, and store in a cool place.

Painting used to be a simple matter. Having sanded the surface till smooth, you opened the paint can and brushed the paint on. Mineral spirits thinned it, and cleaned up the mess. If you wore a respirator you were either playing dress-up or hiding from bill collectors. If you wore gloves, you were a sissy.

Back then, paints were divided into two, and only two, types: oil- and water-based. Probably the first water-based coating was called whitewash, made a household word by Tom Sawyer and later by the Warren Commission. After World War II came the miracle of latex water-based paint, strictly an interior house paint. Since then its uses have expanded, but only recently to boats.

One exception was Easy Deck, or AirBahl, an industrial product adapted for boat use by the cognoscenti. It is water-based, with thicker viscosity than other latex paints, and it's used on wood cabin tops in conjunction with canvas or nylon screening as a deck covering. Incredibly sticky and impermeable, it requires regular re-coating in heavily trafficked areas, but in light traffic areas it lasts almost indefinitely. One of my few regrets is that we didn't discover it till we were at the end of our wooden boat days. This stuff is more a spreadable sealant than a paint.

Modern paints have become far more use-specific and individuated. Each manufacturer insists on its own solvents and thinners. Much of the stuff is so toxic there's a warning on the label that says "breathing fumes can cause brain damage." You'll want to wear gloves, as getting the stuff on your skin is like a dose of Sloane's liniment applied to an open wound. I could almost feel brain cells melting when I was adapting our icebox to a refrigerator, working, as I did, with resin, acetone, urethane paint and solvents, all the while with my head in an unventilated space of about three cubic feet.

Most urethane paints are applied in thinner coats than traditional oil-based paints, but the result is harder and more durable. Nancy used polyurethane paint when she re-did RED SHOES' red sheer stripe. That was three years ago, and so far the color is still bright and fully saturated.

Varnish. When you say 'varnish' in a gathering of yachties, be prepared to cross yourself, face Mecca, and, best of all, if you can find one, sacrifice a virgin. This holiest of theologies has as many sects as there are varnishers. All agree, however, that there is but one god, and She is a Badger. Badger hair brushes occupy an honored place in the sacristy, and used ones are sold as relics.

The faithful use only traditional, oil-based varnish. The hairline that separates how much traditional varnish you apply to make it 'flow' (among varnishers a liturgical term) from the amount that invites a run, drip or sag is known only to a chosen few. (Just heard a tip: for better flow, run the engine while you're brushing on the last coat. The vibration will 'settle out' the brush strokes, giving you a perfect finish.)

When the Vindicated Varnishers came to town preaching polyurethane and the concept of forgiveness, I was the first one in the tent to convert. Polyurethane varnish is indeed forgiving, and even tolerates sponge brush application. (Sponge brushes are made with a special type of sponge called Farris, and the ads always show a handsome klutz applying his varnish with Farris ease. Those of us who varnish with a sponge are considered excommunicants by Onthedocks Badgerians.)

Nancy tried using water-based varnish once, and it's the only time I ever knew her to cry over a varnish job. She found the coats so thin that in re-coating she couldn't tell where she'd been, nor could she see imperfections till the varnish had dried. Then, when it was done, poorly to Nancy's perfectionist eyes, it lifted from parts of the teak, and we had to sand it all off and start over with a different type. Nancy, in order to recover her normally bubbly disposition, wanted to meditate in the wilderness, but as we were in Fort Lauderdale she had to make do with a credit card and three consecutive days at a shopping mall. We are told that there are brands of water-based varnish that are more viscous, but you're on your own here.

Varnish comes in either glossy or matte (dull) finish. Now who in their right mind would want to go to all that work and not have it shine?

Exterior varnish is claimed to be loaded with ultra violet inhibitors which extend dramatically the time it'll last in the tropics. This has yet to be proved. Varnish requires constant supervision, and will deteriorate rapidly if not monitored. The catch-22 is, you don't want to wait till the varnish cracks, flakes or peels before you re-coat, otherwise you'll have to scrape and sand forever in order to take everything down to bare wood. But then, if you re-coat with the varnish still in good condition, you'll never know how long it would have lasted had you waited. The best you can do is to keep an eye on it, and hope that when it comes to brightwork, a watched yacht never spoils.

Whereas varnishing attracts the devout, bottom painters tend to be atheists. Where varnish adds to the boat's beauty, bottom paint is anti-life. A great leap forward was leapt a few years ago when tin-based paints came on the market. Since then ecological shamans have declared that tin-based paint is bad for the planet because it kills things—which is what I always thought was the point. Evidently not, as we're told we can no longer use it unless we haul out in a yard in almost any country other than the U.S.A. So we're back to outmoded copper, which also kills things but not as effectively.

In my opinion, the introduction of ablative paints was another great leap forward. So far no bureaucrat has ordained against it, although what it does is sluff off poison, leaving a trail of death behind your boat. This differs from old style bottom paint, which essentially creates a killing carapace that goes with you.

Because ablative paint wears away till it's gone, some bright person thought up the idea of painting the first coat a different color, so that when it starts to show through, you know it's time for a haulout.

As with choices of mates, automobiles and breakfast cereals, boat owners develop a loyalty to a certain kind of bottom paint. Below is our history of brand use:

Woolsey Neptune, the paint that was on SEA FOAM when we bought her, and which we continued to use. Good stuff.

A paint we bought in New Zealand that looks almost black after it's applied, and which we suspected, but never proved, had an arsenic base. It was a most effective paint, although you might fear a lawsuit if anchoring off a U.S. swimming beach.

Various local bottom paints bought in Costa Rica, Papeete, Samoa, and Kiribati, all of average effectiveness.

On RED SHOES, Pettit Trinidad, a carapace type with over two-third copper, which after three haulouts built up such a thickness that large chunks fell off, along with the scales from my eyes.

Something called Tropikote, I think, which has been superseded by another imaginative but equally misleading name.

AwlStar Gold Label, an ablative paint that although it has less than 50% copper has done the best job of keeping us clean while we've been in the Caribbean. We will use it again. (This paint rated tops in *Practical Sailor* tests.)

To rid RED SHOES of the hard but crumbling shell of the Trinidad paint, we used Peel-Away from Dumond Chemicals, a *paint remover* that was extremely benign, non toxic, and environmentally safe compared to most paint removers. We applied it thickly with a brush, then covered it with butcher's paper to keep the moisture in. Then we went and had a beer. Next morning we peeled off the paper and with a broad putty knife removed the paint, which the remover had reduced to the consistency of butter. Good stuff. The recommended waiting time is 24 hours, but with butcher's paper the paste would have dried. We waited roughly 14-16 hours. A special laminated cloth is now recommended for this purpose.

Bottom paints aren't consistent, and even if they were, users would assess them differently. Two skippers, side by side in the yard, about to re-paint their bottoms, their boats having last been painted with the same brand, might ask each other, "Was it as good for you as it was for me?" To which the answer will range from "Oh yes!" to, "Well, we can always try again," to, "I'll never again deal with such a blatant lack of potency."

CHAPTER 18

Maintenance—The Constant Survey

Dear Herb: We are Maine sailors, and other than the occasional weekend, we manage only a two- or three-week cruise in September. We're busy professionals, and when we pick up our boat from the yard where we store it for the winter, we expect all the systems to work, and barring the occasional failure, to work well all season. We have no time for puttering, and haven't learned the art. However, we are retiring next year and planning a six-year circumnavigation. As we'll have all the time in the world, but no concept of what maintenance chores will be necessary, would you please tell us about some of the things we'll find ourselves doing?

Pampered from Penobscot

Dear Pampers: I certainly sympathize with you. Although being able to pick up a phone and have something done for you is certainly convenient, in your case it has prevented you from getting to know your boat. The difference between how you relate to your boat now, and how you'll need to relate to it over the six years of your proposed cruise, is like shopping at the supermarket versus growing your own food.

You've probably had your boat surveyed by a professional, either when you bought it, or when applying for insurance if your boat is over three years old. A yacht surveyor looks for all the things that can go wrong on your boat and, at the end, hands you a list of recommendations. The list will mention defects or abnormalities that you, had you been an expert at maintenance, would have already known about and remedied.

Okay, I am oversimplifying. A professional surveyor will know more about boats in general than you do, but hopefully you'll know more about *your* boat. Frankly, a person planning to spend a significant hunk of time cruising in a sailboat would be wise to take a course in boat surveying, or at least read some books on the subject. Or alternatively, if you plan to carry insurance and your insurer requires a survey, be sure and be there with the surveyor. Watch, ask questions, take notes.

Rather than try to cover the whole spectrum of a boat survey here, I'll suggest some ways to prevent or at least delay bad things that a survey might turn up. Perhaps our focus should be on 'An Ounce of Prevention'.

Damn! Already I can see, going through my notes, that we're going to get into far more detail than I ever intended. Oh well, if you're game to plow through all this stuff, I guess I don't mind writing it down.

The basic systems on a cruising sailboat are mast and standing rigging, running rigging and lines for all uses, sails, hardware, equipment, finishes, plumbing, electronics, and your electrical systems. We'll ask for each system: "What is it that we don't want to go wrong under any circumstances? What don't we want to happen?" This is one subject where accentuating the negative is the way to get where we want to go, and being paranoid is not considered an affliction.

Mast and standing rigging. What we don't want is the mast to fall down. When a mast falls down, it's usually because some part of the standing rigging failed. So it follows that what we *really* don't want is for the standing rigging to fail.

Prevention lies in inspection. Stainless steel is treacherous and can fail with very little warning. But in most cases, there was a warning and the dismastee just didn't see it. Hairline cracks in swage or other fittings, in tangs and chain plates, signal trouble. Often, though not always, rust is an indication that trouble is brewing.

Recently, an insurance survey revealed a crack in a swage at RED SHOES' masthead, an unusual occurrence. One normally finds them at deck level, where salt water has had a chance at them. This was in the headstay, and we assumed that the continual flexing of the stay under sail caused the crack. We replaced the headstay with new wire and fittings. We carry a spare wire long enough to replace the backstay, and both upper and lower Sta-Loks for each shroud and stay.

If your standing rigging is new and has swage fittings, it's advisable to seal them with a good sealant where the wire enters the swage. This will keep out salt water, and extend the fitting's useful life.

The beauty of Sta-Loks and similar fittings is that you can re-use them. Thus if a swage fails, and you carry backup Sta-Loks, you can use the same wire, making up the difference in length either with toggles or extra long fittings. Unfortunately, by the time a swage fitting fails, your mast has most likely already fallen down.

You also have to watch for burrs on your wire rope. A burr will occur when a single strand breaks. Sometime ago, we had a lifeline fail at a swage fitting at a stanchion. It appears that each time either of us left the cockpit to go forward on that side, or to get into the dinghy, we put our weight on this lifeline. Ultimately the bending of the wire at the inflexible fitting caused enough fatigue that it broke. It broke one strand at a time. I spotted it when there were a couple of tiny strands still connecting it. A burr on lifelines or standing rigging is a signal for immediate replacement.

Spreaders. RED SHOES' mast has only one set of spreaders. As on most cruising sailboats, we have attached padeyes for a lightweight halyard on the bottom of both port and starboard spreaders. One is for the courtesy flag of the country we're visiting, and the other I use either for a special ham antenna in port, or a radar reflector at sea. We used to tie off these halyards snugly, leaving no slack to flutter in the wind.

After six or seven years, the tension on the flag halyard, when on the tack where the standing rig is tight on that side, actually pulled the spreader downwards. This happened in tiny increments until I noticed that the spreaders were no longer tilted upward at the proper angle. By attaching the main halyard to the tip of the spreader, and relying on the eye of a friend in a dinghy watching from way out in front of RED SHOES, we were able to get each spreader angled equally so that it properly bisects the angle the shroud makes as it passes over the spreader's end. We then replaced the stainless steel seizing wire to fix the spreader to the shroud. However, seizing will not prevent moving the spreader if too much tension is applied to either flag or radar reflector halyards.

I pointed out to a friend who owned a ketch that the spreaders on his main were actually tilted down and in danger of collapsing. Sure enough, within the week he motored back to the anchorage, with spreaders collapsed, the mast still standing. He was lucky, and is now a believer in insisting on the proper spreader angle.

You don't want your halyard, sheet, preventer parting at an inconvenient time (or any other time). Maintaining running rigging is a matter of keeping your lines shipshape—ends burned and whipped, eye splices whipped at the throat. All else is a matter of inspection, watching for chafe. Dacron line is a wonder, as it resists sun and mildew.

Most people these days use short (18 inches) pieces of clear plastic hose for dock line or anchor line chafe. Fire hose is excellent, and fire departments are always replacing hose, so get your name with your chief for the old hose. And for the perfectionist, don't forget elk hide or cowhide for those lines and situations where the location of chafe protection on the line doesn't vary, i.e., dock lines, halyard eye splice, etc.

The problem with chafing gear is to keep it in place. With foresight, you can have a couple of pieces of plastic or fire hose threaded onto your rode and pre-positioned. Otherwise your hose will need to be split, so that you can put it around the rode at any point. Then, however, it must be secured two ways—around the rode itself, and then lengthwise, so that it won't slide out of place.

Chafing gear will itself chafe, and will have to be adjusted from time to time so that new material is brought to bear on the point of contact.

With anchoring, one approach we've used is to rig a spring line to take the strain. We use chafing gear on the spring line, which is secured to the anchor rode with a rolling hitch. Now, even if the chafing gear works its way out of place, allowing the spring line to chafe and part, the rode is still intact to take the strain until I can rig another spring line.

You don't want sails ripping or blowing out. Sails will last far longer if always covered or bagged when not in use. Even more than chafe, sun damage is a sail's biggest enemy.

We had a situation on RED SHOES that will happen to few people. Our roller-furling jib originally had a white sun shield. As it was the same color as the sail, we never noticed that half the time we were barber poling: i.e., the jib, rolled up, had a streak of exposed sailcloth that spiraled down the forestay like the stripe on a barber pole. That section rotted out long before the rest of the sail.

Barber poling is the result either of rolling up the jib with too little tension on the sheet, or of a too-narrow sun shield, or both. Since the calamity with our first jib, we've insisted on a wider, colored sun shield. That way, if we've barber poled, the white stripe stands out like the stripe on a barber pole.

If you plan to do a lot of downwind sailing using the main, it's essential to mount baggy wrinkles or some other form of chafe protection on the appropriate shrouds, thus minimizing the abrasive effect of continuous rubbing. PVC pipe or plastic hose are more popular now than the salty look of baggy wrinkles.

Be sure to notice the projections that might tear the jib when you come about—we tore ours three times before we realized that it was catching on the tang of the staysail stay. The ends of the spreaders, if not properly covered, can also be a source of disaster for an overlapping jib.

You don't want gear failure. On our old boat, SEA FOAM, we had only one creaky winch, and I don't remember ever servicing it, although in nine years I'm sure I must have. On RED SHOES we have Lewmar winches: three #16's and two #43's, and each requires servicing about twice a year. The gears need grease, and the little ratchet jobbies, which pick up dust and salt, always need cleaning and lubing. The small parts that make up the ratchet (pawl) use little springs, and I've been in constant fear of losing one, as I have no spares. (Note to myself: get spare springs from Lewmar.) Incidentally, it's important to keep the pawl springs clear of grease. Otherwise the spring may be inhibited from pushing at the pawl, and the winch will not work properly.

For some reason we have cam cleats made by two different manufacturers, and both of them either pack up or become extremely difficult to operate. Salt gets into the works, which are virtually inaccessible. So far I've gotten by with flushing them with fresh water and bathing them in WD-40, but I know that some day I'll have to remove them from the deck and dismantle them completely to do a more thorough job.

Maintenance of roller-furling gear is a problem. The bearings on our roller-furling gear are plastic, which means that they can develop flat spots. Therefore it's advisable to slack off on halyard tension before rolling up the jib, particularly if you're not going to use the jib for a day or more, as continual tension will eventually distort the bearings, and the gear will refuse to operate smoothly.

As with any deck hardware with moving parts, salt will build up in the works and should be flushed away with fresh water; then, if possible, the moving parts should be lubricated with a plastic-compatible stuff, such as silicon or Teflon spray.

With roller furling, the halyard is always in the same place—up at the masthead where you can't inspect it. It makes sense to lower the jib periodically, inspect the halyard, and flush and lube the upper bearings of the roller-furling gear.

Proper headstay tension is essential with roller furling. If the stay curves too far from a straight line and there is too much sag, rolling up the sail in a blow will be unnecessarily difficult. Also, a taut forestay will have less flex and side to side action than a loose one, thus minimizing metal fatigue. And the sail will work better.

You don't want fasteners corroding and freezing. Most hardware on aluminum booms and masts is attached with stainless steel bolts or machine screws. The contact of stainless steel and aluminum invites corrosion. All stainless steel fasteners in the mast or boom should be lubed with a product especially made to minimize the corrosion that leads to freezing up. We use Permatex Anti-Seize. Star brite and Tef Gel make stuff designed to do the same thing. Loktite Removable Thread Locker claims to protect against corrosion as well as to prevent the loosening of fasteners due to vibration, etc. Whenever you add hardware to your boom or mast, make sure that the fasteners are properly lubricated.

We have an Aries windvane, which is made of aluminum and fastened with stainless steel bolts. We bought it used, and as soon as we got it home we dismantled it completely and reassembled it using Permatex Anti-Seize on all bolts and other fasteners.

You don't want propane tanks expiring at an early age. Propane tanks should be kept in a locker that is isolated from the rest of the boat's interior. Because propane is heavier than air, the locker should drain overboard at the lowest point. On RED SHOES, when we are sailing in any kind of sea, salt water comes up through the drains, and spray leaks in from the hatch.

Steel propane tanks should be inspected and painted regularly. If made of aluminum, propane tanks can be left alone. Aluminum will corrode eventually, so the tanks must be replaced when they become pitted. However, if you paint them when you first buy them using a zinc chromate primer, they'll last longer.

You don't want your stove to quit, particularly in the middle of preparing spaghetti during a hurricane. This means that the pressure gauge, regulator, and relay switch will need some kind of protection. Flushing with fresh water and spraying with WD-40 after each passage is one approach. Another is to paint whatever needs protection. We didn't think of this, and as a result of a recent insurance survey have been told to replace them all.

You don't want ground tackle failing. Once again, chafe is the biggest enemy. However, it doesn't hurt to check, when dropping or raising anchor, if the splice is holding up; if there's a thimble, how's the seizing? and do all the shackles still have their seizing wire intact? You have seized all shackles with monel or stainless steel seizing wire, haven't you?

We've found that galvanized anchor chain lasts us about three years, and then must be re-galvanized or replaced. You can eke out another year or two if you can overlook rust stains on your decks. Keep an eye out for line chafe, and for occasional distorted links in the chain.

For people using rope rode who anchor in coral sand: sand gets into the fibers of the rope and exerts abrasive action beyond imagination, thereby weakening the rope. In Tarawa, in what was then the Gilbert Islands, we had a rope rode fail for that very reason. Unfortunately there's no good answer. Either use all chain, but that adds extra weight, or budget for replacing rope rode that's been saturated with coral sand.

You don't want to lose all the fresh water out of one tank while at sea. This plumbing problem will happen on some systems and not on others, but it is rare. Our pressure water system, for example, came with a pump that was too powerful. We were popping hoses off bayonet fittings on a regular basis, suddenly finding all our fresh water in the bilge. This is most likely to happen with hoses carrying hot water, as heat softens plastic hose. We replaced our pressure pump with a less powerful one, but we also went over all the hose connections and tightened the clamps. We haven't popped a hose since.

Hose clamps, when initially installed, have to kind of settle in. We went around tightening the clamps on RED SHOES and at first accused the manufacturers of neglect. However, it wasn't their fault: it's a characteristic of hose and hose clamps. Also, hose clamps can rust, weaken and fail. When you shop for hose clamps you'll notice there are two qualities—buy the better ones. You don't want the hoses attached to through-hull fittings to pop off, allowing sea water to fill your boat, so use double clamps on all through-hulls, and wherever else there's room for two clamps. A cruising friend who mistrusts all hose clamps puts a dab of 5200 on the hose barbs for insurance. Whatever you do, carry spare clamps, and inspect, inspect, inspect.

Engine cooling system hoses age, and can crack and leak, mostly at the site of a hose clamp. A hose that makes contact other than where it's clamped will be abraded and will eventually fail.

Some people swear by the kind of hose that has a continuous wire spiraling through the material. I hate it. A virtually inaccessible bilge pump hose of that material failed within the first six months. Somehow water gets to the wire on the outside, and because it is made of ordinary steel, not stainless, it rusts, the rust rots the material, and lo and behold you have a problem you don't need. In the case of our bilge pump hose, rather than replacing the whole length that runs through the dark and tortuous reaches of interior cabinetry, I cut out the rotted section, took a short piece of PVC pipe with an outside diameter that matched the inside diameter of the hose, and clamped the ends of the healthy sections of hose to it. Not an ideal solution, but it has worked now for nine years.

People use this kind of wire-infested hose because it'll go around corners without buckling and constricting the flow. I recommend almost any other solution: i.e., using PVC for sharp turns, or enlarging the bend so that regular hose can manage it without buckling. Hose with wire in it has been the Benedict Arnold in our war with plumbing problems.

You don't want pumps to fail—but they will. Rather than rebuild pumps, it makes sense to carry a spare for the essential systems. A spare pump for the galley might get you through a drought on a passage. Then, if you have a repair kit for the failed pump, you can while away the calms working on it. Although you probably won't be using the pressure water system once you leave Marinadom, you still may want to carry a spare pressure pump, as they are virtually impossible to repair.

As I mentioned elsewhere, we have an electric bilge pump. Rather than carry a spare, we have a Rule through-deck hand pump as a backup that operates from the cockpit. Because the electric pump has so far taken care of us, we haven't used the manual pump. The diaphragm on the Rule is not exposed to sunlight; I recently inspected and tested it, and it seems to be fine. When a manual bilge pump of the diaphragm type is the primary bilge pump, the diaphragm should be replaced regulary, and a spare diaphragm carried in case of failure. With the exception of the head, which is unpleasant enough to have a category of its own, we haven't had a serious plumbing problem since we've had RED SHOES.

You don't want the head stopping up when you have guests aboard (or any other time). Ours, a Groco model K manual head made by Gross Mechanical Labs, requires dismantling and installing new seals, gaskets, and flapper and joker valves at least once a year. In nine years I have had to do a major rebuild—replacing the shaft and piston rings—only once.

I have had to remove the hoses and beat the accumulated plaque out of them twice. I am burying an awareness that the time to do it again is imminent.

One way to prolong the intervals between plaque removal is to forbid toilet paper or any other cloggery being put into the head. A warning that keeps crew conscientious is, "If you stop it up, you bail it out so the plumber can work on it." An inspired discourse on the joys of handling fresh, raw sewage goes a long way toward enforcing this.

Tip: Pour ½ cup of white vinegar into the toilet and pump the water out of the bowl. Then pour another ½ cup into the bowl. Let it sit overnight. This will help a great deal to take care of the odor that builds up.

Head manufacturers make their profit from their over-priced repair kits. During our nine years on RED SHOES our head repair and rebuilding kits have cost us over $500, and the price of repair kits has doubled. We have an expensive Groco, but I have been on boats boasting inexpensive heads that have worked for years without maintenance, and in my next boat I would buy a cheaper head and replace it with a new one if the old one developed a serious malady. Throwing a diseased head overboard has to be one of life's more uplifting experiences, and one that I look forward to eagerly.

You don't want to come below to a saloon awash. Which leads us grace-fully into *electrical*, as one of the weak links in our electrical system is the float switch for automatic bilge pump operation. Rule makes two types. In our experience, the cheaper one doesn't last long enough for me to get used to having it. The more expensive Super Switch is guaranteed, and ours have lasted the length of the guarantee, but not much longer. There are other automatic switches, and some may be more reliable. I have adopted the approach that it's worth the extra money to buy the Super Switch, but we keep a spare as we've learned that it's bound to fail.

This is actually a good thing. Expecting the switch to fail makes me check the bilges regularly, enabling me to spot debris that might clog the pump, or oil and grease that should be cleaned up.

You don't want to fry either your alternator or your batteries. Probably the most important thing you can do to maintain your electrical system is to check the wires leading to and from the alternator. Engine vibration can loosen them, and if the wrong connection is broken, the alternator can burn up. Also, any connection that might be wetted with sea water should be protected and inspected on a regular basis. Battery connections should be checked regularly for corrosion, taken apart, cleaned, and greased if necessary. A properly greased battery terminal will go for years without attention.

If your batteries need maintenance, you'll have to monitor the level of the electrolyte in each cell. A battery that's treated properly might not need to have distilled water added more than once a year. But if anything goes awry with the charging systems aboard, the electrolyte can be boiled off in a twink. In extreme cases, the battery will be ruined.

You don't want to be an electronics repair shop groupie. The only person I would trust to fix anything electronic on RED SHOES is either the factory that built it, or a man named Merlin, a Brit who's probably dead by now. In my life I have seldom felt despair equal to the feeling I have when I gaze at the innards of an electronic device with a behavior problem. We have all become victims, in the sense that we take electronic devices for granted, depend on them heavily (I'm writing these words on a laptop while monitoring Chan-nel 68, the yachtie's calling channel here on the Rio Dulce), and at least in my case have no knowledge whatsoever about how to repair them.

Fortunately the majority of problems with electronic devices are not electronic, but electrical or mechanical, and in those situations I've been able to make repairs. However three radios (ham, VHF and handheld VHF) and both instruments (speedlog and depth meter) have at one time or another been returned to the factory for service.

Sometimes a company will actually be helpful. We had a problem with our Heart Interface inverter. I called the factory and talked to a technician who was not only knowledgeable, but also explained things in words I could understand. He informed me that the problem lay in a circuit board. Installing the circuit board required, as I recall, techniques learned in Soldering 1-A, plus the mechanical aptitude needed to attach things at obvious places. The unit has worked perfectly ever since.

You don't want your boat to look as if you didn't care—because then nobody else, including insurance companies, will, either. Many boats these

Nancy oiling teak. A tape player, CD, or AM-FM radio helps keep you from dwelling on how much you'd rather be doing something else.

days have no teak trim topside. RED SHOES has some, and we have wavered between letting it weather, and treating it with SeaFin, a product made by Daly's in Seattle. When newly applied it looks like varnish and brings out the natural beauty of the wood. Best of all, re-treatment does not require an extensive scraping and sanding to get rid of old coatings. We had tons of varnished mahogany topsides on SEA FOAM, and alternated between shameful neglect and over-conscientiousness.

A product that recently came to my attention is Cetol, a teak finish that users claim lasts for months. After 20 years of brightwork disappointment, however, I'm caveating any emptors.

Unless you own slaves, nothing you do with outside teak is completely satisfactory. The worst teak solution, in my opinion, involves products which contain pigment, hide the grain and color of the wood, and end up looking as if you'd painted your beautiful and expensive trim with an inferior brown paint. And there are those who actually do paint their teak, resolving to strip it down and varnish it when they finally sell the boat.

Stainless stanchions, bimini frames, chain plates, pushpits and pulpits will develop a patina of superficial rust. Nancy has used various products and now favors Brite Boy metal polish. Whatever she uses, she scrubs with one of those green scrubbies such as ScotchBrite. This is an area where you have many choices. No matter what, try using a green scrubby. We love them for cleaning teak, washing dishes, and for scrubbing any place where dirt or stains are stubborn.

You don't want to waste a haulout. Few things are more discouraging than launching your boat after a two-week purgatory in the yard and realizing you've forgotten to attend to something important. Usually the sight of your boat's exposed undersides will remind you of all the things you wanted to do. However, making a list never hurts, as it helps to focus on the upcoming job.

Yard list: Cosmetics. Work from toe rail down. Sheer stripe need painting? Unless you've decided on an Imron or Awlgrip job on the topsides, clean, wax and buff. Raise waterline (always). Tape and paint boot top, unless you're as slothful as we are and have eliminated it.

Inspect metal parts for electrolytic damage. Replace zincs. Check cutless bearing; shake the prop shaft for play. If in tightening your stuffing box over the previous months or years you've run out of threads, now's the time to add packing. (If you have a stuffing box that doesn't require packing, skip ahead.) On most boats you can repack the gland while the boat's in the water by first diving down and packing something around the prop shaft to prevent sinking when you remove the packing nut inside the boat. If you have a Dynaplate for a radio ground, clean it. Clean transducer for depthmeter; clean paddle for speedo.

Inspect for blisters. Prepare bottom for bottom paint. Time the last coat to conform with the proper interval to wait before launching: it is specified on the can. Paint keel bottom and other spots when the crane lifts it off the support. Launch, and drink to a job well done.

You don't want your bimini, dodger, or awnings to drip when it rains. Sunbrella, the usual fabric used for awnings, etc, becomes porous after a time and needs periodic application of some type of waterproofing. We personally avoid Thompson's Water Seal, as we find it promotes unremovable mildew in the fabric itself. Star brite makes a waterproofer that so far has not produced mildew. There are other brands, Scotch for one, that may be just as effective. Ask at your canvas shop.

You don't want to abuse your boat. A racing sailor pushes his boat to its limits. A cruising sailor will usually try to play it safe. Your boat is your home, your wealth, your envelope of safety. It is also a wondrous structure that will be very unlikely to let you down as long as you keep an eye out for its well-being.

CHAPTER 19

Repairs—A Pound of Cure
(Or Was It Curare?)

Dear Herb: I read your letter to Pampered of Penobscot, and it sounds like you're telling the poor bastard to spend the rest of his anxious days examining his boat—a kind of vesselating hypochondria. You'd be making mother hens of us all. What ever happened to 'kicking back'?

S. Loth of Lompoc

Dear S.: A sailor can continue cruising for a long time, and it would be convenient if his boat continued with him. Every relationship requires maintenance, and maintenance is certainly better than repair. We're not thinking in terms of a six-month cruise and then you sell the boat. We're thinking about the whole experience.

However, for those who persist in the view that maintenance isn't important, below are a few desperate measures.

OF ROT AND TEREDOS

This is primarily for wooden boat owners, but rot can also occur in wood that's used in fiberglass boat construction. Rot occurs primarily in untreated wood living in moist conditions. Trapped water will encourage rot.

When we bought SEA FOAM, a corner post in the trunk cabin was rotten. Nancy had an uncle whose hobby was woodworking, and he offered to make us a new corner post. He used a type of mahogany no longer available in any useful quantity, or at a viable price. He picked it up 40 years ago off the commercial wharf in San Pedro, California. It was a full four by four, but because it wasn't cut true and was short, it had been used as a sticker for stacked lumber and was destined to be thrown away. (A sticker is a piece of waste wood that lies across the pile on which the boards are laid. Stickers allow air to pass through the lumber pile, which helps with the drying.) It was a beautiful piece of wood, no knots, and hard as oak. Forty years ago it was junk, another case of not recognizing value until scarcity forces us to see it. A piece of it became the best and strongest item in the trunk cabin.

The best way to treat rot is with surgery. Cut it out and replace it with sound wood. However, this isn't always possible, or it can be difficult and expensive. In such cases, it may be practical to avoid major surgery through the use of a product called Git Rot. Git Rot is an epoxy resin of thin viscosity that will soak into the rotted wood and harden. The wood must be *completely dry*, as Git Rot will not displace water, and in order to assure total penetration you should drill a pattern of eighth-inch diameter holes through the rot to a depth where you've reached unrotted wood. With good saturation, the repaired area will be as hard or harder than the original wood. Better yet, the spread of the rot will have been stopped. However, the repair, though hard, won't have the same breaking strength or flexibility that healthy, fibrous wood has.

I would never buy a boat fastened with galvanized fastenings. Plugs are supposed to keep out moisture, but as the boat ages, more and more plugs leak. With the slightest bit of moisture, galvanized fastenings have a galvanic corrosive effect on wood. Wherever this happens, in time the galvanized screw will develop an area of rotten wood around it. If I was considering buying a boat that was fastened with galvanized screws, I'd factor the cost of re-fastening into my offering price.

At present, the ideal fastener material is either silicon bronze for screws or copper for rivets. Neither will cause rot to the wood around it, moist or not. I once saw an 80-year old tugboat being repaired—some planks had become rotten through neglect, not because of the type of fastener. In fact, the boat had been fastened with square boat nails made of Swedish iron, and every nail they removed was still, after 80 years of continuous use in salt water, in perfect condition.

Some older boats were fastened with plain old iron boat nails. You can almost always tell by the unsightly rust streaks descending from leaky plugs. Replacing the fastener and re-plugging is best, but even if all you do is remove the offending plug, dry the area thoroughly, and re-plug so that moisture is effectively kept out, there aren't likely be any more rust streaks, and the fastener will probably last the life of the boat.

We've covered *corrosion* of stainless steel exposed to salt water and air. When attaching extra stuff to your boat, never buy what is sold in hardware stores for home use. Don't use brass or, unless it is an emergency, galvanized screws or bolts. That leaves silicon bronze or stainless. Stainless has mostly taken over the market. In old SEA FOAM (30 years old when we sold her, and 16 years later she's still going strong), we occasionally found fasteners that had crystallized—a few in the planks, but mostly in deck fittings. I haven't found a satisfactory explanation for this. Galvanic action, for example, doesn't explain the crystallization of screws on deck or in the cabin trunk—screws that are dry during most of their lifetime. Is there electrolytic action between screws and the fittings they secure because they're made of a different kind of bronze? In any event, older boats produce crystallized bronze screws that can be identified by a pinkish color and a tendency to disintegrate when tapped with a hammer. These, of course, must be replaced.

Engine mounts are the exception to the bronze/stainless imperative. We once sailed with a boat whose stainless steel engine mounts were continually breaking. In my opinion, only mild steel bolts should be used here. Mild steel is far more resistant to the deleterious effects of vibration, or the shakes and rattles that with some engines approach concussion. Fight the battle of rust, and if you lose, plan to replace. Anything's better than having a motor come loose in the middle of a crisis, such as motor sailing to windward in a gale.

Instead of bronze, many modern boats use a material called Marelon for through-hull fittings. Based solely on what I've read, I favor the idea. For one thing, Marelon obviously won't corrode and dissolve if you forget to replace your zinc anodes, whereas bronze might. Another thing is that Marelon, being inert electrically, won't act as a conductor for lightning. Just one story about lightning strikes that have blown out bronze through-hull fittings and sunk the boat has convinced me to consider Marelon. And finally, bear in mind that sunlight, the major enemy of all forms of plastic, will never reach your through-hulls unless you sail differently than I do.

Minimalists will suggest, "Why have any through-hull fittings?" Most wives or partners prefer sinks that drain and toilets that flush. Until they reach a change of heart, most of us will have to continue dealing with through-hulls.

We mentioned in the maintenance chapter that sacrificial zinc anodes need to be replaced when they've been eaten away, and sooner is better than later. Don't wait till you need a metal detector to tell where the zincs were. Serious electrolysis, found most often at docks that provide shore power, can eat up propellers, prop shafts, rudder shafts and through-hull fittings in no time. In most cases, any of these repairs will require a haulout.

Worms (teredos) are a wooden boat's nemesis. If you're a wooden boat owner, you are not paranoid if you fear worms. They are indeed after your hull.

Some woods—teak, New Zealand kauri—are inherently resistant to worms, so if your boat is planked with either, fear not. But these woods are so scarce they're virtually unavailable for planking new boats. SEA FOAM was planked with Douglas fir which prior to construction had been soaked in creosote. We repaired SEA FOAM's cutwater with a wood bought in Papeete that was supposed to be worm resistant, but which turned out to be the only place on the boat that suffered from serious worm damage. When we discovered that, our confidence in our worm-resistant, creosote-treated hull received a boost.

Worms are to wood what gophers are to new lawns. Their presence is indicated by little holes. The more holes, the more elaborate the labyrinth they've created within your plank. When we hauled out in Papeete to renew our bottom paint, our new two-year old cutwater looked like a randomly drilled cribbage board.

My first thought was poison, and I bought some concentrated stuff that must be illegal in environmentally aware countries. Worms, unfortunately, do what gophers do, which is to build barriers in their tunnels. Painting the stem three times a day with a lethal chemical that had the destructive power of Agent Orange was personally satisfying, but I knew in my heart that most of the worms were laughing and scratching safely behind their dams. But I hoped for the agonized death of at least a few.

The next treatment was the blowtorch attack. If I can't poison the buggers, I'll cook them, right? I moved the flame slowly over a portion of the infested area, thereby raising the temperature of the interior of the wood to worm-bubbling levels. Gradually I covered the whole area, imagining worm screams as I worked. *Most* satisfying.

Having successfully completed my 'scorched stem' policy, I prepared the wood for Git Rot. After drilling a pattern of eighth-inch holes, remembering to angle them downward, I flooded the area with the liquid. We owned the boat for another three years, and successive haulouts revealed no further worm damage.

Naturally when it came to worm discussions, fiberglass boat owners gloated, usually in overbearing, supercilious ways, and their presence at wooden boat cocktail parties was eschewed. About this time, in the 70's, *SAIL* magazine (or was it *WoodenBoat*?) came out with an article on the polyestermite, a worm that was said to consume fiberglass like the teredo eats wood. It was a spoof, but it was effective, in that it planted in the minds of fiberglass boat owners a seed of doubt that caused them many anxiety-ridden nights. For a while all gloating ceased, but it resumed when the word reached everyone that the polyestermite was the creation of a sadistic writer.

However, gloating always attracts the attention of the sheriff of karma, whose memory is infinite. Along came blisters, silencing the gloating of fiberglass boat owners forever.

OF BOAT POX AND BLISTERS

A 1990 *Practical Sailor* survey suggests that one in four fiberglass boats will suffer blisters. Blisters occur in fiberglass hulls as the result of water traveling osmotically through the layers of resin and fiberglass. Having breached the outer layer, the water combines with uncured resin, or other agents used in laying up the hull. If there are defects in layup, this can augment the blistering process. When you pierce a blister, the stuff that comes out is not water, but an acidic, pungent liquid.

If blisters were superficial, a kind of chemical acne, there'd be no problem. Unfortunately they are more like metastasizing cancer. Serious weakening of the hull structure can result if blisters are allowed to go unchecked.

Boat hulls are made of fiberglass and polyester resin. Many manufacturers apply an epoxy barrier coat to the underbody before laying on the anti-fouling paint. This barrier coat is supposed to seal off the hull so that water can't get in and blisters can't get a foothold. However, there is some evidence that epoxy, while it's the best solution we know, is by no means impermeable. Water, the ultimate solvent, will in time infiltrate or otherwise reduce any material to its molecular state.

This thin coat of epoxy can be damaged—rubbed off during a grounding, or sanded off either for a repair or during a moment of misplaced enthusiasm when preparing the bottom for re-painting. If you ever have the slightest hunch that you have indeed damaged the integrity of the epoxy barrier coat, *renew it!* Although the real effectiveness of barrier coats hasn't yet been reduced to percentages—it may actually turn out to be more like the Maginot Line—it's our only real defense at the moment.

The recipe for fighting a few blisters limited to a small area is to remove all bottom paint from the area, and clean out the blisters themselves with a Dremel or similar tool. (I have a friend who uses a chisel.) Let the area dry out while you do everything else on your haulout list. It's best if you live in northern climes and leave the boat hauled out for the winter, but how many liveaboard cruisers do this? Finally, prior to painting the bottom, fill the craters with an epoxy filler and cover the whole area with a couple of coats of epoxy barrier coat. Apply bottom paint, launch, and pray.

For help and in-depth techniques for repairing more serious blister damage and other fiberglass problems, Gougeon Brothers, Inc., sell an illustrated booklet, *Fiberglass Boat Repair and Maintenance*, which instructs the reader in the use of their excellent products. Also available from Gougeon is a 48-pager that focusses solely on blister detection, prevention and repair. Videos on the subject are available, but are more expensive. Write to Dept. 25, PO Box 908, Bay City, MI 48707. *Osmosis and Glassfibre Yacht Construction*, Second Edition, by Tony Staton-Bevan, covers in-depth the subject of boat pox.

A serious attack of blisters is best repaired by yard specialists, who may sandblast the hull, or might take an electric planer-type tool and shave a layer or two (or more, depending on the severity of the blistering) off the whole bottom. Then the boat must sit while it dries out, after which it is cleaned of residue (dried acidic stuff), and the barrier coat and paint put on. This assumes a hull thick enough to remain strong after the removal of about an eighth of an inch of material. Otherwise, a new layer of glass, preferably using epoxy resin, must be laid up.

Polyestermites indeed!

POSTSCRIPT: RED SHOES was manufactured just prior to Pacific Seacraft's use of Vinylester resin for the first layer of mat next to the gel coat. Vinylester has been in existence for a dozen years, in use by most quality boat manufacturers for a decade. Interplastic, a major manufacturer of the resin, assures me that on boats where Vinylester has been properly applied, there have been no incidents whatsoever of blisters. If I were buying a used boat today, I'd try to find out from the builder if Vinylester was used.

More information about this resin can be had at no charge from Interplastic, 1225 Wolters Blvd, Vadnais Heights, MN 55110. Tel: 612 481 6860 fax 612 481 9836.

CHAPTER 20

More on Cures,
Or a Glitch In Time Saves Nine

Dear Herb: I'm a single-hander, a widower, and a tailor by trade, and I'm hopeless when it comes to mechanical things. I suppose I can learn the rudiments, but some of the stuff you talk about is definitely beyond my limited talents. What would you suggest?

People Are Not Their Seams

Dear PANTS: If you can tailor, you can certainly learn to do canvas work, mend sails, and probably many other things that you put your mind to. Another suggestion might be to marry a woman who makes her living working on boats. On the other hand, maybe it would be cheaper to just hire her.

Remember that one of the values in servicing and maintaining your own boat is that you look around and notice things. The sailor who merely starts the engine and expects it always to run, or who immediately calls a sail repairman when tears or chafe appear, will never notice the loose or frayed fan belt, the leak in the cooling system, the cracked swage fitting at the top of the mast, or the burr on the headstay wire. He won't see them before they fail, before they betray him while negotiating the entrance to a tricky pass, or during the survival storm that was the stuff of his worst nightmares.

As for those who refuse even to try, I hear a huge 'Hooray' from professionals. Masters of Boatwork (MOBs), known affectionately as 'The Mob', look to the helpless to provide them with highly profitable work.

But even if you try, there comes a time when the diagnosis eludes you, or the necessary tool, product or technique is absent. If you haven't found a boatworker to marry, you'll have to invent, improvise, jury rig, and make do with chewing gum and bailing wire till you get to a port where help is available. Then you can look for a local mechanic, rigger, or whatever specialist you need. Prepare to pay through the proboscis, however, as MOB members are skilled at estimating your total net worth and billing you that plus 10 percent.

The Mob is very jealous of its territory. Remember in the old days, when the cruising fraternity was one of the few remaining environments where 'help thy neighbor' was operative? Mobsters are definitely against this, and they're organized. Guilty of samaritanizing in a Mobster's territory? Beware of 'persuasion' that could well escalate to water balloons.

Enter the GLITCH, or Generous Liveaboard In Transit Coming to Help. A Glitch gets it on by being more prepared than anyone else. He (or she) not only has every tool made, but knows exactly where each one is stored. He carries a huge inventory of spares and can always find quickly the item he wants. If he doesn't have it he can make it. Not only did he design and build his boat, but he rigged it, built all the electronics from scratch, and was a professional motor mechanic for years. An expert marksman as well as a karate black belt, he has no fear of The Mob.

Glitches are unstintingly generous with their time and talents. When a Mobster hears of a Glitch coming his way, he moves on to greener anchorages, knowing that if he hangs around, the CIA (Cruisers In Action) in conjunction with the FBI (Free Boatwork Initiative) can prevent The Mob from resorting to violent enforcement. Mobsters are organizing, however, and groups such as The Union to Prevent Unauthorized Random Samaritanizing (UPURS) are acquiring increasingly large memberships.

But beware! There is one drawback to having a Glitch come to your aid. He or she exacts his pound of flesh in intimidation. Having watched a Glitch in action, a cruiser who thought himself self-sufficient will never feel adequate again. Wives and Significant Others run off with Glitches, as they tend to be superiorly endowed in all departments. When you hear of a Glitch coming your way, better think twice. Many skippers feel it's preferable to pay tribute to The Mob.

Self, Mob, or Glitch, you're at sea, you've just experienced some drastic boat failure and you have to get your beloved/hated yacht into port. Jury rigs are in the category of "what to do till the doctor comes."

In my opinion, this is where the wheat is separated from the chaff. Are we self-sufficient or do we call the Coast Guard? Do we rush to take advantage of our insurance policy's towing clause? Even if there is a Coast Guard within calling distance—for voyagers there usually isn't—it becomes a matter of pride to get your vessel home without assistance. No shame devolves on those who can't, or on those who call for assistance out of fear for the safety of crew; but in all other respects, it's my feeling that a certain taint falls on those who don't even try to help themselves. For instance, I've heard a skipper whose engine has failed call the

Removing and repairing our keel-stepped mizzen mast ourselves meant we didn't have to give up 600 windward miles.

Coasties for a tow—and there's wind, and he's driving a functioning sailboat! Come on.

What follows are some ideas for jury rigs that we or others have used successfully. And if the crises involved happened to occur because of defective maintenance, well, nobody's perfect.

Standing rigging failure does not always mean dismasting. A lower shroud might part, or a shroud could part in light winds, or you could be lucky, blessed, or with your incessant inspections you could spot a problem aborning. Thus it's good to have remedies in mind.

On an older boat, the standing rigging might well be 7x7 wire; 7x7, compared to 1x19, is flexible, and can be secured with loops made over thimbles and held by Nicopress fittings. This is great, because Nicopress fittings and crimpers are comparatively cheap and can easily be used by the do-it-yourselfer. So if a shroud were to part in the middle, you could conceivably cut out the bad part and add a short section.

Usually, however, shrouds part at the bottom or top. If this happens, you could add a short length of wire, but if you didn't have that you could use chain. The anchor rode won't miss a foot or two. I've seen boats with wire rigging and a piece of chain at the bottom added for the sole reason of making it into port. But months or even years have passed and the piece of chain is still there. As my son Philip said when I stumbled for the nth time on the wiggly 12x12 that passed for a front step to his otherwise marvelous house, "All temporary solutions last 30 years."

Modern rigs use 1x19 standing rigging (or rod rigging, a special case); 1x19 won't bend as around a thimble, so its ends must be equipped either with a swage or Sta-Lok type fitting. If a swage, one should probably carry Sta-Loks as replacement in case of failure, as few cruising skippers are willing to deal with the expense or the bulk of a swage press. If the wire breaks right at the swage, or the swage itself fails, the shroud can probably be repaired using one of the special long Sta-Loks. And if by doing this you still end up with too short a shroud, you can make up the difference with extra toggles if you have them, or, *in extremis*, a short length of chain.

I just went out and looked at RED SHOES' set-up. The turnbuckle fits into a toggle that's a fork which fits over the end of the chainplate, and is pinned to it. RED SHOES carries extra wire, Sta-Lok long fittings, and extra toggles, so in the event of a shroud failure we could probably make repairs without having to resort to chain.

It is very unlikely that rod rigging will fail. If it should, however, it must be replaced, not repaired. If we had rod rigging, I would carry extra wire and Sta-Loks to get me home.

A *bowsprit* is a device to 1) increase the effective deck length as it relates to sail plan and 2) to harass, torture, and ultimately kill crewmembers, depending on the length of the bowsprit and whether or not it has a pulpit. Unless very short, a bowsprit is stressed against head-stay tension by a device known as a bobstay, a rod, wire or piece of chain that runs from a point on the bowsprit to the cutwater. SEA FOAM had an 11-foot bowsprit.

I have learned to hate *bobstays*. Our first bobstay, the one that came with the boat, was a length of 1x19 wire secured with swage fittings. No turnbuckle, but on a sloppy rig—ours had deadeyes and lanyards, no hope of modern degrees of tension there—it shouldn't have mattered. However, we had friends on a modern rigged boat who knew all about *their* rig and thought this knowledge applied to all rigs. So in the Galápagos we exchanged our perfectly serviceable piece of gear for a length of ⅜-inch chain with a turnbuckle. Months later in Huahine, in an effort to achieve a headstay that under load looked less like a semicircle, we tightened this turnbuckle. Then, under sail to Raiatea, the deadwood to which the bobstay was attached ripped off. (Read my book *Blown Away* for a full description of that headache.)

It was in New Zealand that we decided our chain bobstay was too funky, and made one up using 7x7 wire with a thimble at each end, the wire secured with double Nicopress fittings. Months later, when Nancy and I were enduring our worst passage alone—Hawaii straight to San Diego in November—that bobstay broke. For 30 minutes, in seas of 12 feet or more, I hung over the bow in a bos'n's chair and tried unsuccessfully to attach the *chain* bobstay I'd made to get us home. Dunked as the boat plunged, blind from wetted glasses, and juggling two strips of stainless, a clevis pin, two cotterpins and washers, I was unable to attach the cutwater end to its fitting. But after a rest I went back and tried again, and on my very first attempt I accomplished it flawlessly. Having initially heaped blame on God for the mess we were in, I was quick to give Him credit for helping me effect the solution.

Why did the bobstay break? We had fastened it to the cutwater fitting using a loop around a stainless steel thimble. What with the constant flexing, the fitting had literally sawn through the thimble and thence through the wire.

I've seen bobstays made out of stainless steel rod, but I would never have one. Hit anything, dock, dinghy, another boat, and you'll likely bend the rod, and then where are you? Back to chain. On your new Shannon 38? Horrors!

I have the same objection to rod rigging and solid lifelines. The advantage in stiffness, in my opinion, is outweighed by the fact that it'll bend and stay bent. Wire isn't perfect either, but at least it straightens after impact.

One of the many other jury rig stories from our old SEA FOAM: On a passage from Tarawa to Suva, Fiji, the raw water pump that cools the engine quit. We ended up turning a five-gallon plastic bucket into a gravity feed tank, plumbing it into the system, and having our then 16-year old son, Craig, keep bucketing in water from the sea. It pleased me because it got us safely to Suva, but Craig would rather I not discuss how he felt about it.

A similar thing happened quite recently aboard RED SHOES. Suddenly there was no water coming out of the exhaust. One of the blessings of paranoia is that you tend to see any change as a threat. Nancy would love to have a dollar for every time I've said of a new sound, "What the hell is that?" Usually it's nothing, the product of vibration, or maybe a porthole falling shut. In this case, grass had been sucked into the raw water inlet for the engine cooling. As I removed the hose from the through-hull, a geyser proved that the stoppage was not there, and I foresaw a pleasant hour or two while I, racked into a twisted and unnatural position, chased the problem down. We were approaching Fort Myers Beach entrance, a narrow channel rimmed by mud bars, and an immediate solution was needed. Using a short length of hose, I bypassed the whole thing—hoses, raw water strainer and all—and went directly from through-hull to raw water pump. We then motored safely to anchorage, where I found and cleared the blockage.

"We'll take care of it ourselves, thank you," is one of the most rewarding aspects of cruising. And at times it has snatched us back from situations that would have ranged from unpleasant to disastrous.

If you have chosen an *inflatable* as a dinghy, there'll come a day when you'll have to *patch* it. Our present RIB, bought used three years ago, has yet to earn a patch. In the meantime, the two-part glue we've kept for making repairs has solidified. This suggests a need for a higher quality glue or a lower quality dink.

Most inflatable repairs make use of a type of contact cement that comes in a one-part or two-part formula. Bostik is one of the better one-part glues, but the best is two-part. If you have refrigeration, glue will keep longer if kept cold. Even kept cold, one and a half to two years is optimistic. We have kept dinks tumescent using ordinary contact cement, but the patches sooner or later come off. A properly applied two-part glue patch is as permanent as the Hypalon you're patching.

Five years ago, while we were cruising the Amazon Delta in RED SHOES, someone tried to steal our dinghy in the night. The thief or thieves swam out, cut the painter, and then, frustrated at discovering that the dinghy was locked to RED SHOES with a cable, slashed one of the chambers. Given a choice of thieves, one would hope for a mature one who'd outgrown such childish vindictiveness. That particular inflatable was built with three chambers, so the two undamaged ones kept it afloat. However, an eight-inch long tear had to be repaired.

In an emergency, far from professionals, when faced with a major inflatable repair, we've opted to use the stickiest stuff I know of, Dow Corning's 5200 sealant. Instead of a patch made of Hypalon, the material of which most inflatables are made, we've sometimes used the mesh-like material you can buy in builders' supply stores, an adhesive-backed, three-inch wide fiberglass tape made for mudding drywall joints. The tape is strong, and adds tremendous tear strength to the 5200. The patch will be ugly, but it works, and there comes a time in an inflatable's life when you have to weigh ugliness against mortality.

The cut dinghy in the Amazon was the most serious dinghy repair we ever did. Using 5200 sealant as glue, we stuck a strip of Hypalon to the *inside* of the tear. Be careful not to use excess glue here, as it will ooze out the side when you clamp it, thus gluing the patch material to the other side of the chamber as well. When that had set up, we stitched the rip for extra strength using dental floss. We then glued a long strip of the drywall mudding tape over the outside of the repair, taking one application of 5200 to glue it, and another to fill in completely the mesh in the tape. Two years later when we finally sold the dinghy, that chamber was still air tight.

CHAPTER 21

"So Now We're Going Sailing"

Dear Herb: We've just taken possession of our new boat, SPRING-BOARD, a Hans Christian 43. I tell you, we're in seventh heaven. We're also worried to death. Now what?

The Fearful Faithful

Dear FFs: SPRINGBOARD! Love that name. Not to worry, everything's going to be all right. You've bought a wonderful boat, and now you have to get used to each other. Think of it as a honeymoon. Did that worry you to death?

Actually, thinking back to my own honeymoon, maybe that's not such a good comparison. . .

My father was an inventor of sorts who had a lot of fun with life. After a summer spent working in a lumberyard in California, I returned home to Maine to find that my car, a little four-door Studebaker that had carried our family through World War II and beyond, had been completely revamped. Ten winters in heavily road-salted New England had reduced the body to rusty scrap. So my father'd had the foreman of his plywood mill rebuild it by welding a ¼-inch boiler plate steel for the floor, topped by a wide plywood body supported by a heavy, angle-iron framework. The result looked like a mini Brinks truck and weighed about the same.

Pam, the future mother of my children, and I worked to install a full-size double bed—after all, it was for a honeymoon, right? We painted the name 'Shackmobile' in dayglow script across the back. The double meaning escaped my bride until we were irrevocably married.

My father always maintained that world travel would mean far more if we first learned something of our own country. I listened for a change, and discovered he was right.

Although Dad had cloned a new body, our vehicle had the same old aging innards. We set out from our Falmouth Foreside reception on our trip across the continent and back. Thirty minutes from home we developed brake trouble. This was to establish a pattern.

137

Instead of a romantic bower, each new campsite became a pit stop, auto parts strewn about in an ambiance of pine needles and grease. I fixed most of the problems myself, but by the time we reached the West Coast, my beleaguered bride cried every time I said the word garage. It was rare that we covered four hundred miles without a breakdown.

Three months later we were in Pennsylvania hurtling down a two-lane highway, headed for home. Pam was at the wheel negotiating an impressive downhill run: we always coasted to save gas. Suddenly the right rear wheel came off. I knew it was the right rear wheel as soon as I saw it rolling past us. Because the axle had broken, the brake drum went with the wheel, so we had no brakes. The only thing slowing us down was the right rear stump. Just imagine dragging your foot to slow an armored vehicle coasting down a steep hill at 50 mph.

The road was straight, traffic was light, and eventually we ground to a halt. A village mechanic had parts shipped in by bus and worked far into the night to get us back on the road. He even took a check. But no matter how much I emphasized to Pam all the warm-hearted garage men we'd met, that was it. As soon as we reached Maine, the Shackmobile went on the block.

So let's avoid 'honeymoon' and call getting acquainted with your beloved SPRINGBOARD something less loaded. Until we can come up with a better suggestion, how about 'foreplay'?

Nancy and I owned SEA FOAM for a year before we cast off for paradise. During that year we went for a lot of daysails. We learned that 1) the wood-burning fireplace filled the cabin with smoke; and that 2) the bilge pump plumbing syphoned water *in* when we were on the port tack. We took care of both before we left on our voyage.

I also learned how many different reactions non-sailor guests can have to sailing. One wife became catatonic if we heeled more than ten degrees; another became frightened and scathing whenever her husband took the helm, no matter how well he steered. And Nancy and I were able to convince even the most novice male sailor that our 27,000-pound vessel would never tip over under any conditions short of a hurricane, but certain female novice sailors would never believe us.

Most interesting to me was how my musician friends took to sailing. Arriving in shiny black shoes, which they immediately doffed at our request, pale of skin, hollow of eye, outrageous in dress, they showed more enthusiasm and willingness to help than any other group, and all showed a natural instinct for dealing with wind and wave. During that year we invited over a dozen musicians and their wives or dates to go out for a daysail, and afterwards each would ask, "Hey, man, when are we gonna do this again?"

Newport Beach, California, has the reputation for being one of the most densely populated harbors in the U.S. We learned to bring our boat under sail to her slip at the far end of the harbor, tacking through mooring fields and Sabot races. We did this without ever making any serious errors. I look back on those days and weeks of learning about our boat as some of the most pleasant of our sailing lives.

There was no such party time when we took possession of RED SHOES, because we had her trucked to Oxford, Maryland. Our days were spent commissioning her. The few daysails we took were just the two of us. The boat had remarkably few problems. The worst one was that our jib's #6 luff tape was too small, and in any kind of a gust the jib would rip free of the groove in the roller-furling extrusion. As soon as we replaced the luff tape with #8, we had no more trouble.

The other problem was that the engine was out of line, making the boat shake under power like the paint can shaker at your local hardware store. I was able to align the engine myself, having learned the process on SEA FOAM. (See Chapter 16.)

We also had trouble with the autopilot, an accessory we'd added ourselves. The pilot has a memory, and if the belt slips, which it tended to do on the knurled drum that comes with the pilot, the pilot's 'brain' gets the wrong feedback and steers badly as a result. Correcting this by adding belt tension put too much side thrust on the motor's bearings. Eventually we solved the problem by taking an old drive belt, cutting it to the proper length, and glueing it, teeth out, to the drum. The exposed teeth meshed with the actual drive belt, which has rarely slipped since.

I deemed our boat's problems minimal, when weighed against all the things that might go wrong with an expensive and complex piece of equipment. Pacific Seacraft's excellent reputation is justly earned, and I can only wish you the same satisfactory experience with your Hans Christian.

Finally, although your shakedown sailings will have a serious purpose, don't forget to enjoy them. And of course the best insurance against *not* enjoying them is to avoid doing things that invite disaster. So:

Always get the most recent weather info.

Know the rules of the road, and sail as defensively as you would drive your car on a crowded freeway.

When piloting, don't cut navigational hazards close—allow good margins for error.

When landing at a dock or threading your way through mooring fields, maneuver slowly.

Knowing that a complex maneuver is coming, talk it through in advance with your crew. Everyone aboard should know what's supposed to happen.

Respect the wind, and reef when the wind *suggests* rather than demands it.

And finally, irrespective of moral or legal considerations, if you or your crew drink alcohol or enjoy funny cigarettes, save it for when the anchor is down and the sails and gear are properly stowed.

I guess what I'm suggesting is, act responsibly, sail conservatively, and pay attention. Use common sense.

On the subject of sailing conservatively, the more experience I have, the more I tend toward restraint, sometimes perhaps overly so. During a passage on RED SHOES from Puerto Rico to Panama, I looked aloft one evening and saw what appeared to be a jagged craze across the bottom of the starboard spreader. Were they stress cracks? I was certain they hadn't been there earlier. The thought of a collapsing spreader was decidedly unsettling. Six- to eight-foot seas prevented going up the mast (at least they prevented *my* going up). The best I could do was to inspect the spreader with binoculars. I studied it from all angles, and though never totally convinced that what I was seeing were cracks, I decided to err on the conservative side.

The beauty of the cutter rig, of course, is that if all the other standing rigging should collapse, the inner forestay-running backstay configuration will keep the mast from falling down. We lowered the main, rolled up the jib, rigged both runners, and raised the staysail. With only 15 knots of wind it'd be a slow night, but I knew that in the morning we'd still have an erection, speaking mastwise.

Next morning, using a looped halyard, I scrubbed the bottom of the spreader. Sure enough, the cracks smeared and then were completely erased. The only explanation that made sense was that, unbeknownst to us, a bird had perched on the spreader the previous afternoon. Wind had smeared its droppings across the bottom of the spreader. My log entry read, "I am probably the first skipper in history to spend the night under reduced sail because of bird shit."

In my list of admonitions above I forgot to mention jibes. You probably are familiar with the term and even the maneuver, but in case you're not:

Jibes (not the sarcastic kind, which is perhaps why Hiscock and others spell it 'gybes') are another major source of dismasting, and perhaps, for your shakedown days, we should mention them. To jibe, of course, means to change tacks by bringing the *stern* through the eye of the wind, as opposed to coming about, which means to steer the *bow* through the eye of the wind. An intentional jibe is also referred to as 'wearing away'. Here we're concerned with unintentional jibes.

Unintentional jibe stories are legion. Sometimes they're benign, sometimes not. We did one on SEA FOAM coming up from New Zealand. The night was dark as death. The wind was blowing about 20 knots, which meant that, sailing downwind, the wind over the deck was about 13 knots. The helmsperson—I think it was Nancy—lost her concentration just long enough to wander into a jibe, and the main boom, crashing across, took out the port running backstay. I was able to repair it when we reached Tubuai, one of French Polynesia's Austral islands, but a disconsolate Nancy failed to be cheered by my pointing out how much worse it could have been.

Besides helmsman error, causes of unintentional jibes can be a sudden wind shift, as when a squall hits; sailing by the lee with the wind too close to the critical point of jibing; and autopilot or windvane malfunction. Depending on the strength of the wind and/or any weak link in your rig, a jibe can be anything from embarrassing to disastrous.

When sailing before the wind on RED SHOES, and particularly at night, we always rig a preventer. Ours is simply a long line running from a boom bale to a bow cleat. This of course means I have to go to the foredeck if we decide to change tacks. A better solution might be a boom vang with a snatch block which, when clipped to the toe rail, can double as a preventer.

Dutchman, a company in Norwalk, Connecticut, makes something called a boom brake which is designed to keep the boom from crossing the deck fast, as in the case of a jibe. If it doesn't clutter up your running rig too much, it might be worth thinking about.

And we haven't even discussed personal injury, man overboard, or even death, all of which at one time or another have been caused by unintentional jibes.

So let's avoid 'em.

A final word: a foresail sail plan for running downwind—one that doesn't use the mainsail—might become a Chinese fire drill in a jibe, but the jibe itself will be far less dangerous to people or rig. It's that damn boom sweeping across the deck that does all the damage.

CHAPTER 22

Self-Steering

Dear Herb: It seems that with GPS, CD-ROM charts, and an interactive autopilot, I could program my boat, step off onto the dock, and a couple of weeks later fly down and meet it in Venezuela. Doesn't all this automation take the fun out of it? Honestly, I hardly even want self-steering. What do you think?

Disillusioned and Distressed in Trenton

Dear DDT: Things change, things change. I myself sometimes resent the speed with which electricity is depriving me of things to do on my boat. (Am I right to blame electricity? Or have my choices caused our present electrified condition?) On the other hand, we sailed SEA FOAM thousands of Pacific miles without self-steering. I have to say, however, that today, on RED SHOES, Nancy and I consider self-steering a must.

There are times, still, when I truly enjoy steering, tweaking the sails, reacting to wind and wave: it's called sailing. But when I tire of this, I'm always delighted to turn the job over to the Navico, our autopilot, or Alice, our Aries windvane. And on a passage, with only two of us on board, we would soon be exhausted without the help of our robotic crewmembers.

Why have a windvane if you have an autopilot? After all, an autopilot will steer when you're under power, whereas a windvane, except in special wind conditions, will not. And of course the autopilot steers to a compass course, while a windvane keeps you sailing at a constant angle to the wind. If the wind changes direction with the windvane steering, the boat changes course. With an autopilot the boat doesn't change course, but the sails will either spill the wind or be too tightly sheeted. In either case, a skipper should be up and doing something, such as adjusting sails or correcting the self-steering.

For six years we had only our Navico autopilot. Our longest passage was upwind from Barbados to Belém, Brazil, and took 19 days. On the return (downwind) trip we made two stops, so our longest time at sea was six days. Three other passages: U.S. Virgin Islands to Bermuda, seven days; Bermuda to Maine, seven days; Bahamas to the U.S. Virgin Islands, eight days. All these were made using the autopilot.

The basic disadvantage of the autopilot is that it uses electricity. It uses significant amounts when actually turning the wheel, and downwind it works particularly hard. At sea, during the night, using running lights, a cabin light, compass light, instruments, GPS and autopilot, our batteries would barely last until morning. Often before the night was over we'd have to run our engine to charge them. And this was before we installed a reefer, and were considering installing a watermaker!

Another disadvantage of our autopilot is that it goes crazy during ham radio transmissions, so that whenever I want to use the radio, Nancy has to steer. The Navico is also susceptible to voltage changes, so it would react when we started or stopped the engine. The battery voltage differed sufficiently between the alternator's charging or not charging to cause a 90-degree change in course.

Finally, autopilots are basically electric motors. Wheel pilots are made as minimally as possible in order to be miserly with amps yet still do the job. Some cruising folk carry a spare autopilot. Others opt for a pilot a size larger than that recommended for their boat. Because cockpit-mounted autopilots are nowhere near as durable as a good windvane, we chose to go with an Aries.

Belowdecks autopilots are much more powerful and durable than belt-driven pilots. If they are solely electro-mechanical they'll probably use significantly more juice. Hydraulic autopilots can deliver as much power as mechanical advantage can provide. Belowdecks autopilots are more expensive than cockpit mounted ones. However, as boats get larger and heavier, an adequate autopilot will have to be upgraded accordingly. For want of personal experience, I've asked two circumnavigators to comment on their autopilots.

Knowles Pittman, co-skipper of BOSTON LIGHT, a Skye 51, had an Alpha Marine Systems autopilot which Knowles asserts was excellent. In an entire circumnavigation they sent for parts once, maybe twice. The problem was electronic: a circuit board had to be replaced. Power consumption was minimal. Knowles was particularly enthusiastic about the autopilot's performance going up the Red Sea: "750 miles running, then 750 miles beating, with winds as high as 50 knots. In spite of the boat's sluing and surfing, the autopilot handled it well."

Single-handing circumnavigator and one-time record holder Dodge Morgan used two hydraulic Wagners on his custom built AMERICAN PROMISE. Redundancy was the theme of AMERICAN PROMISE, and it was carried through with the use of two autopilots which could be used together or separately. They performed 100% after the initial shakedown. Now, however, for his two successive 53-foot cruising cutters WINGS OF TIME, he swears by Robertson. "In 50,000 miles of cruising," he claims enthusiastically, "they've behaved flawlessly."

By the way, there's a demonstrable tendency for someone who bought something to declare that it's the best damn whatever in the world. Would you believe there are still people around who own British Seagulls and who claim, against all reason, that they're great little outboard motors? *Caveat lector.*

In 1993 we were making plans to sail to the Far East. Remember in Chapter 12 when we talked about fuel capacity? I worried not only about autopilot failure, but about how much fuel we'd have to use just to charge batteries on a long passage. Besides buying a Windbugger and considering buying solar panels, I was thinking in terms of cutting down electrical requirements at sea. One greedy device we could eliminate was the autopilot. To eliminate the autopilot, we needed a windvane. When an almost-new Aries came on the market, we bought it.

A windvane based on the same principle and made in the U.S.A. is the Monitor. The manufacturer points with pride to its performance in tough situations like the single-handed round-the-world races. I bought the Aries because it was half the price, and because in Red Hook harbor there were two boats with Monitor windvanes that had suffered structural failure. They were older models, and the manufacturer claims that the more recent models have been improved.

Our first experience with windvanes was in New Zealand, when a friend offered to help us fabricate and install a windvane of his own design on SEA FOAM. He had used his all the way from California. It was the auxiliary rudder type, in which the sail, or wing, reacted to the wind, driving a pushrod up or down, which operated a trimtab mounted behind the auxiliary rudder, which turned the rudder, which was mounted on its own pintles and gudgeons on the transom. The device was aero- and hydro-dynamically sound, and steered us beautifully. But steering our 27,000-pound vessel in all sea and wind conditions involved tremendous forces, and we simply never built the rudder or its mounts strongly enough.

Even after we upgraded the size and strength of the structural members, we were subject to the limitations of third-world welding. This was in the 70's, and stainless steel welding expertise was not as widespread as it is today. From the time we left New Zealand until Nancy and I returned home to San Diego harbor, an interval of five years, repairing the wind-vane was a chore that had to be done during or after most of our passages.

The Aries is a whole different story. Built out of aluminum with strength factors comparable to the landing gear of a 747, it even oper-ates on a different principle. The windvane's sail reacts to the wind, driving a pushrod that turns a small rudder. There the similarity ends. The rudder, or paddle, is actually a servo-pendulum, which means that it swings, pendulum-like, from side to side, this motion being con-trolled by its rudder action as it passes through the water. The pendu-lum is attached to lines which go either to a tiller or to a drum on the

Installing the Aries. Our windvane can be dismantled and stored on deck or in a lazarette, leaving only a small framework on the stern.

wheel, and transmits such power that a strong man cannot restrain it without disengaging the mechanism.

A trick that some cruisers are turning to with their tiller pilots is to attach the arm to the windvane. Autopilot moves lever which turns paddle which moves servo-pendulum which steers boat. The advantage to this deviousness is a tremendous increase in steering power using a fraction of electrical power. The disadvantage is that the number of degrees the wheel can turn or the tiller can move is far less than if the autopilot were hooked up directly. In physics you never get something for nothing.

With the use of so much force, the Aries can steer even large yachts in severe weather and sea conditions. It does have drawbacks, however. Because of the extreme tensions involved, the lines that move the tiller or turn the wheel are subject to chafe, and how they are led is critical. The other disadvantage is that until you've dealt with it for a while, adjusting the steering lines is tricky. Because the arc through which the pendulum swings is narrow, it's important to center it when the boat is balanced and sailing straight. Achieving this in varying conditions under sail can be frustrating indeed. But once it's centered, the Aries will steer better than any human helmsperson.

Once again, in my opinion we're talking about things that are use-specific. If you're going to cruise the coasts and island chains of North America and the Caribbean, an autopilot alone would probably serve you well. However, Dodge Morgan, in his single-handed circumnavigation in AMERICAN PROMISE, used only an autopilot. He had a diesel generator and lots of batteries to power his electric winches and roll-up sails. The crew of BOSTON LIGHT in their round-the-worlder also used only an autopilot. The original makers of Aries in England went out of business some years ago and many cruisers have lamented its disappearance. However it is being manufactured again. Contact Peter Matthiesen, Aries, Ruglokke 30a, DK-6430 Nordborg, Denmark (tel. 45 7445 0760, fax 45 7445 2960).

A windvane requires a big structure on the stern of your boat. Our planned trip to the Far East has been postponed. Nevertheless, if I were setting off on a long voyage and had to choose, I would opt for a vane.

POSTSCRIPT: A windvane on the stern is like a merit badge—it suggests to other sailors that you've voyaged. And while we're on the subject of appearances, *never* wear a captain's hat. Cruising folks will assume that you've never been farther from the dock than an afternoon sail can take you.

CHAPTER 23

Anchoring

Dear Herb: I've read your stuff over the years, and it seems to me that you telling people how to anchor is a lot like O.J. Simpson lecturing husbands on domestic relations. My questions are: 1) How am I supposed to put my trust in advice given by someone who's dragged all over the Pacific, the Atlantic, and the Caribbean? and 2) by the way, have you ever made a list of all the places where you've dragged anchor?

Faithless In South Hampton

Dear FISH: Good questions. The answer to 1) is, you can't. To 2) no, but here are the instances I remember from our SEA FOAM days.

Ensenada Harbor, Mexico. In a Santana with 70-knot offshore winds, we stopped dragging when we put down two anchors on the same rode, after which the only danger was all the other boats dragging past us.

Punaauia, Tahiti. After several weeks the anchor rode managed to wrap itself around the fluke of the yachtsman in a perfect clove hitch. (Two anchors.)

Matauwi Bay, Russell, New Zealand. We had an identical situation.

Raivavae, French Polynesia. During a midnight storm our anchor slipped through the bottom at a slow, but consistent rate. The neighboring yacht warned us with its horn and turned on its lights, giving us a landmark on this dark, rainy night by which to re-orient ourselves. We re-anchored with two anchors and stayed put.

Samoa Harbor. The holding ground where we were was simply awful—no one's anchor(s) held. We moved.

This doesn't really belong on the list. At Tarawa, in the Gilberts, lying to two anchors, we were riding out a blow in a nasty chop (10-mile fetch) when the rode to one of the anchors parted. Known to the initiate as a rode kill, this happens when the rode, in our case ¾-inch nylon, has been abraded internally over the years because of having absorbed coral sand. We had no engine, so our son swam out, found the tail of the lost anchor, tied the two rodes together, and we rode out the rest of the storm successfully.

Here are the ones I remember from our years on RED SHOES:

> Once in the Exumas, a chain of islands trending southward from a point about 30 miles east of Nassau, in the Bahamas. (Two anchors.) See Chapter 24.

> Great Cruz Bay, U.S. Virgin Islands. During a squall, the Bruce tore loose with a huge hunk of grass sod in its 'mouth' and therefore was unable to re-set. This is the biggest drawback of the Bruce. (One anchor.)

> The River Kourou, French Guiana, seven miles to the north of which lies Devil's Island. The tidal flow in this river reaches three knots, the ebb four knots. For reasons we could never figure, we returned from town to find RED SHOES swinging wildly back and forth in the current, finally yanking out first one anchor and then the other. No, the rudder was not turned, and no, no other boat in the anchorage was doing this.

> Roatán, the Bay Islands of Honduras. Identical situation as Great Cruz Bay. (One anchor out.)

> Susanna's Lagoon, a small, landlocked baylet in the Rio Dulce of Guatemala, where nothing ever happens. I anchored with a casual lack of attention, and later, when a violent thunderstorm swept through (the only one of the year), I was reminded that you *always* set the anchor against extreme eventualities. (One anchor.)

I don't count the scores of times that I've dropped the anchor and under reverse it failed to set, because in those situations we always re-set until it holds under the strain of 2000 rpm in reverse. Nor the times when the holding ground was lousy and we knew we'd drag if the wind came up; then we either left someone aboard or watched carefully from the shore. If you live aboard, and if you do any exploring, you're going to run into difficult and unfamiliar anchoring conditions, and you're either going to deal with them perfectly, or you're not. The only moral question is whether or not you're going to lie about it later.

Here's a suggestion that is in fact crucial when you anchor: plan to get to a new, unfamiliar anchorage by mid-afternoon, thus giving yourself plenty of time to work out unusual or difficult circumstances before dark.

I used to have a hard time getting Nancy to go along with this. On our trailer-sailer trip, when we were cruising in uncharted Lake Powell, which is in fact a flooded section of the Grand Canyon, we met unusual situations that we'd never before or since encountered. Nancy would get angry with me when I wouldn't leave for a new anchorage because we wouldn't get there till early evening. At least once we ended up going someplace entirely different because we couldn't figure out a safe way to secure the boat; another time we ended up having to drive pitons into cracks in a cliff and lie against fenders up against the rock wall. The depth there was over 150 feet.

Getting to an unfamiliar anchorage early gives you time to noodle around, and if necessary maybe even find an alternative nearby. Arriving late and having to deal with whatever you find can lead to trouble.

Setting the anchor became easier and more consistently successful after Bruce Van Sant, the author of *The Gentleman's Guide to Passages South*, told me: "Set it like you're playing a fish, with gentle tugs gradually increasing in strength." This is the best advice I ever heard. Think about it. You let the anchor down till it touches bottom. Don't dump all the chain or line out at once, but pay it out only as necessary as your mate backs down with the engine, or as the boat drifts backwards in the wind, tugging gently every so often. What you're trying to do is encourage the point or points of the anchor to penetrate into the bottom. Think of working a stake into the earth without the use of a hammer.

If you give too forceful a tug initially, you'll jerk the anchor out of the bottom, after which it skids along on its side, defying the set.

In places where it's not too deep, I dive down to have a look. Sometimes the anchor is okay as is. But if it's sort of half caught, and, in the case of the plow or Bruce, lying on its side—this happens particularly in hard sand or grass—I'll surface and tell Nancy to put the engine in slow reverse. I then dive down and position the anchor properly, wiggling it back and forth to get it to penetrate the bottom, the tension on the rode pulling it deep into the sand.

Sometimes you find that what appears to be a nice sandy bottom is actually a thin layer of sand over a coral shelf. The anchor will never hold in a blow, so you have to do something. If there's no good sand available, maybe there's a hole or crack in the coral where you can wedge the anchor tip. This will only be secure until the wind changes direction, so you may want to put out another anchor in the opposite direction, wedging it, too, into a hole.

In the mangrove islands of Belize, the bottom often would be mostly grass, with the occasional oasis of sand. Usually these oases make the best and most secure place to drop the anchor. Off Ambergris Cay, however, in places where there was no grass, we found only a few inches of sand over coral. With my fishing spear I went exploring, and by stabbing the bottom found that where the grass had taken hold, the sand would be deep and hard packed—excellent holding as long as I hand-set the anchor. However, once again we had to watch the weather, as a change in wind direction might pull the anchor loose, and no way would it re-set without my help. In the trade winds, wind direction is more stable than in higher latitudes.

All chain rode is preferable in most cases, not only because of its resistance to chafe against rock or coral, but it also adds the advantage of a catenary curve. This is the curve that results from the weight of the chain itself. Using all chain in a deep anchorage of say 40 to 50 feet, the catenary curve will improve the angle of rode to anchor, making the pull while setting more horizontal, as long as you're not pulling too hard. It will also provide a shock absorber in all but very strong winds. When the winds pipe up, you let out more scope, which adds more weight, which increases the shock-absorbing capacity.

The wind strength can reach a point, however, when the chain is out straight, bar taut. Now there is no give, and one wonders about the trade-off—the value of the elasticity of nylon rode versus the chafe resistance and catenary curve of chain. So we add to our all chain rode a snubber, or length of three-strand nylon line bent to the chain with a rolling hitch and cleated on the bow. Then we let out more chain so that the snubber takes the strain. The thinner and longer the line, the more elasticity—and the more chance it will chafe through or break under strain.

On the subject of elasticity: Nancy and I were crewing for my cousin Sandy Fowler on his C&C 39. He had read something in *Yachting* to the effect that a light Danforth on a long rode of light three-strand nylon will hold fast in good holding ground. Nylon is used because it stretches more than other rope materials. We were off Morehead City, North Carolina, on the Intracoastal Waterway, and what Sandy put out was a 10-pound Danforth on 150 feet of ⁵⁄₁₆-inch nylon rode!

I figured it was a stunt, done to impress me. Around 2 A.M. (when else) the wind piped up 25 to 35 knots, and I too was up, bouncing around nervously looking at the lee shore. I finally couldn't stand it any longer and roused Sandy, who said, "Okay, we'll drop the plough over the side leaving plenty of rode coiled on deck, so if we drag it will hold us. But I'll bet it'll still be right under the bow in the morning."

It was.

The other thing besides wind to worry about is fetch. Fetch is the length of open water across which waves can build. Waves cause a boat at anchor to pitch, and pitching jerks on the anchor rode. If the catenary or snubber doesn't absorb enough of the shock, the pitching of the boat will snatch the best laid anchor out of its grave. So when wind and wave pipe up, more scope will soften the effect of pitching.

Some skippers insist on setting two anchors at all times. This is the instruction given to bareboat charterers, the theory being that two anchors reduce by half the number of bareboat skipper anchoring fuck-ups. However, one anchor, properly set in good holding ground, should really do the job. In the list at the beginning of the chapter, most of the times we dragged, we had actually set two anchors. And if you're changing anchorages every night or so, using one anchor instead of two will mean a welcome reduction in work. Some bad situations are made even worse by the need to retrieve (*in* the dark, *in* the wind, *in* the rain) two anchors instead of one. I put out two anchors a lot, but it's not a hard and fast rule on RED SHOES.

When we knew we were coming to the Rio Dulce, we asked a friend who had spent three years there to make notes in our cruising guide. One spot on the river was marked as a good anchorage, but "Two anchors are needed!" was exclaimed in the margin. Dutifully I deployed two anchors, and next morning found that we'd twirled a total of *thirteen* wraps in our two rodes.

Fortunately I had just learned from a friend, Doug Conners on CHINOOK, how to deal with rode wraps. I released the rope rode, and gradually brought all the wraps up to the bow in the form of loops, making a coil with 13 loops which I draped over the bow roller. Now I was ready to raise the anchor that's on all chain, so I needed to attach a snubber to the rope rode outboard of the loops, as that was the anchor that would hold RED SHOES while I was retrieving the other one. Once the anchor with the chain was up, I dropped the loops clear and raised the other one. It worked like magic.

I used to boast that two anchors on the same rode would never drag, but I've been corrected. If the holding ground is lousy, e.g. thin sand over a coral shelf, the only thing that'll hold you is getting hooked into a crevice. However, in cases such as Ensenada Harbor where people were dragging because the bottom, though deep enough, was soft and silty, our putting out two anchors in tandem held us while others kept dragging on by.

Anchor rode loops. The port anchor rode—chain and rope—is looped and snubbed while you recover the starboard all-chain rode.

Here is how it is done: Lay out one anchor about 30 feet outboard of the other, fastening the rode of the outboard anchor to the tripline shackle on the inner anchor. Then pay out rode as you normally would. We don't do this if we feel the wind might change. If we think it might, we lay out a third anchor on its own rode.

Although I no longer make the extravagant claims I once did for this tactic, the few times I've used it, it hasn't failed. What I worry about is having all my eggs on one rode; but if I've maintained my ground tackle as I should, that shouldn't be a problem.

Getting it up. When it comes to coal miners, seasickness, and anchors, we can fly in the face of Newtonian physics, and say that what goes down must come up. One of the biggest errors I made when equipping RED SHOES was not to insist on an electric windlass. Nor did I think ahead enough to have our new boat wired for one.

We had an electric windlass on SEA FOAM which worked perfectly until we had our chain re-galvanized, after which the links no longer fit the wildcat. (Another example of our throwaway society: you can hardly find re-galvanizing plants any more, and when you do, the process is nearly as expensive as buying new chain.)

On RED SHOES we have a Lofrans manual windlass with both gypsy and wildcat. In eight years I've used it twice. It's very stiff even with no load, and with a load it's one hell of a lot of work. I used it several years ago to raise the 35-pound Bruce out of 70 feet of water. With ⁵⁄₁₆-inch triple B chain at a pound a foot, we're talking over 100 pounds. By the time I had the anchor aboard I thought I was going to die.

I always thought that if I removed the windlass and lubricated the innards, it might work more easily. But since we've been anchoring almost always in less than 40 feet, and mainly in 25 feet or less, I just raise the anchor by hand. Nancy and I have adopted hand signals, so that when I scream she knows it's important. We take in the scope by her driving RED SHOES slowly forward. When all the slack is taken in, I make the rode fast and signal "break it out." She drives forward again, pulling the anchor from its nest. Then I pull it up by hand. (Having done heavy manual labor from time to time during my life, I've learned to put most of the strain on my legs and arms rather than on my back.)

Doug, the same guy who taught me to use loops to overcome rode wraps, showed me how he, bad back and all, manually retrieves his anchor. He sits on a large fender of the sausage-shape type, and pulls on the

Doug sitting on fender raising anchor: A tip for skippers or crew with creaky backs.

rode as one would pull on a shell oar, pushing with his legs, using the fender as a roller: it acts like a sliding seat in a rowing shell. I tried it, and recommend it for anyone with a creaky back.

One of the great aids we've adopted on RED SHOES is a deck washdown pump. Made by Shurflo, it's one of the best gadgets for the money on the boat. With a washdown pump, the mud that usually comes aboard with the chain is washed off before the chain reaches the deck. We wash the decks down more often, too. It's actually fun. There is something subtly satisfying about standing around spraying stuff, comparable to the pleasure of fly casting, be there fish or not.

If you're still with me, here's what has worked for us most of the time. On 27,000-pound SEA FOAM, a boat over twice the displacement of RED SHOES, we used ⁵⁄₁₆-inch BBB chain, and ¾-inch three-strand nylon rode. The chain never failed us. As I mentioned, the rope, bathed in rust and saturated with particles of coral sand, parted in Tarawa after five years of use. SEA FOAM's main rode was all chain (300 feet); the other was 50 feet of chain and 250 feet of rope. We carried a 45-pound Danforth, 35-pound plow, and a 45-pound yachtsman.

On RED SHOES our main anchor is a 33-pound Bruce on 100 feet of ⁵⁄₁₆-inch BBB chain shackled to 200 additional feet of ⅝-inch three-strand nylon line. Our second anchor, also stowed on the roller and always ready to deploy, is a 35-pound CQR with 30 feet of ⁵⁄₁₆-inch BBB chain and 250 feet of ⅝-inch rode. A third anchor is a 35-pound Danforth on its own 30 feet of ⁵⁄₁₆-inch BBB chain and 150 feet of ⅝-inch nylon three-strand. Many sailors don't trust swivels in their ground tackle. I bought an oversized one for the Bruce that's ¾-inch stock and weighs close to 8 pounds. Trust that? You bet!

We also have a 10-pound Danforth on 250 feet of ⁵⁄₁₆-inch three-strand nylon rode. I don't trust it worth a damn.

CHAPTER 24

A History of Dragging:
An Open Letter to the Guilty

Dear Herb: Have you ever lied about dragging?

Suspicious in Saratoga

Dear Suspicious: No. For your macho skipper, dragging is more of a loss of face than a non-erection. (Who, me? Drag? You wanna step outside, fella?) When you drag, you feel inadequate, thinking you're the only person who ever does. The fact is, tying a 13,000-pound boat to a 33-pound anchor is a lot like trying to park a loaded dump truck on a steep hill by tying it to a shovel. Inevitably you'll encounter times when it doesn't work.

The history of dragging goes back to when sailors, in order to keep their boats from drifting away at night, would run them aground. The first skipper to think of a better way was a Norseman named Erik Brough (pronounced 'Bruff'). Brough believed in mass, and you could always tell his fleet by the way the ships were down at the bow. Great blocks of granite made effective anchors, but the weight made the ships hard to maneuver, and totally useless in combat.

About one hundred years later, another skipper named Captain Brough (pronounced Brow as in 'eyebrow'—no relation to Brough [Bruff]) developed the anchorboat. Fighting ships carried no weight with Brough, but barges loaded with huge boulders would be sent to an anchorage ahead of the fleet. This system worked well until the enemy discovered the moorings and cut the rodes loose, all of which drifted up on a Greek island which still bears their name.

On arriving at a mooringless anchorage, Brough would have to send divers down to replace cut lines. Divers were reluctant, those being the days of sea monsters, and Captain B's verbal harangues became known as 'Broughbeating'.

The idea of hooking into the seabed first occurred to a Commodore Brough (pronounced 'Broff', and no relation to Brough [Bruff] or Brough [Brow]). One day the Commodore was working in the backyard trying to

155

break up hardpan so his entrepreneurial wife could plant a field of pop-
pies. With a mighty blow he buried the point of his pickaxe in the clay,
and no amount of tugging and wiggling would free it. He finally gave up,
and for years used the pickax as a hitching thing for Boat, his favorite
horse. After months of his wife's reminders to "tie Boat to the hitching
pick," a synaptic miracle occurred, and Brough invented the first yachtsman anchor. His was the first device to depend on something other than
weight to keep boats from drifting away.

Brough's pick worked well enough in rocks, but was treacherously
inefficient in sand. It did not follow as the night the day, however, that
shovel followed pick (synaptic miracles were rare even then). Finally a
descendant of Brough, who insisted on pronouncing his name 'Brew',
found that a shovel worked pretty well as an anchor in sand as long as the
wind didn't change. Experimenting, he came up with the Plough (which
he, and only he, pronounced 'plew').

Other patent anchors such as the Danforth, the Northill and the
Bruce, and more recently the Fortress, also adapted the shovel principle.
Brough, feeling infringed, spent the rest of his life fighting for his royal-
ties. Brough was known as the giggling gladiator and his jousts in court
were called Brough-ha-has.

Down through the centuries, the Broughs (Bruff, Brow, Broff and
Brew) have all slid involuntarily to leeward, ending up with varying degrees of embarrassment. Fortunately, these slitherings almost always took
place in darkness, giving birth to denial, or prevarication on a theme. As
history was primarily oral, the tales whispered down to us boast of a holding power that the anchors they tell of in fact lacked. I am not a muck-
raker, but I have seen too many of my friends made to feel inadequate
("the anchor didn't drag, *you* did."). Therapists will tell you that there's
only one absolute truth in anchoring: stated simply, it says: Every skipper
who has ventured from his mooring on a regular basis for an extended period of time—he whom we call a cruising sailor—has dragged. Most have
dragged more than once, and all are destined to drag again.

Getting skippers to confess to dragging can take months of analysis.
Once unburdened, however, a dramatic change takes place, and it's not
uncommon to see a shriven dragger clicking his heels on the foredeck,
touching down on only every fourth click.

Which is why I'm telling you this story.

We were cruising in the Exumas, a chain of inviting islands that
trickle south from a point about 25 miles east of Nassau in the Bahamas.
Forecasters had called what we were having "a period of unsettled
weather." Violent thunder squalls would sweep through, ambushing all

but the most wary. The first squall to hit the dozen yachts anchored off Staniel Cay caused half the fleet to drag. Fortunately it was early enough in the morning so that we were all still aboard our boats, and the only consequences were some strenuous rode work, and the sounds and swirls of faces flushing.

The incident made me nervous, however, and I craved protection and good holding ground. We moved nearby between the Majors, an anchorage surrounded by islands. Right in the middle was a luxuriant sand bar. We set two anchors against a reversing tidal current, and waited.

The previous storm had come out of the south. This one came with little warning out of the west. Fifty mile-an-hour winds don't whine in the rigging, they scream. RED SHOES careened as if struck by a freighter. Both anchor rodes stretched till they had shrunk to two thirds of their original diameter. For two hours we were buffeted, rain like buckshot, rapacious lightning and imploding thunder nearly continuous.

After the storm, the radio waves were dripping with woes. One skipper had had three anchors down and yet had dragged, wrapping the rodes in an irretrievable tangle. Another skipper had had to abandon two of his anchors, barely managing to buoy them beforehand. RED SHOES, I was pleased to announce to whoever would listen, had held fast.

Next day dawned clear and crisp. If we didn't want to lie cringing in our protected hole forever, it was time to move on. Someone had drawn an anchor on my chart at a cove on the north end of Thomas Cay and marked it 'good', so north we sailed. Picking our way nervously across shallow banks and through narrow, switchback channels, we arrived at the anchorage about 5 P.M. and entered the cove through a narrow channel. Once inside, we found ourselves in a cramped space, our swinging room restricted by a shallow bar.

Our storm anchor is a 33-pound Bruce. I believed it infallible, and I was surprised when, after two tries, it still hadn't set. On the fourth try, however, it caught. I swam over it and could see that it was on its side, one tip only partially buried. I wasn't happy, but everyone was bored with anchor drill, and we couldn't drag it with the engine, could we? I deemed the set the best I could do, put out the Danforth near the beach to keep us from being blown onto the bar, and placed my bet on the squalls being over.

That night the worst squall yet rousted us out of bed with winds that were clocked at the Staniel airstrip at over 55 knots. The downpour smothered RED SHOES in blackness and bedlamian wails. We could see nothing, and we were all shuddering at the jarring of the keel bouncing on the bottom. Were these waves crashing against rock close behind us? We plugged in the spotlight, and through the curtain of drenching rain I could see a small cliff only a boat length away.

I didn't dare use the engine—there was no way to know how our second anchor line lay, and it could easily have wrapped itself around our propeller. Later we concluded it must have been trapped under the keel, as it was nearly chewed through. So we bounced; lesser boats might well have suffered serious damage. I was thankful for the shallow sand bottom, which was keeping us from washing onto the rocks.

For two hours we absorbed the storm's fury, wondering if morning would find us wrecked. Finally the wind dropped to where I dared take the plow out in the dinghy. I dropped it way out over the sand bar, which gave it an uphill pull, and it immediately caught and held. The tide was flooding, RED SHOES was floating, and we were able to pull the boat into deeper water. It was no comfort, however, to realize that had I put the plow out over the bar in the first place, we'd have been okay.

Next morning, having first checked that RED SHOES had suffered no visible damage, I asked on the radio if anyone else had dragged. No one had. They had all had their anchors buried in "our" sand bar. I mentioned that we had dragged, and had spent the night awake and fearful.

"What a shame," said one. "No damage?" asked another, sounding disappointed.

Having confessed and repented, I've become lighthearted, sailing serenely along, my course strewn with discarded guilt. The age of the lie is drawing to a close, fellow draggers. As the laser of truth will seek you out anyway, why not come out of the closet voluntarily and join us mortals, basking in sunlight?

CHAPTER 25

Where Are We, Already?

Dear Herb: You've admitted you have neither the tables nor an up-to-date almanac aboard. What are you going to do if your GPS packs up?

Anyway, I've never felt that finding major hunks of land was a problem. Far more of a problem is finding your way close to shore without getting in trouble. How about a word or two about piloting, too?

Skeptic in Saskatchewan

Dear Skeptic: T'anks. You've reminded me to run my computer nav programs to see if they still function, and if I still can function with them. But for now, what I'm going to do if my GPS packs up is to get out my backup GPS.

You may be right about piloting. The secret of both navigation and piloting, however, is keeping track of where you are and what your boat is doing *all the time*. It's called paying attention, and you'd be surprised how many situations this applies to in successful cruising.

Unfortunately none of us pays attention all the time. And then there are mistakes. And the unforeseen. How about the uninformed? And the sudden devastating surprises sprung by the unknown. . .

All of the 'un's above overlap, or may even have a common meaning. For example, as we approached the mouth of the Para River in Brazil, we discovered that a wreck which was on our chart and on which I was depending as a reference was no longer there. This was certainly unforeseen. Had I kept up, as a merchant ship's navigation officer must, with all the notices to mariners, I would probably have been informed. As it was, I was using copied 20-year old charts and got what I deserved.

Most cruisers on a budget simply can't afford to buy new charts for all the places they intend to go. Right now, in anticipation of our aborted voyage to the Far East, we have aboard roughly 400 charts. Two hundred of these are borrowed. As for the rest, most are photocopies. Twenty or thirty have the corners cut off, because I got them from a friend who was

159

working in a marine store in Florida. The store was instructed by NOAA to replace certain charts, to mark the obsolete ones by cutting a few corners, and ultimately to destroy said obsolescence.

A chart hand-inked on parchment may be assumed to be out of date. The only new charts we have are the Better Boating Association charts and Waterway Guide chart books, which are copies and compilations of U.S. charts, all of which are in public domain and not in copyright. We've used charts that turned out to be inaccurate, but we expected that: after all, the small print said the data was collected in the eighteen hundreds.

I don't recommend using old or superseded charts. When I tell you what I do, I'm assuming you're going to find out what other people do and make an informed decision. This book is not an instruction manual, it's a discussion.

Incidentally, cruisers in commercial seaports have sometimes made friends with officers aboard one of the ships, and occasionally the officer in charge of charts has had to replace all charts of a certain area, but had yet to throw out the replaced ones. He'd be happy to get rid of them, and some cruiser was delighted to take them off his hands. We never struck it that lucky, but we knew at least two cruisers who did.

I rationalize the use of old charts because after all, rocks, rills, or reefs don't move, do they? If buoys are in a different place, painted a different color, with a revised numbering system, we can handle that, can't we?

Where this rationale fails is in the ever-changing mouths of rivers, and where dredging and shoaling of sand and mud have occured. But then, no save-money scheme is without its downside.

Let's see, if we'd bought 400 new charts at an average cost of $16, we'd have spent $6,400 instead of maybe $500 todate.

BBA chart books cost $50 to $100. Good copies are three to six dollars. Borrowed and discarded out-of-daters do not cost anything. We trade for some. And a few we've traced.

I take it back. We still have original coastal charts from California to Panama, as well as the Galápagos Islands, bought new for our voyage in SEA FOAM at a cost of about three dollars each. They're only a quarter-century old. For everything west of the Galápagos we bartered or bought used from returning and retiring voyagers. You guessed it—they're even older.

When the U.S. Government suddenly raised the prices of charts by a factor of better than five in order, they said, to offset the cost of updating geodetic surveys, they eliminated most of the cruising population as potential customers. I'd like to know if their receipts for charts went up at all. I'd like to know if the genius that thought this up calculated the potential cost of an air/sea rescue of skippers using out-of-date charts?

I have a friend who cruised the Straits of Magellan using only a Chilean chart catalog. The catalog is a compendium of all Chilean charts, but reduced to about half size. My friend said he had to use a magnifying glass, but that all the information was there. If I remember correctly, he paid the equivalent of $15 for the catalog, a fraction of what he'd have had to pay for individual charts. Furthermore, he had them all, and didn't run into the situation so common among cruisers who bought only what they thought they'd need.

There are times when you would wish your depth meter would give you soundings from 100 feet ahead, or 500 feet ahead, or whatever. We have one that does—me, in the dinghy with a lead line. But in most cases, such as during a river entry which I'll discuss below, and during almost all land-falls, we come from sea with the dinghy lashed on deck and the outboard stowed on the pushpit, the whole thing difficult to launch and assemble even in the calmest of conditions.

We once buddy-boated with a friend who had a portable depth sounder. We'd just throw a 12-volt battery in the dinghy and go explore a prospective anchoring spot. It never worked very well, but I thought the idea was neat. At a recent boat show, an exhibitor was offering a hand-held, battery powered depth sounder the size of a small flashlight. You stick the end of it in the water, then raise it to take the reading. It is available from Speedtech Instruments, 10413 Deerfoot Drive, Great Falls, VA 22066.

Entering the Para River was one of the maybe half-dozen times in our cruising in the tropics when I wished we'd had radar. Radar would have shown the land configuration, would have picked out the beacon long before we could see it. Radar has become much less expensive and there are new types that use far less current than the greedy old monsters—those that employ LCD (liquid crystal) displays instead of CRTs (cathode ray tubes). A prospective cruiser with an extra $1,500-$3,000 for electronic aids should consider it.

I'm sure I would love it if I had it. As it stands, however, we have to plan our unfamiliar landfalls to coincide with daylight and good visibility. In darkness or occluded weather, we stand off and wait.

By the way, while we're roaming through the catalog of electronic exotica, how about electronic charting? Well, if the price of original charts is daunting, the price of electronic charts is a stone wall. The cost can be amortized, I suppose, if you're a cruiser who always cruises in the same limited areas. The main thing about electronic charting is that it's lots of fun. If it interfaces with your GPS it puts your boat on the screen and

Craig throwing lead line from the bow of *Sea Foam*. A lead line backs up a dead depth meter, and requires no electricity.

makes navigation a little like watching yourself on TV. However, everyone I know who has it insists on having the paper charts too. The screen is small, and zooming in for detail reduces the area covered to pinhead dimensions. Given a choice, I'd rather have radar.

For piloting and all landfalls, one of the greatest aids you can have is a good quality pair of binoculars. If they contain a built-in compass, so much the better. Our compass disagrees with the ship's compass by as much as five to ten degrees, depending on our heading, but we don't care, because we mostly use it for relative readings.

The Maroni of French Guiana was a river we entered with trepidation and near disaster. After threading the tortuous outer channel over the bar, we pointed south for the six-mile journey to the river mouth. The next two charted buoys (reds) were missing. The remaining buoys were green, but invisible against misty, distant foliage on shore. No problem, we had a compass and could steer to a course.

There was one high point of land with a tower on it, Galibi, on the Suriname side. Trouble was, we didn't want to head for it, we wanted to come in on the other side of the wide river mouth. It was too far ahead for triangulation: i.e., the difference in consecutive compass readings would be so small as to give insignificant results.

Then the depth meter gave shrinking readings—do we turn port or starboard? Because I remembered friends telling us they had gone aground well to the right of the inbound course, we turned to port. This was a good guess, as the bottom fell slowly away. Not too long after that we picked out the greenie with the binoculars. We had been pushed over a mile off course.

Radar would have shown us both buoys, the one we'd left and the one we were headed for, and it would have been obvious that we'd been swept to starboard by the two-knot cross-current. But we didn't have radar. What I could have done was watch the outer red buoy as it dropped astern and take *rear bearings*, using our binocular compass. A change in the bearing would indicate that we were drifting off course to one side or the other. I knew this, but at the time I forgot. Since then I've taken rear bearings often, sometimes for the fun of it, and a couple of times merely to save the boat.

When you leave a buoy or other landmark and head for your next invisible waypoint on a compass heading, you take bearings aft on the buoy you've left. Provided you're on course for at least the first few hundred yards, you've got your benchmark bearing as a referent. (It doesn't have to be a buoy—when you set out on course, any landmark dead aft will do. But usually I use this on a leg between two buoys.)

The next most valued instrument after compass and binoculars is the depth sounder. It warned us in the two previous examples, giving us time to do something. It can also guide you along a coast. By following one or another of what are called fathom lines—a matter of keeping the depth sounder reading more or less constant—you can stay in navigable depths even in occluded visibility.

Using a single landmark, triangulation can give you your approximate distance off shore. Let's say you're sailing along parallel to the coast, and you spot ahead of you a landmark that's on the chart. Note your compass course. Take a bearing on the landmark. and draw the bearing line on the chart (in the example I labeled mine AF). While you're at it, draw the line from the landmark that will meet your course line at a 90 degree angle (AD). Note the log reading, as later you're going to want to know the distance you've traveled.

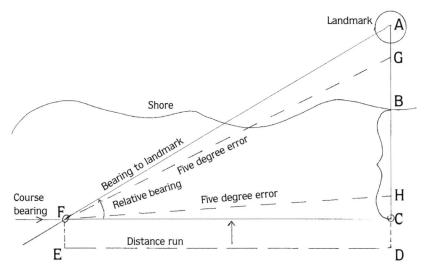

Take bearing at F. Draw line on chart.

When landmark A is abeam at C, note distance run on log.

Draw line AC.

To scale, set dividers to distance run.

Keeping straight edge parallel to course bearing, move dividers up till the points meet at F and C.

In a perfect world, distance off is BC.

Lay off dashed lines FG and FH indicating five degree error.

To allow for cumulative five degree error, subtract distance AG from distance BH.

Because hand bearing compasses often differ from the ship's compass, take all bearings using the same compass.

Cleave as accurately as possible to your course until the landmark lies abeam. Note the distance you've traveled. From the edge of the chart, set your dividers to the distance run (a degree of latitude equals a nautical mile). Call this distance ED. Lay your parallel rules along your course bearing and move distance ED till its length meets lines AF and AC. Letter C will be your approximate position, given zero error, drift, or current. Again using the dividers you can ascertain your distance off.

A more common method requires two charted landmarks.Take bearings on the two landmarks. Draw the bearing lines on the chart. Inasmuch as your boat lies somewhere on each line, your position will be where they cross, give or take some compass error, and your ability to take an accurate bearing.

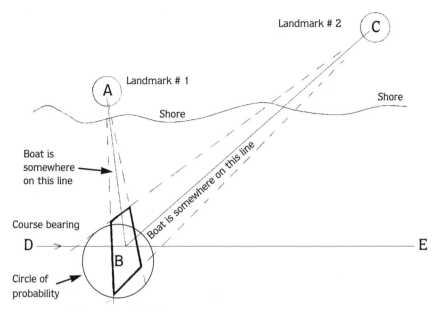

Draw course line DE.

Draw line on chart bearing BA, and another bearing BC.

In a perfect world, boat is at B.

Draw lines indicating five degree error. The boat is likely to be anywhere within the parallelogram around B. Rather than plot all the lines, I usually plot one, and using that as the radius, I draw a circle of my probable location.

Which brings us to the *most important concept* in this game of staying off the rocks. It involves accuracy, and margins for error. Assume a probability that your bearings in the second example are five degrees off either way. Draw lines on the chart that represent this. Now you have an area *within* which you *probably* are, rather than a point *at* which you *certainly* are. This is called reality.

But we all have working GPS's, don't we, so none of this is necessary.

I used to laugh listening to people under way checking into the radio nets and reading their positions off the GPS in degrees and minutes, the minutes to the third decimal place. The most a minute can be is a nautical mile. Minutes of longitude become shorter in higher latitudes, so let's just stick with latitude. The third decimal place in minutes equals $\frac{1}{1000}$ of a mile, or six feet! If the reporting vessel is going six knots, it's covering ten feet per second, so that by the time the person giving his position has uttered the words, the third figure is meaningless.

Believing in insignificant figures gives rise to false precision. Let's take the GPS reading and put our position on the chart. If I'm at sea, using a large scale chart, the width of my pencil mark probably equals a quarter of a mile. So what, I wonder, is significant about minutes to even one decimal place, where the first decimal place equals less than half a pencil line width?

Math probably has rules for determining to what decimal place a number is significant. To me it's a matter of common sense, and if you think about it, I hope it will become that way for you, too. Because how you rate what's significant will determine what you allow as a margin for error.

When we left Bora Bora in SEA FOAM and headed for Tonga, six hours out we were in a full gale. We couldn't run before the gale until we'd passed Mopelia, an atoll to the southwest of Bora Bora. With only 1000 yards of visibility, I plotted a course to miss the atoll by 20 miles. If I had to do it over, I'd make the distance even greater. As it was, I was accused of over-caution by the crew. But I didn't hit it, did I?

I know of several instances where yachts have run up on the reefs on one of the Aves in Venezuela. The Aves are two atolls that are mostly submerged coral reef. They lie about 15 miles apart. The westernmost one is roughly 30 miles due east of Bonaire. When you're leaving Venezuela's Los Roques for Bonaire, the Aves lie right on your path. As long as it's daylight and visibility is good there's no problem passing them, or you may even want to stop at each one.

But at night, or in bad visibility, what do you do? Or better, what don't you do? You don't continue on the same course. You head northwest or southwest, or maybe even north or south, anything to get out of the line of danger. And remembering that the easterly trades and the current will push you west, you don't heave-to till you're well above (or below) the latitude of the Aves. What's well above for you? For me it would be five to ten miles, depending on how close I was to the nearest of the Aves when I made the decision.

In her book *Sitting Duck* Betsy Hitz-Holman writes of leaving Bequia in the Grenadines bound for Bonaire in the days before GPS and SatNav. The sky was overcast, no sun for sextant shots, and the crew were relying solely on a radio direction finder, with results that were not to be trusted.

If you had been unable to confirm your dead reckoning position for three days and were heading for an island landfall, what would you do?

I'm sure you'd do everything possible to make a daylight landfall. And if you're uncertain, and if danger lies east and west of your destination, from which direction do you approach? Did you say north or south?

Good. Best of all, I hope you'd heave-to well clear of danger and wait for a position fix.

What's well clear? If you steer consistently one degree off course, after 60 miles you'll be a mile off. Neither you nor your autopilot/windvane can steer that accurately, never mind how accurate your compass is. So let's use five miles off. In three days you've sailed maybe 300 to 400 miles, and could easily be 25 to 30 miles off course. Well clear of the danger, then, would mean 30 to 35 miles.

True, for you to be 30 miles off course, all errors would have had to be cumulative, and that's practically never the case—at least some balance out. But why take the chance? What does it cost, a few extra hours? It took Hitz-Holman and her crew two weeks and significant money to get her boat off the rocks, and more time and money to rebuild it. They were lucky it wasn't a total loss.

CHAPTER 26

Radio

Dear Herb: I've never done much with radio before. We're on a budget, and I want to get by with the absolute minimum. But I'm also interested in what you've had on board, and why you made the choices you did.

Frankly Curious Cruiser

Dear FCC: When we first cast off on our South Pacific voyage in SEA FOAM, radio telephones were a new thing for me. As I became used to it, however, it became one of my pet subjects. In the beginning, we had an old type radio telephone (RT) that operated on frequencies in the two-meg band. You don't know about megs and bands, and you probably don't care to. Suffice it to say that bands are segments of the continuous spectrum of radio frequencies, and the higher the megs, the shorter the waves. And what this means to you will come out, I hope, as we go along.

Anyway, the two-meg band is a long wave band, and is almost totally superseded by other, shorter wave bands for marine radio communication. For one thing, AM (amplitude modulation), the old way of transmitting voice signals, used a wide carrier wave, which means that the available space was crowded—so crowded, in fact, that if sidebands hadn't existed, we would have had to invent them.

The other thing about the two-meg band was that transmissions made uncontrolled skips. It was funny when we were in Tahiti to pick up Hong Kong police department transmissions. It probably wasn't so funny when some gossipy mariner's transmission from the Indian Ocean cluttered up the emergency frequency on which the Oshkosh volunteer fire department depended.

Leaving aside exceptional conditions, the range of the two meg-band was around two hundred miles. We buddy-boated with friends on the yacht SCALDIS from Acapulco to Tahiti, and talked to each other by radio on a regular schedule. A schedule is essential, because unlike with a phone no bell rings when you call somebody on the radio. Someone has to be listening, so you arrange to call at a certain time.

VHF marine radios were introduced in the late 60's. By the time we reached Tahiti in 1973, however, they were still so rare that cruisers who had them hardly ever found anyone to talk to. These radios used Very High Frequencies (VHF), and like TV their range was termed 'line of sight'. This meant that if you had a masthead antenna, your transmission, traveling in a straight line (not following the curvature of the earth), might be heard 20 miles away. (There's a very rare condition called 'tropospheric bending' that's kind of like an electronic tunnel, through which your VHF signal can follow the curvature of the earth for two to three hundred miles. Sound like the two-meg band? No. The two-meg band did this most days or nights at some time, whereas I've heard distant VHF stations maybe three times in our nine years aboard RED SHOES. And we monitor constantly at sea, and most of the time when we're at anchor.)

The marine VHF band provides over 80 channels, all of which are allocated to specific uses. Channel 16 is for calling and distress. Channel 13 is monitored by, among others, most of the bridge tenders on the Intracoastal Waterway. Channel 22 is the U.S. Coast Guard. Yachts generally call each other on 16, and once contact is made, move to one of the ship-to-ship channels—Channel 68, for example. There are several ship-to-ship channels, and for a while VHF relieved the cloggery that afflicted the two-meg bands.

But like Southern California freeways—soon after you build a new one it's used to 110% of its capacity—VHF is overcrowded. Channel 16 gets jammed up with yachts trying to contact other yachts, to the point where distress signals often suffer from interference. So now the FCC has designated Channel 9 as a new calling frequency. Channel 16 will be solely for distress.

But guess what? If you're listening for a call from your buddies on Channel 9, you're not going to hear my SOS on Channel 16. Damn!

Technology to the rescue. New radios are being marketed that can monitor both. Some 'scan' either all the channels, or a few selected by you. Eventually all radios sold will no doubt be required to monitor both 9 and 16.

In most places where we've been in the Caribbean, there's an informal agreement among yachts to use Channel 68 as a calling channel, from which you move to another channel once contact is made. But this is a convention and has nothing to do with contravention, the latter referring to misuse of channels and lack of proper license and, and, and, any of which can earn you a whopper of a fine.

So you're out there, doing it, but your friends are all more than 20 miles away. You can either cross them off your list, write a letter which might catch up to them someday, or buy, for anywhere from $1,500 to $2,500, a single sideband marine RT (SSB). Marine SSBs cover a wide range of bands and usually have a number of pre-set channels, as well as a feature that allows the owner to key in channels of his own. Frequencies are electronically controlled in the form of 'presets', which means that you push buttons and are right smack on the money. Not only that, but shore stations such as AT&T's WOM in Miami and KMI in San Francisco use duplex— different frequencies for sending and receiving. With marine SSBs, when you punch in Channel X, *both* frequencies are spot on. The importance of this feature will become more evident a bit later on.

The popular marine bands are six, eight, and 12 megs, with other options being four, 16 or 22 megs. Lists of legal frequencies are available— you can either write to the FCC, or maybe your marine store will have something. Or, if you bought your radio new, maybe the literature that came with it will tell you. (Because of the compulsive nature of bureaucrats: "We're not doing anything today, let's change the rules," a list of legal frequencies doesn't belong in a book which both my publisher and I hope will be relatively enduring on the shelves.)

In any event, the same customs for VHF use apply to SSB marine RTs: each band has a calling channel. After reaching your contact, you're expected to move to a different frequency. Sometimes you'll even go to a different band. Yachts are pretty good about doing this. Some commercial fishermen aren't, and will often occupy a calling channel using illegally high power and blanking out your best efforts to reach your faintly audible friend. Commercial fishermen are to marine SSB what truckers in the U.S. are to Citizens Band (CB) radio. And I'm talking *Texas* truckers.

Different bands work better over different distances and at different times of day. I won't go into sun spots, solar flares, and other electromagnetic storms, but they and other mysterious circumstances can drastically enhance or diminish radio reception. Usually six megs works best for distances under 1,000 miles, whereas 12 megs can cross oceans. The eight-meg band has more of the characteristics of six than of 12 megs. Recently a bunch of new legal ship-to-ship channels have been added to the four- and eight-meg bands, relieving the ever increasing congestion on the air waves. Bureaucrats predict that further steps will be necessary as yachts proliferate.

Why marine band SSB? Well, besides keeping in touch with your friends and getting the latest gossip on outrageous romances, bitter divorces, drug arrests, bargain marinas and crooked officials, you can make trans-oceanic phone calls (expensive), receive weather world wide, and get accurate time (for sextant navigation).

And if you don't want to contribute, but would rather pass through the revolving door of gossip on someone else's push, you can buy a set for $50 to $400 that only receives. I would suggest getting one with an outlet for an external speaker, as this is the source that will enable your computer to do marvelous things. If your radio doesn't have such a jack, it's a simple matter for you or your local electronics expert to install one.

A *license* to own and operate a marine RT used to be free, but at some point the FCC started charging a fee. For a while it was $35 for a five-year license. Then, amid screams of yachtie protest, it became $115 for ten years. I believe there was an interval when they wanted $175 for ten years, but the above-mentioned screams effected a reduction. FCC license application forms 506 and 753 are available from the FCC. The forms themselves are still free.

For now, pleasure yachts operating in U.S. waters don't need a license for their VHF, but who knows what the requirements will be in the future.

Ham radio deserves its own section. Ham or amateur radio began with a group of buffs who understood tubes and coils and things. They built their own radio sets (rigs). The FCC allotted hams unused portions of the frequency bands to play in. Initially, hams communicated only in Morse code. Now voice transmissions predominate, and you can tune in to almost any ham conversation and learn more than you ever wanted to know

Herb and Misty at the radio. Nancy never got her license, but she enjoys telling Herb what to say.

about antennas. When they tire of talking about antennas, hams talk to each other about resistors and capacitors. Cruising sailors often tune in on ham conversations as a sure cure for insomnia. Hams do make an important social contribution, however. During floods, earthquakes, and other disasters, ham operators bring portable gear to the scene and provide emergency communication.

Tiring of their own arcanities, and natural disasters being all too scarce for jaded adrenal glands, hams turned to cruising sailors for excitement and purpose. When SEA FOAM suddenly developed a major leak during our voyage home from Hawaii, I checked in with a California ham and asked him to keep track of us on a daily basis. I didn't feel endangered, but I worried that if our electric bilge pump stopped working, or if the leak got a lot worse, we might have more water coming aboard than we could easily handle. Before I knew it, a Coast Guard cutter was offering to steam north 1500 miles to bring us a pump. (We refused the help, but we were comforted that they were there, and that they cared.)

Gradually rigs (I use ham words, and soon I'll have you doing it too) became more sophisticated, and started incorporating transistors and logic modules and circuit boards and integrated circuits and other stuff that mystifies and intimidates. But they also became more reliable and more user friendly. Antenna tuners, magical devices that turn whatever antenna you're using into a one-size-fits-all thing, became fully automatic. Push-button hamming came to the marketplace.

At which point cruisers who couldn't even spell transistor, who couldn't define logic let alone module, who were bored by circuits and who resisted integration, bought profligately. Insulated backstays, the antenna of choice, that used to be famous for failing when the old-fashioned ceramic insulators cracked under strain, were upgraded, as Sta-Lok and other brands of insulators brought back insulated backstay reliability. And although hams like to talk to each other, and ham nets are fun, the impetus driving the cruiser toward hamdom was the *phone patch.*

The phone patch is an electronic device that links radio conversation to the telephone. On your boat, anchored in the crystal clear water of the blue lagoon off the idyllic, palm-fronded, coral sanded tropic isle, while cuddling with a topless Tahitian, you could call Mother! For the amount AT&T charged for this service we could cruise for a week. Hams did it for free, out of the milk of human kindness.

So you would call your ham friend on schedule, first making sure that the country you were in had a reciprocal third-party agreement with the U.S., and give him the phone number to call. (Hamming used to be almost totally male, as women were far too sensible to get hooked on tubes and coils. With the advent of user friendly rigs, that, too, has changed.) The calls, of course, had to be collect if the ham didn't live in the same telephone area that Mother did, as the ham wouldn't pay, and you couldn't, which made calling the folks an even greater bargain. Now comes the good part: teaching your 80-year old mother to say 'over' each time she'd finished saying something to which you were supposed to respond.

Eighty-year old mothers have been using the phone since Alexander G. rang his first bell, so here's this poor ham, who has to throw a switch each time the talker becomes the listener, trying to deal with a beloved matriarch's insistence that after all, this is a phone, isn't it? What's the matter with you? Add to a total absence of 'over's the fact that we're dealing with a lady for whom interrupting offspring on the phone is a way of life, and you have a chaotic conversation.

And we haven't even discussed static, or the distortion introduced by the boat's batteries not being fully charged, or the unfamiliarity at the best of times of the sound of radioed voices, particularly if the pitch is altered by one or the other radio being slightly off frequency. I have spent several difficult-to-arrange patches devoted entirely to the topic, "but it doesn't *sound* like you, dear."

I was convinced that I could beat the high cost of ham equipment by going to a 'ham fest' and buying used gear. Used equipment is used equipment, however, and I ended up with a set that later proved to be electronically challenged. No island repair man could cure it, so eventually I found a dealer who was willing to take my set in trade for the exact same old model, but working. (By now I'd invested enough money in ham rigs to have bought myself a brand new transceiver.) I also settled for an economy tuner that you have to adjust with knobs—cheap, and perhaps not as effective, but it gets you on the air. My antenna is a piece of heavy wire used in construction, gift of a friend, as I refused to pay for backstay insulators. All of my gear could be improved, however, and will be, starting tomorrow.

Having make-do equipment has had unforeseen results. Shore-based hams, with nuclear powered stations and antenna arrays that look like NASA's Control Center, delight, with their stallion-grade signals, in telling me what a weak signal I have. Although I would never go into therapy simply because of this, the topic of an inadequate radio signal has come up several times while seeking counsel in other matters.

CHAPTER 27

Information Please!

Dear Herb: When emergencies come up, or in ticklish situations, where can I get reliable information?

An Empty Vessel Yearning to Be Filled

Dear EV: With ham radio you're in touch with experts from all over the world. This can be both good and bad, because ham operators can also be theatrical hams and as such will do almost anything to be in the limelight. One night, I overheard a North American doctor ham, who was either a dropout or had fallen asleep in class when they talked about tropical diseases, advise a cruiser suffering from dengue fever to take aspirin to get the fever down. This was before aspirin alternatives. I broke radio silence to caution the cruiser against this, as there are several types of dengue fever, one of which can make you a bleeder. I knew this because one day in Tahiti I drove with a friend to the hospital while he filled a salad bowl with blood from his nose. The nosebleed, initiated by a sneeze, was the result of having taken aspirin for dengue. The French doctors cautioned us never to take aspirin for dengue until we had had a blood test to determine the type.

Another near disaster resulted from a letter in an SSCA Bulletin. Entering Ahe, in the Tuamotus, depending on wind and tide, can be tricky, and it's possible in certain conditions to roar through the pass at 10 to 12 knots. At least that's how we did it, looking for a reef on the right (or was it left?) and narrowly missing it because it actually was on the left (or was it right?). The letter had it backwards, an easy enough thing to do if you're dyslexic, learning-impaired, or misanthropic.

Diving accidents are dangerous at any time, but particularly when you're thousands of miles from help. We on SEA FOAM were involved in one in Vavau, Tonga, in 1979. Three men, our 17-year old son included, went on a quest for black coral. Jewelry quality black coral was being found only in ever deeper places. This dive went down 180 feet. One diver, Don, ran out of air on the bottom. Steve, the second diver, didn't run out till he was halfway to the surface. Craig was the only one who surfaced with air left.

No need here to go into the mistakes and errors in judgement that led to this.

When Don, the fellow who had run out of air, surfaced, he had a slight headache. Soon, however, he went into what appeared to be a stroke. He became immobile, his facial expression painfully distorted. We were afraid we might lose him.

Steve had worked for an oil company in the North Sea, where he regularly dove to depths of 500 feet. However, his knowledge of recreational diving was sketchy. He took Don down with a fresh tank to a depth of 30 feet and stayed there with him till all the air was gone. When Don surfaced, he seemed completely recovered. We non-divers thought Don's troubles were over, but Steve warned us, "We're not out of the woods yet."

Back in Vavau later that afternoon Don started feeling a tingling in his feet. Meanwhile I had returned to SEA FOAM. Ham radio—should I get on the air or shouldn't I? Don is my friend, but do I have the right to start wheels turning without either his or his wife's knowledge or consent? It can't do any harm, and ham operators love to be helpful in emergencies. At 6:45 P.M., nearly five hours after the accident, I went on the air for what would turn out to be a nine-hour marathon.

Why didn't I get on the air sooner? None of us had any idea how serious Don's condition would become. Yachties in general are self-sufficient cruisers who tend not to call for help until they've exhausted their own resources. During the long night Don's condition gradually worsened. Thanks to the ham net, we were able to consult with decompression specialists in Honolulu and in Sydney, Australia. Treatment of decompression sickness is a highly specialized aspect of medicine and the local doctors had no experience or competence in dealing with it. It was essential, the doctors all agreed, to get the patient to a decompression chamber as quickly as possible. In the meantime, his wife was to administer oxygen (we got some from a local welder, the only oxygen available); give aspirin with copious fluids; give an injection of 10 milligrams of Decadran or other suitable steroid; and keep Don's feet up, head down, and keep him still.

By morning Don could barely move his head, and nothing else. An Air Force New Zealand plane on maneuvers in Fiji agreed to pick him up. At 1:30 P.M., 24 hours after the accident, he was flown to American Samoa. There he was tranferred to a commercial jet bound for Honolulu, where he was met by a U. S. Navy ambulance. He was taken immediately to the decompression center at Pearl Harbor and was kept in the chamber for seven hours—at the time, the second longest duration in the history of decompression treatment. Don is now completely recovered, and ham radio played a part in saving his life.

They never did find any black coral.

Whereas in the early 70's few cruising yachts carried SSBs, many do now. Electromagnetic intercourse among yachties is just as easy and successful on SSB as on ham bands. With SSB you can do most of the things you can do with ham radio. The main difference will be you won't have access to free phone patches, and you'll have far fewer nets to participate in. And because many SSB-ers don't have ham rigs, whereas almost all cruising ham operators have SSB (marine band) capabilities, SSB alone is sufficient for most cruisers' purposes.

However, except for various official or licensed commercial installations, shore-based SSBs are illegal, so if you have friends ashore to whom you wish to talk, ham is the medium to use. If your friend is a ham, you're in business. If not, there's always the phone patch, or, as a last resort, a 'one way', which means the shore-based ham will relay your message to its recipient, and relay his or her message back to you. This works with about the same reliability as the rhythm method of birth control.

A shore-based ham with a phone will often allow you to leave his phone number with a relative to be used in case of emergency. We had done this with my brother. A ham who regularly came up on the East Coast Intracoastal Waterway Net called us one morning with the frightening message, "Call home, it's an emergency." I hopped in the dinghy and rushed to a pay phone. My brother, whom we were going to visit within the month, wanted to know if I wanted a big party for our homecoming, because if I did, he'd have to get busy with the invitations.

I thanked him, then spoke gently of the difference between 'urgent' and 'emergency'.

VHF radio will get you current weather reports anywhere along either coast of the U.S. and on the Great Lakes and many other bodies of inland water, but if you wander offshore you'll need either ham or SSB radio, or a short wave receiver capable of receiving either. Since weather reports can save your boat and your life, you might even tell your accountant to enter radio expense in the insurance column. It makes sense to me.

CHAPTER 28

Weather

Dear Herb: We're going to have weather, whether or no. How do you deal with this? And while you're at it, would you please explain fronts and things? A word to the wise will be sufficient. I just don't want to be caught with my pants down.

Better Safe Than Sorry

Dear BS—TS: Good questions. Already you stand head and shoulders above the crowd in knowing that forewarned is forearmed. Into each life some rain must fall, and most of the folks I talk to think it's better not to have your head in the sand. There are, of course, those who'd rather not know beforehand, claiming that prior knowledge of stuff hitting the fan spoils not only the time you're actually getting splattered, but the time you spent worrying about it.

On RED SHOES we used to listen on SSB to transmissions coming from station NMN (November Mike November) out of Portsmouth, Virginia. A synthetic voice, it sounded like Hal in the movie *2001*. When we were in the Pacific we listened to WWV out of Hawaii. Lately we've been receiving weather info in code—Sitor, for all you technobuffs—which is translated by our computer into plain language. The advantage of this over voice is that you have a printed copy of the weather report, so that if your mind wanders, or your crewmember coughs at a crucial moment, you won't miss a detail. You take output from the external speaker jack of any all-band SSB receiver, run it through a simple electronic device called a demodulator, and let your special computer software decipher the code.

With a better computer I could also get satellite photos, as does an acquaintance here on the Rio Dulce. He was so pleased with himself and his technology that he'd come up on the local morning net and, using his satellite image, forecast the weather. It got to be a joke, as he was wrong so often that when he predicted rain, nine out of ten sailors who'd planned to varnish went ahead with it, successfully. It takes skill and experience to abstract reliable info from a satellite photo. Ineptitude, however, fails to dampen the high-tech ardor of most of us who love gadgets and expensive toys. Weatherfaxes covering the Atlantic, the Gulf of Mexico, and the Caribbean are presently being transmitted from station NMG in Belle Chasse, Louisiana. On the West Coast, they are transmitted from NMC at Point Rey. You need either a weatherfax machine; or an all-band SSB receiver, a demodulator, and a PC with special software.

Because frequencies and schedules are changed almost as compulsively as the weather itself, up-to-date information is best found in a book that's updated yearly called World Wide Radio Facsimile Broadcast Schedules, published by Cortex (800 862 4761).

Deadlines, schedules, commitments: I figure these are the biggest threats to cruisers other than bad luck. Weather, not deadlines, should determine whether or not you leave. If you have to be somewhere at a certain time, allow yourself plenty of slack. Having to leave in a storm or when a storm threatens is stupid, and can be suicidal. A distant cousin and her husband lost their lives in a gale off Cape Small, Maine, because he, a doctor, had to be back to work on Monday. It was before the days of GPS, so there's no way of knowing whether they sailed onto a reef because they didn't know where they were, or they miscalculated when seeking shelter in a nearby cove.

Unless your name is Nixon and you simply have to get back to the White House to deny something, there's seldom a reason urgent enough to send the skipper of a small boat out into a storm. If you're young and don't give a damn and perhaps even relish the challenge, that's one thing. But most of us don't ride a motorcycle off a ski jump just to see if it can be done, and with common sense in control we don't head out into bad weather voluntarily.

In general, in the trades, squalls move with the wind—that is, from east to west. But cold fronts move from west to east. Or south. Someone in Tahiti who wants to know what the future holds, weatherwise, should pay more attention to what's going on in Tonga and Samoa than in the Marquesas. Sailors in the Western Caribbean should pay as much attention to what's going on in the Gulf of Mexico as in the Leeward Islands. Frontal systems are relatively stable (and implacable), whereas squalls can build up and dissolve while you watch them. In sailing SEA FOAM from Hawaii to San Diego in November 1979, we enjoyed westerlies in what are normally trade-wind (or easterly) latitudes—plus or minus 16 degrees north. The westerlies were the result of a cold front that brought us a gale that bore us eastward for ten days. . .

Waterspouts are miniature hurricanes—tornados, if you will. They are lethal, willful, and awful. Like wolves, they tend to travel in packs.

When you see one or more coming your way, confess all your sins. You may not get another chance.

There are always local weather phenomena. For example, there are cold fronts that move from west to east across the North American continent, then dip down into the northwest Caribbean. Known as northers, these winds blow out of the north-northwest and often reach hurricane force. Anyone sailing Yucátan, Mexico, Belize, or the Bay Islands of Honduras who has experienced the fury of a norther has learned to fear them.

You can tell a few things by looking around you. Puffy cumulus clouds portend, but don't guarantee, stable weather. Squally clouds and thunderheads bring unstable weather. An overcast sky can portend either bad or benign weather. A long, dense line of black clouds on the western horizon warns, "douse all sail and duck."

The North Pacific High is the best example of what a high pressure system is and does. When it's stable, in the spring, you can count on winds revolving clockwise around its center. In the actual center there's no wind at all. We've been there, too.

During the season when the North Pacific High is unstable, it's really unstable. When Nancy and I sailed SEA FOAM from Hawaii to California in November (wrong season!), we listened to the weatherman and noted the High's location. In 24 hours it could be found 600 to 1000 miles from where it had been. This is not to say it moved there, but rather, like Lewis Carroll's Cheshire cat, it would dissolve, or be absorbed, then re-form somewhere else. We gave up trying to use it and were content to ride our very own gale for roughly half the passage.

In the northern hemisphere, the winds revolve around low pressure centers in a counter-clockwise direction, opposite to the way they blow around a high. Low pressure systems include but are not limited to hurricanes. In the southern hemisphere, the direction of revolving winds is reversed: they blow counter-clockwise around a high, clockwise around a low.

This knowledge can be very helpful in passage planning. Using your knowledge of the North Pacific High, you can take advantage of its clockwise winds in sailing from Hawaii to North America. To do so, leave Honolulu in April or May when the High is very stable and head northeast, planning to steer a giant curve over the top of the High. You'll then finish by approaching San Francisco on a southeasterly course. And you'll have had fair winds all the way, unless you run into exceptions.

Pilot charts are a mix of information based on averages, and over the years have taught me the real meaning of the word *exception*. Wind roses graphically indicate what sporadic reports from ships at sea have led the chart maker to believe happens at a particular place during a particular month. Arrows show wind direction and indicate by their length the number of days (as a graphic percentage) during the month you might expect it to blow from that direction. Arrow feathers indicate the likely wind strength. A number in the center indicates the days you can expect calms. But the wind rose is a statistical average, and should be taken as an indication only. Remember all those times you visited Dorothy in Kansas? And she insisted, "Gee, this weather is unusual—we *never* have tornados in October?" Sure, Dorothy.

Ocean waves tend to stay the same until they change, and sea change usually precedes wind change. If the waves start to come from another direction, expect the wind to change to that new direction. If the waves have been two to four feet and they start to increase in size, that means stronger wind is coming your way. Big, loopy swells mean a distant storm is out there somewhere and may have your name on it. After a while, and without really understanding all the mental processes involved, you get a weatherish feeling from waves that's right at least most of the time. Which is certainly as good a success ratio as the U.S. weather service prognostications.

You seem to like sayings. There is a saying in Maine, and other locales have adopted it, that if you don't like the weather, wait five minutes. My experience is that Maine weather is not nearly so changeable. Varied, yes; cyclical, even; but the saying connotes whimsy, which is a misrepresentation. If you pay attention, Maine weather holds no more surprises than weather elsewhere.

What Maine has that the deprived tropics do not is fog. Fog usually comes in the morning and burns off in the afternoon. Since the advent of Loran and GPS, Maine sailors no longer hit the reefs in the fog—only each other.

When we cruised the coast of Maine, we noticed that many of the lobster fishermen had radar. And of course they all had Loran. They would happily go roaring through the fog, and I remember one particularly awful day when we were on a well-traveled route in Penobscot Bay hearing lobster boats, invisible in the dense murk, passing at high speed. I assume they could see us on radar, but that was never proven.

Maine lobstermen now listen to the radio. They used to stick their finger in the air, sniff, nod, and either leave port or not, depending on how they felt. They had a better success ratio then, and I can only surmise that instinct, unused, declines in strength, until finally you don't even notice its presence, let alone understand what it's trying to tell you.

Nancy keeps our accounts, and for this relies heavily on a calculator. Even simple problems, like dividing 636 by 6, will send her to her electronic aid. Most of the time I can give a ball park figure close enough on which to

Fog in Maine. I've wished for radar maybe a dozen times in all our years of cruising. (There is no fog in the tropics.)

base an informed decision. But Nancy hates ballpark figures, and determinedly seeks arithmetic accuracy. As a cocktail waitress in busy night clubs, she used to take orders from four tables, bring 16 correct drinks to the proper people, collect the right amount from each, and never write anything down. Now her penchant for exactitude has gone electronic. Never is $3.75 and $4.10 about $8.00. "It's seven eighty-five," she'll say, accusingly.

Don't, however, confuse the accuracy of an electronic device with the reliability of its input. The two have nothing whatsoever in common. Just because you receive a weather forecast on $2,000 worth of radio and process it with $4,000 worth of computer doesn't mean the forecast is worth more than two cents.

Our cat, Misty, is a lousy sailor. She hates heeling, she hates the noise of the wind, she hates waves, and if I get tense she senses it and hates that. Fear, hatred, and vertigo combine to give vomitous results. Because she's always seasick, she's worthless as a bellwether at sea. But occasionally she will throw up as we're preparing, in a totally calm environment, to raise anchor. This has happened three times, and in two of them we went on to have horrendous passages in bad weather. So now, when the cat throws up either before or during weighing anchor, we just drop the hook and wait another day. Her nausea is at least as reliable as any other item in our bag of tricks.

I love the weather rock, a rock the size of a softball which hangs with its explanatory sign on the porch of the French Harbor Yacht Club in Roatán, the largest bay island of Honduras. The sign says:

If wet—raining

If white—snowing

If swinging—windy

If bouncing—earthquake

If gone—hurricane

Don't let all this uncertainty deter you, however. It's an ill wind that blows no good, and every squall must have a sunny aftermath. Weathering weather is part of the grand scheme of cruising, so you might as well prepare yourself for it.

CHAPTER 29

Hurricanes

Dear Herb: Having done most of my sailing on the Great Lakes in our C&C 38, I've never experienced a hurricane. I have managed to scare myself silly reading about them. I know that you've survived at least one hurricane without getting blown away, and would like to hear about what you did and what you would do next time. Can you set my mind at ease?

Chicken in Chicago

Dear C'n C: No. I wouldn't attempt to ease your mind. Apprehension is a real response to a real threat, and lack of it might well cost you your boat and your life. And don't feel embarrassed about 'Chicken'—we all fear hurricanes. Or perhaps a better word is respect.

As far as surviving hurricanes is concerned, we've been through three, although for none of them were we at sea. In the first one, Hurricane Meli, although we thought we were going to be nailed, we actually were hit by the edge of the storm and endured no more than 60-knot winds. For Hurricane Bob we were in Falmouth, Maine, where a kind cousin offered RED SHOES the use of his mooring, a monster designed to hold a 60-foot yacht. Bob brought hurricane-force winds, but failed to hit us with his knockout punch. We also elected not to remain aboard.

Hurricane Hugo was a true test of Seek Shelter tactics, and we'll get around to discussing that. For now, I'll say only that Lady Luck played a part in all cases, aided by a few ideas which I'll pass on to you.

Hurricanes are circular storms with a low pressure center. In the Northern hemisphere, winds revolve around the center in a counterclockwise direction. Wind arrows on a circle would not be tangent to it, but would angle roughly 15 degrees toward the center. During hurricane season in the Caribbean we keep track of tropical waves—lines of low pressure that move westward across the Atlantic from Africa. If a wave develops, it becomes first a tropical depression, then a tropical storm, then a hurricane. In a hurricane, winds are clocked at a minimum of 64 knots—over 75 statute miles per hour.

That's what it has to blow before it even earns the name *hurricane*. Hurricane Hugo's winds were more than double that. But because the force of the wind increases as the square, the force exerted on any stationary object by 150-knot winds is four times that exerted by 75-knot winds. And the force of 75-knot winds is *nine* times that of 25-knotters. The force of 150-knot winds *on your boat* is 36 times that of 25-knot winds. Going to weather in 25 knots of wind, RED SHOES is already reefed down; or if we're in an anchorage, we're thinking about putting out a second anchor. The fact that any boat has ever successfully lain to anchor in a Category IV hurricane to me is a miracle.

In such forces, things happen of which you've never dreamed. Mature trees, snapped off at their base, go ballistic. Panels from corrugated iron roofs, ripped from their rafters, turn into flying scythes. Twigs and bits of leaves become shrapnel. The wind screams, and waves become tumbling skyscrapers.

And within a hurricane system there can be tornados boasting 200-plus knot winds. (Two hundred and ten knot winds have nine times the force of 70-knotters, and forty-nine times the force of 30-knotters!)

Why do I play with these numbers? To keep myself scared spitless. I want to know the enemy's power. Only then will I take drastic action. And what is drastic action? Paying whatever to be hauled out by a shipyard, or sailing 400 or more miles south is in my opinion pretty drastic; drastic is spending three days tied up in sweltering, windless, bug-ridden mangroves.

Hurricanes are named, and the names progress alphabetically through the season. The hurricane season in the Caribbean is June through December, although hurricanes have been known to occur in other months. Months of highest frequency are August and September.

A hurricane report from NMN in Portsmouth might sound like this: "At 0600 Zulu, Hurricane Zebediah (boy, was that an active year!) was at 15 degrees north, 55 degrees west, moving west-northwest or 290 degrees at 15 knots. Maximum winds are 100 knots. Radius of 64-knot winds: 75 miles northwest quadrant, 75 miles southwest, 50 miles southeast, and 50 miles northeast. Radius of 30-knot winds: 125 miles northwest, 125 miles southwest, 100 miles southeast, 100 miles northeast." The synthetic voice will then go on to predict coordinates and wind strengths for up to three days. Reliability decreases radically with later projections, but it's been my experience that the 24-hour prognosis is extremely reliable, and that the extended forecasts are more often accurate than not.

Tropical waves are tracked from Africa all the way across the Atlantic. If a wave develops into a storm, reports are given every three hours.

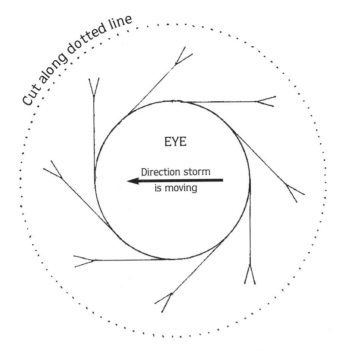

Approximate winds revolving around circular storm, such as a hurricane.

Place this on a small scale (large area) chart using Hurricane Center prognosis. I made mine on transparent plastic (cut up Ziploc baggy). Flipped over, it works for the Southern Hemisphere as well.

Drawing of circle with wind arrows. Make one of these to lay on your chart to predict the direction of cyclonic (tropical storm, hurricane) winds. Estimating the direction from which the storm cell will come and how far away it will pass is crucial.

Satellite imagery gives Portsmouth most of its information, but the U.S. still sends pilots out to fly through the eye of the storm to locate it and report wind strengths accurately. Our government in its wisdom suggested cutting out these overflights, but Caribbean countries pleaded for their continuance, saying that the accurate warnings save both lives and property. So we're still doing it, and God bless those pilots.

A revealing exercise is to cut a circular disk out of clear plastic and with a marking pen ink in the wind arrows. Lay the disk on your chart of the Western Atlantic. As an example, pick an island, let's say Martinique, to receive a direct hit with the storm moving due west. The first winds will be out of the north-northwest. Moving the disk westward, you'll see that after the eye passes, the winds will be out of the south-southeast. Antigua, to the north, will first get north winds with maybe some east in them. As the storm (disk) moves west, you can see that the wind will veer more to the east. Bequia, to the south, will start off with westish winds, which will then back around to the south.

Keep in mind that the storm is a cell, often with a definite rim. When you are in the path of a hurricane, you won't necessarily get gradually increasing wind strengths. In Hugo, the wind arrived with a 'wham' that'd knock your socks off.

Notice also that as the storm system moves westward, the speed at which it moves is added to the speed of the easterlies, and subtracted from the speed of the westerlies. This gives rise to the terms 'dangerous semicircle' and 'navigable semicircle'. Although the idea of a navigable semicircle in a category IV hurricane is more fantasy than fact, you do what you can, and at sea, a skipper would want to make every effort to sail out of the path of the hurricane in a direction that would put him in the navigable semicircle rather than the dangerous one, even if neither is navigable, and both are dangerous.

But let's now put the disk due south of the Virgin Islands, and move it gradually due north. St. Thomas will first get east-northeast winds; then, following the passing of the eye, wind out of the west-southwest. Notice that the wind shifts 180 degrees with a direct hit, and closer to 90 degrees with a near miss. Also note that if St. Thomas received a direct hit from the east, the winds would arrive from a much different direction. The direction of the winds will be subject to the direction of movement of the storm itself, and where you are on its rim.

Had the skippers who chose to anchor out in Bahia Honda, Culebra for Hurricane Hugo, done this exercise, they would have seen that the wind might come out of the south (which it did) and take that into account (which they didn't). The fetch caused by the wind coming directly into the mouth of the bay wielded the *coup de grace* to many.

For Hurricane Meli, we were anchored off the Tradewinds Hotel in Suva Harbor, Fiji. We laid out three anchors 120 degrees apart. After the windshift we hung off in a way I'd not foreseen. Not only were several boats dragging all over the place, but they were also able to re-set anchors under power, which never could have been done in stronger winds. We found ourselves one boatlength behind a ferro-cement boat that was on a mooring and engineless. Our anchor was directly underneath. As long as I couldn't raise and re-set our anchor, I would have liked to let off more scope, but the boat behind us was only a boatlength away, and behind him, also about a boatlength away, was a rockbound islet. We and the skipper behind us were up all night with engines running.

Even with winds of only 60 knots, there was considerable minor damage, and all of it boat-to-boat. Boats that went up the river were joined

Hurricane Hugo. A huge percentage of hurricane losses result from the domino effect of one boat dragging.

by 150-foot tugboats and commercial fishing boats, formidable opponents in the bumpcar battle of bulwarks. Fifty miles to our south at the Astrolabe Reef, two yachts that had elected to make a stand were destroyed and sunk. Two people drowned, the other three made it ashore and hid in a cave, watching palm trees with trunks over a foot in diameter hurtle past. Not far to the south, a stone church collapsed, killing a couple of dozen villagers who'd taken refuge there. Winds were estimated to have topped 120 knots.

Until you've experienced it, the force of the winds in a major hurricane is unimaginable. It was apprehension that caused us to learn all we could about hurricanes and to study all the ways in which other sailors have combatted them, both at sea and in hurricane holes. I consider it a blessing. If it had led instead to existential apathy, I could have been just another victim. It's one more of the many cases in the cruising experience where leaving your destiny to fate will more than likely prove fatal.

There's a computer program called 'Storms' put out by Utopia Software, P.O. Box 420324, Houston, TX 77242. The one I have tracks over 300 Atlantic, Gulf, and Pacific storms on a computer-generated map of the appropriate area. You can zoom in, enlarging a section. You can ask the program how many hurricanes threatened a certain port over the last x number of years, and restrict the question even further by specifying a month or months of occurrence. You can specify what strength of storm you want the program to list—tell it, for example, not to list anything less than 64 knots of wind, and to list nothing that passes the specified port by more than x miles. You can ask it to list all the plotted positions of the storm, and it will come up with a table that gives its position every three hours from birth to death; gives latitude and longitude of each position; and gives the wind strength and the speed and direction in which the system is moving.

If you're monitoring a storm or a season's storms, you can plot the positions you receive. While huddling in fear and trembling in your preselected hiding hole, you can watch its progress as it marches inexorably in your direction. When it's all over and you've survived, *your* hurricane will join the list of those included with the program, so that later if you want to remember what it was like, you can call up the storm track and relive each terrifying moment.

In 1989 Hurricane Hugo became the most expensive storm to hit the United States, causing $7 billion in property damage in South Carolina. Then Andrew became the champion with damages amounting to over $20 billion.

Hurricanes form in the Western Caribbean and the Gulf of Mexico in the early (June) and late (after September 15th) part of the hurricane season. In July, August, and half of September, more form in the Eastern Atlantic.

In 1974, Hurricane Fifi became one of the worst natural disasters of the Western Hemisphere, killing an estimated 5,000 persons in Honduras, El Salvador, Guatemala and Belize.

In 1988, Hurricane Gilbert hit Cancun as a Category V. The 20-foot storm surge picked up a Cuban freighter several miles offshore and tossed it ashore like a toy.

THE SAFFIR/SIMPSON HURRICANE SCALE

[From information contributed by the National Hurricane Center in Miami, Florida, in the form of a NOAA pamphlet titled *Hurricane! A Familiarization Booklet.*]

THE SAFFIR/SIMPSON HURRICANE SCALE attempts to relate hurricane intensity to damage potential. This scale, which ranges over a scale of one to five, is summarized below.

CATEGORY 1:

Winds 75 to 95 miles per hour: Damage primarily to unanchored mobile homes, shrubbery, and trees. Some coastal roads flooded. Minor pier damage. Storm surge to five feet.

CATEGORY 2:

Winds 95 to 110 miles per hour: Considerable damage to vegetation, mobile homes and piers. Small craft in unprotected anchorages break moorings. Marinas flooded. Storm surge to eight feet, flooding low-lying escape routes two to four hours before arrival of center.

CATEGORY 3:

Winds 110 to 130 miles per hour: Some structural damage to residences. Mobile homes destroyed. Storm surge to 12 feet. Terrain lower than five feet above sea level may be flooded inland eight miles or more. Low-lying escape routes flooded by rising water three to five hours before arrival of center.

CATEGORY 4:

Winds 130 to 155 miles per hour: Extensive damage to roofs, windows, and doors. Storm surge to 18 feet. Flat terrain lower than ten feet above sea level flooded as far as six miles. Major damage to structures near shore.

CATEGORY 5:

Winds greater than 155 miles per hour: Major damage to buildings. Storm surge greater than 18 feet. Massive evacuation within five to ten miles of shoreline may be required.

INCREASING WIND FORCES COMPARED TO
22-KNOT WINDS

	mph	knots	multiple	force against 4x8 sheet of plywood in lbs/sq foot
Good sailing	25	22	1	50
Gale	41	36	3	150
Hurricane	85	74	12	600
Category II	100	87	16	800
Category III	120	104	23	1150
Category IV	142	123	32	1600
Category V	160	139	41	2050
Reported gusts	200	174	64	3200

A boat 34 feet long with 2 foot high topsides has roughly twice the topside area of a sheet of plywood, and would be subject to twice the force!

CHAPTER 30

Fear and Trembling in Culebra

Dear Herb: Tell us your scariest hurricane story.

Eager Tyro

Dear E.T.: I'll read from RED SHOES' log:

September 17, 1989, 3:24 P.M.: Sunday, Culebra, Puerto Rico. Hugo is upon us. Seventy miles east of St. Croix, it's forecast to make a direct hit. Four known dead on Guadeloupe. Maximum winds are 140 miles per hour, or 120 knots, with gusts to 140 knots. There is a ten-foot tidal surge forecast, and at sea, 20-foot waves.

We have lashed the mainsail to the boom, but otherwise stripped the decks, relocated all halyards, lashed oars, tied down the bimini frame, and I have eight lines ashore into the mangroves. I've changed to the full propane tank, even though there was a little left in the tank we are using, as I don't want to run out. We have plenty of water. Diesel tank full, batteries charged. Dinghy is partially deflated and full of water. Outboard is on the pushpit.

Civil Defense folks came around to suggest that we leave our boat and take shelter ashore. We feel we're as safe aboard as we would be ashore, with far less chance of having a building fall on us. We are one of the several crews that stayed.

September 18. Maydays all night long. One guy: "I'm being hit by an island of mangroves with a house on it. I'm breaking up!" Another: "This is EL CAPITAN, 98-foot Broward motor yacht—45-foot ketch in front of us, you're dragging down on us. I'm shining a spotlight on you, blowing my horn at you. (Yelling.) You are dragging down on us." He was later swept away by over a half dozen sailboats, washed up on the beach, his two props fouled with anchor lines. In the process he cut another sailboat in half, heard the screams, helpless.

"Mayday, Mayday, we've broken loose. We're drifting through the anchorage. Nothing we can do. Wish us luck."

Red Shoes tied up in the mangroves. A mangrove creek protects from fetch, the huge, anchor-snatching waves that can build up over open water.

The wind indicator on the Marine Resources Center blew off at 200 knots. Another Hugo-spawned tornado lifted a house 20 feet in the air, where it exploded into bits.

We are *interdependent*. Independence was for storms of yore, when you could act without bringing consequences down on others. Now, with all the boats there are, it's different. "I'm fighting for my life," came over the VHF last night. But that's what we all were doing. Perhaps we should have prepared more as a team than as individuals.

Fury best describes the wind for me. The wind screams a crescendo, reaches a peak, then shrieks even louder. Suddenly comes a moment of calm, the inside edge of the eye, when the wind drops, when everyone thinks, "It's all downhill from now on." Dreamers.

After the eye passed, the winds became even more furious. Because the storm's northwesterly movement had slowed, it took nearly 11 hours to pass us. Blasts whooshed straight down the throat of Ensenada Honda, causing waves that snatched anchors from their graves. Imprisoned in a tangle of trees, impaled by rocks, or hurled up into the town's main street, boats became the corpses of dreams.

The radio tells the story. How brave are the people who came on the air to warn others that they have lost control and are dragging through the anchorage! Who among us can imagine himself heading for disaster, yet having concern for the welfare of others?

The tidal surge raised RED SHOES partially above the shelter of the mangroves, exposing us to the full strength of the wind. The whole boat is covered with mangrove leaves, twigs, and stained with tannic acid from bark and crushed leaves. Tops of the mangroves are twisted off, drawn and quartered by the storm. In a few cases, the mangrove trees someone had tied to broke away. Lines part from chafe, from age. Among the owners of the boats who have elected to remain aboard, skippers swim, then scramble through slippery branches to re-attach the parted line to another tree. One friend, in order to save his own boat, was forced to save the unoccupied boat across the creek from him, swimming to the empty craft and putting out extra lines.

Misty feigns sleep, her eyes snapping wide in the gusts. Nancy is afraid. Twice during the night I went out to inspect the lines for chafe. None was discernible. But in making my way up to the foredeck, my body was battered, my eyes squinched shut to protect them from birdshot rain. One friend said he used to carry a motorcycle helmet with a Plexiglas visor. After two trips up to the foredeck against leaves and twigs driven like shrapnel by the wind, I began to think it was a good idea. Some wore diving masks on deck, but I preferred risking twigs to shards.

At least two trimarans were flipped over. One flew kitelike to a hilltop near the Marine Resources Center.

The radio tower blew away. The De-sal plant has been severely damaged. Electricity and phones are out.

The shrouds thrum in the gusts, vibrating like taut strings. Protected though we were, often we heeled till the rail was under water. Out in the bay, disasters come in rapid succession. Calls for help elicit only words of encouragement—there is nothing anyone can do. In a few cases, people whose anchors were holding threw lines to those whose anchors weren't; but in no case was such generosity successful.

September 20. Wednesday, 4:59 A.M. Yesterday we took the dinghy around the harbor and took pictures of the damage. Of the over two hundred boats anchored out, a mere fraction survived. A few were blown into the mangroves at the foot of the bay and suffered reparable damage. But by far the largest number were high and dry, virtually destroyed. Some sank. We counted over 190 boats either on the shore, sunk, capsized, or seriously damaged—roughly two thirds of the yachts here.

One sailor said, "I weigh nearly 300 pounds, and when I went up on the foredeck during the height of the storm, one of the gusts found me stretched out on deck, hanging on with both hands, the wind literally lifting me and flogging me onto the deck like a telltale in a breeze." Another sailor told me he was blown over the side, and was only held to the boat by his safety harness.

HAPPY HOOKER, a steel day-charter boat, tried to fight the storm under power, never dropping an anchor. It carried only one. Out of control, it wiped out the ground tackle of several boats and ultimately was driven ashore, taking several more boats with it. Later in a bar the skipper bragged about the damage he'd caused. One of the victims overheard, and decked him.

September 22. Friday, 6:41 A.M. We charter a plane and take pictures of the destruction from the air for *SAIL* Magazine. Pilots of private planes are picking up extra money by charging exorbitant prices to fly people off the island. Most of those in trouble can't afford it.

Captain Gary (Fatty) Goodlander, a St. Thomas talk show host who lost his boat, ran a three-times-a-day radio program on VHF in order to provide facts and scuttle rumors, and also to coordinate aid and expertise with those who needed it. A friend on BRIGADOON sailed round trip to St. Thomas, bringing back fiberglass and resin to help those whose boats might be patchable. Another friend, Mark Reigal, piloted his research trawler all the way from the west end of Puerto Rico in order to offer much-needed potable water and a small crane.

Looter stories: One guy caught two people going through his steel boat, closed the hatch and locked them in, then went for the police. Those looters went to jail. One Civil Defense guy spotted a looter on a high-and-dry boat and yelled at him to come down, he was under arrest. The looter shot and wounded him.

Bob, owner of GRACIE, came to his boat to find a fellow cruiser taking his winches apart. Caught red-handed, the thief stammered, "I'd like to buy your winches." All Bob had left was what he could salvage.

The morning after the storm, a friend we'll call George went to visit a cruiser we'll call Benedict Arnold. Bennie had already been scuba diving and from the bottom of the bay had scavenged anchors, winches, lines, chain, and other gear. George said, "If I find one piece of my gear on your boat or in your pile of stuff, I'll put a bullet right between your eyes." Bennie, suddenly reformed, went ashore and told people what he'd found, and that they could have their stuff if they'd come by his boat. Exposure had convinced him to be honest. But the incident makes me wonder how many others who weren't caught kept what they found.

But there were white hats, too. A white hat announced on the radio that he and others had organized a water taxi service for cruisers who'd lost their dinghy. Wealthy boaters from the main island brought food. On the other hand, a shipment of baby stuff, diapers, food, etc., was hijacked off the wharf during the night. A drama of contrast.

No phones, no mail service; the ferry only started working three days after the storm. Skippers of surviving yachts were busy collecting facts, making lists of those boats that were disabled, those that survived, and those that were totaled. Local residents offered their houses for use by folks who'd lost their boats. Cruising hams spent hours at their rigs putting people in touch with loved ones. Skippers whose boats were intact took the cruising homeless aboard as non-paying guests. Hearing that most of the island water was polluted, the U.S. Navy sent a barge carrying huge tanks of water.

So that the displaced could have electricity ashore, skippers of wrecked yachts offered the use of their generators. Hearing of this, people came over from the main island to steal them.

Kay Crist, the owner of schooner FLYAWAY, was missing. She and her husband were swimming to safety, both wearing life jackets. He reached shore, turned to help his wife, only to see a wave take her out to sea again. Her body was never found. Kay was Hugo's only Culebra victim.

Tears and hugs, heroes and thugs. The things people believe and live by were put into bas relief. Friendships were forged that will last a lifetime. And all of us became better acquainted with the enemy—nature on a rampage, helped occasionally by our fellow man.

Some called it the 'no fault' storm. There was a sense that if you'd decided to swing to anchors, the blitzkrieg of the storm could not be denied. There is some truth in this, but in fact the storm was fraught with fault. Some skippers were irresponsible. They suffered, but all too often they brought down the responsible ones with them.

What did we know that others didn't? Nothing. We merely estimated that the mangroves would eliminate fetch and provide the best shelter. And acted early.

We hid in our mangrove creek days ahead for two reasons. One, we were free to make our decision. Two, we drew only four feet, a shallow enough draft to get us deep into the mangroves. And three, we'd already been through two hurricane scares and knew that to get the place you felt was safest, you had to be one of the first.

Getting in early required a willingness to brave discomfort. While waiting for Hurricane Dean to pass, we learned that in the mangroves you have hot, humid, breezeless nights, spawning armies of vampiric mosquitoes and gluttonous no-see-ums.

But even during the storm, the mangrove creeks were far from full. Some skippers preferred to trust their anchors. Others had too deep a draft. Still others saw yachts tied to both sides of the creeks, their mares' nests of lines blocking passage, and figured there was no way they could get through. But the fact is, for those who tried, all the moored boats dropped lines and did whatever was necessary to help the late-comer in.

Other skippers made their moves later than we did usually because of jobs. No one wanted to leave before it became certain that the hurricane was a real threat. The previous two, Dean and Gabrielle, curved north before reaching us, and left behind the unfortunate feeling that the weather forecasters were crying wolf.

Charter companies are accused of waiting till the last minute, and then hastily mooring their fleet in slapdash fashion. Although such tactics aren't fair to neighbor boats, there's something to be said for the charter company management. Not only are they reluctant to lose money for a false alarm, but also we must credit them with some concern for the customer who has a two-week vacation and is paying dearly for his charter. To haul the crew off the boat and stash them in a hotel, or worse, send them home, is a real shame if the threat doesn't materialize. The truth is that you have the freedom to make an early decision only if you are free of business constraints.

A month ago, we asked a Culebran friend to watch our boat when we planned to fly to the States. Yesterday he came alongside and told us he wouldn't be able to. Losing three of the six boats for which he was responsible had shattered him. He told us this on Thursday, and we were flying out on Saturday. Casting around for alternatives, we finally invited Larry and Sherry from CAROUSEL to live aboard till we returned. A two way street—they get a place to live that's less like a refugee camp, and we get someone to take care of our boat.

We went to a cruisers' meeting to talk to Larry and Sherry. It was a round robin, each skipper or couple telling the group their tales of loss. After several such stories, the presiding cruiser asked us to tell our story.

"I feel guilty," I said. "We were back in the mangroves and didn't get a scratch." And they *applauded*, happy that we had made it, even though they'd lost most or all of what they had.

The day came when we were to leave to catch our plane. As we sat waiting for the ferry, three 45- to 50-foot Puerto Rican sport fishermen arrived from the main island loaded with bags of flour, beans, rice, and other staples. A chain of about thirty men unloaded them and put them on a truck. They were to be distributed free on the island.

Fajardo on the east end of the main island of Puerto Rico was a mess, and the marinas that we could see from the ferry were destroyed. It was six days since Hugo, yet electricity was still out, although en route to San Juan we could see it was being reestablished in random fashion.

The San Juan airport, in addition to losing its control tower, suffered serious roof damage and was leaking like a sieve. Hundreds of adults and children were camped out on the floor. All the toilets were stopped up.

Hugo marched through Puerto Rico like Sherman, stripping men and women of pretenses. Survival was important, but some survived with an attitude that inspired. I was thinking of this as our Eastern Airlines flight arrived in Atlanta, where people had no concept of what hundreds of us had been through, and certainly no understanding of how anyone could leave such a scene uplifted rather than depressed.

But how could I not? He was a modern phoenix rising from the ashes, a young man named Tom whom I barely knew. Just as we were leaving, he rowed by RED SHOES in his dinghy. I asked him how he made out. His boat TAWI TAWI had been totaled. No, there was no insurance. But Tom smiled as he said, "Hey, I found my tools; they weren't even wet. I have everything I need to start over: my tools and my hands."

CHAPTER 31

Lessons Learned—
Eyewitness Accounts of Hurricane Hugo

Dear Herb: I know that RED SHOES survived Hugo. But sometimes you learn more from people who didn't—why they didn't, and what they feel they'd do next time. How about telling us some of their stories; you have my attention.

Skipper Hooked On Disaster

Dear SHOD: If you're truly hooked on disaster, I've accomplished my purpose—not if you feel immortal, but if you see that there but for the grace of forethought go you. Bear in mind that no one is immune, and prevention is the product of paying attention, acting early, and having good luck.

We've briefly mentioned what happened to some of the other boats in Culebra. Hugo was the third storm of the season to seriously threaten the islands. The first two, Dean and Gabrielle, turned north before reaching the Caribbean, instilling in some skippers a false sense of security. Hugo hammered the Virgin Islands and Puerto Rico for nearly 12 hours, producing heartbreak, heroics, and humility. Every skipper who stayed aboard and did battle has a story. These tales, with their flashes of humor and courage, were told in various cockpits over coffee or sundowners. Although coppery sunsets and gentle trade winds have returned to blunt the edge of wariness, the stories that follow remind us that cruising can never be danger-free.

When Hugo threatened, Wright and Louise Saylor took DDRAIG, their center cockpit Freedom 40, way up into the north end of Ensenada Honda, Culebra, where a small islet gave some protection from the south. Wright's main concern was to stay away from other boats. DDRAIG was not hit, but three of her five anchors were wiped out by yachts that had broken loose. Wright was up all night checking lines. For chafing gear he used nylon-reinforced hose, but prefers exhaust hose, with the wire spring inside. The wire spring crushes and keeps the chafing gear in place.

198

As soon as the wind clocked into the south, the waves had over a mile to build to 10 to 12 feet, and were breaking over the foredeck. The last anchor rode—1¼-inch line—finally parted 50 feet from the boat. It was stretched out so far the chafing gear was five feet in front of the bow. DDRAIG had held out for eleven and a half hours—just one half hour before the end of the storm.

When the last line parted, Wright was able to turn DDRAIG and steer her up a mangrove creek, where she came to rest with her bow on dry land. Most of the damage was cosmetic: paint, pulpit, lifelines. One year later the boat was back in Red Hook, St. Thomas, fully found and chartering again.

What would they do next time?

"Sail south," said Wright.

"But," I said, "last year there were three threats. Each means sailing south three days, three days to get back. That's six days away from work. Will you really sail south for each one?"

"I don't know," was his reply.

A couple we'll call Frank and Edna took five years to build PSEUDONYM, their 40-foot sloop, from a bare hull. She was launched in June of '86.

During Hugo, PSEUDONYM lay to her mooring in a cove near the western shore of St. Thomas harbor. Frank put out four additional anchors. PSEUDONYM was doing fine until around 11 P.M., when a 65-foot steel schooner broke loose, wiping out their ground tackle and smashing broadside into them. The schooner then went on to take out several other boats.

PSEUDONYM had a spotlight and foredeck lights, and since another boat also had a spotlight on, Frank could see enough to steer toward the beach. With a draft of 6'4", PSEUDONYM grounded several boat lengths short of shore. Frank and Edna donned life jackets. Edna took a waterproof pouch of papers and valuables. Lashed together, the couple made it through the surf to safety. They spent the remainder of the night in one room of a house more than 50% destroyed during the storm.

"I was at work when the schooner first arrived," said Frank. "A neighboring skipper warned the schooner captain that he was anchoring too close. 'I'm going on vacation,' was the reply. He left his vessel lying to only two anchors, all sails still bent on, two windsurfers on deck, six scuba tanks lashed to the stern rail. All that windage." The Pseudonyms are taking the owner of the boat that hit them to court for damages.

"Our boat is all we own", said Edna. "They shouldn't be allowed to get away with this."

Edna and Frank plan to be out of the hurricane area during next season. "But if we were still here," said Frank, "we'd head for Ensenada Honda in Vieques. All the boats there survived in the mangroves with minimum or no damage. And the eye passed right over them."

"I've talked to a lot of skippers who've come to that conclusion," I said. "What if it's crowded?"

"I don't know," he said. As we were leaving, he added, "If I ever again have to ride out a hurricane at anchor, I'll be much more aggressive toward people that anchor near us."

Cruisers Rob and Jill Eberle believe in training and preparation. Before going cruising, Rob took an 18-month course in diesel mechanics, while Jill quit her regular job to become a sailmaker. During the four years they'd owned VALKYRIE, a Contest 38 sloop, they sailed her back and forth twice from the Virgin Islands to the Northeast.

"They call him Hurricane Rob," Jill said, "because we're always earlier than others leaving our jobs to prepare for an approaching storm. Rob would listen to Portsmouth weather and track the storms all the way across the Atlantic from Africa."

Doing their homework, long before the first hurricane threat, Rob and Jill explored most of Hurricane Hole, St. John, in a dinghy with a lead line, looking for a place that would accommodate VALKYRIE's 6½-foot draft. By the time Hugo threatened, they had had two dress rehearsals preparing for Dean and Gabrielle. Thinking ahead, they topped off VALKYRIE's tanks, figuring that after a hurricane, water and fuel might be unavailable. They also went to the dive shop and got full dive tanks.

Once in Hurricane Hole, Rob dropped a 60# CQR in 18 feet of water and laid out 300 feet of 5⁄16-inch hi-tensile chain. Lying stern to the mangroves, VALKYRIE was ultimately secured by a web of eight shore lines. One line went to a chain around a huge boulder, which moved during the storm! In addition to the plow, Rob later set a 60# Danforth and a 30# deepset hi-tensile Danforth. Using scuba gear, he hand set all three.

"It's best if you can pick your neighbors," said Rob. On one side they had an experienced friend whose competence was known. On the other was a smaller, lighter and unoccupied sailboat which, if worst came to worst, would not mount as damaging an assault as a heavier boat.

Once VALKYRIE was secured, Rob went diving and re-set the anchors of nearby unoccupied boats when necessary. When their air tanks were empty, Jill caught a ride to Cruz Bay, commandeered more tanks, then enlisted other scuba-qualified skippers to help with the anchor-setting job. In addition, Rob and others went aboard untended yachts and rigged chafing gear out of rags, and added whatever extra lines they could.

"Anchors dropped from a dinghy almost never set properly," Rob said. "We thought of what we were doing as being like defensive driving—you have to watch out for the other guy." Jill: "One thing we've thought of doing next time, if there is a next time, is ringing our boat with tires." VALKYRIE didn't need such protection during Hugo, however, as all the boats but one in the anchorage held fast. That one, an unoccupied Tayana 37, broke loose and became a threat to the whole fleet, at which point an unidentified skipper hopped aboard, started the engine, and drove it up on the mud in a mangrove, where it stayed for the rest of the storm.

Rob slept some during the hurricane, feeling that being rested was an important part of defense. Jill, wondering how he could sleep, stood watch and monitored the radio. Frequently Rob would get up and go topside to check for chafe, wearing plastic safety goggles. VALKYRIE's chafing gear—two and a half foot, double-layered lengths of elk hide sewn on by Jill—never chafed through. They had even rigged chafing gear on the mangrove end of their shore lines. Jill and Rob maintain elkhide is the best chafing gear you can get, and far superior to plastic hose.

Rob: "During the height of the storm, huge sections of mangrove, including some very large trees, were torn loose by other boats. Heavier boats especially have to spread the load. The safest course is to run multiple lines to as many different big trees as possible and tension them evenly."

Rob figures to use much the same tactics during future threats. "Frankly," he said, "I'd rather spend next season in Venezuela. But the cruising kitty is growing, we have good jobs, and it looks like we'll stay here for another year. After that, we hope to head for the Med."

SUGGESTIONS

The best knot for a bollard, samson post or tree is two round turns and two half hitches. It doesn't jam, and it produces far less chafe than a single loop, such as a bowline.

Many spoke of the chaos below. In preparing for a hurricane at anchor or at sea, don't forget that belowdecks is going to be like the inside of a cocktail shaker. Extra care must be taken to secure anything that moves.

No one spoke of having prepared food ahead of time, or of having filled thermos bottles with hot coffee or soup. Having fruit, cheese, hard boiled eggs and other cold food available makes it easier to keep up your strength.

If you're not too busy in your own defense, stay tuned to VHF Channel 16. Although there is seldom anything you can do for someone in trouble, you can encourage, and often a suggestion made by an experienced skipper can help a less experienced sailor avoid a mistake or weather a crisis.

It's frightening to think how little you can do; the good news is that oftentimes the little you can do can make a big difference.

As with the destructive Cabo San Lucas storm of the early 80's, bow rollers are all too often a weak link. Your boat should be equipped with ways to lead shore lines and anchor rodes without using the bow roller.

Many experienced sailors were surprised when the wind turned and came out of the south. When a circular storm approaches, it's helpful to make a sketch of the storm, the direction the storm might be traveling when it hits you, and your location. Wind directions and strengths you might experience will also depend on whether you're hit by the navigable or the dangerous semicircle.

CHAPTER **32**

Storm Tactics at Sea

Dear Herb: I've read articles and books about what you should or shouldn't do at sea in a storm, and I find some areas of serious disagreement among the authors. I might well add to my confusion by asking for your ideas, since as far as I can see, when the wind reaches a certain strength, there's nothing you can do anyway. Please don't bullshit me.

Cynic from Cincinnati

Dear CynCin: I'm both glad and sorry to say I'm not going to be as much help as you'd expect—sorry, because I'm a writer sharing ideas gleaned from experience, and glad because after two decades and over 50,000 miles of ocean passages, I've only been at sea in a few storms, and the worst of those blew no more than 50 to 60 knots. This says to me that although many sailors have sailed and survived worse, being caught out at sea in those conditions is part luck of the draw, part lack of weather information, and if you believe in such things, part karma.

Prospective cruisers who read about the Smeetons pitchpoling their way around Cape Horn in TZU HANG should realize that pitchpoling is indeed a rare event, an event to fear and avoid, but not one to monopolize our defense plans. There are other, far more likely battles with Neptune for which we should be loin-girding. However, if pitchpoling is one of your bogey men, let's put it at the top of the list of *things we don't want to happen.*

The only time I can remember when we might have been in danger of pitchpoling was a passage aboard SEA FOAM from New Zealand to the Austral islands of French Polynesia. I'd called the weather bureau in New Zealand and was told a big front was coming through, but the wind would be fair, and at that point I wasn't really sure of what a front was. So we left, with the result you might guess: 150 miles out we started getting winds of 30 knots, increasing to between 45 to 50 knots before we were through. We had a windvane, but fortunately it broke—you'll see why I say 'fortunately' in a moment. We tore our staysail, which might be called fortunate also, as it kept our women busy sewing and therefore less afraid. We were five aboard, all capable helmspeople; the crew was able to stay relatively rested. And SEA FOAM, big old tubby sweetheart that she was, was strong and buoyant.

The wind, of course, was behind us, so that trying to get back to a harbor in New Zealand was pretty much out of the question. Besides, the wind was pushing us the way we wanted to go, wasn't it? So we, or the weather gods, decided that we'd *run before it under bare poles*.

The waves grew to some of the biggest I've ever seen. However, we were in deep, deep water, so none were breaking hard, and SEA FOAM seemed well able to deal with the few that broke at all, little coamers that tipped over harmlessly behind us. We realized, though, that surfing down the biggest waves was a little like pushing SEA FOAM off the Matterhorn— no real problem until we reached the bottom. Although we did schuss a few waves straight down, plunging our bows into the wall of water that was the next wave, SEA FOAM was so buoyant that we popped up like a cork. The ride was scary, and we were never sure when we buried the bow that it'd come back up complete with bowsprit. We learned that a diagonal course down the backside of the biggest waves was the best way to handle things. And although we didn't all perform perfectly at the helm thereafter, we did plow into the valleys far less frequently.

The other danger, of course, was broaching, which means turning too far across the wave. The wave tries to push the boat sideways, but the keel resists. The turning moment can result in a *knockdown*, also something *we don't want to happen*. A lot depends on how well the helmsman steers. Though we never had the chance to try it, I don't believe it's a job that a windvane can do adequately. If I were short-handed, I might try it, but not in such strong winds.

If you're hand steering you might try taking the downside of big waves at a 30- to 45-degree angle from straight down, much as you'd traverse a steep ski slope to control both your speed and your angle of descent. Then, if you're still going too fast, you'll probably want to stream warps.

We could have streamed warps. We had plenty of line, and carried two used tire casings lashed to the bow pulpit for just that purpose. I guess we just didn't believe speed was the problem. And of course, uppermost in all our minds was making port as soon as possible.

A word about waves: they are as individual as can be imagined. Some factors determining their size and shape are the distance they've traveled before reaching you; the depth of the water; the tides or currents involved; the obstacles, islands, reefs, capes, they've passed; and whether they're the product of winds coming from one direction or several. The waves we were dealing with in this storm were huge but consistent, with sloping rather than precipitous surfaces, and I imagine they were formed by a single front, as there were no rogues. A rogue wave is exceptionally large. Weaned on multiple steroidic forces, it is the result of two or more terrorizers (read 'storms') conspiring to make one terrifying offspring.

I've been in smaller waves in the Atlantic that I feared more. Square-faced and breaking, they punished our doughty RED SHOES mercilessly. And crossing the Gulf Stream in the 50-foot BOSTON LIGHT during a Marion-Bermuda race, we endured for a while waves generated by 30 knots of wind against a two-knot current. No fun, but it was a race, so we pushed harder than we might have otherwise.

SEA FOAM was 36 feet on deck with a 32-foot waterline and a 13-foot, 9-inch beam. Stubby and fat as she was, I'm sure her buoyancy was a significant factor in our not pitchpoling in those 30- to 40-foot waves. A longish, narrowish hull would have been in danger of diving deeper into the next wave, with who knows what results.

During another bad storm, perhaps our worst, we *laid ahull*, which means we furled all sail and went below, and again I'm sure that it was SEA FOAM's buoyancy that made lying ahull a successful tactic. The wind was coming from the direction we wanted to go, so running before it was not at the top of our list. I went to sleep, the lee cloth in place, and was bounced out of bed to land on my head, so I guess we had some hairy moments. I don't remember, as the blow to my skull knocked out my memory, a case of amnesia which took several hours to recede. Nancy reminds me that it was so scary on deck we simply didn't want to go out there till the wind lessened. We and the boat survived, but not because of any marvelous tactic.

I believe there are winds too strong and waves too high for the tactic of *heaving-to* under sail alone. When you're up on top of the wave, the wind hits you with its full force. In SEA FOAM, we have been laid over 45 to 50 degrees with only the tiny staysail up! In the valleys, there can be little or no wind, or a backwind. The two alternating extremes could drive you crazy, and might well defeat what you're trying to do.

We have hove-to both on RED SHOES, off Cape Cod, Massachusetts, in a 35-knot gale—the winds were on the nose, as we've successfully run and reached in similar conditions—and in SEA FOAM off Suvarov, a northern Cook Island in the South Pacific. I read recently that heaving-to properly should result in drifting half sideways, always staying in your boat's slipstream. I've read elsewhere that heaving-to will result in a scallopy motion, forward as the close-hauled reefed main or mizzen pushes you, then falling off as that sail luffs up, and the backed staysail or storm jib pushes your bow off the wind. The latter illustrates our experience.

Most of the bad weather we encountered was in the 30- to 40-knot range, and heaving-to was always an option. In long-lasting bad weather, heaving-to provided us with essential rest. Storms that last for days reveal the weakness in single- or even double-handing, as fatigue can be an even bigger enemy than the storm. We've often found it better to let the boat take care of itself, either hove-to or lying ahull, while we recharged ourselves physically and mentally.

Lin and Larry Pardey have successfully used a tactic involving a parachute anchor, a bridle attached bow and stern, and a snatch block by which they adjust the bridle and consequently the attitude of the sailboat as it lies to. For a comprehensive discussion of this and other tactics, read their book *Storm Tactics Handbook: Modern Methods of Heaving-To for Survival in Extreme Conditions*.

I'm convinced the Pardeys have come up with something important, a tactic we might call the Pardey Parry (or—no, please, not the Larry Parry). We have a parachute type sea anchor called a Para anchor and for our next passage I'll have it on deck. One of the two anchors that normally ride on the roller will be stowed, and its rode readied for the Para. I'll experiment with leaving the 30 feet of ⁵⁄₁₆-inch chain on, as it will tend to keep the Para submerged, a desirable result. We don't have a snatch block—too sexist—so we'll thread our one heavy block on the rode beforehand. This will be known as the Payson Policy. When the storm hits, we'll deploy the prepped Para using the Payson Policy with the Larry Parry and go below and go to sleep.

That's the way *I* like to deal with storms.

Before leaving California on our first cruise, we had read Adlard Coles' *Heavy Weather Sailing*, as well as everything Eric Hiscock had written about storm tactics. Devices that have been improved since those gurus sailed are the drogue, and the sea anchor. We carried a sea anchor on SEA FOAM but never used it. From what I know now, it was far too small for our 27,000-pound boat, and lying to it we would have been pushed backward far too fast, thus risking damaging our rudder.

The Para anchor, today's version of the sea anchor, is much bigger. It is indeed like a parachute, and the instructions recommend deploying it on 400 to 600 feet of line, depending on the periodicity of the waves. Frankly, without tying a whole bunch of lines together, we don't *have* six hundred feet of line on RED SHOES. But on a bigger boat, we might consider carrying the Para anchor with its own rode. The Para anchor is much bigger

than any sea anchor I ever saw, and should definitely slow the boat's leeward drift to a safe and manageable speed. The Pardey's idea of an adjustable bridle which holds the boat at an angle to the wind sounds like a
winner to me. This, they say, is better because you're providing your own
drift slick, plus you're at a better angle to the waves, and you're not drifting
straight backward with the concomitant strain on the rudder.

Lying to a sea anchor introduces the danger of chafe, as the stresses
on the rode (and on the Pardey harness if you use it) will be severe. The
same problems in the use of chafing gear that apply to land anchoring will
apply doubly to sea anchoring. It would be smart if you have a sea anchor
pre-rigged for deployment to have chafing gear secured to the line at the
proper place. Otherwise, you'll have to rig it after deployment, which will
be both difficult and dangerous.

I like the idea of DDRAIG's skipper to use wire-wound heater hose for
chafing gear because the wire is crushable and will clamp the hose in
place. I've often tried to keep nylon-reinforced plastic hose in place using
small stuff and tying a rolling hitch around the rode at each end of the
piece of hose. This is a poor solution in a big storm. Stretch makes the
rode thinner, the rolling hitches come loose, and the hose slips out of
place. The only secure way I've found is to work the small stuff around
two strands and under one. Then, the tighter the pull on the rode, the
tighter its grip on the small stuff. But even this, with the rode stretching,
may put the chafing gear in the wrong position.

But I'm also going to try DDRAIG's idea—that is, if I can figure
something out: once the wire in the hose is crushed, clamping it to the
rode, how do I get it off?

Maybe the very best way would be to secure the hose in the chock or
hawsehole, and let the rode slide freely through it as it stretches, although
this doesn't provide as much chafe protection as having it secured to the
rode. In any event, use a longish piece of hose to allow for the rode's
stretching under load. How you secure it is your call.

It is really sad, but at least two instances of single-handers losing their
boats *after* the storm has passed come to mind. Grateful that the ordeal
was over, they dragged their weary bones to bed and never woke up till
the hull was smashing and grinding to its death on a coral reef. Having
survived the immediate hazard, they failed to account for other dangers or
were too exhausted to care. Nowadays with GPS these wrecks probably
would not have happened. If you rely solely on sextants, 72 hours or more
without a sight could easily put you 100 miles or more away from where
you thought you were, in danger rather than safe in open water.

All of our storm tactics have evolved from paying attention, assuming the worst, and preparing for it. We douse sail or reef down when we think the weather is worsening, not after it does. One of our more dangerous moments aboard RED SHOES came when we were sailing downwind with the jib poled out and the mainsail wing-and-wing and prevented. Struck by a white squall with winds of 40 knots or better, all we could do was steer to prevent a jibe, and hang on. I was finally able to release the main halyard, and although the sail didn't come down all the way, it was scandalized enough to reduce some of its power.

It was one of those freak squalls. I'd no sooner looked over my shoulder and wondered aloud to Nancy if we should reduce sail when we were hit. It was too late. We rode it out, our knot meter pegging at ten knots, and I lost a few more hairs.

MAYDAY! A Last Resort. Three men who were bringing an Endeavour 37 from Florida to the Bay Islands of Honduras ran smack into Hurricane Alison off the southwest coast of Cuba. One crewmember became incapacitated through sea sickness. The other injured his arm, rendering it useless. The third, after 20 hours at the helm, was at the end of his tether. When a freighter answered their distress call, they thought help was on the way.

But it came at great cost. The first attempt at rescue was an effort to put the sailboat under tow. Bringing the two boats together caused a great deal more damage to the sailboat, rendering her unseaworthy. The problem then became "how do we transfer people from the sailboat to the freighter?"

Experienced sailors would not have gotten into this mess in the first place. For one thing, they put off reefing the main until things were so bad they didn't dare go forward on deck to do it, so they were trying to deal with 60 plus knot winds with the full main up.

All three were definitely incapacitated, exhausted and terrified, and because of that unable to think clearly. The helmsman had the most experience. He was frantically worried, not only about their situation and his ability to continue, but about his son, who was helpless below with seasickness and fear. The boat owner was the one with the injured arm.

"Next time," said the owner, "I'll tell the freighter captain what we want him to do. He took charge, coming close to us in order to take a line, intending to give us a tow. He came too close, and in the process my boat was dismasted and most likely holed."

The freighter moved off, and the three men managed to escape into the liferaft. The freighter then tried to maneuver close enough so they could climb a ladder to safety. The side of the huge ship was a wall of steel that plunged and rose in 15- to 20-foot cycles. There was a time during the backing and filling when the freighter's propeller, coming clear out of the water, threatened to chop the liferaft and its occupants to bits. Dealing with the freighter turned out to be far more dangerous and frightening than the actual storm.

"We learned later," said the yacht's skipper, "that there were two other sailboats in trouble. In both cases, freighters were requested by the U.S. Coast Guard to stand off to windward, giving the sailboats a lee. They did so for several hours, and the beleaguered yachts survived the rest of the storm in good shape. Naturally we'd do that too, if there's a next time, God forbid."

Once a crew actually abandons the yacht, the problem becomes how to get the raft alongside the ship without harm. It should be up to the freighter to pass a line—they'll have monkey's fists and heaving lines to handle their huge hawsers, and a higher vantage from which to throw. Once the yacht crew has the line, the freighter crew should be able to pull them alongside without having to maneuver the ship. A hand-held VHF in a waterproof envelope is invaluable in such a situation, and the captain of the yacht should be sure to take it with him when he and his crew take to the liferaft.

A crewmember who for some reason is partially incapacitated would do well to wear a safety harness. That way the crew of the ship could help pull him up the Jacob's ladder with a line.

Herb steering with a handheld VHF. A handheld VHF is not only convenient, but it can also save your life.

The Coast Guard deserves high marks. A Coast Guard plane flew over the scene several times, and only left when the transfer of people was completed. They had requested the other two ships to stand off and give lee and would have done the same for the Endeavour, but the yacht had already been wrecked by the time they arrived on the scene.

Not having been there to evaluate the conditions (wave shape, wind direction, distance from lee shore etc.), who can say what tactic might have worked? Certainly, getting the sail down, even if it took a shotgun blast to do it, would have been the number one priority. Maybe then they could have lain ahull, or run before it. They had choices before their encounter with the freighter, when the yacht was still seaworthy, but after it was smashed up, of course, they didn't have a chance.

The thing that interested me, one that no one writes about, is how *do* you most efficiently transfer people in a storm? How *do* you deal with a ship that offers assistance? It's the yachties' lives that are on the line, so the skipper should tell the ship's captain, who may never have thought about this, what he wants the ship to do: stand by, provide a lee, take off crewmembers, whatever. Certainly not provide a tow.

Other people's experience and our own inventiveness and decisiveness is all we have to go by. My mother made a remark when I was young that has stuck for all these years: "Life is a series of lessons with no chance to practice." This is certainly true in many cases, but imagining scenarios, developing options, planning, reading, observing, and above all, using common sense and precaution can often make the difference between life and death.

CHAPTER 33

And We Shall Have Lightning

Dear Herb: The last thing I want is to be struck by lightning. What are the sure-fire means of avoiding it? Or if struck, minimizing its effects? Please don't hold back to try to comfort me. Tell me everything. I'm capable of dealing with facts.

Mature in Montana

Dear M&M: Maturity in this case has less to do with dealing with facts than with the lack thereof. Encouraging statistics about avoiding lightning strikes simply don't exist. Think about it—if they did, your question wouldn't be necessary. There would have been four-inch high banner headlines in the sailing magazines, and all newly constructed boats would include whatever it took to make them lightning-proof.

And if there really were a sure-fire way to prevent lightning strikes on yachts, what do you think insurance companies would do? Did you say "insist on it as a condition of insurability"? Bingo!

Where there are challenges at sea or at anchor, Nancy and I work hard at achieving and maintaining confidence. There's a direct ratio between knowledge and confidence. In the case of lightning, however, you soon learn the difference between the meanings of confidence and faith. Confidence comes from belief in things that have been proven empirically. Faith is belief in creative guesswork.

Without faith, each thunderstorm would bring us to the catatonia that seizes animals like deer or rabbits when a spotlight is shined in their eyes at night. Faith stands up to ignorance, bravado confronting the schoolyard bully. The chain of events goes: confidence takes us to sea, bad luck confronts us with lightning, and faith takes over, be it in wishful theory, rabbits' feet, universal consciousness, or that bearded old man in the astral throne that Catholics, Southern Baptists, and other fire-and-brimstoners evoke to scare their children.

To some people, faith can bring as much confidence as knowledge. I'll never forget the Polynesian spear fisherman who stood in the shallow lagoon pass, and who, while up to his armpits in water, stored his bloody catch on a wire at his belt. This flies in the face of every theory about shark danger, so I asked him about it. "My brother protects me with his magic," he told me. When we left the area he was still fishing in the same fashion, uneaten.

Just for fun, take this logic test: does the fact that the fisherman had so far remained safe from sharks prove conclusively that magic works? No? Well, that's about where we are with lightning theory.

People who insist they know the whole truth about lightning have given rise to the phrase 'nuts and bolts'. So if you're mature, as you claim, that's the state of ignorance you'll have to live with.

You can make lightning. Scuff across a wool carpet wearing leather soled shoes, then touch a metal lamp. The spark that you see and the pain that you feel are caused by a nanobolt, ions (electrically charged particles) traveling at the speed of light. A bolt from the sky is infinitely bigger, probably caused by one of Thor's obstreperous children scuffing his feet on an Olympian carpet and giving earth the finger. A pleasanter theory has it that an electrostatic charge builds up in the sky (clouds rubbing together? what fun!) till it climaxes with a leap to earth.

A recent article in *Practical Sailor* adds to my murk and gloom about lightning by saying that it doesn't conform to direct current (DC) laws (about which I know a little), but to radio frequency (RF) or high frequency alternating current laws, about which I know a great deal less. All I got out of it is that a lightning strike is analogous to the first shot in a game of pool. The cue ball is the path of the initial bolt (DC). The break, where the balls go every which way, is what happens electromagnetically at the strike site (RF). I hope this analogy is more helpful to you shooters than it is to me.

There are two approaches to dealing with lightning on boats: a) preventing strikes, and b) minimizing the effects when a) doesn't work. Let's take b) first.

If you're struck, it will likely be at the masthead. To make this even more probable, people used to install a lightning rod. The idea was to attract a strike to the masthead so that it wouldn't choose to hit you elsewhere. If you have an aluminum mast, it will conduct the charge to its base. Wooden masts should be equipped with a heavy duty conductor. From there one should provide a path either to a keel bolt that's attached to external ballast, or to a grounding plate, or both. Why? Because the lightning bolt wants to get to earth, and we want to provide an easy path for that to happen. Without that path, lightning leaps, and the leaps cause hull damage.

Don't get smug just because the boat you're thinking of buying is already equipped with a grounding plate. There is evidence that a grounding surface consisting of a long, one-inch strip of copper running the length of the keel would be six times more efficient at dissipating a lightning strike than a one-foot square plate. It seems that lightning may prefer to escape via sharp edges rather than flat surfaces. Got that?

Because we're dealing with extremely high voltages, as high as a million volts, we need to provide an adequate pathway. For this, heavy cable (at least #4) is recommended. Having the right gauge wire is half the battle. The other half is the quality of the connections. A corroded or otherwise deteriorated connection is like a roadblock, causing lightning to seek a more destructive detour. Because these connections will be between dissimilar metals—aluminum mast, copper wire, steel or bronze bolt to keel or grounding plate—exposed to salt water (at the mast base and in the bilge), they will be extremely vulnerable to corrosion and must be monitored and maintained. Finally, the cable should be led as directly as possible, as the lightning that strikes you is in such a hurry to get to earth it can't make sharp turns.

Although lightning rods coupled with a heavy conductor leading to a rod stuck several feet down into the earth may help avoid damage to buildings on land, a boat's access to ground is not nearly so straightforward. Between the keel or grounding plate and earth is water, and to get to earth the charge must pass through it. This may explain why boats in lakes sustain more damage from strikes than those in the ocean, salt water being a better conductor than fresh.

Besides providing a path to earth in the event of a strike, another desirable move is to try to equalize the potential (voltage) among all the metal components of the boat. This is because voltage differences encourage electrical leaps, called side flashes, within the boat. In an attempt to avoid these leaps, bonding has become standard practice with most boat builders. Bonding involves connecting all major metal and electrical systems, standing rigging, lifelines, auxilliary engine, rudder, binnacle, and all electronics to each other and to ground. This supposedly keeps every bonded member at the same potential.

The trouble with electrical bonding is that even the best systems are imperfect, and the high voltages and magnetic effects that resonate during a lightning strike will create voltage differences anyway, but far less, if your boat is bonded.

Does this mean we should abandon all hope for lightning protection? No. Tests indicate that struck boats that have a lightning protection system (LPS) fare *somewhat* better in avoiding hull damage than boats without.

When it comes to electronics damage, however, the advantage difference is insignificant. Is bonding worth the extra cost? Yes, on the premise that anything we can do to lower the chance of lightning damage is worthwhile. So if you're buying a new boat, you'll probably want to insist on a bonding system, as it's much easier to put one in while the boat is being built than to add it later.

There's a theory, now relegated to myth, that lightning will strike the highest mast around. A newer theory states that lightning 'sees' height differences in 150-foot increments. Thus a mast under 150 feet high is the same height as sea level. Or, to put it another way, the difference in height of masts under 150 feet has little or no relation to a likelihood of being struck. However, the height theory is still true when it comes to larger differences, such as skyscrapers, radio towers, etc.

And if you believe that masts, tall or short, make no difference, the question becomes: "Is a boat that's struck by lightning the victim of random choice, or is there some feature that made it more attractive to a bolt than the surrounding surface of the earth or the ocean?"

It's presently agreed by most theorists that strikes are encouraged by a buildup of an electrostatic charge on the struck object. Boats passing through the water and masts passing through moist air are thought to collect ions. Does this attract lightning?

A long-standing theory still held by the American Boat and Yacht Council (ABYC) concerns the so-called 'cone of protection'. With a lightning protection system, the tip of the mast is like the apex of a cone, of which the surface of the water is the base. The area of protection varies in size depending on which expert you talk to. The ABYC still goes with a cone whose apex angle is 90 degrees. In most cases, this means that your whole boat is in it. Many two-masted boats mount a lightning rod on each. Owners of stubby masted boats should be aware that the whole hull may not be in this protected zone. But don't worry too much about it: its existence is uncertain anyway.

Another approach to understanding what's happening might be this: A thunder cloud builds up a negative charge on its lower surface. (If it were a positive charge, the polarities we're talking about would be reversed.) The negative charge organizes the ions within its sphere of influence—i.e., the surface of the earth underneath it. This 'organizing' consists in attracting the positively charged ions and repelling those that are negatively charged. On a boat, when a thundercloud passes over, the positively charged ions are sucked up to the top of the mast. The air acts as an insulator, however, so there are no leaps (bolts) until the potential difference reaches a certain point. Or until humidity and rain make the air a less efficient insulator; or, or, or. . .

The above would be fairly easy to deal with if it were all that was going on. Unfortunately, we have to consider another phenomenon—the fact that unless you provide what a bolt considers a more desirable alternative, lightning will seek out electrostatically charged places anywhere on your boat. Lightning has been known to strike a burr on a screwhead, or a broken strand of wire on a shroud. This is because pointy places are thought to act as venturis, in the sense that electrical potential builds up there. Where there is a point, the potential can build up to a degree that the ions explode upward in what's called a streamer, which attracts lightning bolts. The sharper the point, the greater the charge buildup.

Enter the wire brushy thing, or static charge dissipator. The theory is that by putting what is essentially a special type of wire brush at the masthead, all the little pointy ends will expel (or allow to leak) the static charge from your masthead into the air in sub-critical quantities. The many points mean that no one location is going to build up a charge sufficient to attract a bolt. By bleeding off positively charged ions, we've supposedly neutralized the boat electrostatically.

And if true—lo and behold magic occurs—the yacht adopts the same electrical potential as the surface of the sea. It makes no difference that your mast is the highest thing around, lightning can't strike you even if it wants to *because it can't find you.*

Now that's my idea of good lightning theory. Right there under lightning's very nose you've donned an electrical camouflage suit and become invisible to bolts. Nancy says disdainfully that the comfort I get from this is analogous to the belief in magic claimed by the Polynesian fisherman.

Probably mounting an ion dissipator (referred to above as a wire brushy thing) at the masthead isn't a bad idea. That plus proper bonding and grounding is the best that the creative theorists can come up with for the moment. Note, however, that while the proponents of dissipators claim that the charged ions are blown away, another expert claims that they in fact can hang around, thus supercharging the air around the masthead. If true, this would *increase* the likelihood of a strike. Here logic tells me to embrace the 'blown away' theory—thunderstorms are windy, aren't they?

And yet another expert uses murky stuff like E fields and volts per meter and impedance and inverse proportion to prove that the earth provides energy 4,000 times faster than a dissipator can dissipate. If true, does this make dissipators virtually useless?

A final word about wire brushy things: statistics prove that radio towers and cellular phone installations have shown a dramatic decrease in lightning strikes after installing them. This is fact, so maybe we're making headway in the protection game after all.

Personal safety during thunderstorms. By bonding all large metal systems together electrically, you've taken a giant step toward personal safety, as bonding is a defense against side flashes, or random leaps that might strike you.

Even with bonding, you will want to avoid touching two different metals, such as shroud and lifeline, or wheel and binnacle. At the instant of a strike, voltage differences may still occur, and you don't want to be a conductor.

Think of all the metal items that aren't included in a bonding system. I'm looking around the cabin and seeing bronze portholes, a propane cabin heater, a fire extinguisher. Best is not to touch any.

Steps to take to avoid becoming a conductor: stay dry, or if you must be outside, wear foulies—oilskins are better insulators than fabric. Either install a leather cover on the wheel, or wear gloves, preferably rubber, or both. Never go barefoot.

Somewhere I read about a guy who, in order to avoid conductor-hood, developed the habit of always steering with one hand in his pocket. I consider men who do this suspect.

To throw a final twig on our growing blaze of confusion, an article in the December 1993 issue of *Practical Sailor* advises us "to remain low in the boat" during a thunderstorm, while an article in the June 1994 issue advises us to "stay as high above the waterline as possible." Thus in the case of a couple with dependent children, one of you should probably stay in the cockpit while the other hides below. But to hell with that, I say. Nancy and I no longer have dependent children, but even if we did we would continue (high or low) to hold hands (bond) during a thunderstorm. And keeping our voltages equal has nothing to do with it.

One might think boats with wooden masts would be immune to lightning strikes, certainly far more immune than the metal-masted variety. Not true. There are many instances of yachts with wooden masts having been hit by lightning while they sat in a marina stuffed with aluminum masts. There go myths 5a and 6b: Lightning always strikes the highest thing around (nope), and will always choose a metal path to ground over a wooden one (double nope).

Let's go back on land for a minute. We used to think that trees were hit because they are tall. Now one theory is that twiggy branches provide points, and we've already discussed how bolts are attracted to points. Or perhaps trees, caressed by a moist wind and falling rain, build up an irresistible static electrical charge. The latter theory, I suppose, could apply to a wooden boat's mast.

I remember once seeing Saint Elmo's fire during a passage on SEA FOAM. It happened when the sky was alive with electronic hanky-panky, and I felt as though our old lady, wanting to be a part of it, had put a flower in her hair. Saint Elmo's eerie glow, obviously electric in origin, was a kind of green, radiant ball at the mainmast head. It grew in size and brightness, as invitational as the knowing grin of a woman of the night, and I was sure I was about to witness SEA FOAM's deflowering.

Then, as mysteriously as it had come, it went away. I can only conclude that unusual conditions built up a static charge at the masthead which then, somehow, was bled off. What activated it? Darned if I know. What de-activated it? Same answer. I only know the masthead turned on like a middle-aged housewife at a Barry Manilow concert.

This, of course, was a wooden boat with a wooden mast, and no lightning protection system. Hiscock, who wrote of the phenomenon, also had at the time a wooden boat with a wooden mast. I don't know of any boat with a grounded metal mast that's experienced the awesome wonder of Saint Elmo, but I'm told it happens.

But if Saint Elmo's fire is the result of a buildup of electrical potential, why isn't every occurrence of it a precursor to a lightning strike?

A cruising friend, an electronics professional, told me of a time when he was at sea in his aluminum-hulled, aluminum-masted boat and saw a black cloud approaching. He next noticed a dark line running through the sky from his masthead to that cloud. As the cloud approached and then passed him, the line connecting it to his masthead followed, and only disappeared when the cloud was far behind him. He was able to put names to the phenomenon, like 'charged moisture particles' and 'ion stream'; but no, he couldn't explain it.

Protecting the electronics. If somehow you forgot to put aboard a large lead container for carrying radioactive materials, you won't be able to put your electronic devices inside it during a thunderstorm. Some folks, lacking such a box, hide as many of their electronics as possible in their stove's oven. Hiding them in the stove is a very satisfying tactic. The fact that this won't necessarily save them from ambient radiation if the boat is hit is of secondary importance. Mother didn't worry about the efficacy of mustard plasters on the chest, either; it was the 'there, there' that was important. By enstoving the toys, the skipper and crew feel in control, and the act of nurturing gets their minds off their plight. If you do this, however, try to remember to remove the toys before starting a recipe that tells you to preheat the oven to 450 degrees.

For enstovers: it's a myth (sayeth a guru) that motorists are protected from strikes because they're insulated from earth by rubber tires. The truth of the matter (the guru continues) is that the driver and passengers are protected because they're encapsulated in a metal box. (Such as a stove? Hmm.)

In my opinion, one of the best discussions on lightning protection is *Lightning and Boats: A Manual of Safety and Prevention*, by Michael V. Huck, Jr. Huck claims that the *metal* box that contains the device is its best protection if *the box itself is tied into the grounding and/or bonding system*. The ambient radiation, made up of what are called side flashes, generates a surface charge, which, if drained off to ground, is less likely to allow damage to electronics within. And Huck points out that the ground wire in the power cord is not enough; the box must have its own ground.

Thought for enstovers: if such be true, why not use a heavy cable with alligator clips such as an auto jumper cable—every boat should have one—to *ground the stove* during thunderstorms?

And a question I'd like to have answered: of the sailboats I know of that have suffered lightning damage, several have been under way, and all those under way have been motor sailing. Is the friction of the churning propeller in the water building up a static charge, much like scuffing leather soles across a wool carpet? Is it worth considering *not* to motorsail in a thunderstorm? I think so.

Disconnecting electronics from power, ground and antenna might save the stuff from spikes. But unfortunately the tremendous radiation that accompanies a lightning strike is what's most likely to cause damage. We usually do disconnect, but we keep one GPS operating, simply because thunderstorms often come at night and blow like mad, and if I'm dragging anchor, I want to know where and how much.

We were sitting in a small bay in Belize a few months ago when a bolt and its thunder occurred simultaneously. I have this feeling that if you're hit by a lightning bolt, you'll know it, so my guess is this was very close but not a bullseye. Thereafter our depth meter didn't function. If you're into *post hoc, ergo propter hoc*, a case can be made for radiational damage. I guess I'm too suspicious of theories to buy that, but any alternative relies pretty heavily on coincidence, of which I'm also suspicious. Your choice.

One last RED SHOES lightning story. We originally installed a strobe light at the top of the mast. When it stopped working several years ago, I decided the expense of replacing it was more than my rare use of a strobe light warranted, so I disconnected the positive lead at the breaker panel.

Recently, while anchored off Key West during a thunderstorm, we had a few very close strikes. After the storm I looked up and saw that the strobe was flashing! Because it wasn't connected except to ground, I wasn't able to turn it off till I'd reconnected it.

And, reconnected, it still works.

A final final suggestion: you should be aware of your hair. If during a thunderstorm the hair on the nape of your neck stands up, you can bet that a lightning strike is imminent. So look for an NFS (Necknape Field Strength) meter to come on the marine market in the near future. (On the other hand, hair awareness might do nothing more than warn you that tomorrow's reports of your death will not be exaggerated.)

That's about it for lightning, except that I generally add a few strategically timed "Now I lay me"s during thunderstorms. Episcopalian parents scare their kids, too.

CHAPTER 34

Man Overboard

Dear Herb: I have nightmares about my husband falling overboard at night. In my dream I wake up and he's gone, and I'm all alone. I can't go cruising until I've dealt with this particular, consuming fear.

Anxious Mate

Dear AM: I hope before leaving you will have become PM (Prepared Mate). You're certainly worrying about something real. But before we move on to the subject of your letter, I want to congratulate you on the success of your marriage. You'd be surprised at the number of letters I get asking not "how can I help my husband who's fallen overboard?" but "how can I help him *fall* overboard?"

Let's talk about some things you can do as preparation, many of which are simply common sense.

Have the person on watch wear red or orange foulies, or, if it's hot and tropical, a red or orange tee-shirt. We did a little experiment on SEA FOAM before ever leaving California. You might want to try it with your husband. In broad daylight, with a two-foot chop and three-foot swells, we threw over a blue cockpit cushion, continued on course for a mere five minutes, then turned and held a reciprocal course. We did the same thing with an orange cushion. We found the orange cushion with no problem. *We never found the blue cushion, even after a half-hour search!*

At night, have him or her carry a flashlight. Some people say to carry a whistle, but if the engine's going you're not likely to hear it. And in most cases the searcher (as opposed to the searchee) will have taken the sails down and started the engine for easier maneuverability. On the other hand, if I've fallen overboard while clipped onto the jackline and am just dragging alongside on my tether, perhaps a whistle would worm its way into Nancy's dreams.

Herb at mast. We often wore a harness, but the cumbersome bulk of most PFD's, plus tropical temperatures, lead most sailors to do without except in extreme conditions.

When leaving the safety of the cockpit, make it a rule to wear some kind of flotation device. Most people, even those who are religious about wearing a safety harness and clipping onto a jackline, don't do this. Of course, the higher the latitude, the more clothes you're likely to be wearing, and the more important flotation becomes.

Many people trail a long line behind the boat at night. A polypropylene water ski tow rope (it floats and has a handle on the end) would be perfect, but any line will do. Tie a large knot at the end of it to facilitate hanging on.

We suggest this because we know of two cases where a man had fallen overboard and was saved because of either a trailing line or a fish line. In case one, a single-hander hung on for several hours. The boat was sailing too fast for him to be able to pull himself to safety, so he just dragged along till it went up on Australia's Barrier Reef. In case two, the man hung on until the wife woke up for her watch and missed him. Then she cut the line . . . (just kidding.)

A worthwhile refinement of the above might be to have an alarm sound as soon as the weight of the man overboard puts extra drag on the line. Radio Shack and other stores sell an alarm that sounds when a pin is pulled out of the socket, activation analogous to that of a hand grenade. Something with such an alarm, a slip knot and a trip line should be easy to put together.

If the boat is sailing slowly enough that the searchee can haul himself up to the stern, is there a swim ladder that can be lowered by a person in the water? If not, how does he get back aboard?

All the above assumes the searchee is conscious, uninjured, and able to act on his or her own behalf. When this is not the case, the problems of both search and retrieval are increased geometrically. It's too bad they haven't come up with an electronic diagnostic device that transmits the physical condition of the searchee. If you got a message like "the subject broke his neck and has gone down for the third time," you wouldn't even have to turn around.

Let's say it's my off watch and I come up to find Nancy missing. Given the present state of our relationship, I'll be concerned. Frantic, even. However, the procedure I'll follow will have been discussed thoroughly between us so that a) I don't panic, and b) I have a step-by-step plan.

1. We're probably on autopilot or windvane, so first I note the course we're sailing, and add 180 degrees to get the reciprocal.

2. I punch the 'event' or 'mark' button on the GPS, entering our present position as a way point. I write down the way point number.

   (The 'man overboard' button on our GPS is a pain in the neck. It locks the instrument into an alarm mode wherein it beeps incessantly. I can't think of anything more effective at making me lose my cool. I'd choose to use the 'event' button, which does the same thing without locking up or beeping.)

3. I turn the boat around. The situation: wind strength, direction; are we running or reaching? will determine whether I take all the sails down or not. The important thing is to follow, if at all possible, a reciprocal course. If it's blowing hard and I make little progress dead against it under power, I must make short tacks.

   There's a question here about what to do with the sails. What kind of rig do we have? How strong and reliable is the auxiliary? I'm going to have to douse all sail when I'm trying to get Nancy back aboard. With that in mind, I douse all sail now. Or, finding that I need sail to make any progress, I leave only the roller reefing jib out and motor sail.

About now I'm feeling the pressure of time and it's making me frantic. I tell myself to relax. A few extra minutes can result in an organized search rather than a helter-skelter one. An organized search is far more likely to succeed, and the few minutes needed for preparation will make far less difference than I fear. This is true in the tropics. In colder climates, speed becomes of vital importance because of hypothermia.

4. Let's say it's possible to run the rhumb line of the reciprocal course. Because the autopilot will steer better than I, especially when I'm distraught, I set it. Then I check the log.

Nancy was supposed to have logged our GPS position every hour. By noting the last position, I know she went overboard after that time. And now, in addition to, and more accurate than, a reciprocal compass course, I have a GPS way point (her logged entry) to head for. Having entered that, even if I'm tacking I can stay pretty close to the rhumb line by using the off-course feature of the GPS.

5. We've probably been sailing with just the masthead tricolor for navigation lights. Nancy will see it, and if she's not disabled she'll shine her flashlight at me. I turn off all other lights, as they inhibit my night vision.

6. If in spite of all this, maybe because of current, strong winds, big seas, I fail to find her on the first pass, I do a one-eighty and head back toward the way point I punched in just before turning around.

7. Worst case: with all the care I've exercised so far, I still haven't found her. Now I build a grid on the chart, I figure that current and wind are flowing in the same direction (the usual case, except in oceanic rivers such as the Gulf Stream, or the Guiana Current, or the like), so my next pass will take that into account. From then on I make overlapping passes, much like mowing a lawn. By this time, unless she's sunk or is wearing blue or green, I should have found her.

One thing that keeps me hopeful happened to us aboard SEA FOAM on a passage from Suvarov in the Cook Islands to American Samoa. SEA FOAM had name boards. They were red, matching the sheer stripe, and the lettering was in gold leaf. For some reason I can't remember we lost both the name board and the smaller home port board. I was for sailing on, but Nancy was insistent that we at least try to recover them. So we turned back. Hand steering a reciprocal course, we powered against the trades, and after 45 minutes we found both boards. This has stuck in my mind, the fact that sailing a reciprocal course works, and that the color red stands out on a blue ocean like a bare nipple in the front pew.

So, is it okay to fall overboard?

No, no, and no!

Let us say we did the above and the person overboard has been found. Now all we have to do is get him or her aboard. This is when the money you invested in a Lifesling gets paid back. We deploy it. We also lower the swim ladder in case we have to go overboard. But Nancy, although too weak to climb the swim ladder, is able to get herself into the Lifesling, so we don't.

What's the situation now? Let's say it's the worst: the wind is blowing 20-25, the seas are up, and RED SHOES is God's hackey sack. We've taken the sails down and are lying ahull, which means that we're wallowing in the troughs, rocking through an arc of 40 degrees. If I use the main halyard to retrieve Nancy, she'll swing like a pendulum and crash into the hull. So I've clipped the main halyard to the end of the boom just in case the topping lift fails, and have prevented the boom outboard with the Lifesling tackle rigged. This takes long enough that Nancy begins to think I'm fluffing off. Nancy clips herself on and I winch her up. Now she's hanging outboard. With a little luck I can control the boom, and am able to bring Nancy more or less amidships and lower her to the deck.

I wonder how much of this Nancy could do if our positions were reversed. Rigging the Lifesling tackle is something we haven't practiced. Oh well, maybe I'd be strong enough to come up the swim ladder on my own.

In the case of an older couple with no extra crew, a man overboard situation in rough weather at night, though not hopeless, is certainly desperate. If the searchee is injured, the situation imagined above becomes far worse. So? Common sense says, *do everything you can think of to reduce the risk of falling overboard.*

We always wear a safety harness at sea on night watch. If I have to go forward in rough weather, I get Nancy topside—neither of us is to go forward alone at night even clipped on. I always have a handhold, and it's never a lifeline.

I strongly recommend having sissy bars (more commonly called a mast pulpit) at the base of the mast. Although we've tried to obviate the need to leave the cockpit, things come up. The clevis pin came out of the gooseneck, for example, and in rough seas I had to put it back together. Sometimes a batten gets caught in the lazy jacks when raising the main, and if the sail won't shake itself loose when I loosen the halyard, I have to go to the mast. I always have to go to the mast to attach the halyard, and to douse the sail. We don't have sissy bars on RED SHOES, and as a result I've spent far too many hours hanging on with one hand and attempting impossible feats with the other.

With both an autopilot and a windvane, it's unlikely either of us will be glued to the helm. If we were, and I had to urinate, I would use a can or just pee into the cockpit. If it were Nancy, she'd have to call me to steer while she went to the head; or, as a last resort, pee in her pants. It's a truism that half the drowned men whose bodies are recovered have their flies open. Would someone please explain this to me?

RED SHOES' rig has been described. The watch stander is almost never required to leave the cockpit. Maybe on a tack the jib sheet catches on something. I must leave the cockpit to rig a running backstay, but usually I do this before sunset, while Nancy is present. If we must tack during the night, thus requiring shifting runners, we're both awake and topside. I can't think of anything else, and deem our ability to reef from the cockpit one of our best defenses against falling overboard.

We didn't install a mast pulpit. This was a mistake. Although I can do two reefs from the cockpit, dropping the mainsail completely always requires me to go to the mast to haul down the sail. To furl it I must work at the boom. This is a time at which I am most vulnerable. At night, it is rarely necessary to drop the main completely, but it has happened. Nancy is always summoned to the cockpit while I go to the mast.

The roll-aboard. I have stretched my imagination countless times replaying the drama of retrieving a partner in rough seas. Only one of my *what ifs* has a happy ending.

Since 1970 my brother Mike has been disabled by a paralytic disease called Guillain-Barré's syndrome. Mike and his wife, Barbara, have visited us several times. They both love to snorkel. Mike, however, can only get back into the inflatable when he's standing in shallow water. This eliminates most good snorkeling spots.

For his last visit I had a friend, a canvas worker, put together something we'll call a roll-aboard. It's made from a three- by seven-foot piece of strong, canvas-like fabric, Sunbrella. One end has two grommets, which are secured to the inside of the dinghy—our RIB has conveniently located padeyes. The other end has a broomstick in a sleeve. The sleeve is interrupted in the center, so it's possible to attach three lines to the broomstick: one at each end, and one in the middle.

We lay the roll-aboard out on the water. Mike swims into it. Then two people in the dinghy pull on the lines. The fabric makes a kind of cradle, or sling. Pulling up the one side gives the pullers a mechanical advantage of 2:1. In fact, Nancy and Barbara were able to bring Mike aboard with incredible ease.

Two points: the canvas needs a couple of strategically placed weights so that it will sink and form a cradle. Point two: we learned immediately that Mike was going to roll like a log as he's pulled aboard, and that it worked best when he lay with his back to the dinghy at the onset. This brought him up onto the top of the tube on his stomach.

There is no reason that a similar device wouldn't work to bring someone aboard a yacht. The dimensions might have to be changed. But I can see that one person on deck, having clipped a line to the safety harness of the person overboard, could, from on deck, maneuver him or her into the cradle of the roll-aboard. Then, with the help of a halyard, he could easily roll the person aboard. There would be no pendulum action to bang the body around, as the device would keep the body pressed to the side of the yacht.

In rough seas, canvas material could have drawbacks. As the yacht rolls, the canvas can act as a sea anchor. Its interaction with the water might be inconvenient. Therefore a net, or some net-like material, or a cross-hatch made from nylon strapping, would doubtless work better in rough sea conditions. It could bring other things aboard, too, such as one of those bales of marijuana people tell me they've seen floating at sea, or a mermaid, or that 150-pound tarpon you played for the last three hours. With such potential for usefulness, how could you not cram one aboard?

POSTSCRIPT: The November 1996 issue of *SAIL* Magazine had an article on man overboard stuff, and it looks as if the roll-aboard is an idea whose time has come. Write, phone or fax *EasyLift*, C-level Inc., 58 South Gate Lane, Southport, CT 06490, tel. 800 998 8683 fax 203 254 3770 or *Jason's Cradle* (high tech and expensive), Land and Marine Products, Inc., 77 Third Street, Newport, RI 02840, tel. 401 841 9800, fax 401 841 0771 for their raising-from-the-drink devices. But there's one thing to remember about building or inventing your own—you'll play around with it until you feel comfortable using it, a factor that could make a crucial difference in an emergency.

CHAPTER 35

Abandon-Ship Bag

Dear Herb: My husband wants to know what we should put into our distress bag?

Written for Pessimist out of Pascagoula

Dear Poop: That's a good question. How long do you plan to be out there?

If a couple of days, then maybe an Alice Hoffman novel, a Walkman, six of your favorite tapes, a Sterno stove, a couple of saucepans, four gallons of water, and a half dozen Seal-a-meals.

If a couple of weeks: a watermaker, six novels, a Walkman, 24 of your favorite tapes, extra batteries, a Sterno stove, a couple of saucepans, fishing gear, four six-packs, and enough trail food for an extended hike.

If a couple of months: a watermaker, a large notebook and pens (you write your own novel), a Walkman, 96 of your favorite tapes, fishing gear, a Sterno stove, a couple of saucepans, 9 Seal-a-meals for Sunday dinners, trail food, C-rations, vitamins, and a case of rum.

If a whole year: a watermaker, 2 large notebooks and pens, fishing gear, trail food, C-rations, a portable hydroponic garden, a dwarf lime tree (bearing), and, unless you're an obstetrician, two gross of condoms. You might also bring a copy of the book *Alive*, which rationalizes cannibalism, although hopefully the question won't come up.

All this presupposes you have a second grab bag with the EPIRB, flares, handheld VHF, handheld GPS, extra batteries, sunblock, hats, long sleeved shirts, long silk trousers, sun glasses, and everything Dave Barry ever wrote.

Damn, I forgot the cat. Bring cat food, litter and litter box, and at least one toy.

There.

Nancy and I attended Weight Watchers for several weeks. The national sales rep, an attractive woman with a sensational figure, spoke to our group about temptation. Hers was Snickers bars. Whenever she flies, which is often, she carries a carton of the candy bars with her. If the pilot ever announces, "Fasten your seat belts and prepare for a crash landing," she's going to eat the whole box.

I feel the same way about mayonnaise. You might include a similar treat for the day you give up hope. But don't give up hope. I believe it was the Baileys who, their yacht having been attacked by whales, took to the life boat and were adrift for 117 days. They spent much of their time discussing designs for a new cruising boat!

I would plot novels, short stories; maybe mentally rehearse jazz tunes on the piano. Nancy might imagine recipes, or, if that proved to be too stimulating, invent a mental bridge game. Bring a Rubicube.

Bring passports, boat papers, and your insurance policy. You may be washed up on the shores of Singapore where it's very expensive, so bring money and credit cards. Don't leave without American Express. And bring your driver's license in case you want to rent a car.

To inspire survival, bring pictures of your children and grandchildren. You wouldn't want to miss their growing up, would you?

Just to be on the safe side, forgive all those who have trespassed against you.

And of course, before leaving home, both of you made sure that the executor of your estates had copies of the following documents:

Will or Trust.

Living will, which states that in the event of your (natural) death, any of your organs may be used for food.

Promissory notes.

Mortgages.

Insurance policies.

Social Security numbers.

Any other financial documents.

Diskettes of backed-up computer files.
      Include your highest Tetris score.

It's a fact that people can survive a lot longer without food than without water, so the Power Survivor watermaker should be a number one priority. Sunblock, and perhaps an old parachute to keep you in the shade (which slows dehydration) would be good. Dehydrated foods are concentrated, and with a watermaker they'd be space-saving practical.

With the modern EPIRBs that tell searchers not only where you are but what you're wearing and your mother's maiden name, you shouldn't be out there all that long. Bring along a handheld VHF radio so you can chat with your nice rescuers as they approach. Take along a handheld GPS so you can tell whoever's coming to rescue you exactly where you are. With the information network expanding daily, you're safe. So don't worry about getting rescued. It's all part of new age cruising.

A nervous peek at the future: Cassandras and I-Chingers are warning that eventually there'll be so many of us out there taking to our liferafts, rescue resources will be overwhelmed. They see it coming down to, "Are you worth saving?"

Thus, in preparation for ocean cruising, sailing schools are recommending that you add the following info to your EPIRB registration (you did register it, didn't you?): A list of your Sea Scout merit badges; any marooned cruisers you've rescued; and a sworn statement that you've never created large wakes in five mile-per-hour zones, flushed your MSD in restricted areas, or illegally painted your bottom with tin-based paint.

CHAPTER 36

Insurance

Dear Herb: I really don't understand you. You said in your lecture that you and Nancy put all your eggs into one boat, as it were, yet you left as inexperienced sailors without insurance. If there's any logic to such a decision, I surely don't see it. You preach common sense, but in matters financial you don't show a shred of it.

Heavily Insured and Cautious in Kingston

Dear HICK: You have stumbled and fallen face first into the dreamer's dichotomy. Common sense only applies to the steps we take to safeguard our boat and our selves. The decision to go cruising in the first place was, I grant you, quixotic.

On the other hand, maybe it wasn't.

Let's pose a few questions. I'm not an adversary in this case, but rather a fellow seeker of answers. It is indeed a radical decision to turn everything you own into cash, which you then turn into a boat. But more and more people are doing this. Why? Specifically, why did we do it?

I'll answer the insurance question first. Before leaving on SEA FOAM, we investigated blue water coverage offered by various companies, and found them all too expensive. We could have cruised for six months on the price of a year's insurance. Did we have enough money to start over in the event of disaster? No, we barely had enough money to start. We didn't buy insurance for the simple reason we couldn't afford it, and that's about as practical as you can get. Instead, we took extra care, which is a form of insurance in itself.

But why did we put all our eggs in one boat in the first place? That's the real question.

Remember the cartoon character Alfred E. Newman in *MAD* Magazine, with the balloon over his head that said "What, me worry?" In fact, he worried about everything. And he was me, and a lot of other guys. I worried about tomorrow as if it were guillotine day. I was a paranoid hypochondriac with deep feelings of insecurity for which I could never find a reason.

Looking back, I've come to believe that it takes more courage of a certain kind to stay in suburbia and do the expected thing than it does to sell out and sail off. I came to a point where I realized that my talent was modest, that I would never become a star in the galaxy of fame. If I didn't change I would, for the rest of my life, do my best, pay my debts, and finally die the mediocre middle class man that I really was. And if that sounds a little strong, I intend it to, because those are some of the feelings that *allowed* me to act quixotically. And for those feelings I shall be eternally grateful.

Money is not the only thing one has to spend. The other thing is a life. The difference is that you never know how much is in the bank, or what your balance is. Your life is your inheritance. As soon as you realize this, you start trying to spend it wisely. Nice, round, imposing thoughts. But what do they mean? They meant, to me, make changes. Radical changes. We made the changes blindly, having no idea what we'd discover about ourselves in the process.

I've said this before, but I'm going to repeat it in case you, too, suffer from the same thing I did. Middle class malaise is more than discontent. It's being worried and unhappy without being able to pinpoint the cause. It's anxiety.

I suddenly realized that I haven't used the word anxiety more than a dozen times since we went cruising. Because anxiety to me has a special meaning. It's a general angst. Some of it stems from my upbringing, which said that if you make regular trips to the doctor for a checkup and keep up with your insurance premiums and make yourself enough money to keep you in beef and gin and attend services at least on holy days, you'll be safe. So you do those things, but the Truth, which lives within all of us no matter how badly we treat it, says it's a lie. You aren't safe, you've just managed to bury any and all recognition of what the threats are.

So I worried about cancer, and monetary debt, and why my palms would run with sweat whenever I drove in rush hour traffic, and the sins I was piling up, and all the other stand-ins we invent for Death. "You'll never get out of this life alive," is the barstool wisdom. As soon as you admit that there's going to be an end to your life, you begin to be concerned with what, to my mind, is the only existential concern: what do I want to do with what I have left?

Of course the answer to that is different for everyone, and this is a good thing, as there're too many of us out here already. The waters are crowded, and all the neat, secret places are being filled up. But that's okay. Doing something is one thing. What's important is how you do it, and knowing why you're doing it. When a man sails his Columbia 45 to waypoint #352, drops his anchor in a lonely lagoon of glass-clear water and looks around at whispering palm trees and beaches of golden sand and asks, "What's all the fuss about?" you know that GPS or not, that man is lost.

For us the decision to cut loose and go cruising was radical and wrenching, and I'm grateful for that, too. It was a time of changes, many of which were painful. After all the pain and problems, I was damn well going to discover something important, whether it was out there or not.

And of course it wasn't out there, ever; it was inside me, and out there was merely the environment that allowed me to see it. Because cruising is an environment where cause and effect are tangible and identifiable. For someone who is always going to worry no matter what, cruising is the greatest possible medium. There are so many real things to worry about on a voyage, and real things to do about them, who in his right mind would need to create more?

None of this came to me in a Eureka flash. It came in bits and pieces. One piece: We were delivering a leaky boat that would surely take on water beyond our ability to pump it out if we ran into a serious and enduring storm. I was worrying, as usual, about every little thing. Tired of my fretting, Nancy finally brought me out of it.

"Come on, Herb, what's the worst thing that could happen?"

"We could die," I said.

"Exactly," she said, and went back to her book.

Insurance exists as a symptom of our middle class desire for safety. But the safety it offers, in my opinion, is a chimera. Because we decided against insurance as being too expensive, I discovered that sailing uninsured was part of the package. To perform on the high wire without a net is risky, but it sure motivates you to practice.

Today aboard RED SHOES our situation is different. We don't own the boat, so we have a responsibility to the people who do. Here are a few facts:

> In the nearly nine years we've had the use of this boat, we've paid out over $13,000 in premiums.

> Because one company that insured us went belly up, there was a two-month period when we were not insured. Guess when we incurred our only coverable damage?

> After our original policy was canceled, we aborted our decision to transit the Panama Canal and cross the Pacific to cruise Asia primarily because we couldn't find another company that would insure us.

Some insurance companies have a bad reputation when it comes to honoring claims, but that coin has two sides. I remember the professional skipper who had two boats to care for during Hurricane Hugo. He brought both into the mangrove creek and tied them up right behind RED SHOES. We talked about what we were doing, and how, and I guess he was satisfied with our defense just as I was satisfied with his.

During the storm, the skipper checked his charges while wearing a motorcycle helmet with a Plexiglas face shield. At one point, a line to a mangrove tree either parted or came loose, and he swam into the mangroves to re-tie it. We talked on the radio during the storm. When it was all over, neither his two boats nor RED SHOES had suffered damage.

After the storm, the skipper was able to get in touch with the boat owners by radio, and to reassure them that due to his sterling judgement and performance, neither had suffered any damage. One of the owners asked him, "Gee, can't you fake something? I'd sure like to get a nice, fat check from the insurance company." The skipper, furious, told the owner what he could do with his boat.

Six years later we were in the Bay Islands of Honduras, anchored in the outer section of French Harbor, Roatán. A nasty squall came through at

A motorcycle helmet with Plexiglas face shield protected this skipper's face from flying debris during Hurricane Hugo.

2 A.M., and our anchor, which had been tested in various conditions over a period of several days, was snatched out of the bottom. We dragged down on a beautiful Amel 48, and our Aries mount did serious cosmetic damage to its right front topside.

On our arrival in Roatán, we collected two months of accumulated mail. It contained a notice that our insurer had canceled all yacht policies due to financial problems. The owners of the Amel had had their policy canceled as well.

Next morning I pointed out the damage to Edwin, the skipper of the Amel, and we assessed it glumly. Edwin had had his topsides painted with Imron in Venezuela less than two years before.

A local Roatánian, Sherman Arch, was known for his excellent fiberglass work. The problem would lie in matching the color, a shade the Venezuelans had arrived at by adding a bit of this, a bit of that. There was a small amount of the original paint left over, but either because of its age or the way it was thinned, it refused to dry after Sherman applied it. Removing it took forever: the gluey mess was totally resistant to solvents.

The Amel owners were understandably worried. If Sherman couldn't match the color, what would we do? We were lucky. Sherman finally got the bad paint removed and was able to match the color perfectly with other paint. The Amel owners were satisfied. Sherman's bill was only $240. Had we been back in the States, in similar circumstances, a damaged party would have insisted on a new Imron job, and the bill would have been thousands of dollars.

Even legitimate claimants no longer think in terms of inexpensive solutions. Scratch my boat? Nothing less than repainting the topsides will do, as long as the insurance company is picking up the tab.

If we all acted responsibly and honestly toward our insurers, the problems of high premiums and stringent qualifications would shrink. I'll never forget when, while we were cruising the South Pacific on SEA FOAM, State Farm came out with an affordable blue water policy. I'm sure they based their premiums on the then available statistics for yacht losses. What they failed to account for was the gleam in certain eyes. During the two years the inexpensive policies were offered, the loss of yachts by sinking or grounding on coral reefs in remote areas of the Pacific increased dramatically. Some boats would sink within weeks of their owners having stripped them of equipment. We once saw an insured skipper rowing shoreward, his dinghy piled high with sails, sheets and halyards. "My boat just sank," he told us, grinning happily.

The Seven Seas Cruising Association tried to organize coverage for their members. You become a Commodore of the SSCA only after having fulfilled certain conditions involving passagemaking. You're recommended for Commodorehood by other Commodores who know and respect not only your seamanship, but your determination to 'leave a clean wake' with all its shades of meaning. The board of the SSCA went to underwriters with the notion that the members, being experienced, would be preferred risks. For some reason, associate members were included, although all you needed to become an Associate was the ability to write a check for $29.

One underwriter agreed to the deal. I understand that during the next two or three years, in addition to the predictable number of claims for loss or damage, the company paid claims for over *four hundred* 'lost' dinghies.

The SSCA-sponsored blue water policy had been interesting to us because boats of any length were covered even while crossing oceans; and the third crewmember requirement, standard with most U.S. insurers, was waived. Furthermore, the first year it was even less expensive than the cheapest local coverage. However, in three years the premium more than doubled, and the deductibles and restricted areas increased. As an example, we would have had a whopping 50% deductible if we suffered a loss during a named storm, usually a hurricane.

After that company's demise, we actively sought new insurance. Two European companies turned us down because we were a U.S. flag vessel, and European insurers were leery of U.S. citizens' penchant for taking everyone to court. As my London editor pointed out, we could have registered RED SHOES in another country and reapplied, but that would have presented a whole different set of problems.

The coverage we finally were able to get at a price we could afford was for the coasts of North America and the Caribbean, excepting, however, Cuba, Haiti and Colombia. The unused portion of the $1,700 premium we paid to the defunct company? We're still trying to get some of it back.

CHAPTER 37

Planning the Cruise

Dear Herb: What's this nonsense about planning? I want to go with the flow. I want to kick back, cast off and *cruise*, man. Poke my prow into the here and there. Mosey. The bore of planning is much of what I want to get away from. Capiche?

Siddhartha At Play

Dear SAP: If you lived on Casco Bay, Maine, you wouldn't go sailing in January, because most of the time ice would prevent your getting away from the dock. Best to plan for a thaw.

Okay, you say, but that's part of going with the flow. If the bay's frozen over, the river ain't flowing for sailors. When it thaws, you'll go with the flow.

Sophistry. Few if any cruisers disregard seasonal weather. When you walk down to the dock and see that your boat is locked into the ice pack, and you say, "Guess I'll wait for the thaw, hoar hoar," you're not only kicking back, you're planning. So let's assume that at least some aspects of planning are compatible with going with the flow. One cruises Maine in summer, and maybe in spring or fall. Guess I'll choose fall. That's plan A.

A friend informed me that cruisers don't have plans, they have intentions. But even intentions are subject to a concern for, if not subservience to, weather considerations. So you plan.

When you cast off, kick back, and cruise, do you have food on board? Spares? Fuel and water? Hey, man, that's planning. When you leave the harbor, do you turn left or right? North or south?

Enough nitpicking. We'll talk about *degrees* of planning. And if you still feel at the end that none of the shoes fit, you can go barefoot for all I care.

In an earlier chapter, I listed many of the places we visited in RED SHOES, but none of the Pacific islands we cruised to in SEA FOAM. Those destinations, of course, were the ones that inspired us to do all those anti-middle

Craig with seals. The Galápagos provided Craig and all of us with many wonderful experiences early in our cruising life.

class things we've discussed before. And first among places to visit were the Galápagos Islands of Ecuador.

The Galápagos had been the subject of at least one National Geographic article. Then there was Robin Graham's stopover, and William Robinson's, and almost everyone's who'd written articles about their South Pacific cruise, and the book *Galápagos, The Flow of Wilderness*, with its incredible color photos by Eliot Porter and text by Loren Eisley. If that weren't enough, we had 10-year-old Craig, whose rosy boa and king snake and hamsters and gerbils and guinea pigs were the bane of our Mexican housekeeper's existence, and who, when hearing we were going to the land of iguanas, interrupted his normally serious mien with a huge smile. I had read Charles Darwin's *Voyage of the Beagle*. We all longed to experience God's Disneyland, where the animals had yet to learn to know man as the enemy.

So we planned to go there. It wasn't hard—it is, after all, on the way to the Marquesas. Ah, the Marquesas, reputed to be the land of love: of canoes paddled by topless women bearing gifts of fruit; of wild, sexual dances that pique the most jaded imagination; of singing and hand-carved ukeleles; of lush, mountainous islands opening their arms to us voyagers. This in spite of the fact that centuries earlier, when the locals had opened their arms to whalers and pirates, they'd been given in exchange smallpox and the clap.

We planned to go there, too. And the beat goes on. As I write these words, I'm reminded that now, in the Galápagos, you pay royal fees, you're restricted to two harbors unless you take a guide aboard, and you're only allowed a short time to visit.

As for the Marquesas, all the French Polynesian islands now restrict cruisers to six months of the year. The other six months they've gotta be outta there. This is because there was a bad year in the 80's when several hurricanes roared through, damaging many cruising boats, leaving many cruisers in distress, and presenting the French with that which they most hate and which they'll go to almost any length to avoid, problems. Also, significant amounts of money are required from cruisers these days, either as a deposit in a French bank, or in the form of airplane tickets to the States, so that if you become a nuisance or a neck-hanging albatross, they can ship you out at your own expense.

Given the French xenophobia, the high prices, and the other restrictions, why would anyone want to go there?

The answer is July 14th. Bastille Day is the Polynesian answer to Carnival. Everyone turns out and turns on. There's dancing and parading and contests of strength and canoe races and costumes and consumings and carnalities. So if you're going to go there, you really ought to plan to be there in July.

That sort of covers the advisability of weather planning and event planning. It briefly suggests a need for money planning. You might think about putting aboard enough food, water and fuel to last till you get wherever you're going, and you might investigate what'll be available when you get there. Don't forget medical supplies.

If you move as slowly as we do, you'll need to renew your boat's anti-fouling paint along the way, so you might want to try to find out what haulout facilities are available, if the yard in question drops many boats, and what kinds of anti-fouling paint you can buy and at what price.

If you enjoy reading, don't forget to bring plenty of books. Your favorite novels, be they gothic romances, sexy and violent adventures, mysteries or technotales—you can never have enough. And bring a few serious books you've always wanted to read but haven't found time for. Time you'll have, and motivation aplenty when you've run out of pop fiction. Puzzles and games? Why not?

Once you've established where you want to go, and when you'd best be going there, it's time to make lists. Lists are like the Magic Pudding, and exemplify perfectly what is meant by a renewable resource. The more you take off the top, the more it grows at the bottom. Lists will never become endangered. The only time a list comes to an untimely end is when you've run out of paper.

Cruise Planning List:

1. Where are we going?

2. When's the best time to go there?

3. If there's a logical choice, what's the best route?

4. How long a passage does it entail?

5. What do I need to take?

   a. To eat and drink

   b. For the boat

   c. For fun

   d. To trade or give to locals

6. How much money do I need?
   How do I move it from point A to me?

7. Who fields my mail, pays my bills?
   If I don't do this, I'll need to cut up all my credit cards (thereby cutting myself off from a popular and effective way to move money around) and make a calendar of bills and other stuff that require periodic attention. In my case, these would include: pay veterans insurance; return the Coast Guard's yearly query regarding my boat documentation (and without which my document will be canceled); pay boat insurance; pay my memberships (SSCA and Authors Guild); and other things of which I'm reminded only when the bills and notices come in.

8. What shots do I need?
   The U.S. Bureau of Health will tell me, and give me my yellow card documenting compliance.

9. What shots does my pet need?

10. Passports; documentation of all the above.

11. How will people get in touch with me in an emergency?

    a. Ham friend? Ham net control operator?

    b. ATT marine telephone base (WOM in Florida, KMI in San Francisco). This would mean I'd need to check their traffic list regularly.

12. Foreign dictionaries and phrase books, if appropriate.
My friend learned Tahitian, and thereafter never had to pay for his drinks in French Polynesian bars. I knew French, and paid for all of mine.

About credit cards: the easiest way to get money in a foreign country is by a cash advance on VISA or MasterCard. These can of course be debit cards, where I put money in before I can take it out. (This should satisfy anybody's desire for debtlessness.) I can then arrange to have all expected checks that come my way to be automatically deposited to my debit card account. Any unexpected windfalls would be fielded by my friend or agent in the States.

The only credit card we decided to keep for our South Pacific cruise was American Express. It came in handy unexpectedly when the Fijian authorities in all their wisdom suddenly chose to require proof of financial responsibility before granting a visa extension. We didn't have nearly enough money, and were always on the edge of penury, waiting for the mail that would bring me notice that an article had sold. I did have my American Express card, however. I showed it to the officials, one of whom had a general idea of what it was. "Go ahead and give him a visa—when you have one of those cards, you can write a check for cash any time you want." His knowledge had a significant gap which I wasn't about to fill—that there had to be money in the bank on which the check was drawn.

You can dial ATT direct from most countries. By making calls on my ATT card, I pay roughly half what I'd pay if I went through the host country's operators.

So you may want to re-think dispensing with plastic.

Before we left for the South Pacific, Nancy and I hired a tutor to teach us celestial navigation. We later took a course in CPR. Both these skills, like any technique, require either practice or regular refreshing, otherwise we forget. With the advent of GPS I've become rusty with a sextant, and although my almanac has work forms in the back, we no longer carry the tables. I think I have somewhere a computer program that'll solve the navigational triangle, but the last time I looked I couldn't find it. That prompted me to buy a backup GPS. As for CPR, you'd better not rely on me if you have a heart attack, as I'd probably break your ribs or do something else vaguely inappropriate.

Cruise planning: it may sound too formal to someone who wants to escape the rigors of schedules and other exigencies. But the fact is, planning is inescapable. It's the degree of planning that's optional. Although careful planning may seem to deprive cruising of spontaneity, in the long run it will make your cruise safer and more pleasant.

By the way, as an ex-professional entertainer I can make a good case for "all spontaneity is rehearsed." Certainly, for most of us, spontaneity is a skill that must be learned and practiced like any other.

CHAPTER 38

Charts, Cruising Guides and Books

Dear Herb: I don't have a computer on board—wouldn't have one of the damn things. My boat is a Crealock 34. What reference books should I carry? As a matter of fact, could you talk about books in general? I'm a year away from casting off, and I love to read.

Space Conscious

Dear Spacey: So much depends upon your level of expertise. I'll make suggestions for various topics, but you alone can determine if those particular practical books are the ones you need.

Another consideration is "how can I enrich my visit to this place"— a sort of "beyond getting there" thought that gets us into a discussion of travel in general. I have a few ideas on this topic as well.

And, of course, while you're cruising you're a liveaboard. Is there a subject you've always wanted to explore more thoroughly? I mean, besides diesel engine repair? Because if you move at the snail's pace of most cruisers, you'll have many moments for contemplation.

I can't believe you don't like computers!

How to sail: No, I'm not being a smartass. There's a real difference between knowing how to make your boat move to the wind, and knowing how to sail. Knowing sail trim, sail shape, boat balance, weight distribution, and other fine points you might think are the bailiwick only of racers will enhance all those days you're going to be under sail. And yes, it's true that as often as possible we'll be sailing off the wind, where the fine points are pretty much superfluous. But no matter how often we say, chortling, 'Gentlemen don't sail upwind', the fact is we often have to. And when we must, doing it well not only shortens the time we have to spend doing it, but for me it adds much to the enjoyment.

I'm not going to suggest titles here, but rather that you go to your local marine or book store or library. You can also write to Armchair Sailor, Bluewater Books and other nautical book specialists for catalogs.

If you have the opportunity, thumb through a few books by different authors and choose one that appeals. I suggest this because for me, the tone the writer adopts is as important as the information provided. "Does he know what he's talking about?" is certainly important, but "does she have a sense of humor?" is a close second; is he opinionated beyond belief (so many of us are)? Does she sound snottily superior? If I'm studying this expert's ideas I'm going to be spending a lot of time with him.

I suppose here is as good a place as any to mention a cruiser we met in the Marquesas. Over the years he tore out informative articles from sailing magazines, and filed them away to take with him. We were delivering LISSA, a boat that sailed beautifully, and we knew we had a lot of weatherly sailing ahead. The rig, however, was improperly tuned, as the mast was kind of pretzelly under load. Because our own boat at the time was SEA FOAM, a boat with deadeyes and lanyards instead of turnbuckles, tuning was more a matter of taking out the slack than it was of applying tension. SEA FOAM's sloppy rig was forgiving, but it left me knowing nothing of the art of rig tuning. My dilemma was known throughout the anchorage, and the cruiser came to my aid with an article he pulled from his files.

Articles lose their value in direct proportion to your forgetting where they are. He had one of those expandable files and an exhaustive index, and went to 'Tuning the rig' without hesitation. His files were numerous, and covered about any nautical subject you could think of.

CHARTS AND CRUISING GUIDES

We talked about *charts* in an earlier chapter. I'll add one thought: My feelings about enough charts compare with Nancy's feelings about enough food. If she can't provision for six months, she's unhappy. I know of cruisers who voyage blithely with an obviously inadequate chart supply. One we heard of cruised the Kiribati Islands using commemorative postage stamps with pictures of the lagoons. They showed him where to look for the entrance, didn't they? Which is why we have over 400 charts aboard. The cost of charts could most certainly be accounted for under 'insurance'.

Incidentally, I try to keep all my charts, except those I've borrowed. If you get rid of your charts, you've taken a serious step toward canceling a dream or a memory.

The course lines and fixes on your old charts will push recall buttons that pictures miss. Recently, for example, we gave a slide show that included our passage on SEA FOAM from Suvarov to American Samoa. We showed dramatic shots of the harbor taken from the top of the tramway. Seeing these pictures evoked scenes from our visit; but the other day I picked up our old chart of Pago Pago, and forgotten feelings came rushing back: the anticipation of cold beer, fresh veggies, and mail, that accompanied our early morning landfall; and, after six days at sea, how welcoming and protective the harbor felt, bathed in the reds and shadows of sunrise.

Which is why new charts of places you've already been can never take the place of the old ones. The mind needs the x's, the course lines, the coffee stains, the scrawls of stress, the jottings of achievement. When I view our ocean charts with their fixes and tracks, vivid replays of passagemaking adventures leap off the page.

I also hang on to charts of places I haven't been yet, even if it's unlikely I'll ever go there. In 1973, when Nancy and I and four of our children set sail from San Diego bound for Tahiti, we intended to harbor hop all the way to Panama before going offshore to the Galápagos. But the weather was cold, so we scrapped some planned stops on Baja's west coast in order to get to the warmth of Cabo San Lucas. A half dozen unused charts of Baja's harbors remain in storage, and a dozen or more of unvisited Panamanian islands attest to Nancy's assertion that regrets in life stem far more often from the things you didn't do than from those you did.

As long as I have the charts, just maybe. . .

Although I've referred sarcastically to *Pilot Charts* as statistical accumulations having little relevance to reality, from the perspective of one who always encounters exceptional conditions, they are still the best planning guides we have. Pilot Charts are month by month records on wind direction, strength, days of calms; currents; gales; hurricanes; and icebergs. They also give water temperatures, data I've never found useful, perhaps because we have no thermometer on board. If you're one of those unlucky skippers who lives the exceptions, Pilot Charts will make you angry. Actually, however, more often than not you'll find conditions to be what they predict.

A study of Pilot Charts will tell you when *not* to be in a certain part of the world. Most areas of most oceans have storm seasons. Even in those areas that tend to have storms every month, you can expect fewer in certain months than in others.

Most information in cruising guides and passage planning books is derived from Pilot Charts. You can probably get along without them if you want your information chewed and digested by others. Personally, I enjoy studying the source and distilling the data, even though nine times out of ten I'll come to the same conclusions as are in the guidebooks. But every so often there'll be a place I'll want to go 'off season', and Pilot Charts will give me the conditions to expect.

Cruising Guides. There are two sides to the cruising guide story. We've come to depend on them in the same way we depend on GPS. Cruising guides dispel mystery and reduce risk, two essential elements of adventure. When I try to imagine what it would be like to cruise without a radio or a cruising guide, I get a kind of tight feeling in my stomach. Cruising without information, without prior knowledge of where you're going, is too Columbus-like. Take away charts and all electronic aids, and re-imagine. Are you getting a feel for the size of the cojones of early voyagers?

Imagine having a yen for sailing to a certain place, and running into someone who's cruised there. "What's it like?" you say, and he or she tells you. "How do I approach? Where do I anchor? Is there good shelter in case of storms? Where do I check in? Do I wait on the boat or go ashore? What did you have to pay? Are the locals friendly or hostile? What haulout or repair facilities are there? What supplies? What kind of money do they use? Medical facilities? And once I'm there, what's there to do?" With the answers, you have the beginnings of a cruising guide for that place.

Where cruising guide authors fail is in trying to do too much, or perhaps we drive them to this by expecting too much of them. We come to see them as coast and geodetic surveyors, but they are not; they're cruisers like ourselves, who have been there and done that, logging their lead line or depth sounder readings, taking note of landmarks and hazards. There are things they miss, and human errors creep in.

Guide writers use various methods of getting information about places they haven't been to but wish to cover. Sailing Directions and Coast Pilots are helpful in the larger view. Charts help, but in many places in the world they're unreliable. Articles and cruising books fill in some blanks, as do SSCA Bulletin letters. Some guide writers ask other sailors to keep records and pass the info on to them so they can include it in the guide. Sometimes I've had the feeling that the emissary forgot, and tried to write the information from memory after the fact. As long as lack of knowledge doesn't appear in the title, I'd appreciate the candor of a guide writer who occasionally admits, "Actually I don't have any idea where that damn reef is, but it's in the area, and you probably should only sail there in good light."

Cruising guides are less useful when it comes to information that's subject to change: Rocks and stuff don't, but fees and entrance procedures may and often do. Visa requirements change. "Should I go ashore or wait on board?" changes. Facilities start up or die, and, in some areas (Galápagos), the rules for cruisers change frequently.

Not all errors are limited to changing rules, however. A certain chart of Venezuela shows a submerged reef where in fact there's a high, humpy island. Both of the popular and excellent guides to Belize and its neighbors wrongly locate Glovers Reef by one full mile of latitude *and* longitude.

In spite of the limitations of some cruising guides, don't leave home without them. Used with caution, they are invaluable aids.

The best cruising guides we've ever used are the Waterway Guides that cover the U.S. Intracoastal Waterway. They come out with a new one every year, so errors get corrected, and the info is as up-to-date as possible.

Already some cruising guides include GPS-derived latitude and longitude coordinates. GPS way points will make cruising so easy that just about everybody will be coming out here. Then our main worry will be, who's home minding the store? And my main worry will be, how come everybody's out here and *writing about it?*

BOOKS

The following is a list of suggested books. I've starred the ones we have on board. The lack of a star doesn't mean we wouldn't *like* to have it, but means it's in storage in some relative's basement or we haven't the room on board or the money or all three. The list is far from complete, and is included merely as a guide, not a library's card catalog.

My computer doesn't have the memory for some of the neat stuff that's available. CD-ROM for reference material solves the space problem. The money problem is never solved, and perhaps happily so. A book or CD-ROM disk for which you've saved will get far more attention than one that's part of a bulk-bought library. But then, you said you didn't like computers, didn't you?

BOOKS ON VOYAGING, NAVIGATION AND PILOTING

Ocean Passages for the World
We don't own this, but I've always wanted to. Deterrents are the price and size of the book. I've studied borrowed copies, though.

* *Cruising Under Sail*, Eric Hiscock
Two books now combined into one. A classic. Some of the stuff is out of date, but much is pure gold.

* *Heavy Weather Sailing*, K. Adlard Coles
   This too is a classic, updated from the one we own. Essential for stimulating "what if's".

* *Storm Tactics Handbook*, Lin and Larry Pardey
   This is new. The bridle/Para Anchor theory sounds good, but I haven't tested it yet. Biggest problem for me is having a parachute sea anchor ready on the recommended 600 feet of rode.

Chapman's Piloting
   Essential reference (you'll notice we don't have one) for the basics in seamanship. Periodically updated.

* *Bowditch American Practical Navigator*
   This is still the best bargain in any seagoing library. Published by the U.S. government and now in two volumes, it's thorough and accurate on hurricanes, weather seasons, and all kinds of stuff. There is a heavily abridged version published for boaters, but after reading it I was left with wanting more.

* Books for Celestial Navigation
   Here you're going to have to decide on whether you go with tables (bulky) or a calculator (fallible).

DON'T FORGET

Tide and Current tables
   A computer program exists for this. But then, you *still* don't like computers, do you?

* Light Lists
   See Tide and Current Tables above.

* Coast Pilots and Sailing Directions
   Although these are intended for ships, there's good stuff for yachts, too.

Reed's Nautical Almanacs
   There are several, covering the East and West Coasts of the U.S., the Caribbean, Europe, and the Med. These are also excellent bargains, and cover currents, tides, harbor charts, aids to navigation, communication information, and more.

* The Yachtsman's Almanac
   Cheaper and better than the government publication. The appendix always has good info, which is periodically changed. In fact, if you

can deal with the compressed data, you won't need any other navigation book. Last one I read told me how to solve the navigational triangle. It required a calculator, which of course can fail. However, it provided a method that didn't require all those tables.

* Chart Catalogs
These show you all available U.S. Charts, from the largest to the smallest scale, by areas. As of their 1996 master catalog, these were available free from West Marine.

MAINTENANCE BOOKS

Marine Diesel Engines: Maintenance, Troubleshooting and Repair, Nigel Calder
I'd get this one rather than his *Boatowner's Mechanical and Electrical Manual*. The latter is a good book, but at 518 pages it's very big. I read the part on alternators and found it kind of murky. Accurate, though, as far as I could tell.

Living on 12 Volts with Ample Power, Dave Smead and Ruth Ishihara
I've read parts of this and found it clear and thorough. However, I consider it overly fussy in its recommendations for charging and maintaining gel cells.
I also like *The 12-Volt Doctor*'s books.

Sail repair and canvas work
Can't help you here. Nancy has made all our hatch awnings, and has done much of our sail repair. Both require a strong sewing machine.

Knots: *Chapman's Knots*, Brion Toss. Also, *The Ashley Book of Knots*
Toss's book is clear and concise. Ashley's book is exhaustive, and finding the answers to simple questions can be exhausting.

AND OF COURSE

* Language dictionaries and study books
Larousse makes the best dictionaries, but may be more than you need. For fun, if you're heading for Spanish speaking countries, get *Breaking Out of Beginner's Spanish* by J.J. Keenan. It gives you idioms, idiosyncrasies, and insults. *The Yachtsman's Ten Language Dictionary* by Barbara Webb and Michael Manton is very valuable for the cruiser.

* World Almanac
  This and the following two books would be best on CD-ROM for space considerations. World Almanac should be bought every couple of years. It's amazing how much information it contains.

* Atlas

  Encyclopedia

  History

AND

* A good book on fishes
  There are area as well as general coverage books. Get more than one, and check the quality of the pictures. You'll haul these books out every time you come back from snorkeling. Don't stint here.

* Shell book
  This became less important as the ecological impact of collecting live shells hit us. Prior to that, Nancy probably bought four or five books.

* Bird book
  Audubon is still the best, although this may change. Birds in different parts of the world have local names, so you can count on being confused.

* Flora and Fauna book
  Trees and flowers and herbs and things, especially if you're into medicinal and edible wild stuff. Be careful about mushrooms.

* Flag book (although our World Almanac has an adequate flag section)
  Some countries are very fussy about flying a proper courtesy flag. Flags can be expensive, and as long as you have the sewing machine for sail repair. . .

AND, AND. . .

* Cookbooks
  Because of Nancy's need to research recipes, we're overloaded with them. Her cookbook, *Beyond Peanut Butter*, coming out in the fall of '97, is special because it includes what to do with a lot of local and foreign foods.

* A consumer book on drugs, including generic names
  Drugs are cheaper in many countries than in the U.S. and often can
  be bought without prescription. You'll want to know about them,
  what they're used for, their side effects, contra indications, and
  generic names. A drug sold in Venezuela that I take for hypertension
  costs one third the price of the same drug in the U.S. Sold under a
  different name, it seems to accomplish the same things its more
  expensive counterpart does.

  I hate the U.S. attitude that overprotects customers (or doctors?) by
  requiring prescriptions for almost everything. The Central and South
  American Countries we've visited don't suffer from such nonsense.

  A physician's reference book, such as the *Merck Manual*
  You'll want a compendium of diseases, symptoms, treatment, and the
  disease's expected course. Be careful reading it, however, as with the
  slightest tendency toward hypochondria you'll end up believing you
  have them all.

* *Advanced First Aid Afloat*, Peter F. Eastman, M.D., and *Your Offshore Doctor*, Michael Beilan
  These two are helpful when you're in Phuket (phonics can really get
  you in trouble with that word) and the local medicine man neither
  speaks English nor makes boat calls.

YOU'D ALSO LIKE TO HAVE

* West Marine, Boat U.S., and other boating catalogs
  These are the dream books, as is the *Computer Shopper*, which I
  haven't given a place on the list because you say you hate computers.

* Shop manuals (as opposed to 'Owner's Manual') for both the yacht's
  auxiliary and the dink's outboard motor
  And it might be wise to get a parts list if the shop manual doesn't
  provide it. Parts suppliers love numbers, and don't respond well to
  the likes of "please send me the little knobby greasy thing that's right
  under the black box in the back."

  A book of radio frequencies
  You'll want to know where to find weather forecasts and weatherfax
  transmissions; which ship-to-ship and ship-to-shore channels you
  can use on SSB; and where to find Voice of America, the BBC, CBC
  (Canada), and Christian Science Monitor broadcasts. Reed's Almanac
  has some of this, as do some of the cruising guides. The problem here
  is that much of the info changes on a regular basis.

WE TOOK SOME OF THE HARVARD CLASSICS

* *Moby Dick*, Herman Melville
  Great to read if you need just one more anxiety on your first ocean passage.

* Anything by Joseph Conrad
  One of the greatest sea story tellers of all time.

* *Two Years Before the Mast*, Richard Henry Dana
  Dana tells us what it was like to cruise back in the eighteen hundreds.

* *Voyage of the Beagle*, Charles Darwin
  A must, if you're going to the Galápagos.

* *Satan Came to Eden*, Dore Strauch
  This is an out-of-print book, but if you're heading Galápaward you'll love it. It's the true life story of Floreana and its mysterious murders, by one who was there.

OTHER CLASSICS

The Moon and Sixpence, W. Somerset Maugham
Based on Gauguin's dropout from Europe and drop-in to French Polynesia.

Rain, by the same Maugham
Set in Western Samoa. May I say 'Maugham's wrath outgrabe'? I'll probably never get another chance.

Mutiny on the Bounty, Charles Nordhoff
This classic is a must for Tahiti or Pitcairn bounders. Three movies that I know of have been made based on this book, and Bligh is a boathold word, especially among distaffs.

Also the sequels, though not as dramatic, are interesting as fillers-in of blanks. Bligh's voyage home, halfway around the world in a lifeboat, has to be one of the most extraordinary adventures.

IF YOU HAD A BIGGER BOAT—FOR THE SOUTH PACIFIC

* *Wake of the Red Witch*, Garland Roark
  Fiction, but it's a great story set on sailboats in the South Pacific.

* *Trustee from the Tool Room*, Nevil Shute
  Nevil Shute's wonderful tale about a model train buff who leaves his London Post Office job and travels to the South Pacific on a voyage

that will save his niece's inheritance. Good example of the networking that can occur among people with similar hobbies, as the hero is
helped along the way by other model train enthusiasts.

* *Hawaii* and *Return to Paradise*, James Michener
Michener's early and best 'area' books.

Kon Tiki, Thor Heyerdahl
Voyage of the ultimate minimalists, guaranteed to make a reluctant
pussycat feel better about the pea green boat you talked her into
setting off in.

Fatu Hiva, also Heyerdahl
Heyerdahl has taken enough critical crap about this account of his
visit to the Marquesas. The history is fictitious, and gives the reader
a negative picture. But there isn't much out there on these islands.

HUMOR

* *The Boat Who Wouldn't Float*, Farley Mowat
The funniest book about boating ever written. I have yet to decide
whether I hate or love it, as it inspired me to become a cruising writer.

* *Three Men in a Boat*, Jerome K. Jerome
A small boat classic and a must for Anglophiles. It was given to me
by Alphonsus J. Murphy, one of the world's most discerning God-
fathers. I was five, and didn't appreciate it till ten years later; but I've
remembered it, and him, for a long lifetime. A recent re-reading revealed that the humor is dated, but there are still many funny and
timeless scenes.

* *Blown Away*, and *You Can't Blow Home Again*, both by Herb Payson
What can I say? These sequential tales are of a family's early mis-
steps as voyagers in an old wooden boat. At best they're a barrel of
laughs.
    With apologies to Thomas Wolfe and all that, I must confess that
You Can't Blow Home Again was a poorer, bowdlerized version of
my preferred but publisher-rejected title, *Sucked Back*.

FOR THE CARIBBEAN

* *Caribbean*, James Michener
Late, verbose, hastily written Michener, but there isn't much else out
there, either.

The Night of the Silent Drums, John L. Anderson
Recently re-issued, this exciting but sad historical novel is about a slave revolution on St. John in the U.S. Virgin Islands—a slave's eyeview of earlier, less praiseworthy times.

* *Don't Stop the Carnival*, Herman Wouk
Herman Wouk's fictional account of a man who buys and tries to operate a hotel on Water Island, right off Charlotte Amalie in the U.S. Virgin Islands. It's not about boats; it is, however, about frustration, on which much boat humor is based.

* Anything by Fritz Seyfarth
Fritz, now dead, was a friend and a true sea gypsy (his term) who lived aboard his old wooden ketch, TUMBLEWEED, in the British Virgin Islands. His books are small paperbacks that contain whimsical vignettes on islands and pirates.

GUATEMALA

I, Rigoberta Menchu: An Indian Woman in Guatemala
A Mayan's eyeview of the oppression that's been going on in Guatemala during the last couple of decades.

Any book on the Mayans (Honduras, Guatemala and Mexico.)

FOR FUN—SOME RECENT FAVORITES

The Bean Tree, Barbara Kingsolver
This is an absolutely charming book. Unfortunately I've not enjoyed her succeeding novels as much.

Seventh Heaven, Alice Hoffman
All of her books are different in style and tone, and for me all succeed admirably. *Seventh Heaven*, perhaps the most accessible, is fun and wise. *At Risk*, a story about a daughter with AIDS, is quietly tragic. *Property Of*, which I believe is her first novel, has a raw, unforgettable power. If you've gathered that I love this writer's work, you're on the money.

Woman Lit by Fireflies, Jim Harrison
A recent discovery by me, this book contains three novellas by a funny, sensitive writer who picks off-the-wall things to write about, and soon has you deeply involved in them.

Shipping News, E. Annie Proulx
As you begin, you wonder why you're bothering with these people. By the time you're through, they'll be dear friends.

Brazil, John Updike
I never enjoyed this writer more.

A Thousand Acres, Jane Smiley
To be savored, not gulped.

This is the kind of list that could go on and on. If you're not now a reader, perhaps long passages will turn you into one. And if that happens, I hope some of the above suggestions will offer you some pleasant experiences.

CHAPTER 39

"My Wife Doesn't Want to Go"

Dear Herb: I'm in a quandary. For years I've been talking about retiring and sailing around the world, or at least doing some long distance cruising. My wife has been sort of quiet about it. Now, with my retirement and pension only a year away, she's saying she doesn't want to go. I don't want to scrap the dream, but I don't want to scrap a 35-year marriage, either. Do you have any suggestions?

Perplexed

Dear Perpy: You have hit upon a ticklish subject which, to those who aren't in your shoes, is funny, and to those who are, it is not. Our first boat, SEA FOAM, was built in California in the backyard of a man with a similar dream. He launched her and sailed with his wife into the sunset. On reaching Hawaii, Wife said, "It's the boat or me, Jerkoff." ('Jerkoff' sounds Russian, but was actually a nickname.) The man chose the boat, but died before he could cast off the lines. The cast-off wife came out winners, as she sold the boat for a good price and tripled her stash in Las Vegas.

A similar but happier story, husbandwise, concerns a cruiser we met in the Bahamas. He was in his early sixties, victim of a 40-year marriage. I took an instant dislike to him, finding in him no redeeming characteristics—he didn't like going ashore, he didn't like snorkeling, he didn't like passages. And although his wife served us coffee and cake, I got the distinct impression that he didn't like visitors, either.

Two years later we met him again at a bar in Tobago. He was smiling and bubbly, full of fun stories, buying us drinks, and obviously enjoying his life of sailing, snorkeling, and something else which became plain when a lovely young Trinidadian returned from the ladies' room. Where was the wife? We didn't ask.

A fellow named Dick (we're having to disguise everyone here) was from a country which shall remain nameless. We met him in the Caribbean as he was completing his circumnavigation. His crew were two beautiful young Scandinavian women, and it was plain after being with

255

him for a while that he was bedding each in turn, although the terms of rotation were vague. Dick's wife would fly to join him in the various major ports along his route, at which time the Scandinavians would disappear, only to return when the wife flew home. We don't know about the wife, but Dick was one of the happiest men we've ever met.

Another young couple—we'll call them Bert and Bertha—were having marital problems. He was a Bligh-like captain. She had been a bright and successful professional. They went cruising to patch up their relationship. Within a year she flew back to the States and filed for divorce.

Why didn't it work? Think about it. Here are two people who had gradually grown apart. Their shore routine had each going to work after breakfast and maybe coming home for dinner. Maybe. The trend was to spend less and less time with each other. So to solve this they go to sea? Live together 72 hours a day in a space the size of a large closet? And in an environment where she, formerly an independent decision maker in her work, has to love, honor, and obey? Come on!

Fear is one of the major reasons why women don't want to go voyaging. We were friends with a couple: A was frightened of sailboats and the sea, while B loved it. Did you guess which one was female? However, there was something else going on here. She was pretty much okay when Nancy or I were at the helm. But when her husband was steering, she would hold on to the binnacle till her fingers were dead white, all the while throwing up on her neighbors. If the wife thinks her husband is a total incompetent, she'll never entrust her life to him in a sailboat on the high seas.

The Asinine Spouse Syndrome (acronym deleted) is prevalent in many marriages. How often has she seen him approaching, grinning stupidly, with his jockey shorts around his ankles? Who in her right mind could respect that? These wives roast their husbands for the identical traits they find fetching in an attractive male guest.

Many women who go sailing with their husbands and hate it get pregnant, usually by the husband, so that he can be forced back to land and fatherhood. A couple we met in Tahiti (a port known to many as 'Cruiser's Cusp') were at an impasse—he loving it and wanting to sail west, she hating it and wanting to sell the boat and fly home. The impasse was resolved when she told him she'd missed her period for the second time.

Occasionally an inventive and desperate woman, looking for any man who'll take her out of all this and return her to a normal life, will get pregnant by whomever, not caring whether or not she ever sees her compulsive, rude, and dictatorial husband again. These women go on to lead happier lives than they'd ever dreamed of, having learned to appreciate hearth, home, and harnessed husband in a way many malcontented wives never do.

The sad stories come from women who are afraid to speak out about their relationship. We were in Papeete tied up to the quay when I decided to do a series of interviews of married women cruising with their husbands. At first the husband would hang around, determined to monitor his wife's responses. I learned early on to make my first twenty questions innocuous and boring. Before long the husband's eyes would glaze over and he'd think of something he should be doing and go away. Then the wife would lean forward, her eyes slanted slits, and *sotto voce* snarl, "If you print this I'll kill you, but I *hate* sailing, and while we're sailing I hate *him*!" After three or four interviews I felt like a nudist in an apiary, banging on hives with a stick just to see what would happen.

Women have made great gains in their struggle to achieve equal opportunity in the job market, but in most cases they're still not seen as equal by men. We men inherited this archetypal Adam/Eve, Anthony/Cleopatra mindset and are uncomfortable when we consider giving it up.

And of course one of the last bastions of male machismo is a boat. There can be only one captain and that role is filled by the man on the majority of cruising boats. Whoopee, guys! See me swashbuckle! Take note of my witty, biting sarcasm when my crew does something wrong. And later on down the line, watch me single-hand.

Herb washing dishes. When couples cruise, he who doesn't cook is doomed to this.

For the moment, we'll assume the long-suffering-in-silence wife, not the 'you never do anything right' harpy. Statistics on the latter are lacking, no doubt because so many of them are tragically lost at sea.

Why do we find sharing so difficult? Perhaps we don't share because as captains we can't distinguish between the necessary and the optional. Take the anchor: I drop ours and pull it up, and am responsible for insuring that it stays where I set it. So, *faute de mieux*, I'm sheriff of choosing our holding ground. All of the irritation is removed, I'm told by Nancy in no uncertain terms, if I announce in advance good reasons for my unilateralness.

When it comes to ambiance, however, we run a democracy. On RED SHOES democracy means Nancy chooses. Do we want to be close to the mangroves and bugs, or farther out? Do we want to cuddle up to the town's generator plant, or should we move on up the coast? Do we want to anchor *in medias* fleet, or solo? In all such decisions I defer to her, not the least of my reasons being that in such matters she's usually right.

Should we pull up the dinghy? When anchored in areas where theft is a problem, we raise the dinghy up alongside using the staysail and mainsail halyards. It's a two-person job. The outboard is locked to the dinghy transom and the dinghy is locked to RED SHOES. Nancy is always conservative in such matters, whereas my conservatism is moderated in direct proportion to the amount of work involved, especially at cocktail time.

And at sea, should we reef? In general, if you think you should reef, you should reef, and it's fairly certain that Nancy will say, "Yes, we should." Even sharing decisions when I *know* Nancy's response will agree with mine gives her the option to participate, and why should I deny her that?

As to where we go, the secret is knowing what bait will work. "Would you like to sail to the San Blas Islands of Panama?" "Isn't that where they make *molas*?" "Why yes, darling, I believe it is." The outcome is foreordained.

Bait can work against me. Once we'd reached Panama, I was reluctant to sail to the Rio Dulce of Guatemala. I could envision the 200-mile beat against trade winds and currents to get back around Cabo Gracias a Dios, all of which would be necessary to return to Panama. But Nancy had heard of the Mayan huipils, backstrap looms, and their preserved customs and costumes. Unless I lied and invented sea monsters and piracy, no way was I going to change her mind.

When we got there I loved it. If Nancy has heard of a reason to go someplace, I should quit dragging my feet and set sail. I've seldom regretted following her lead.

In 1971 I was the one who suggested buying a boat and cruising to exotic lands, but thereafter it was Nancy's determination and enthusiasm that carried me over the shoals of doubt. It was she who inveigled me to cross the country in a motor home, although I'll take credit for insisting we drag a sailboat so we could earn part of our expenses with articles and photographs. In the mid-eighties it was Nancy who decided that land life was becoming dull, and why didn't we go cruising again? And it was she who arranged getting RED SHOES, which made the cruise possible.

Many women are adventurous. But care is warranted here. Once a certain kind of woman's imagination is given free rein, no recanting on your part will be tolerated. It could well wind up that you stay home and *she* single-hands to Paradise.

Women have always had goals but have usually achieved them through guile, temptation, and seduction. (A woman friend recently described women's most effective tool as 'the vaginal wrench'. They still use this, all right, but they've added all the power tools as well.) Planted in the soil of her man's mind, her goal would be achieved in Macbethian fashion. Now, however, it's the man who must attempt to realize his goal with guile and seduction, along with judicious use of the tumescent drill.

Given that, Perpy, if your wife's reluctance is based on lack of interest, try bait. If bait doesn't work, a routine of 'you sail, she flies' for the long passages is possible, with whatever crew arrangements you can manage between ports. (Communication may mean 'no lies', but it doesn't necessarily mean 'reveal all'.) And if even *that* doesn't appeal to her, you might consider moving to a non-community property state.

Your wife, Perp, seems reluctant to go cruising at all. But if you manage to persuade her to try it, here are a few situations in which a little thoughtfulness can make it work.

The man is on the bow, the woman steering. The boat is perhaps coming to a dock for a landing, or approaching a spot for dropping the hook. Or, if you're lucky to have made it thus far, you're visually picking your way around the coral heads in a tropical lagoon (called 'eyeball' navigation). This is the perfect setting for the total annihilation of a relationship. In any of those circumstances, a misunderstanding can result in intensive yelling.

Whether the woman admits it or not, one of the things that really pisses her off is to be yelled at. It doesn't matter that the yelling is claimed by the skipper to be non-accusatory, but merely fueled by frustration and invoked to be heard over the noise of the engine and the 30 to 40 feet that separate you. In her mind, the very act of yelling *presumes* anger and criticism, either of which can raise the hackles of the most complaisant female.

You're leaving a slip in a crosswind, or you're busy stowing the anchor and the helmsperson must on her own steer carefully out of the constricted anchorage. Well, you knew well in advance you were going to do this operation, didn't you? You thought it through, pictured each move you'd need to make, right? But did you go over it with your partner?

This is something about which Nancy is definite, and I still manage to forget to do it sometimes. "Tell me the plan," she'll say. If she's at the helm, does she come in at an angle? Does she steer 230 degrees to get out of here? Once the mainsail is up, will I want her to fall off to starboard or port? Going over these things with her in advance prepares her mind, and will avert the panic-laden surprise. Often she'll ask why we're going to do it that way, and occasionally she'll object to my decision. Explanation soothes reluctance. We'll omit the rare instances when her objections saved our collective asses.

Probably the most voracious teredo in the hull of marriage is the belief in "If you love me, you're supposed to know what I'm thinking." The cost of therapy for learning that partners are not mind readers, that you must speak your mind out loud, has been huge.

I've run across couples who use handheld VHF radios (CBs would be cheaper and work as well) for passing info from bow to stern, or from crosstrees to helm. The problems with that are numerous. For one thing, you have to use your hand or hands to operate the radio, and unless you've grown more hands than I, you can't afford it. One hand for the job, one for the ship, and one more for the radio. It doesn't compute.

Our answer is hand signals. But hand signals take hands too, and there are times, notably during anchor drill, when there are no hands available for signalling. During those times I yell, and for each yelled command expect a response (usually 'okay', but sometimes 'what?') This is the best we've been able to come up with, so in order to smooth any rough edges the system might generate, we've been working on developing a loving scream.

One other place to avoid panic is during a night watch. Encountering a ship at sea at night is never fun, but if the watch stander, through lack of experience or for other reasons, can't figure out its course early on, it can lead to an emergency. If the ship is passing harmlessly in the distance, you'd rather be allowed to sleep. Holding a seminar with your partner on lights, and on how to judge if you're on a collision course, will help. Early in our cruising two situations arose in which the watch stander didn't want to wake me until finally the situation had become an emergency. So at first, ask your partner to wake you for all ships. Sit with her until the ship has passed, pointing out the navigation lights, the changes in compass bearings, and estimating the distance away. Eventually she'll become comfortable, or at least as comfortable as anyone can be about passing ships, and will be able to make most decisions on her own.

And finally, a thought that might appear to be promotion, but in fact is intended to be helpful: Time after time, men attending our seminars have said that their wife or Significant Other was persuaded to give cruising a try after reading my book, *Blown Away*. As mentioned earlier, it's an account of our beginnings, with all their problems and rewards. Nancy plays the prominent role she deserves, and women seem able to put themselves in her shoes. I'm certainly no model of applied sharing (more by virtue of self-centeredness than by intention), but Nancy's insistence on an equal partnership has been unrestrained and persistent. Over the years, a zigzag course toward equality has worked for us, and maybe it can for you.

CHAPTER 40

Cruising with Kids

Dear Herb: Having read your book *Blown Away*, I know you cruised with some or all of your combined family. How would you rate the experience in the children's lives? How do they? Do you have any suggestions for a couple planning to voyage with a girl and a boy, ages 9 and 10 respectively?

A Fumbling Father

Dear Fumbly: Is there any other kind of father than fumbling? If so, I'll bet they're either dogmatic or few. You're way ahead of the pack by admitting it.

As a grandfather now, I have some of your concerns in perspective. There are problems; kids are people, and differ in their wants and needs. Your economic situation and their prospects for a decent education at home are both significant. Your relationship to them is crucial—your willingness to relate to them more than just as little passengers aboard. One or both parents will have to teach school, or at least provide some kind of program for learning. And all of the above is useless if temperaments clash, either with each other, or with the environment of boat living. Your question isn't easy.

On SEA FOAM, we found a boat family to be much like a farm family in a remote area, or a frontier family. There the interdependence of family members was crucial to survival. On a boat this means that everyone shares the work—who cooks and who washes the dishes. On SEA FOAM sharing the labor was by no means limited to that. Cleaning, taking care of your personal stuff and berth, fish cleaning, sail handling, and watch standing were shared. No one gets a free ride, which in our society is a lesson in itself. Your children are pretty young, but certainly old enough to take care of their own quarters and take dish duty on rotation.

Watch standing is doubtless the most important job you can give a child. Common sense dictates that you start with supervised daytime watches of short duration. If they have to steer, so much the better, but if not, there should be definite routines: an alarm that goes off every ten

Daughter Sarah and son Chris on steering watch aboard *Sea Foam*. Earphones console Sarah and protect us from sonic intrusion.

minutes, at which time the person on watch stands up in the cockpit and slowly turns and inspects the horizon through 360 degrees. At specified times, the watch stander writes in the log whatever information you require, and, as soon as possible, on a schedule determined by the captain and initially with supervision, plots the position on the chart. If the skipper is navigating by sextant, a child can handle a stopwatch, write down numbers. It takes patience to involve a child, but it takes a tireless robot to run your boat yourself 24 hours a day. When you encounter resistance, remember that by training assistants you're doing this for yourself as well as for your children.

There is something to be said for SEA FOAM's primitive equipment— no autopilot or windvane, and navigation at sea by sextant only. A child raised on a boat with electronic steering and navigation misses a great deal. Even an electric windlass deprives him or her of direct contact with reality.

Watch standers on even a robotic boat must note approaching squalls, changes of wind, ship traffic, and must keep a written record of progress against the time when all aids fail. The more training you give them, the less supervision is required, and the more responsibility they can take.

There is something about standing watch that lasts a child a lifetime. With Craig, it was a lot like putting a 12-year old on sentry duty. Just as the battle can hinge on a single sentry, the boat and everyone on it depend on the person on watch. So the skipper's instructions must be comprehensive and explicit. At first it's "call me if anything unusual comes up. That's *anything*." Eventually, with experience, the child can decide to add or reduce sail, or to change course to give a passing ship a wider margin.

But even then, every change should be logged, and every situation that's remotely uncertain laid in the lap of the skipper.

The grossest misapplication of the above happened in a South Pacific island. A cruising yacht was approaching landfall at night, sailing parallel to the fringing coral. The profusion of lights ashore confused the watch stander, and the boat went up on the reef, where it was destroyed. The people were saved, so was most of the gear. For the next month, the skipper hung around selling off the equipment and what remained of the boat. When describing how the disaster happened, he pointed to the watch stander: It was his daughter. She was alone on watch, approaching land, at night. She was ten years old.

How do you think his daughter will rate *her* cruising experience, with Daddy putting all blame for its demise on her young shoulders? Or, for that matter, how will she feel about him?

Cruising with kids is a complex issue. There are far too many variables for cut and dried rules. You understand the goals and work toward them, tacking as necessary.

When we left San Diego on SEA FOAM in 1973, our children were Lee (age 22), Philip and Connie (20), Chris (19), Sarah (16) and Craig (10). We left with Phil, Connie, Chris and Craig. Connie left us in Acapulco, to sail on SCALDIS, a boat with whom we buddy-boated as far as Tahiti. Sarah visited in Costa Rica. Philip sailed with us as far as Tahiti. Lee visited in Tahiti. Chris stuck with us till New Zealand. Craig stayed with us for the duration.

Our problem was to maintain dignity and control when our older children considered our decisions or behavior stupid or outrageous. Our other problem was to have home school with Craig using the Calvert School program. We did our imperfect best.

The Calvert program worked well for us. Craig was an unusually serious child. (He's an unusually serious adult, although this in no way means he lacks a sense of humor.) Nancy became a perceptive and inspiring teacher. I was the authority in math, and the stern voice of discipline (cat-o'-nine-tails were out that year). Calvert took us through the eighth grade, after which we encouraged Craig to read, and to learn navigation. We gave him scuba gear, and encouraged his writing. He wrote and sold three articles to sailing magazines.

He left us and went from eighth grade Calvert straight into a California Junior College. Finding students "not serious," he joined the Navy and became a nuclear technician on the sub WILL ROGERS. After three years of submarine duty, during which time he married, he was transferred to Orlando, where he taught enlistees. There, along with his naval duties and buying a house and raising two children, he put himself through night school, earning an MBA. After nine years service he left the Navy for private industry. At the time of his discharge he had three IRAs. I mean, the kid is *serious*.

Which could possibly be considered the downside—missing growing up with his peers. While cruising, most of his friends were adults. Did the boy grow to manhood too fast, too soon? Is there something to be said for a carefree childhood?

After leaving SEA FOAM, Philip went to wooden boat building school, then got into post and beam house construction. His house and barn buildings bridge the gap between artisan and artist. He's gone back to university and taken a masters degree so he can teach school when an opening comes up in a locality where he and his artist wife want to live. They have two children.

Chris left SEA FOAM in New Zealand and crewed for another skipper back to Hawaii, where he decided to live. Four years later he was managing a chain of seven stores. He's now married with three children and working in a supervisory capacity in the Alaskan gas fields.

What do these three men have in common? A refined sense of responsibility that our society finds valuable, and a strong urge toward independence and self-sufficiency. And all three value community, the interdependence of people in groups. For all except Craig, there was certainly far more to their upbringing than voyaging on a small sailboat. But given all their experiences over the previous two decades, just how much influence standing watch on a big ocean had on their characters is hard to judge.

Craig conning from *Sea Foam*'s bowsprit in Fiji. Cruising kids learn responsibility. With experience, eyeball navigation is like reading a colorful road map.

Of the three daughters, two were with us for only a few weeks. Connie has since made seagoing a part of her life. She has crewed as cook on private yachts and on sponsored whale watching expeditions, during the course of which she's sailed the Pacific from Alaska to Hawaii to New Zealand and Chile. She's now married, and with her husband spends half of each year cruising on their Nor'Sea 27 in the Sea of Cortez.

One cruising couple's ten-year old son came along for a year, and was only too delighted to return to land and regular school. Another couple's cruising daughter's first formal schooling was in New Zealand, where she was put into the seventh grade with her age-level group. She passed everything with A's and was bored with the lack of challenge. Her father had stopped playing chess with her a couple of years before because she beat him regularly.

What's it like cruising with kids? Who can say. Your experience will be your experience. I remember our voyage with our children as having many difficult moments. But most of the time it was rewarding for us as parents. Was it as good for them as it was for us? Craig has said it was the most influential segment of his life. The others, who experienced voyaging as adults and for a far shorter time, haven't said much about its overall impact on their lives. Maybe one of these days I'll find the courage to ask them.

CHAPTER 41

Cruising with Pets

Dear Herb: We understand that you have a cat on board. What are the difficulties you've encountered? Our cat, Pussy-Wussy the Hussy, is more than a pet. She's a member of the family. Obviously we won't change our minds about cruising simply because of her. I'm sure we could find a good home for her. But if it's not *too* much of a hassle, we'd prefer not to leave her behind.

Pussy-Wussy the Hussy's Parents

Dear PWHPs: Where you want to cruise will figure heavily in your decision as to whether to keep Pussy-Wussy the Hussy on as crew—or, as in our case, keeping her as crew will determine where you cruise. We've considered transiting the canal and taking RED SHOES to the Pacific Northwest via Hawaii. But if we do this, we'll have to do it without our cat, a blue-point Siamese we call Misty.

We found her, a gutter cat, so thin her bones rattled, one eye weeping with herpes. In spite of the problems involved in cruising with pets, we brought her along. One of our concerns was that she might fall overboard. She has fallen overboard three times. The first time she was fishnetted out by a neighbor. The second time she climbed a piling and rescued herself. Last night Nancy and I fished her out with our cat retrieval gear: a fishnet.

She used to roam the foredeck when we went to sea, looking for a quieter, less lumpy lair, and we bought lifeline nets to protect her. Since then she has always remained below while we're sailing, maybe coming up to the cockpit for a look around, but never venturing out on deck. We've since dispensed with the nets.

Knowing litter to be a problem, we trained Misty to use the toilet. People used to ask why we had duct tape on the toilet seat. It was to give the cat purchase for her claws. This was a great situation for us, but evidently not for Misty. Several months at a dock in Ft. Lauderdale re-trained her to sites where scratching the earth after excretion was a ritual act. When we put to sea again, she would postpone using the toilet until we

Nancy with Misty. Our little stray and reluctant crewmember (the cat, not Nancy).

worried about her health. We finally gave in and put a litter box aboard, and her habits returned to normal.

Which was good for her peace of mind and better for her health, but it meant we had to deal with litter. In many places where we've cruised, litter is not to be found in stores. So we've learned to wash and dry Misty's so that it'll last five to ten times its normal useful life. We also have to deal with the litter crumbs that escape the box when Misty really gets into scratching. All in all it's an adjustment that has enhanced the cat's quality of life and sullied ours. I don't think this worries Misty.

She hates sailing, and particularly motor sailing. I don't just mean a little bit, she *hates* it. She throws up, if possible on our bunk, and when she's done doing that she drools copious fluids. She also loses hair when she's anxious, and I don't understand why, after a day at sea, she isn't completely bald. I do know that the saloon and everything in it is covered with cat hair. (For all you technopoops, I *know* cats have fur and not hair. But what Misty distributes about our boat is mentioned casually in scenes like, "Damn it, Nancy, there're three fucking cat hairs in the butter," and substituting 'fur' simply wouldn't make it.)

A strictly Siamese trait is her refusal to eat whatever we give her. Turning up her nose is an inherent need. If we find a good buy on dry food, she'll refuse to eat anything that doesn't come out of a can. We've tried going head-to-head with her, leaving her dish full of whatever she's rejecting. We put up with the miaows, the lovey-dovey beseechings, the pitiable looks, but finally are forced to give in when she practices dramatic leaps onto the chest of whoever is sleeping or napping. In a war of determination with Siameasles, you can't win.

Given all of the above, why do we cruise with her? Because most of the time she's a good friend. I enjoy her company. Besides, when did it ever become ethical to banish a family member simply because he or she was difficult?

But that's Misty, not Pussy-Wussy the Hussy. Many cats don't throw up at sea, and you can find cats that'll eat what you've gone to great effort to buy for them. So let's move on.

Problems with having a cat on board: We have crossed from Florida to the Bahamas several times. To enter the Bahamas with a cat, you're supposed to present a veterinarian's certificate that she's healthy and has had rabies and feline leukemia shots. The certificate must be dated no earlier than 24 hours before your arrival. But sailboats have been known to hang around Biscayne Bay for days, even weeks, waiting for a weather window. The law, it appears, was written while considering airplanes and other means of travel that follow schedules. Sailboats definitely don't.

Pet owner sailors have taken various steps to deal with a law that is stupid from a cruiser's point of view, but which appears to be applied inclusively by Bahamian officials as a source of fines. (Why is the law stupid? For one thing, if the cat receives a clean bill of health from a licensed vet and then never gets off the boat, which is usually the case, she is no danger to the rabies-free Bahamas.) In any event, we succumbed to minor extortion one time when our certificate was 24 hours overdue. "We'll take your cat away from you and put her down," was the threat which took US$20 to neutralize. Another time the U.S. vet was kind enough to leave the date of the certificate blank and give us his pen. A third time we actually made it within the allotted 24 hours.

Bermuda, which I thought was going to be the stickiest, took a fairly intelligent view. Although we had a health certificate from a vet in the U.S. Virgin Islands, Misty did not have a tick clearance. I have never before or since heard of such a thing. However, the official was lenient, and all we had to do was promise to anchor out, something we intended to do anyway as marinas are normally not our style.

In our four visits to Belize, only once have we been asked about pets. In that case, our vaccination certificate was one month past the year's validity. The quarantine official picked up the phone and tried to reach a vet with whom he had an arrangement, but he wasn't home. After various explanations of what he had the authority to do to our cat if he chose to, he let us go with our promise to have her vaccinated as soon as we reached Belize City. There, however, the cat doctor had no vaccine, and all of the vets we reached practiced on large animals and had nothing for cats.

We left Belize at the end of our month's visa and sailed to Honduras and the Bay Islands. There, we figured, we could get Misty legalized. However, the vet on Roatán was also a large animal vet and couldn't help us. In desperation and using my computer I took our most recent certificate from the U.S. as an example and made a counterfeit one which I printed in fine style using a very official looking font. We returned to Belize for a delightful two months and were never asked for pet documentation again.

Don't get me wrong—we *wanted* our cat to be legal and protected with all the inoculatory skill that modern science can offer. When a Guatemalan vet who practices in Guatemala City arrived on the Rio Dulce and announced that he would inoculate pets during his one week visit, we immediately rushed over, pussy in hand. As he was filling out the certificate he said, "Did I hear you say you were going to Belize? Yes? Well then, I'll predate this certificate. They insist that she have her shots at least a month before you go there." Which proves that people in general find ways around pointless red tape.

I'll never forget our friends, a pair of Aussies from Tasmania. They arrived in New Zealand with a cat, which was immediately quarantined on their boat for a period of six months. During that time, an official who deservedly earned the name Pussy Inspector would come by at random times to see that the cat was on board. When their cat went into heat and swam ashore, they were frantic, as the fine for being catless was NZ$500. Their solution was to borrow a cat until their own reappeared. This worked, although one wonders what would have happened had the pet returned while the owners were off the boat and the PI had arrived to find *two* cats aboard.

Hawaii is as strict as any place I know. A crewmember on a boat in Papeete was leaving permanently for the States and wanted to take her newly acquired French cat with her. She'd planned a three-day stopover in Hawaii. Having no intention of putting her scaredycat in quarantine, she got some tranquilizers from a French vet, tucked the cat in the front of her pants, and on the plane passed herself off as pregnant.

We haven't discussed dogs and birds because I know nothing about them. I imagine the regulations for both bear investigating. The thing to do, I suppose, is write to each country asking for their rules, and then do your best to conform.

Here is a story about a problem with dogs that has nothing to do with foreign countries, but it's a concern that's stymied many cruising dog owners.

We first passed SEA BIRD, a smallish green cutter, motoring down the Intracoastal Waterway just above Little River. When we spotted her a week later aground, pinned sideways by wind and tide against a mud bank in Minim Creek, we felt we knew her. Her single-handing skipper, a mid-sized, compact woman with blond hair cut short, whose name we later learned was Polly, stood, hitched up her pants, and waved.

Actually our destination was 15 miles further on. But we had already seen one boat ignore SEA BIRD's plight. Nancy and I looked at each other, sighed, turned RED SHOES around, and anchored in Minim Creek.

It took us two and a half hours to get SEA BIRD off the mud. When she was finally floating free I asked Polly if she'd like to come aboard RED SHOES for a drink.

"I've lost 15 pounds," she told us as she climbed aboard, one hand holding her belt. "None of my clothes fit. When you're single-handing, you don't make every meal.

"For 24 years I worked in Sarasota as a hospital lab technician, but I always wanted to go cruising. Now I'm 51, and I figured if I'm going to do it I'd better get at it."

Tristan Jones was Polly's hero. She had met him some years ago at a boat show, and bought two of his books, which she already owned, in order to have autographed copies. Polly used to raise pug dogs, but for her cruise she got a black labrador and named it Nelson, same as Tristan did. Nelson had not yet learned to use the deck for a toilet, and Polly was forced to stay near land in order to take him ashore daily.

"I could give him away. A friend would love to have him, but I'd miss him. I don't know *what* I'm going to do.

"I began thinking about cruising when I was 20, looking at this boat or that, and finally decided I wanted a steel hull. Ten years ago I bought the plans and had the hull and deck built. I did the inside myself. I'm no carpenter but I don't care. When you want to do something badly enough, you don't worry about it much, you just do it."

Later on I dinghied her back to her boat. As she climbed aboard, she let out a whoop! There, standing proud on the starboard deck, was a pile of feces. Nelson, ashamed, jumped into the dinghy and hid behind me, but Polly was overjoyed.

"Nelson, you wonderful dog!" she said, hugging him. And to me, "Do you know what this means?" I said I thought it meant regular cleanup, but she said, "It means I can go *offshore*."

At daybreak, as we motored past, Polly was hard at work scrubbing the mud off SEA BIRD. She waved, hollered "Thank you." I pictured SEA BIRD's bookshelf bulging with the works of Tristan Jones, two of them autographed, and I had a vision of one day meeting SEA BIRD at sea, the windvane steering, Nelson barking a happy, unstressed greeting from the foredeck, Polly hitching up her pants and gaily waving her plastic shovel. It warmed my heart's cockles, this vision of fulfillment in a world too often littered with abandoned dreams.

To get back to your problem, I can only tell you that having a cat on board will definitely affect your cruising plans.

Because we have Misty, we've ruled out a visit to New Zealand or Hawaii, places we know and love. I guess we're just fond enough of our feline friend to make parting with her more difficult than giving up certain destinations.

But if she doesn't eat what I give her this morning, I'm darn well going to reconsider.

CHAPTER 42

Money

Dear Herb: My wife and I are semi-retired, which means we have given up our regular jobs, but must still do some part-time stuff to keep our minds and purses adequately fed. We're thinking of living aboard our Whitby 42, mostly in the Caribbean, with sojourns up to Maine for the summer, and maybe spend the spring in the Bahamas. We're trying to figure out if we can swing it financially. How much money will we need?

Inadequately Funded

Dear IF: If I knew how much money you had, I could tell you to the penny. Some people make budgets work on boats, and I suppose to a certain extent a budget of sorts is necessary. But generalizations work better than exact amounts. A person without unlimited funds is always scrimping here in order to be generous there.

Our income comes in small bits from several different sources. It also varies with the fortunes of a freelance writer. Like the tide, neaps and springs are merely pairs of small and large opposites. What comes in will go out. The good months we live well. The lean ones, we tighten belts.

But we're not *quite* as orderly as that. What we in fact do is go along merrily spending what we feel like spending, and every so often have a reckoning.

Just talked on ham radio to friends who approached their cruise differently. They worked in the Virgin Islands for several years, putting aside money while never actually living on the cheap. In other words, they had fun while they stockpiled. It takes longer that way. With this system, however, one never knows when to stop. "A little more money and we can have this or do that" keeps you on the treadmill. It's here that keeping your eye on your objective makes sense. As you know, there are those who prefer to stop at 'ready, set' rather than continue on to 'go!' But that's about goals and honesty, not about money. Is your objective to leave, or to prepare to leave? If the former, make a list of the equipment you want for your boat, and don't let impulse or a windfall persuade you to delay leaving.

273

And if you have a kitty which you plan to spend over, say, a five-year voyage, you'd better figure on its running dry in four. What you thought would be adequate in most cases won't be.

I have a friend who's going to laugh at all this. He has no personal vices, is content with simple fare, can maintain everything himself, and is able to squeeze a penny till the copper melts. Picking up extra cash is not a problem, as he can fix anything on a yacht.

Most of us have some capital (large or small) and some credit (ditto) to cover sudden unexpected expenses. We manage to get into trouble when we consider a trip we want to take as a sudden unexpected expense, and reach into the emergency funds. Fly now, pay later may be economically immoral, but our most exalted government is providing us with a superb example.

In talking about money, we need to list spending categories. In essence they're food, fuel, fun, family, luxuries, and boat. As the boat is a capital investment, we can divide its requirements into repairs, maintenance, and capital improvements. There. Bravely forward.

Food: There are people to whom food is not important, merely a means of staying alive. They can exist happily on beans and rice, or yogurt and tofu, or nuts and fruit, finding their enjoyment elsewhere. But if food is important to you, as it is with us, you'd better budget for it.

Nancy is a wonderful cook, and we eat well on board. This puts our food budget on the high side—actual numbers vary with the country we're in.

Depending on where we are and what we're doing, we have *fuel* costs for propane, gasoline, and diesel. If we're anchored in a place where shore or store is a long dinghy ride away, we use a lot of gasoline for the outboard. On a passage we use none. A 20-pound tank of propane lasts us six to eight weeks. Presently we run our diesel engine one and a half to two hours daily to charge the batteries. When the Windbugger is working we run it less. With solar panels, we'd run it even less. Although we sail when we can, we don't hesitate to run the auxiliary in calms. Often when heading for a weather mark we motor sail. Our engine fuel consumption averages .5 gallons per hour. 4800 hours = 2400 gallons at an average cost of $1.50 = $3,600 divided by the 8 years we've been out = $450/year for diesel. This, too, varies. Furthermore, our charging time has increased since we added refrigeration. See what I mean about numbers? They can be indications, but no more.

Fun for our purpose means extra stuff—there are plenty of cruising activities that are fun, but here we're talking about things like leaving the boat and traveling inland; entertaining aboard; eating out; and a portion of our trips to the U.S.A. Although all of these trips so far have been made for business reasons, we manage to include a lot of fun things. This sometimes includes rental cars, a great pleasure in a foreign country.

Speaking of rental cars and trips home, there are advantages to keeping a car and putting it up on blocks while you're away. The obvious one is that you have a car when you visit home. A hidden advantage, and one we didn't calculate thoroughly enough before selling our own car, is insurance. It costs next to nothing to keep fire, theft and liability on a car that's garaged or on blocks and is guaranteed not to be used. Various insurance companies have rules about this, but ours covered us for liability in rental cars. They covered us for a maximum of two weeks a year, but that was two weeks we didn't have to spend the $10 or $11 a day for the rental car company coverage. Other insurance companies may have a more or less liberal policy in this regard, but it might pay to look into it.

How much goes into the *fun* category is a function of what we have plus ten percent. For months afterward, in order to get even we try to cleave to what we have minus ten percent. This usually works. Spending what we have minus ten percent to pay for an upcoming trip does not work.

Family is a broadsword. It includes what we spend on kids and grandchildren, Christmas, birthdays, and phone calls home not related to business. It overlaps into *fun* when we fly home and go out of our way to visit children in California, Washington state, Alaska, Maine and Pennsylvania.

Luxuries include our VCR, TV, tape player and books, which we devour. Our cameras and computer are both business expenses. Other luxuries might include items that are more than minimal, such as a better dinghy and more powerful outboard than we actually need. Some might say a percentage of our food bill should be in the luxury column, but they're mostly ascetics with pinched faces and haunted eyes.

All of the above is a result of personal choice, but to give you an idea, I'll include here a year of RED SHOES' expenses. Useless on a practical level, it may nevertheless be a comfort to you.

Boat. We can make a few generalizations here. Sails might last five to eight years depending on their use and how you care for them. Wire rigging the same. Plan on a haulout every year, although some people manage one and a half year intervals and more. Lines need replacement—figure new lines all around every five to eight years. You may not replace them all at once, but gradually that's what it'll come to. Our outboards have stood us well for four years each, and might have done better except for the fact that our needs changed. An inflatable dinghy's life will depend on its quality when new, and how you treat it. We went through four dinghies from 1987 to 1992. From 1992 to 1996 we've been using our RIB AB, and it shows no signs of giving up. A quality inflatable dinghy bought in the States will cost $2,500-$3,000, depending on brand and style (RIB or not). A RIB AB bought in Venezuela will be roughly half that price. Outboards bought in St. Maarten, in Venezuela, or in Guatemala will cost 30 to 40% less than in the States.

Repair and maintenance expense depends on how much you can or intend to do yourself. Over the years you can save thousands doing your own work, even though you'll spend a little more on tools and spares.

Bottom paint can be bought at a deep discount, but many boatyards in the States offer low haulout prices while insisting that you buy all your materials through them at list. As with anything in the boat business, you save money by comparison shopping with a calculator in hand. For example, our bottom paint costs $160/gallon list, and I can buy it for $100 or less. For three gallons the difference is $180. Other stuff like thinners, brushes, paints, varnishes, zincs, tape, painters' jumpsuits, gloves, sandpaper, etc. can add up to another hundred dollars. Stuff that you already have on board, as long as it's not too obviously a scam, is okay with most yards. For us this means brushes, sandpaper, masking tape, zincs, etc. We've tried to include paint, but it didn't wash.

Some yards won't let you do your own work. Others will, but won't let you bring in outside labor. Some yards charge a small sum for in and out, but hit you hard for laydays. A little research on the radio nets can save you money.

It's impossible to calculate disasters, breakage, or failure, except to say that they will occur, and the cost of repair or replacement will again depend on who does the labor, and how good a shopper you are, at home or abroad. A lightning strike can cost you thousands, a hurricane, tens of thousands. How can I recommend an amount for your disaster fund, having no idea of your capacity for financial anxiety? Unless you're a wealthy man, there's no way you can cover all bases.

If lightning strikes and hurricanes are covered by your expensive insurance, you can still have costly disasters that aren't: a ruined engine because of an oil leak, or a cooling system failure; a ruined transmission; hull blisters; blown out sails.

And finally, add-ons. On RED SHOES, we installed refrigeration because Nancy wanted it. Then we bought a wind generator because the batteries needed it. We bought a TV early on because on the Intracoastal Waterway you could often get a local station. Then, when we went out of range of TV, we thought we'd enjoy a VCR. We bought a SatNav in '88, a GPS in '93, and a backup GPS in '95. I bought solar panels last year and carried the bulky things down to Guatemala on the plane, got them through customs, and laid them on RED SHOES' deck. The ones I'd bought were too big, there was no place to mount them, so I sold them. But in general, one thing leads to another. For tax purposes, all add-ons are capital improvements if you sell them with the boat.

Records: Nancy keeps a running cash account book. She can tell me what we spent each year all the way back to the year we were married. Her cash account book of 1971-2 was the only evidence that U.S. Immigration would accept when our Mexican housekeeper Augustina was trying to become a legal alien during the amnesty of the 80's. It solves arguments. It remembers the exchange rates of various currencies. It should help us make a workable budget, but it doesn't. Each year is different, some years radically so.

So what would I do in your shoes with a fixed income? I'd make a first-year plan, and try to draw up a budget from that. At the end of that year I'd make a second-year plan, and so forth. I'd establish credit and also try to have a cash account for the unexpected. If my income was small, I'd try in all ways to stretch it. If moderate I'd still try to stretch it, and live well within it. If large, I'd live as I chose, and not worry about it.

Here is a record of our expenditures on RED SHOES for the year 1994, a year in which we sailed from Puerto Rico to Panama, then north to Providencia, the Vivarillo Cays, the Bay Islands of Honduras, and Guatemala's Rio Dulce. Although the amounts will have changed, the things we spent money on will give you an idea of what's involved. Good luck!

BOAT EXPENSES

NEW OUTBOARD MOTOR $1,190.71
Evinrude 15hp Commercial, bought in Guatemala.

MISCELLANEOUS   523.70
This includes bolts, screws, machine screws, plugs, masking tape, brushes, goop (Permatex, 5200, Boatlife) glue, light bulbs, fire extinguishers, hoseclamps, hose, some rope, sandpaper, Scotch scrubbies, sponges, shackles, flashlight and other drycell batteries, etc.

BATTERY FOR ICOM HANDHELD   89.25
Batteries for the little handheld radios are dear.
Remember to fully discharge and fully charge all Nicad batteries, as they'll last far longer that way. Interrupting the charge in the middle, or recharging before it's dead, shortens battery life.

YARD/ELECTRIC   35.00

In St. Thomas, we arranged to tie up to the boat yard dock and use the electricity to do some repairs.

WINDBUGGER PRODUCTS   34.00

Cost of shipping blades, which were guaranteed. All other costs were rebated.

CABLE/LOCK DINGHY   35.18

Essential for security. The outboard has its own lock. The cable was ¼-inch lifeline (covered) with a small loop at one end, a large loop at the other, both loops secured with Nicopress fittings. We lock the dinghy at all times.

LAUDERDALE MARINE/EVINRUDE   125.40

My fault—I hit a rock and broke the driveshaft. In repairing it I learned more than I ever wanted to know about an outboard's lower unit.

PINION GEAR (OUTBOARD)   10.77

NEW PREVAILER BATTERY (on sale)   199.95

PLYWOOD FOR ARIES WIND PADDLES   18.00

I made these. We used to lose vane paddles on SEA FOAM on a regular basis, so I wanted extras. One is smaller, with two-inch holes in it, for heavy air.

REPAIR BOSUN'S CHAIR   10.00

Done by a pro. Can you imagine a manufacturer who offers a quality chair putting hardware on it that rusts out? Grrr.

SPARKPLUGS AND FUEL PUMP   67.37

MORE SPARKPLUGS   7.80

AND YET MORE SPARKPLUGS   12.00

I was going broke buying sparkplugs, one of the many reasons we bought a new outboard motor.

GASOLINE FILTER (OUTBOARD)   10.00

GASOLINE CAN   6.85

PAID TO HAVE ALUMINUM SOLDERED   35.05

This was to repair damage to our Aries

SAIL LOFT—THREAD   10.00

BOLTS FOR STORM SHUTTERS 3.50

I made plywood storm shutters for two portholes. If we break more than that, it's time for the Lord's Prayer.

WATER 3.75

This was in Providencia, an island that belongs to Colombia, where our insurance forbids us to go (ridiculous). In the Virgin Islands we paid from seven to ten cents a gallon for water. Once in the Bahamas we paid 50 cents a gallon for de-salinated water, and had to jerry jug it a quarter mile besides.

FREON 26.25

I know, owning this is naughty, but if you need to have your fridge recharged in the outbacks you'd better have some.

1 SMALL AND 2 LARGE TOTE BAGS 35.85

We use canvas tote bags for everything. If you haven't discovered them, try one. You'll be hooked.

2 PAIRS OF SUNGLASSES 24.00

2 SWIVEL BLOCKS 51.90

7 STA-LOK TERMINALS 286.65

6 RACOR FUEL FILTERS 43.50

Should have bought more. We bought a half-pint of Biobor, a diesel fuel algicide, in 1989, and we're still using it. It goes a long way.

6 FRAM OIL FILTERS 47.70

NAUTICAL ALMANAC 12.95

RIGGING AND MASKING TAPE 28.85

RULE SUPER SWITCH 25.99

Automatic bilge pump switch, guaranteed for one year and probably won't fail till day 366.

PR SPREADER BOOTS 15.75

DECK/STEAM LIGHT 61.50

I ordered the same brand, same model as the one that broke, but the factory had changed it slightly, and none of the holes matched those on the mast.

LPG REGULATOR 39.95

Surveyor insisted.

WRISTWATCH   22.95
    Goes with the almanac.

SHOCK CORD AND SHOCK CORD ENDS   29.00

SCOTCH SCRUBBIES   55.00
    We use a bunch of these.

FISHNET   32.95
    This is part of our cat retrieval system.

THERMOSTAT   25.00
    A spare for our ABSCM.

FUSES   6.36

STA-LOK WEDGES   16.95

STA-LOK WIRE FORMERS   13.50
    When you re-use Sta-Lok fittings, it's best to use new wedges and wire formers.

2 HEAD REPAIR KITS   146.00
    Outrageous, and they are now even more expensive.

2 CHEEKBLOCKS   38.50
    These were incorporated into our single line reefing system.

MISCELLANEOUS FISHING GEAR   1.09
    Given my talent, all this activity deserves.

FLAG   5.00
    We buy some. . .

FLAG MATERIAL   13.33
    But Nancy makes most of them.

GALLEY EQUIPMENT   32.44
    Neither of us can remember what this is.

S. LLOYD (BOAT INSURANCE)   1,890.00
    Our first year premium with AW Lawrence was $900 and covered us for the world. This policy covers us for the Caribbean and the East and West Coasts of North and Central America, excluding Cuba, Haiti, and Colombia. Is that inflation or what?

SHERMAN ARCH   240.00

For an excellent repair job to a boat we dragged down on during the time our insurance was not in force. (See chapter on Insurance.)

ISLETTA CANVAS   20.00
We bought closed cell foam to cover the freezer compartment, and to make a cat lair. The latter never worked out.

SAIL REPAIR   65.00
Stu, on LOOK FAR, is a single-hander we met in the San Blas Islands. He turned out to be a real pro and charged reasonable prices. The kind of person you follow around.

TOTAL $5,782.19
We didn't do a haulout this year, but we did do a lot of extra stuff thinking we were leaving for Asia.

OTHER COSTS

VARIOUS BUSSES $35.27

CAR RENTAL AND GAS   54.75
Half the cost of two days in Panama shared with another couple. We'd love to be able to afford more of this.

AMEX FEE FOR ME   55.00

AMEX FEE FOR NANCY   30.00
After I was pickpocketed in Belém, Brazil, and had to cancel all our credit cards, we figured we ought to have at least one account where Nancy had her own number. It's kind of like insurance.

MASTERCARD FEE   20.00

CUSTOMS/IMMIGRATION   221.47
This includes entering/leaving Panama, Providencia, Honduras' Bay Islands, and Guatemala. The price for entering and leaving Honduras has just been increased by an additional $60.00.

DENTIST   295.00
We found excellent dentists in Puerto Rico and Guatemala City.

DRINKS   56.85

GUIDEBOOK   10.62

FERRY   17.00

FOOD—YEAR TOTAL   2,016.54

WATER/FUEL   439.71
   Sorry, some water sneaked into this figure.

LAUNDRY   19.17

SHOTS/YELLOW FEVER/TYPHOID   524.00
   The figure includes doctors. You'd think the shots'd be for Asia, but
   they were mostly for Panama.

TOTAL EATING OUT   1,883.00
   Guess you know where our priorities lie.

TOTAL OFFICE   273.00
   A lot of writer stuff in here—computer paper, computer battery,
   printer ribbons, etc.

FAX TOTAL—SEND AND RECEIVE   246.15
   A business expense.

ATT CARD AND COIN PHONE   808.00
   Most of this is business.

FILM, PROCESSING, ETC.   227.68

CAMERA: OLYMPUS INFINITY TWIN PHOTO   114.95
   Replaces one that was stolen. We now have another one that replaces
   this, which was stolen. And now yet another (total of four), also due
   to theft.

TOTAL POSTAGE   556.91
   This includes a lot of writers' correspondence that most people
   wouldn't have. However, in St. Lucia we paid $135 for three 9x12
   envelopes stuffed with mail, and decided then to forego magazines.

BOOKS, NEWSPAPERS, CHART COPIES   77.68
   We get a lot of our reading material by trading books.

REPAIRS   294.00

PILLS/VASOTEC/PLAQUENIL   808.00
   Nancy has rheumatoid arthritis, which Plaquenil has put into remis-
   sion. I have hypertension, controlled by Vasotec, which is called Lo-
   trial or Renetec in South and Central America, and is one third the
   U.S. price. And we can buy them over the counter.

WEST MARINE/SHIPPING   52.37

ICE CREAM AND OTHER GOODIES   14.37

SURVEY FOR INSURANCE PURPOSES   263.50
As your boat gets older, most insurance companies will insist upon a survey every three years. This becomes hilarious in places like the Marquesas, where licensed surveyors are as numerous as priapic eunuchs.

TAXIS   152.00
Mostly in Panama.

INLAND TRIPS/GUATEMALA   448.00

WATER/MOSTLY IN VIRGIN ISLANDS   34.00

TOTAL OF 'OTHER' EXPENSES $10,048.99

GRAND TOTAL FOR YEAR $15,831.18
This includes the major and unusual purchase of the outboard, camera, and new Prevailer battery, and an insurance premium of $1,890. But there's always something, isn't there?

CHAPTER 43

Earning While 'Doing It'

Dear Herb: For the past 30 years I've worked as a U.S. postal employee. Having retired, I'm now planning to act on my dream of a South Pacific voyage in my own boat. I know that you have managed to earn while you cruise by writing articles and books. What other ways of earning while cruising have you encountered in your travels?

By the way, I have for years had a hobby of collecting and repairing old clocks. My wife is a professional electrologist, and has recently been very successful sculpting women's hairlines to conform to modern bikini styles.

Priority Male, Portland, Oregon

Dear Pry: As a postal employee you've already learned one of the most important traits of a successful cruiser, and that's to do everything at a leisurely pace.

It's true that not everyone who goes cruising has sufficient funds to keep going indefinitely, and only a few lucky people have enough retirement or dividend and interest income to sustain them without additional earnings. As a result, your question comes up again and again. If you're ingenious and industrious, the answer is yes.

My first question is, do you have one of the many skills we discuss below (or perhaps one we haven't thought of) that would be useful to other cruisers? I say 'to other cruisers', because in foreign countries authorities generally will leave you alone if you're servicing only yachties, whereas they tend to get huffy about work permits if you're serving locals, thus taking work away from their own citizens.

An exception might apply to a rare specialty like yours. A couple of retired school teachers joined the Peace Corps and were sent to Nukualofa, Tonga. The man had taught shop, and he too had a hobby of collecting and repairing antique clocks. He quickly gained favor with the king by repairing two tower clocks and seven of the king's own household clocks. As that was over 20 years ago, you might consider stopping by Nukualofa and selling the king a maintenance contract.

Marketing is important. In Honduras and Guatemala, the skipper of a junk named CONCUBINE offered to repair ailing diesel engines. The interesting thing was the name 'Dr. Diesel' which he used every morning on the local net. If you had a diesel engine problem, he was the first person you thought of.

My second question would be, do you have the knack for spotting opportunity? Do you have the merchant's eye for buying low and selling high? Can you spot a need that isn't being filled locally or at home? And if yes, can you tell if filling the need calls for a one-shot deal or an ongoing business?

The third question: are you creative? Can you, or your wife, design and make specialty items?

The most obvious ways to make money fall into the first category—a skill you have that other yachties from time to time need. There are many (see list in this chapter). You'll need to carry on board a complete set of tools, plus an inventory of supplies and spare parts.

A fellow we met in Tahiti who built his own 70-foot steel ketch was set up to do all arc welding, including stainless steel and aluminum, as well as brazing bronze. He'd named his boat THE ARC. He charged U.S. prices, but was fast and expert, and best of all, *there*.

The single-handing owner of the sloop LOOK FAR carried on board an industrial sewing machine, various weights of sail cloth, and a selection of grommets, cringles, and sail slides. Nancy usually does our sail repair, but the tear in our jib was major and required material and more skills than she felt she had.

Many people have a pet on board, and occasionally a pet will get sick. We knew a veterinarian and his wife cruising French Polynesia on a trimaran. You couldn't forget them: she had a beautiful figure and always wore a bikini; he had a wooden leg, wore kilts, and always played his bagpipes on entering or leaving an anchorage. Although most Pacific Islanders raise only maintenance-free chickens and pigs, our peripatetic piper occasionally found a chance to vet a pet ashore as well as on yachts.

We know a sign painter who put a notice up on the Panama Yacht Club bulletin board saying he would paint or repaint boat names or hailing ports. He mentioned casually that he could make custom designed decals, as before leaving the U.S. he'd had the foresight to equip himself with a large supply of various colored sheets of adhesive vinyl suitable for boat graphics.

In the off-the-wall department—we don't recommend this, as it borders on fraud—is the male surgical nurse we knew who assisted in sex change operations in his country's capital. He figured he knew female genitalia thoroughly: after all, hadn't he helped create complete sets for males-in-transition? Convinced that he had sufficient credentials, he sailed to Tahiti, where he rented an office and hung out a sign, 'Gynecology Spoken Here'. He did a rousing business with women who preferred a sense of humor while being specularly (and perhaps speculatively) explored. His patients were only partly dismayed when later they learned that he was qualified only as a nurse, and that perhaps their paps had been inadequately smeared.

Also in the unusual column, but strictly legitimate, we'd put the yacht MOLAR MECHANIC, on which a retired dentist installed the equipment necessary for most dental work. He charged U.S. prices to yachties, but gave his services free to the local poor.

A good varnisher is worth his/her weight in gold. He/she will own several badger hair brushes, the cost of which would shock you. He will know the best brands of varnish for each purpose (interior, exterior, work surfaces, the sole) and may even have some to sell you. He will explain why you need the expensive thinner that the varnish manufacturer recommends, thus answering the question of why, the last time we varnished, it came out looking like psoriasis.

Cruising sailors who know carpentry and fiberglass work seem always to find jobs. We recently left a port where a friend stayed behind— he had a couple of weeks work making cabinets for a fellow yachtie. And several months ago, in the Bay Islands of Honduras, a friend strengthened his cruising kitty significantly by designing and building a fiberglass bimini for the owners of an Irwin 58.

A couple of caveats, before we move on to other ways of earning while cruising. Offering a skill for money implies that you do indeed have that skill, and that you're willing to take responsibility for your work. Recently a man offered his mechanic's skills in helping rebuild another man's engine. The two worked side by side. The story goes that when the parts were put together and the motor run, due to an error in assembly there was insufficient lubrication, and the engine was virtually destroyed. Each blamed the other, ruining what had been a long-term friendship. The moral, or one of them, is don't pretend to skills you don't have.

Everyone makes mistakes, however. In a popular marina, a cruising rigger we know was helping the owner of a 48-foot ketch to re-rig. Rigger put owner up mizzen mast; but rigger had neglected to secure a few important fittings. You might think that when toppling mizzen dumped owner into drink, rigger would have gone out of business. Not so. Her resultant notoriety, coupled with her panache in describing the affair, brought her a backlog of jobs that stretched into months. She was fortunate in that the dunkee was unhurt, had a sense of humor, bore no malice, and generously took part of the blame.

Less utilitarian, but definitely more fun, are the stories of those who see a need often unrecognized, or who create a desire where none existed before. Silk screening tee shirts may not sound imaginative, but when you decorate them with a cartoon that mocks a ham radio pest whom all legitimate ham operators detest, you have a huge stockpile of potential customers. This couple's 'We Survived Hugo' and 'Antigua Race Week 1990' tee shirts were winners as well.

A woman named Jennifer, on OCTOBER, an Ericson 38, makes marvelous canvas hats. You can get one plain, or with original paintings around crown or brim, or, priciest of all, with a snake skin hatband. I asked for an anchor on mine, and when it came, to celebrate the fact that I'm a musician, the anchor rode was entwined in the shape of a treble clef.

Would you say that becoming a successful painter of island scenes while raising a family was exceptional? A Canadian family of four lived on a home-built, motorless steel cutter in which they cruised the Caribbean for years. Today Ann Miller's paintings hang in several island galleries and command substantial sums. Her husband manages a sail loft, but this is a job job, not of the kind we're discussing here. An indication of their success is that recently they bought a 60-foot aluminum sloop, and it even had an engine.

On a boat named CUCHARA (Spanish for spoon), a woman makes beautiful and unusual, yet useable, spoons using coconut shells for bowls and small bits of curved driftwood for the handles. Imaginatively designed and impeccably finished, her least expensive spoon sells for $30. A friend of ours, spoon smitten, bought four of various sizes. I don't dare let Nancy near them.

And recently Nancy insisted she had to have a charm carved by a South African cruiser. Made from bone, it is pure white, a sensuous intertwining of fluid curves which the artist calls 'procreation'. Other carvings included dolphins, whales, and a selection of most imaginative earrings, some made from white bone, some from bone inlaid with black coral. The carver was only present at one swap meet, but from what I could see, he could re-provision on what he took in.

The carver's wife made what Nancy called 'breakaway shorts', an ingenious wraparound garment secured with Velcro that can be doffed or torn off in a twink. Once the clowning dwindled down, everyone admitted to the garment's attractiveness, and many women bought, some hopefully.

In the late seventies, probably the finest living scrimshander, Miles Cortner, on the wooden schooner SEA SWAN, which he built himself, was in Fiji selling custom pendants of ivory (not yet illegal) engraved with a likeness of the customer's yacht. Our son, Craig, then sixteen, went over one afternoon and watched him work. One week later, Craig had purchased tools and materials and was in business selling the same thing. The quality was admittedly not as good, but the likeness of the customer's boat was recognizable, and Craig's price was less than half what Miles was charging. Impecunious cruisers who had given up the idea of affording such an individuated charm couldn't wait to get their names on Craig's list of customers.

Another of Craig's ventures is worth including. In Russell, New Zealand, it was common knowledge that the local butcher hated cruisers, would sell them inferior cuts of meat at superior prices, and was even known to charge for the weight of his thumb. Craig found an honest butcher in Paihia, the town across the bay, and made a deal. He would row around to all the cruising boats in the two Russell anchorages and take

Craig's scrimshaw work. No longer legal, slices of whale's teeth bought in Fiji provided Craig with the material for scrimshaw.

meat orders, phone them to his supplier, who would send *his* kid down to the ferry with Craig's order. Craig would pick the meat up off the ferry and deliver each boat's order, charging 10% or 10 cents, whichever was more. Craig was twelve.

Perhaps Craig inherited some of his entrepreneurial bent from his mother, who in Tahiti made and sold shirts and shorts, using the decorated flour sacks one could buy at the bakery. The sacks came in several designs, the two most popular being a palm tree or a lobster. As with anything that's an obvious gold mine, soon others began doing the same thing. It got so that competition for buying sacks at the mill became so strenuous, you felt like going there armed. At that point, Nancy moved on to making designer clothing for a Moorea boutique.

Mother and son for a while were involved in a joint venture, collecting, cleaning, and mailing coral to a cousin back in the States who owned a pet store and sold coral to his aquarium buyers. On the side, Craig contacted an Australian shell dealer and learned that the tiny, beautiful shells called Tahitian Gold Ringers were worth 50 cents each. He enthusiastically collected, watched the price drop to 25 cents with the shell's abundance, and learned an important theorem of commerce: Don't flood the market.

Have you noticed the little knitted balls in bright colors that the kids are playing with? Called hackey sacks, they sell in the U.S. from five dollars at check-out stands to as much as nine dollars in sports and toy shops. They can be bought in Guatemala, where they're made, for less than a dollar. A friend buys them in quantity and wholesales them in the U.S. Paying the duty to get them into the U.S. adds 40% to his cost. Our friend has fed the fad by importing hackey sacks for the last two years, to the extent that he recently completely refitted his cruising sailboat. Greed here can be disastrous, warns our friend. Milk it too long and you'll end up with a boat full of hackey sacks.

We've been to swap meets in several locations, primarily Venezuela and the Rio Dulce of Guatemala. Swap meets can be held anywhere where cruisers gather, and are always well attended: a yachtie's appetite for junk must be seen to be believed. Not only can you display boat stuff you want to get rid of, but you can display arts and crafts that you make or have bought to sell.

Nancy, in the San Blas islands of Panama, definitely lost it over molas. A mola is a square of material used to decorate the front and back of the blouses of the local Kuna women. Molas are made with bright and wonderful colors using a technique called reverse appliqué, and spiced

Herb rowing hard dinghy, wearing a flour sack shirt. Flour sacks in Tahiti were emblazoned with either a lobster or a palm tree, and from these Nancy made shirts and sold them to cruisers.

with embroidery. To my knowledge, there isn't a woman who isn't captivated by them. When her shopping frenzy spent itself, Nancy found she had twenty-odd more molas than she needed. She had also honed her taste, and there were early purchases in her collection that no longer pleased her. She sold them at swap meets for bargain prices, and still turned a handsome profit.

It's not easy to journey to the Guatemalan highlands by bus, but if you do, the travel is incredibly cheap, and Mayan fabrics and clothing can be bought at the source for rock bottom prices. In the Rio Dulce there is a cruiser's swap meet that turns out to be one of the big social events each week. A couple who found their funds dwindling took the time and trouble to bus inland, buy Mayan goods, and sell them at the swap meet. Their taste was excellent, and we were not the only ones who bought from their attractive selections.

Unless you're as famous as, say, Jimmy Buffet, a traveling musician/ entertainer probably won't make enough to be included here; third world musicians work for peanuts. But we met a couple traveling on a little sloop, both of whom played instruments and sang. They'd sail into port, then offer to play in bistros where yachties congregated. Their wages from the bistro owner ranged from 'zip' to a free drink, but the harvest from their tip jar made their best evenings worthwhile. The incalculable benefit was the friends they made, and the help they'd receive whenever their needs were made known.

Writing articles won't startle you with the amount of money you'll earn, but it's something you can do on the boat, and if you enjoy it, and can target a market, you can take pleasure in earning part of your cruising budget. The person who wants to break into the small circle of people who regularly sell articles to magazines should read the magazines; note length, style, and range of topics; and aim at a particular slot (feature, how-to, department). But above all, note the illustrations, be they photos, drawings, or art. Many of my articles sell because of the excellent photos Nancy takes. Her contribution pleases her, as does any venture or project that involves sharing.

Writing books is considerably more speculative. Nancy is still work-ing on the cookbook for which she's been doing research for two decades. Called *Beyond Peanut Butter*, it too is pure speculation, profitwise. She intends to publish it herself when we return to land life.

Other cruising people who have been successful authors are the Pardeys with their narratives, and Donald Street with his cruising guides. Nigel Calder, Jimmy Cornell and Katy Burke are among the many others who have helped support their cruising through writing.

An enterprising couple on the KATIE G II could see that new boats on Guatemala's Rio Dulce were hungry for local information. Using their com-puter and a Pagemaker program, they now regularly publish the *Review*, a pamphlet that contains ads from local businesses; articles on health, local customs, and services; tidal information (for boats entering and leaving the river over the bar); and a local calendar of holidays and events.

And then there's bungee jumping. Called "suicide for those who in-sist on changing their minds," customers pay $20 for the opportunity to

Herb writing in *Red Shoes'* saloon.

hurl themselves off an 80-foot high bridge, while harnessed to the end of a rugged bungee cord. Best to go into this business in countries where liability suits are unheard of. All you need to start business is a bungee, a winch, a harness, and a bridge, preferably high, and preferably over water. If you could also charge for photo opportunities, you'd make a fortune.

I've specifically avoided mentioning three possibilities:

Chartering usually requires a home base, and a broker to get you business. The only successful liveaboards who charter and still cruise are people who, when back home, have made prior arrangements for 'friends' to visit, thus avoiding hassles with laws restricting chartering to citizens.

Many cruisers who try chartering discover that it's a high stress job, as far from the laid-back objective of tropical cruising as you can get. Any job is stressful where you have to maintain a positive and energetic mien for your customers, no matter how much they drink. Twenty-four hour turnarounds—cleaning the boat and re-provisioning for the next arrivals—can strain the closest marital relationship. Perhaps hardest of all on the woman is that you'll be sharing your home with a succession of strangers.

Yacht delivery requires that you leave your boat, sometimes for a matter of weeks, as most yacht delivery skippers insist on surveying the boat to be delivered, and having all problems remedied. It helps to have a Captain's license. I may be wrong on this, but I have never met a delivery skipper who cruises and is still able to land more than an occasional delivery job.

Dive trips will restrict you to locations where diving is good, and because of this will most likely put you in competition with shore based and entrenched operations.

I saved the best for last: bikini bathing suits and underwear custom designed and made by an attractive couple on a trimaran in the Bahamas. To advertise, every afternoon the woman played volleyball topless, the man in a string bikini that left almost nothing to the imagination. The games were well attended by both sexes, and the wait for a fitting was a matter of weeks.

LIST OF SKILLS/TALENTS WE'VE SEEN
TURNED INTO INCOME WHILE CRUISING.

Some may now be seen to be ecologically irresponsible; others may run the risk of local competition.

Diesel repair

Electronics repair
   Don't forget TV, VCR, tape decks

Electrical
   Alternators, generators, etc.

Carpentry

Rigging

Refrigeration

Sail repair

Varnishing/painting

Metal work/welding

Canvas work
   Biminis, awnings, covers

Chartering

Yacht delivery

Dentistry

Writing
   Articles/books: adventure, how-to, guides, local color

Computer skills
   Publish local directory for new yachts

Photography

Music playing

Painting, drawing, etc.

Carving/jewelry
   Scrimshaw

Design and make unusual clothing

Design and make bikini bathing suits

Design and make spoons

Silkscreen and/or paint tee shirts

Design and make tie-dyed clothing

Make canvas hats

Make clothes from flour sacks

Sell bungee jumps (needs bridge)

Market local goods (buy low, sell high)

Export local goods (ditto)

Deliver meat and grocery orders to yachts from local stores

Collect and sell sea shells to dealers

Collect and sell (cleaned) coral to aquarium dealers

CHAPTER 44

Cooking and Provisioning

Dear Herb: In your book *Blown Away*, you described how Nancy's security blanket on SEA FOAM was to have six months' provisions on board. Has that changed? And does she still provision in the same way?

A Practicing Epicure

Dear APE: I'm going to have to get Nancy's help on this one. She is the expert, a super cook, and author of a soon-to-be-published cookbook called *Beyond Peanut Butter*, in which she makes a point of including recipes using local foods. Because she's using every opportunity to test her recipes, and because she insists she loves to cook, I never prepare a meal unless for some reason she's off the boat. I'll include here a couple of my standby recipes.

Lunch: A can of B&M baked beans smothered in ketchup, along with a side dish heaped with lettuce lathered with lavish allotments of Hellman's Real or Best Foods mayonnaise.

Supper: Hamburger, cooked rare and juicy, with maybe a touch of Worcestershire sauce, and a side dish heaped with lettuce lathered with lavish allotments of Hellman's Real or Best Foods mayonnaise.

Breakfast: Milk, sliced banana, and a choice of one of the following: Wheaties, Corn Flakes, Grape Nuts, Rice Krispies, or Shredded Wheat.

This menu comes from my childhood memories and brooks no substitutions. From time to time Nancy has tried to introduce me to some kind of bran flakes (you need *roughage*), or Froot Loops (for variety), but I can't choke them down. Frankly, without the childhood association, I'd never eat cereal at all.

The supper of hamburger and lettuce and mayonnaise was what the maid or sitter would cook for me on nights when my parents went out. Lunch with B&M beans has a less direct association. As a child, our

Sunday breakfast was B&M baked beans and B&M brown bread, the latter smothered in thick cream that had to be spooned from the bottle. These days we almost never find B&M brown bread in the markets except when we're in Maine, and cream such as that which came from my grandfather's prize Guernsey herd is no longer available unless you live on a dairy farm. Besides, even though I'm past the age of caring about cholesterol, I still feel twinges of guilt when I eat something with heavy cream. My grandfather lived to his eighties and had spoonable cream most days of his life. Ignorance, at least where food is concerned, was bliss. Anyway, all that remains of that ritual is my taste for B&M baked beans.

How did we get onto the subject of food and associations, anyway? Ah well, might as well continue. My paternal grandparents were wealthy. Granny was a talented amateur pianist, and I've inherited her Steinway grand piano. I also inherited her volumes of classical piano music, all of which she'd had bound in leather and embossed in gold. Their summer house was on a peninsula in Casco Bay, Maine, and the property is still in the family. The farm and hay fields, however, are now covered with houses.

When my family visited Thornhurst, breakfasts were served by a butler and a maid. If it wasn't Sunday, we'd have cereal with the yummy cream, followed by toast, and thick cut, bitter marmalade. The butter was fresh from the farm, unsalted, which the butler rolled into little balls between two wooden paddles and served in a bed of ice in a silver dish. The toast was yummy white bread, none of this whole wheat nonsense, and the crusts were cut off. Although the toast arrived on the table in a serving dish with a lid, it was always cold by the time I was ready for it. Hence, I love cold white toast, cold, unsalted butter, and bitter marmalade.

In these egalitarian days, it's politically incorrect to remember such luxury with longing. Butlers and butter balls, where they still exist, are spoken of only in whispers. So what does all this have to do with provisioning? Only that my clearest and dearest images of childhood are kindled by food. And perhaps it'll explain why we always have tons of Hellman's Real Mayonnaise on board, and a dozen or more cans of baked beans, and a half-dozen jars of thick cut marmalade, and no cutesy cereals. I can't tell you how much comfort this brings me.

I have a hard time in a supermarket with Nancy. The usual pattern is I push the cart and make impatient noises while she, calculator in hand, compares prices, notes the additives, examines for weevils, and then retreats mentally into some sort of private place for reflection and decision-making.

Herb: "What are you doing?"

Nancy: "Looking at this stuff."

Herb: "It's not even on the list."

Nancy: "I just like to see what's here."

Herb: "You're wasting time."

Nancy: "I'm *shopping*."

Herb: "No you're not."

You see, I've shopped with my son, pushing his cart at a full jog while he strides down the aisles snatching cans and boxes off the shelves. His list, scribbled at home, even groups items as to their location in the store. We're in and out of there with the speed of men who've mistakenly entered the ladies' rest room. Now that's shopping!

Nancy: "Look, why don't you go next door to the computer store and come back for me in an hour."

Herb: (Resigned) "Never mind." So I stay, foot-tapping and throat-clearing, to make sure she doesn't buy margarine instead of butter, or Froot Loops instead of Corn Flakes, or forget to buy spaghetti.

Scene: The West Marine outlet in Ft. Lauderdale. I'm standing in front of a display rack, my eyes glazed as I try to absorb all the different prices and types of sealants. Nancy arrives, her shopping cart overflowing, everything on our list checked off.

Nancy: "What are you doing?"

Herb: "Looking at sealants."

Nancy: (Sealants have yet to capture her imagination.) "They're not on the list."

Herb: "I just like to see what's here."

Nancy: "Do we need any of that stuff?"

Herb: "Not now, but we might, someday. Look, why don't you go next door to the fabric store, come back for me in an hour."

Nancy: (knowing that if she does, I'll come carward laden with im-
pulse credit card purchases.) "Never mind." And she stays, irritat-
ing me with overt signs of impatience while periodically pointing
out that it's way past lunchtime.

The result of Nancy's patient and exhaustive food shopping is that we eat
very well on an economical budget. However, her attraction to bargains
has occasionally led to errors. In St. Thomas, in the U.S. Virgin Islands,
we once found a whole carton of unopened boxes of pasta by the marina
dumpster. Bonanza! Sure, there were a few weevils, but she could take
care of that, going through each box and picking them out one by one.
What she didn't figure on was the weevils' fertility. They strew eggs like
a farmer sows wheat. We left the boat for a month and came back to find
all horizontal surfaces aboard solidly black with weevils. It took us
months to get rid of them, and their progeny, and their progeny's progeny.

Once, in Tahiti, Nancy came back from a shopping trip, her face
alight with triumph. "What a bargain," she said, holding up four pounds
of fatty hamburger, "but I never heard of this cut before—*pour le chien.*"
When I told her it was dog food, she was embarrassed, but philosophical.
"The French would never sell anything good this cheap," she said. And
later, when she returned the meat to the store, the butcher laughed till he
cried when she, with the help of a friend, told him her mistake.

Nancy's turn.

When you're cruising and you get to a place where you can buy stuff,
you're going to buy what you like to eat. So the question really is, what
do I provision the boat with that differs from my weekly shopping list?
And why?

We use milk for cereal and for cooking, not as a beverage. Outside
of the U.S.A. we look at milk differently. Fresh milk is usually not available, and when it is one wonders about quality. So I buy long life milk,
powdered milk and canned milk for two months.

We don't eat canned fruit on land or in port, but it's marvelous on a
passage. It goes down easily, doesn't come up easily, and should you have
to throw up, canned fruit tastes more or less the same as it did going down.
The sugar in which most fruit is canned provides a lift. Also, the presence
of sugar in canning eliminates any fear of botulism.

The size of the freezer in our refrigerator allows two people to have
fresh frozen meat every night for two weeks. One reason we can do this
is that I buy boneless cuts or packages of meat and chicken, remove them

Nancy at a local market. At first, many of the vegetables and spices seem mysterious, but Nancy's cookbook, *Beyond Peanut Butter*, will lead you through the maze.

from their styrofoam packages and put them in less space-consuming freezer bags.

We had no idea how much pleasure we'd get from having ice every evening! When the freezer unit is packed, we keep only one ice tray, but as the meat is used up we can add more if we wish. Except for entertaining, however, we seldom feel the need for more than one.

Canned meat is mostly a disappointment. Hams are okay. Bacon, though extraordinarily salty, is okay, particularly if you leach out the salt before cooking. Canned shrimp is good for hors d'oeuvres, casseroles, salads, and linguine. Tuna fish for salads or sandwiches is always a standby. Canned salmon works well. Some specialties such as canned clams or smoked mussels are a good hors d'oeuvre treat. Canned chicken or turkey only comes in small cans. Many of these products can't be bought in countries outside the U.S.A., and if you do find them, they'll be expensive. While provisioning in foreign countries, if you see something you like, buy a lot of it. Chances are you won't see it again for a while.

Many countries don't can their own meat, so what's on the shelves will be imported. This will be expensive.

Hard to find are cans of boiled beef or pork, which are usually okay if made into casseroles. Try before you stock up, however. Most canned meat has to be doctored. You can't just take it out of the can and enjoy it.

A salami will last months if air is allowed to circulate around it, or if refrigerated. Canned corned beef works in hash, and in a few other recipes. We don't like it much, so we don't buy it.

Because the only canned meat available in New Zealand was corned beef and lamb's tongue, we decided to can our own beef and chicken. Five of us spent two days canning hamburger, chicken, sausage, filet, New York steaks, and stew beef. All three kinds of beef came out tasting like pot roast, but it was far superior to any commercially canned beef we've found. The chicken was superior to any canned chicken we've tasted.

Beans, rice, and flour tend to have weevils. These are staples that are available everywhere, so we don't stock up with a large supply.

Pre-passage preparation: Because I usually do not feel like cooking during the first few days at sea, I always prepare food ahead of time. Often I make bread pudding, a nourishing, tasty dish that requires no re-heating. I make sure that cookies and other snack foods are available. Cheese and bread make a good lunch. Fruits that require no preparation are apples, bananas, oranges, pears, plums, and grapes. Herb loves apples with cheese, and bananas with nuts, so I try to have cashews, walnuts, pecans or almonds at hand. On occasion I'll make a large potato salad.

Granola mix or trail food make a good snack. We used to buy Granola bars, but we grew tired of them. Raisins and dried apricots are great, too.

Once the first few days are over, I cook as I normally would ashore. I use those fresh veggies that are likely to spoil first. Longer lasting veggies include cabbage, beets, carrots, potatoes, and onions; also winter squash (pumpkin, acorn squash, butternut squash) and christophenes (chayotes).

When the time comes, I start on either freeze dried veggies or canned. Freeze dried veggies can be bought from Mormon supply houses, and taste far better than canned.

We cook on board more than we do on land: Aboard, even in port, I bake bread often. We use very few prepared foods, such as packaged cake mixes, macaroni and cheese, Lipton's noodle mixes, or Uncle Ben's wild rice. We prepare specialty or ethnic food more often than we would at home, where we'd usually eat it in a restaurant.

CHAPTER 45

The Great Provider

Dear Herb: My husband wants to supplement our larder with the bounty of the sea. I simply *adore* seafood, as long as someone else cleans it. Could you talk a little about how you catch fish, lobster, and conch?

Awaiting Neptune's Garden Salivating Torrentially

Dear ANGST: Nothing makes me feel inferior faster than being around cruising sailors when they're talking about the fish and lobsters they've speared. My ego shrivels like manhood on ice. After twenty years of cruising I have yet to spear either fish or lobster. Truth to tell, I usually can't even *find* lobsters in places where they are supposed to abound.

There was some reason for this in the beginning. For the first year, SEA FOAM sailed in the company of a yacht with a couple of hotshot grown sons aboard, and as long as we stuck with them, we were up to our hips in fish. Our sons learned from their sons, so I saw no reason to get involved with sharks, morays, and other undesirables. Let the children do it—with my cautionary advice, of course.

Memories from that seven-year cruise: approaching Suvarov atoll trolling our boat line and catching a dorado and two tuna in the pass; sharing the spoils with the four boats in the anchorage, and during the rest of our stay having great white hunters drop off gifts of speared fish.

Still on Suvarov: hunting lobster on the reef with son Craig and Nancy, Nancy holding the light while Craig and I leaned over and grabbed the blue-eyed beauties. I'm pretty good with gloves—just don't hand me a spear. You had to grab quick and not miss; you never got a second chance.

Trying to spear crayfish in a fresh water stream at the south end of Tahiti. Refraction was something I'd learned about in physics, but theory never did translate to practice. Craig shot 27 to my one, and the only reason I speared that one was that I blinked.

Our children are now beyond the reach of parental exploitation. A Fagin with no urchins to deploy, I've been forced to try to do my own food-gathering. We occasionally catch something on our boat line, but whatever pride of achievement that brings me is dispelled the minute I pick up a spear.

In the beginning I bought a simple spear, a six and a half foot shaft with a lethal point on one end and a loop of surgical tubing seized at the other. Inserting your right wrist in the loop, you pull your right hand as far toward the point as your strength allows, and at the point of maximum stretch of the tubing, you grip the spear. The left hand acts as the guide through which the spear is supposed to track toward the kill. When the fish appears, you point with the left hand and release with the right. The elastic tubing provides the thrust, theoretically impaling dinner.

Theoretically. In practice, the fish swims away, and having bounced the tip of my spear off a coral head, I retreat to the dinghy where, with a file, I re-sharpen the point to its original keenness. The one good thing about my lack of skill is that I do virtually no harm to the fish population.

At Isla Blanquilla, Venezuela, a friend and I went on several fishing expeditions. After an hour or so of trying to corner a shy squirrel fish, I started taking long shots. I trust that coral damage was slight, but soon my spear tip was so blunt it would probably have bounced off the surface of a jellyfish, had I been skillful enough to hit one.

My friend blamed his lack of success on his spear gun which, he maintained, was too short; it was about a foot long. I stored this information away, so that when I should finally trade in my spear for a gun, I wouldn't make the same mistake.

Because, as man's thinking so often goes, if I had a decent tool I could do a decent job. Spears are to modern spear guns what the sling David used against Goliath is to a rifle. With a spear gun I could really spear fish.

I decided to begin a process in which till recently I put total faith. It's called networking. In every conversation you manage to insert the fact that you're thinking of buying a spear gun, but you don't know anything about them. People rush to advise you, and what's supposed to happen is that sooner or later the picture of the gun you should buy comes clear. I'm here to attest that the process is not foolproof.

After a week, this is what I'd written down:

Get a long one.

Get a short one.

Get one with two rubbers—one rubber won't do the job.

Get one made in France.

Get one made in Italy.

Be prepared to spend some money.

Get a cheap one—they're all made pretty much the same.

Bewildered, I took the middle course and bought a medium-sized spear gun for a medium price. It felt good in my hands. It was French. It was red and lethal looking. Visions of lobster danced in my head. My heart sang with expectation.

Our very next cruise took us to the Islas Tortugas off the Venezuelan coast. With a friend I snorkeled the reefs. I watched as he drifted, dove, pointed and shot. He never missed. I drifted and dove, but always the fish spooked. The few shots I took were too far away, and my aim always went wide of the mark.

"Your spear gun is too short, that's all." His was the longest they make; he could practically touch his prey while his looming shadow remained too distant to scare the target. As we cruised Los Roques and Los

Kuna holding crab. One of these San Blas (Panama) beauties fed us both generously.

Aves (two beautiful Venezuelan island groups), I continued to snorkel with my gun at the ready, spear cocked with both rubbers, Nancy drifting prudently behind me. I developed this sinking feeling in the pit of my stomach, this absolute certainty, that I could go out with a ten-foot spear gun and the results would be the same.

Then suddenly our whole perspective on fishing changed, and smiles returned to RED SHOES. A friend with a 30-gallon per hour watermaker told us that in Venezuela's arid islands, fishermen will gladly swap fish for water. We have no watermaker, but we've discovered that rum will tempt the most recalcitrant lobster from the fishermen's tank. Neither Nancy nor I smoke, but we carry cigarettes, a few of which will pry a good sized fish from a fisherman's catch. They will always over-trade for a can of corned beef, a change of taste that pleases fish-weary palates.

So let successful spear-fishing cruisers continue their macho maundering. I'm proud that I'm no longer seen as a poacher, stealing the locals' livelihood. Instead I'm enjoying economic intercourse, the game that has best cemented discrete people throughout history.

POSTSCRIPT: Here's a list of all the seafood I've speared in twenty years of cruising:

Grouper: 0	Snapper: 0	Crab: 1
Hogfish: 0	Lobster: 0	

CHAPTER 46

Guns Aboard?

Dear Herb: I've got a brother who's setting off on a round the world cruise, and he tells me he's not going to take a gun. He won't listen to me, but he reads your articles all the time, so I'm hoping he'll listen to you. Going off to all those primitive countries without a weapon is just about the damn foolest thing I ever heard. I've got a whole arsenal he can pick from. Just tell him which type gun is best, and I'll see that he has it, okay?

Brotherly Concerned

Dear BC: You obviously care about your brother, so I'll ask you to think over your answers to the following. How many people have you shot? How many have you killed with a gun? If you're not a soldier who's been in some war or other, your answers are probably 'none'.

Perhaps the most dangerous act of all is to threaten without the means or determination to carry it out. If your brother takes along a gun, he'll need to *know* that if he brandishes it at intruders, he has to be ready to shoot—and shoot first, as this is a game in which second place doesn't make it. I'll assume he never used a gun in self-defense. A lot of people I've talked to think they can, or could. Let's talk about that, first.

Scene One: The darkest, most overcast of nights; an anchorage. A sound wakes you—is someone coming aboard your boat? Do you get the Magnum now, or wait until the intruder has the drop on you? Better get it now. Sounds like he's on deck. You remember Betsy Hitz-Holman's book *Sitting Duck*, and the guy who boarded their boat wielding a machete, out of his gourd on some uncontrolled substance. The skipper was badly cut up and took months to recover. You'll be damned if that'll happen to you and yours. You jack a bullet into the chamber. Looking up the companionway you see a shadow. Sumbitch is coming down the companionway! You yell "halt," or if you're really into this, "freeze, motherfucker." Sumbitch takes another step toward you, raises his hand. Is there a gun in it? Can't wait to find out. You shoot, and after turning on the light you see it's a friend.

He sails (looking at the wound you'd better say 'he sailed') a yacht that's the same model as yours. With his wife away, he had the habit of going to the disco and letting it all hang out. He must have thought he was boarding his own boat.

Scene Two: The darkest of nights. A third world anchorage. A sound, you get the gun. The shadow comes down the companionway. You yell "stick 'em up" or "don't move." He's raising one hand, does it hold a pistol? Can't wait to find out: BLAM! The sound of a 12-gauge shotgun exploding in the confines of a small cabin disturbs your wife. As you turn on a cabin light, she appears in the stateroom door, takes in the scene, and throws up.

At least this time you were right, the guy did have a gun. Was he going to shoot or merely hold you up? You'll never know. What you do know is you've just shot the brother of one of the local cops. In your mind you run through a few explanations. You imagine a third world jail. Better simply get rid of the body. You've been saving 100 feet of rusty old chain for just such an eventuality.

Damn, there's blood everywhere. Your wife has finally finished cleaning vomit off herself and the saloon carpet. You ask her if she knows how to get rid of bloodstains. A sudden dry heave obscures her answer, so you ask her again, louder this time, and she nods her head.

Eventually the two of you try to wrestle a 200-pound sack of long pig up the companionway stairs. It takes awhile, and is only successful after you've rigged a tackle using the multi-purchase main sheet. With Ricardo swinging from the boom and dripping blood all over your boat, you motor out into deep water, wrap him with chain, and cut him loose. And while you're at it, you'd better get rid of the gun.

Your wife is below scrubbing the carpet, trying unsuccessfully to remove incriminating evidence. It's comforting to have her involved. You console her by telling her you'll take the carpet ashore first thing in the morning and burn it. For some reason she bursts into tears.

At first light you see where the blood has dripped onto the teak decks. Experiments prove beyond a shadow of a doubt that you've discovered a permanent and effective stain for teak. Unfortunately you don't have access to enough fresh human blood to finish the job, so for the next few months, the droplet stains will serve as mementos of your rich cruising experience.

Okay, the humor is black, but I think these scenes are worth including, as some people have never visualized and extrapolated what carrying and using a gun for self-defense really involves.

I have a friend, an ex-police officer, who suggests carrying a shotgun because it makes the most noise and does the most damage at close range. It would also make the biggest mess, if fired on something with blood in it. "When you hear the intruder," says my friend, "you stick the barrel out a porthole and let off a round. If you hear the intruder leave, you win. If you don't, you lose, so you throw the gun out the hatch and come out with your hands up."

In the latter case, there's some doubt that you'd make it through the night. If you'd shoot first because you *thought* the intruder had a gun, an intruder, knowing that *you* had one, probably would too. In any event, sayonara.

In the last couple of years we've heard of two cases of shootings involving cruisers in Central America. In the first instance, the man, we'll call him Jack, and his wife (might as well call her Jill), were boarded by two unarmed men. Jack went for his gun, and brandished it. Evidently it wasn't cocked, or the safety was on, or he forgot where the trigger was, or he didn't get to it in time, because in fact the intruders, convicts escaped from a nearby prison, overpowered him and shot him dead with his own gun. They then forced the woman to dinghy them ashore, *which was all they ever wanted in the first place.*

In the second case, a couple (we'll call them Tom and Mary) were hanging out in a lonely anchorage in Central America when three young men approached in an open boat. After a few minutes of conversation, one of the men pulled a pistol and covered Tom. Mary, below decks, called to Tom that she was going for Tom's handgun, which was kept loaded beside their bunk. Hearing her call, a second man went below to subdue her. Moments later Tom heard her scream, and dove down the companionway to come to her aid. The first gunman shot but missed. In the ensuing fight, however, he did in fact shoot Tom, wounding him in the thigh. The men then tried to abduct Mary, but the couple resisted so determinedly that ultimately the intruders fled.

Tom has recuperated. I asked him how he felt about having a gun aboard now, and he said he was still in favor of it. Cruising in third world countries, he and Mary will be less inclined to anchor away from other yachts. But if that should happen, he would definitely be more wary.

"A better scenario would be to have the woman topside so that the man, who is probably more familiar with weapons and perhaps more mentally prepared to shoot someone, could be below, armed and ready."

There's no way to know how these two unfortunate events would have played had the boats been unarmed.

What the two above incidents indicate to me is that having a gun aboard isn't enough. What's exponentially more important is having a plan. Sailing couples should talk through all the scenarios they can think of, and perhaps even act some of them out. Whatever tools your plan requires should be at hand, not tucked away in some locker.

Fire drills, man overboard drills, defense drills—you say that's paranoia at work? Or is it common-sense preparation?

We carried a Ruger pump action .22 caliber rifle on SEA FOAM. One time we anchored near a Costa Rican shrimp boat whose crew were eyeing our nubile daughters. They gave us shrimp in exchange for girlie magazines, the prevailing commodity for bartering with local shrimpers. Then we watched them as they all bathed and shaved. "We'll be over later," said the primping shrimpers.

We moved anchorage. They followed. We got out the .22 and plinked at bottles. They did not come over to bother us. Would they have bothered us had we *not* had a gun? Would they have done any more than visit and talk? We'll never know.

In other situations, letting the world know you keep a gun on board could itself attract thieves. In many countries, guns are so difficult for ordinary citizens to get that a thief might take big risks to acquire one.

The life-sustaining by-product of carrying our Ruger was the exorbitant price it brought from a Chinese storekeeper on Tubuai in the Austral Islands. Gun running was left out of my chapter on "Earning While Doing It," as it involves a certain amount of risk if pursued diligently. As a one-shot affair, however, it kept us from starving for another month. With the money we bought a lot of food from the same Chinese storekeeper, making the whole thing a heartwarming if cameo experience of economic hands across the sea.

Later we carried an ancient single-shot .22, a gift from a friend. We sold that to one of the officials on Penrhyn, this time with government sanction acquired by radio from Raratonga. We never had a chance to brandish either gun in the face of an intruder, as during the nearly seven years we carried them the opportunity never arose.

I'll be the first to admit that statistics are no comfort to those whose destiny it is to live the exceptions, but we still make decisions based on them. To tip the odds more in our favor we wear seat belts when driving or riding in a car; we don't walk the streets of Harlem or Watts alone at night; we wear a money belt in third world cities. But on our RED SHOES cruise our decision has been not to carry a gun, and we're comfortable with our choice—for the moment.

If you decide to carry a gun, do you declare it with customs when you enter a foreign country? We always did, and almost always it was taken away from us and held in bond until we left. Right there, most of its usefulness as protection was negated.

If you declare your gun and it's taken from you, you have to reclaim it when you leave. This can be a real pain in the neck, as there is always a policy as to how you retrieve it. It's usually time consuming, but it's also committing. Say you decide to check out, arrange to have your gun returned to you, and then the weather turns bad.

And if you don't declare your gun and you're found out, the consequences can be grave. A yacht leaving Tahiti was approached by a boat load of officials whose intent was to board and search for drugs. The crew threw a small arsenal of guns, including fully automatic rifles, overboard. The officials didn't find any drugs, but they did send divers down for the guns, and having found them threw the whole crew in jail. For all I know they may still be there.

If we had carried a well-concealed gun on RED SHOES and decided not to declare it, we would so far not have been caught. Officials have never torn our boat apart in a search. If they come aboard at all, it's merely for a cursory look around. What do you say to the police after shooting an intruder with an undeclared gun? That you wrested it from the intruder in a hand to hand? Yes, but then he was unarmed, wasn't he? (I know, you're going to shoot him dead, wrap him in rusty chain and sink him, clean up the blood, and never mention the act to anyone.)

The yeas and nays of gun carrying seem unresolvable. But if your brother decides not to carry one, he has other means of defending himself. Many yachties carry mace, or some form of pepper spray. Others feel that a flare gun would be useful, although it's absurdly inaccurate, and more likely to burn up your boat than ignite an invader. A fishing spear or spear gun might deter an intruder who wields only a machete or knife. My little spear gun was confiscated as a 'dangerous weapon' during our time in Bonaire.

We've installed a dead bolt in our companionway hatch so that at night, in a spooky anchorage, we can lock ourselves in. Radio Shack offers various types of alarms, the scream or wail of which might scare off an intruder. Or, take along a dog as second mate: I've never heard of a well-dogged boat being burgled or robbed.

You can see where my sentiments lie at the moment. One incident of violent intrusion could change my mind. No one wants to be a victim, yet carrying a gun is no guarantee that you won't be. My advice is to tell your brother to decide for himself whether to take a gun or not. That way he can't blame you if his choice turns out to be wrong for him.

We raised the dinghy for the night and locked it with a steel cable. The most common crime against cruisers is dinghy and/or outboard theft. Raising the dink every night using one or two halyards is good insurance.

In some parts of the world, having a gun on board may bring you a greater sense of security, and I certainly won't deny that that's important. One night in the Amazon Delta, where we cruised alone for six weeks unarmed, we found ourselves tucked into an isolated cove. Sometime during the night someone tried to steal our dinghy. After cutting the bow and stern painters, the thief learned to his chagrin that the dinghy was cabled and locked to RED SHOES. In what must have been a fit of frustration, he slashed one of the chambers with a knife or machete. When we discovered this the next morning, I wished we had carried a gun. On the other hand, what good would carrying a gun have done us? Both Nancy and I slept through the whole thing.

Finally, we know of sailors in Venezuela, and have met several cruising crews since, who have lain quietly in their bunk during a boat theft. They were robbed by one or more armed men, but they were left unharmed. In one case, the cruising couple was bound and gagged by armed men, and subsequently robbed, and left unharmed.

I think it's important to be aware of the concept of escalation. Let's imagine a confrontation. At the first level it's verbal. One of you starts to yell: level two. Enraged, you throw a punch: level three. He pulls a knife: level four. You pull a gun: level five. Someone ends up hurt or dead.

Nobody decrees that if you carry a gun you'll have to use it. You might feel better carrying one even if you never bring it out. You could for example leave it in its hiding place until and unless you were sure that using it would tip the balance against unarmed invaders. A gun is a tool, and its prudent and practiced use is no more dangerous than the prudent and practiced use of a chain saw.

CHAPTER 47

Medicine at Sea

Dear Herb: When I asked our family doctor to prescribe antibiotics, pain pills, and local anesthetics for our trip, he said "I wouldn't give you or any layman anything stronger than aspirin." We're going to see a different doctor next week, but in my heart I know our doctor is right. We aren't trained in the use of powerful drugs. However, if someone gets sick in mid-ocean, I want to be able to do something. And what about tropical illnesses?

Fed Up Currying Knowledge of Endemic Diseases

Dear (Acronym deleted): You're right and your doctor is wrong. Even if you know nothing, but you manage to reach a doctor by radio, what do you do if he says, "Give the patient two Percodans before setting the bone," or "Get out the xylocaine; that wound must be lanced." Or, in the case of a disease that he's decided from your description is malaria, "As you caught it in Panama, take Fansidar, three tablets in a single dose."

"I don't have any of that stuff."

"You mean to tell me you went to sea without a proper medical kit?"

"Yes, because my doctor wouldn't. . ."

"Fool!" (or its Latin equivalent.)

I've been there. Nancy and I, newly married, each had our family doctors. Mine was a cruising sailor, so I went to him with a list culled from Peter Eastman's *Advanced First Aid Afloat*. He wrote out over a dozen prescriptions, which I gave to our druggist, saying we were going to San Diego for a month, and that when we came back we'd be pressed for time. So could he please have the prescriptions ready?

There followed a whole china closet full of fah-cups. (Fah-cups: a clay-daubing daughter's euphemism for glazing mistakes.) The pharmacist, knowing we wouldn't be picking them up right away, delayed filling the prescriptions. At that time in California, all narcotics prescriptions had to be filled within five days of their having been written. Holding a sheaf of now-void prescriptions in hand, our pharmacist, a busy but conscientious man, drove to another town to get my doctor to re-write them. He happened to arrive in the office during an emergency with a badly cut child. Busy druggist was impatient, doctor was distraught, and the scene ended with both people angry. We returned from San Diego to find the prescriptions unfilled, and my doctor on vacation. Nancy's doctor refused to prescribe anything. As a result, we left with only the drugs we had in our medicine chest.

We were sailing down the west coast of Baja. Son Chris, 19, had cut his thumb, and it had become infected. Swollen, red, and ugly, with no doctor for miles, we knew it had to be lanced. There was no xylocaine, so we fed him rum. Nancy, who thrives on attacking pus, lanced and squeezed, at which time we learned that rum as an anesthetic wasn't worth anything.

The only other serious illness at sea was a bladder infection I had. We treated it with tetracycline, out of date and the wrong drug, and of course it didn't work. A bladder infection, if not corrected, can cause death. Fortunately there was a good UNICEF supported hospital in Southern Tonga. The New Zealand volunteer doctors, after finally having been convinced that what I had was not a venereal disease, gave me the proper antibiotic, and my infection was cured in magically short order.

Prevention is the place to begin. Our boat has screens on any port or hatch that opens, and in tropical countries, where mosquitoes are known to carry disease, we're religious about using them. We use mosquito repellent when appropriate.

Staph loves the tropics: the salinity and temperature of tropical seas are so like blood that staph infections flourish. Once you have it, staph is extremely difficult to get rid of. It's again a matter of common sense to disinfect all cuts, no matter how minor, before they have a chance to worsen.

A couple of years ago we visited a beachside restaurant on the northwest coast of Guanaja, in the Bay Islands of Honduras. After lunch we went swimming, and although I noticed sand flies and knew I was being bitten, the bites seemed innocuous. That night, however, I itched so badly I couldn't sleep. The bites, now red welts, completely covered my arms and legs. I was up all night and tried everything to relieve the itching: soaked the bites with water so hot I felt parboiled; next tried applying pure Clorox; then pure ammonia. All of these remedies brought relief for maybe five minutes, after which the itching came back with sanity-destroying intensity.

In the morning, sympathetic friends suggested Benadryl, an antihistamine, and Valium. With the help of these two drugs I slept that night. Although only once in all our years of cruising did I suffer bites to such a degree, I could have saved myself a night of hell had I known what to do.

Drugs are continually being discovered or improved, so I'd suggest checking with your doctor for the best antihistamine to have on board. As for Valium, I had never had one before, nor have I taken any since. Nevertheless, having experienced the relief it brought, I would not now leave home without it.

The medicine that people take to ward off cholera is only 50% effective. The one time we went into an area where cholera was endemic— the then Gilbert Islands, now Kiribati—we took it, and did not get the disease. However, we were also extremely careful of the water we drank. Had there been fresh locally grown leafy vegetables available we would have washed them in a solution of Clorox and good water. None were available so the problem never came up.

Boaters are much less subject to cholera, as they either treat, make or catch their water. Dengue fever is carried by mosquitoes, is no fun at all, and the only prevention we know of at this time is screens, bug killer, and repellent. We read that the little vampires are attracted to cologne and deodorant, so RED SHOES has a new but far from improved smell.

We are presently in Guatemala where malaria is endemic. Tourists who come here for a short time can take an anti-malarial preventive. However, people who live here don't, and this includes gringos with unexceptional resistance to malaria, as the danger of liver damage caused by continuous use of the drug outweighs the benefits.

Malaria, by the way, comes in different garbs, each of which requires a different defense. In Panama, where the disease is rife, there is a different type on each coast. The best place to get up to date info on malaria is the U.S. Department of Public Health, or the International Association for Medical Assistance to Travellers (IAMAT). Either organization will advise you what immunizations you should have before leaving. The U.S. Department of Public Health advised us to have yellow fever boosters, and to make sure diphtheria, typhoid and tetanus shots were up to date. IAMAT can be reached in the U.S. at 417 Center Street, Lewiston, NY 14092-3633. Tel. 716 754 4883.

Another disease that is particularly relevant to cruising is ciguatera, a debilitating and occasionally fatal malady acquired from eating fish containing the ciguatera toxin. Reef fish collect the poison from coral, and are the most likely to be contaminated. However, the toxin doesn't leave the fish, so if it's eaten by a fish higher up the food chain, that fish is poisonous too. In some areas, pelagic fish that you would think were safe have been found to be poisonous—the most common example is barracuda. At present, the rule of thumb in the Caribbean is not to eat a barracuda that's over two feet long, but the incidence of ciguatera has been on the rise, so be careful, and try to get local knowledge.

In addition to the informative monthly Bulletin, the SSCA has available for its members many pamphlets and brochures on cruising subjects, ciguatera being one of them. In the December 1989 issue, Dr. Richard Lewis described two treatments: Amitriptyline tablets, and for the more severely affected, but only if skilled medical/nursing assistance is at hand, intravenous mannitol.

If you scuba, decompression sickness must be a concern. Why dive deep, when almost everything you'll want to see is rarely deeper than 30 feet? Keeping your gear in perfect repair is only common sense.

The only other malady we got at sea was seasickness. I was never seasick. Nancy usually felt ill to varying degrees during the first three days of a passage. We had Dramamine, but she never used it. By the time we'd learned of remedies that worked without knocking you out, she was basically over getting seasick at all.

It was from Ed and Laurie McKeon, the two friends who cruised with us aboard SEA FOAM for eight months, that we learned of a remedy that really works. Laurie was troubled by seasickness and had tried patches, Dramamine, everything that was available in the mid-seventies, until she discovered Phenergan. It is available in suppository form, and Laurie could wait until she was feeling lousy and then take it. Most seasickness medicine won't work unless you take it before you feel queasy. Phenergan does.

A few years ago a couple of friends took 24 hours to sail the 30 miles to windward from Curaçao to Bonaire. Christmas winds were a steady 25 knots, gusting sometimes to 40. A two-knot current was also working against them. After 30 minutes at sea the wife became violently and continually seasick, and observed, "I never knew a person had so much bile they could get rid of."

There are two main causes of seasickness: psychological, usually fear; and physical. An example of the first would be the wife who deems her husband incompetent, and suddenly realizes her life is in his hands. This insight has been known to cause projectile vomiting.

The second kind is physical, vertigo caused by inner ear disorientation. Quite often seasickness results from a combination of causes. Chronic seasickness can inspire the meekest helpmeet to put her foot down, squashing all hope of future cruising as a couple. That was the way it seemed to be heading with our friends.

She: "I'm never going to sail again."

Nancy: "I have this terrific remedy, it's a suppository."

She (tone expressing a combination of amusement and revulsion): "I would never stick anything up there."

Nancy: "Why not?"

She: "Because."

Many people have a prejudice against taking medicine anally. Not the French: they have suppository technology down to an art. In France, suppositories are available for anything, from aspirin to a dry martini.

We met a cruising couple in Puerto Rico who were sailing a beautiful old wooden ketch. After scrimping and saving, after years of work bringing their boat back from dereliction, they set sail from Florida. Too late, they learned that the man was subject to chronic, acute seasickness. He was useless and miserable at sea. They were on their way home to sell the boat. We gave him some of our Phenergan, and three years later he is still enjoying cruising.

Because most remedies tend to make you drowsy, people who use Phenergan also take a mild stimulant—Ephedrine sulphate if you can get it. Although both medicines come in pill form, if you wait till you're queasy, you're likely to regurgitate a pill before it can go to work. (If you find yourself vomiting a suppository, you're in serious trouble.)

Note: If you take medicine regularly for other problems, you'll need to consult with your doctor to see if any new medicine will conflict.

And finally, if you find that you or your crew does get seasick, I hope Phenergan works for you. There's nothing worse than a dream abandoned when the problem might have been solved.

POSTSCRIPT: Our Siamese cat gets seasick. We tried unsuccessfully to introduce her to suppositories, but, uh—does anyone have any falconry gloves we could borrow?

CHAPTER 48

Problems When Visiting Foreign Ports

Dear Herb: My husband and I have never traveled beyond the borders of the U.S.A. You hear all these stories about unreasonable officials. Have you ever had trouble with officials in foreign countries? What can we expect?

Virgin Vagabond

Dear VV: Good question, but don't let the molehill become a mountain. Checking into foreign countries, while seldom actually pleasant, is rarely unpleasant. And when you consider that the time spent in dealing with the officials is a tiny percentage of the traveling experience, you begin to see things in perspective. To have your fear of officials diminish your anticipation is a lot like losing the joy of life because you occasionally have to go to the dentist.

A big problem for me is rejecting negative expectations. So many stories paint officials as grasping, crooked, autocratic bureaucrats—small minds with a little power. I have to prep myself against striding in with jutting chin, determined to stand firm against victimization. I think of my door-to-door salesman days, don a real smile, and treat Mr. Official with the respect his uniform and office deserve.

This works most of the time.

Radiating pleasure at being in Colón, Panama (a major feat in itself), I was subjected to a 20-minute tirade from—was it Customs or Immigration? I can't remember. In any event, when a U.S. yacht departs the U.S.A., no *zarpe* is issued. (A *zarpe* is a paper that says you cleared out of country X legally and owing no official fees. A country is not bound to admit you without a *zarpe* from your last port. Theoretically a *zarpe*-deficient skipper could be condemned to remain at sea forever.) I was told in no uncertain terms that if I ever arrived in Panama again without the proper papers, I would not be admitted.

Many, but not all, countries with a British heritage want you to anchor off the port of entry with a Q-flag prominently displayed and wait for officials to board you. Some offer dock space (Bermuda, New Zealand),

316

but still you must wait for the official to come to you. In some ports, if you don't go ashore, you'll wait forever. In one of the French Islands—was it Guadeloupe?—you go ashore, find the empty office that harbors the visitors' book, and sign it. End of procedure.

Irritation with official fussiness can reach vein-bursting proportions. Due to bad weather and contrary winds, a passage on SEA FOAM from Samoa to the Gilbert Islands took us 46 days. We arrived around midday, dropped anchor, raised the Q-flag, and only then did we initiate a libationary festival of thanks.

Next day by noon there was still no sign of an official. We had arrived with a broken windvane and a non-functioning transmission. So what would you have done? Exactly. Ashore we went, papers in hand; kissed the earth; could not pass an ice cream store without parting with a bit of money; and were told, when we reached officialdom, to get the hell back on our boat and wait for the officials to come to us. Late that afternoon, nearly 30 hours after our arrival, the officials appeared.

I'm told that the Cayman Islands officials are murder. You must anchor off Georgetown, the main town in Grand Cayman. Fellow cruisers who go to the Caymans often told me that if you drop your anchor on coral it's a $2,000 fine. The safest move is to pick up one of the unoccupied dive boat moorings and wait. If you make the mistake of going ashore to clear in, you pay a $5,000 fine. Expensive for the unenlightened.

In Belém, Brazil, Immigration and Customs are roughly two miles apart along the commercial waterfront. During siesta, usually between

Bird landing on *Sea Foam*'s taffrail. A tired bird visits on our 46-day passage to the Gilberts, and stays on and off for three days.

noon and 2 P.M., the offices are closed. Often the officials quit early and come back late. Sometimes during office hours they have to go aboard a ship, so they close the office. You're lucky if you can find the office, and when you do, if the door is open, and if it is, that there's someone there who can help you. In Belém, anchored off the yacht club with Q-flag prominently displayed, you could wait 20 years and no official would ever come.

We had to go to the Navy to get a cruising permit. The Navy's office is not on the waterfront with the other officials. Fortunately we were warned that if you show up wearing shorts they won't deal with you. Deep in the steamy Amazonian jungle, aswelter in equatorial sunshine, this is the only country we've visited that insists you wear long pants when dealing with officials.

Many are the horror stories of foreign cruisers trying to deal with U.S. officials. Why anyone would want to put up with them in order to cruise our over-regulated shores is beyond me. Cuban criminals, plus hundreds of illegal Haitians and Mexicans can swarm into our country, but middle class Europeans with enough money to own a cruising boat and go sailing on it have often been treated badly indeed. When I'm dealing with an official in a host country who doesn't like yachties from anywhere and particularly those from the U.S., I try to remember what cruising friends from other shores have had to put up with in my country.

Correction: Checking in with Customs in Key West recently, I overheard an official dealing with an elderly British couple. He treated them with deference and respect, while informing them that they'd broken U.S. law by coming here from Cuba—having spent money there, they were in violation of our embargo. However, the official was only politely giving information, not hassling the couple.

Most problems with foreign officials are niggling. In Placentia, Belize, there was, for a while, a medfly invasion. Some yachts checking in from Guatemala were forced to give up their fresh fruits and vegetables to the officials. A medfly invasion is certainly serious, and whatever steps are necessary to curb it should be followed with grace and tolerance. However, the application of the regulation was inconsistent. Some yachts had their larders confiscated, others didn't. Nobody warned you, so several yachties went to the local stores and bought produce, only to have it confiscated when they were about to dinghy it out to their boat.

It began to seem like the rule was applied only when a given official's larder was low. Supporting this theory was the experience of a friend. The officials came aboard, took his veggies, and then wanted to confiscate all the meat in his freezer. He said, "Okay, you can take it, but

I'm going to soak it in diesel fuel first. If it's contaminated, that should fix it." For some reason the official lost interest, and my friend was allowed to keep his meat.

When we checked out of Belize at Punta Gorda, a testy Customs man told us we needed seven copies of a crew list, and told us that a secretary two doors down would fix us up for ten dollars. After visiting all officials, we were left with three unused copies. Since then I've always arrived to check out of Belize with seven copies of a crew list I generate on my computer. No port has ever used more than three.

Because of our recent experience checking out of Belize City, I now will go to almost any lengths to check out somewhere else. The process requires hiring a taxi. As directed, I went first to Customs and the Port Captain, then cabbed two or three miles to Immigration. There I was told I'd have to go back to Customs: "They forgot to stamp this."

"But it's not my fault. Can't you overlook it?" (No.) "Don't you find this ridiculous?" (Shrug.)

I managed to bargain my driver down a few dollars, but it still required going back to Customs for one and only one rubber stamp imprint. A further problem was it was getting on toward noon, when Immigration would close. I made it in time and was properly and thoroughly cleared out. I then told them I thought their inflexibility was unnecessary, and that the burden of solving the unstamped form problem should have been borne by Belize officialdom, not by a poor, downtrodden visitor to their country.

On our last visit to Venezuela, we arrived at Puerto la Cruz from Bonaire, and were told by our agent and friend Marisol, who for a reasonable fee will take care of all the unreasonable paperwork, that if we were only staying a few days we'd be better off not to bother to check in and out. The fees had gone up, each official was insisting on an on-board inspection, none of them would come on board with any other, and it just wasn't worth it. I'm paranoid when involved in this kind of thing, but took her advice. In a few days we completed our business and left.

I wasn't worried about our lack of paperwork when checking into the U.S. at St. Croix. In the past we'd always checked in with a simple phone call, so the absence of a *zarpe* from Venezuela shouldn't be a problem. Except that this time the dockside office was open, the official there.

"Clearance paper from your last port, please?"

As I hadn't ever checked into Venezuela, I still had my *zarpe* from Bonaire. The lady accepted it, glanced briefly at its official appearance, and fortunately didn't notice that it was dated a month ago. (Sailboats are slow, but not *that* slow.) I left, brow-moppingly relieved.

In Guatemala, our bus has been stopped twice and all the men ordered to get off. Uniformed men patted us down. The first time gringos were excepted. The second time we all were searched. I guess they were looking for guns. Whatever they were looking for they didn't find.

It takes a year of red tape to get a Guatemalan driver's license. A friend has been driving licenseless for months. He's been stopped several times, but says 20 Quetzales (U.S.$3.50) always solves the problem.

We have never offered a bribe, and I can count on the fingers of one hand the number of times we've had to pay *mordida*, most of which were in Mexico. Offering a bribe is dangerous indeed. If you're in trouble in a Central or South American country and you believe the only way out is with *mordida*, you may be tempted to try it. I'd say, don't. The consequences might get you off the grill and into the hot coals.

During our years on RED SHOES we've checked into 30 different countries, many of them repeatedly. We've seen fees rise and rules change. We try, usually successfully, to smile and shrug and accept it all as part of the deal. As I said earlier, most of my experiences with officials have been, if not pleasant, at least benign. Even the worst of them wouldn't constitute a sufficient reason to stay home.

Given our vast voyaging experience, here are a few suggestions for making official intercourse as good for you as it is for them. You might pass these ideas on to your S.O.

Frown. Be intense. Let them know you're ready to flare up at the slightest hint of a problem.

Make no effort to speak or understand their language. Talk English only. If they don't understand, speak louder. Banging your fist on the desk is good.

Get their respect by telling them who of their superiors you know, and how you won't hesitate to go over their heads if they give you a hard time. (You can get their superiors' names from the local paper.)

Let them know that you're from the U.S.A., a powerful state that makes their insignificant little dirt patch look like a sharecropper's nightmare. Point out that you pay their salaries through loans made either by the World Bank or the International Monetary Fund.

If you're of European descent, and if he or she happens to be of another race, or a woman, be sure he or she understands where you're coming from, white male supremacy-wise.

When all else fails, throw a couple of hundred dollar bills on the desk. If you can manage a sneer, now is the time.

Remember that this, too, shall pass, and that soon you'll be free to roam their country at will—whenever they get around to giving you back your freedom.

Happy voyaging.

CHAPTER 49

Recreation Aboard and Abroad

Dear Herb: What do you *do* all day at sea? Even in port, on days you don't go ashore, how do you occupy your time? I'm used to doing things like horseback riding, playing golf, and hiking. I need projects. Cooped up in such a small space, I can see myself going nuts. Help?

Worried Mate

Dear WM: It sounds to me like you're being a loyal partner and supporting your husband's dream. Admirable as this is, it's not enough. And I'm not talking about marital vows, I'm talking about you. If you see yourself as being deprived of your favorite pastimes, you'll end up being miserable. Wouldn't it be terrific if you could enjoy it too?

In port, or at anchor, there should be no problem being active. Swimming and snorkeling are recreational mainstays, with hiking a close second. The only time we were denied both was when we were cruising in the Amazon Delta in Brazil. Hiking was out, as all the land was dense, marshy jungle, and all local transport was in canoes. There simply weren't any paths. Swimming, because of anaconda snakes and piranhas, was a matter of a quick dip.

Keeping in shape during passages is a subject that gets too little editorial space. Except for running in place in the saloon, or doing jumping jacks on the foredeck, there're few opportunities for aerobic exercise. However, stretching and tensioning exercises are certainly possible. I've met several women who regularly do yoga aboard, at sea or in port. I know, the things you enjoy doing are kinetic, whereas yoga calls for stillness and contemplation. But you might consider trying it while you're cruising. Women who regularly practice it, though a bit skinny, have always looked pretty desirable to me.

I realize too that with riding, hiking, and golf, exercise is a by-product of the activity. Exercise for its own sake can be damn boring. Almost every treadmill, ski machine, or exercycle is sold with a TV. Joggers all have Walkmans. Enthusiasm for exercise as exercise is found mostly

322

Snorkeling in Hobbity Ongea. Erosion has made Ongean (Fiji) anchorages eerie and wondrous.

among professionals, and I find even theirs suspicious. So the only thing going for you is determination, which for most of us is a soon exhausted, non-renewable resource.

I'll bet you could be happy exercising your mind on passages, and being physical in port. Let's go with that assumption.

READING

When I'm on a reading binge, which I was during a recent two-week bout with pneumonia, I devour what I call distractive paperbacks—novels by the likes of Dick Francis, Michael Crichton, and Ed McBain—at the rate of one or two a day. I mean, who wants to lie around contemplating pneumonia?

Serious novels take longer, as I find myself slowing down, enjoying the turn of phrase, the twist of plot, the insightful development of characters. One, for example, that I just finished, is *A Thousand Acres* by Jane Smiley. The difference between reading this book and a distractive paperback is the difference between gulping and savoring. To be savored, a book must be worthy, and such books aren't all that common.

Of course there is reading for information, or to get the feel of a place or event. When we were contemplating transiting the Panama Canal and continuing west, I was fascinated by a book about the canal's history. I confess to preferring fiction, however, unless the subject of the non-fiction book is something I'm focussed on.

I don't know what people do who don't read.

WRITING

Whether you write articles for publication, a newsletter for family and friends, personal letters, or your journal, writing is an act that clarifies your thinking and distills experience. Writing is an exercise in leaving things out. Does anyone really care that I used floss this morning? That energy was down and flatulence up?

Aboard SEA FOAM, we asked each child to keep a journal. Absolute privacy was part of the deal, so if a son or a daughter felt that a parent or sibling was behaving like a jerk, it was okay to write it. Their journals not only allowed true expression, they acted as safety valves.

Just as lying to one's intimates erodes relationships, lying to one's self erodes character. A journal provides an arena for honesty, and patiently waits for its author to rise to the occasion.

The big thing to avoid in writing is the stylistic harumpf. I have a friend, a professor, whose conversational style is rough and ready, colorful when expressiveness needs color, and almost always acute, perceptive, and funny. But ask him for an opinion on a serious subject and his voice changes from conversational to pontifical. Podiumese. Harumpfic. Warrawarrawarra.

So how to avoid harumpf? Listen. And write daily and a lot, until you are no longer conscious of writing. Do not wear a writer's hat. Remember your childhood—did you have an imaginary companion? Think that. Have conversations: with your partner, parent, inner voice. Let them have real lines.

> Self: "When I spoke to him, he ignored me. Where does he get off, anyway?"
>
> Inner voice: "Maybe he had something other than you on his mind."
>
> Self: "Is that possible?"
>
> Inner voice: "Of course it's possible, you conceited ass."

The other advantage to having a conversation is that it allows you to deal with two sides of a question. Should a writer publish an article giving the location of a wonderful, secret anchorage, encouraging other cruisers to go there? Believe it or not, there are two sides to that and to almost every question, and the dialogue is a great way to explore both sides. After all, if the format was good enough for Socrates, who are we to disdain it?

Why don't I use it here? Well, I'm talking to you, aren't I?

If you write something that other people are going to read, you have certain responsibilities. Rumor and gossip, and in particular harmful or slanderous bits, are out. Opinions should be labeled as such. Funny but embarrassing scenes should be totally disguised. No one should be exploited, particularly not friends. Accuracy should be the goal. Exaggeration is okay if the goal is a different kind of truth, or if it's humor. (Actual truth: The wind was blowing 50 knots; Psychological truth: Hard enough to fanfold your eyelashes. . .)

If writing is the distillation of experience, then what is experience? In the sense we're speaking of, it's something that had meaning in your life. From the experience (which is a process) or set of related experiences came a conclusion. You say, "Too many inexperienced sailors are out cruising these days." You tell anecdotes to support this, and invent a Devil's Advocate to blast away at your cherished idea.

I recommend keeping a journal. If your inclination pushes you further, follow your curiosity.

GAMES

Nancy and I have experimented with gin, cribbage, Rummycube, Othello, and backgammon. Nancy beats me at every one, and refuses to play Scrabble, the only one at which I have a chance. Of the games we've tried, only backgammon had significant longevity. I taught Nancy the game, and before long we were keeping a cumulative score. After a year of my winning consistently it grew top heavy, and I gave her a birthday present of a clean slate. From that day forward she consistently beat me. After two or three years, during which I never again took the lead, for the sake of our relationship we gave up the game.

Nancy used to play a lot of solitaire games. Since acquiring a bridge game for the computer, however, she prefers that. Presently, from the beginning of cocktail hour till dinner, I play Tetris, a game in which different-shaped objects fall downwards on the screen. Using three keys, the player tries to pile the objects up without leaving any holes. I'm pretty good at it, but Nancy isn't, so I play and she watches.

A typical evening might be: During dinner Nancy reads, and I play bridge. After dinner I do the dishes, and Nancy takes over the bridge game, usually playing right up to bedtime.

A friend living ashore asked, "Don't you talk to each other?" I asked Nancy why we didn't converse during meals, and she said, "When you spend twenty-four hours a day together, 'How was your day, dear?' doesn't make much sense. If we have plans or decisions to make we do talk to each other, but it's usually after bridge."

PHOTOS

Nancy takes most of the pictures, but claims them all unless the fact that I took a certain one is incontrovertible (she's in it). Her photos illustrate all my articles, and will illustrate this book. We have two Olympus 35mm single-lens reflex cameras, one of which is automatic, the other manual; and one point-and-shoot Olympus which takes excellent pictures and on which we rely more and more.

At the risk of straying into the mystical, I contend that carrying a camera changes how you relate to the host country. There are cultures whose members truly believe that a photo takes something away from them. It obviously does, but what's debatable is whether or not it leaves the subject diminished. Certainly when you stride through a village snapping shots you are a taker. A picture taker? An image thief? "I'm going to take something of this place—demonstrably your property—home with me."

Where did we get the idea that we have the *right* to take pictures? Do we have the right to record conversations? Take fingerprints? Aren't we here on their sufferance?

However we feel about our right to photograph, having a camera hanging around our neck sets us apart. Without a camera we might have been thought of as a guest. Hospitality might have been forthcoming. But with a camera we're seen as tourists, as fair game. In some way we become visitors to the local zoo, they the zoo's inmates.

As a result of these purely speculative conclusions, we alternate. Sometimes we storm the bastions of privacy as photographers, and sometimes, camera-less, we visit as guests. And frankly, if we were solely recreational travelers and not in the business of writing and taking pictures, neither of us would ever carry a camera.

A picture should have a reason for being: a Mayan cemetery with its colorful, above-ground crypts; a flame tree in bloom; a dolphin coming to play. We give a lot of slide shows, and the slide or sequence of slides we show must inspire a story. Usually the story is an answer to "why we took this picture." At carnival in Trinidad we captured the winning costume; the sexiest dancers; the packed stadium. For Christmas in Hog Island we caught the flavor of participation—our dinghy loaded with the coconut husks, fuel for the barbecue.

Ideally I would like to experience a culture without the barrier of a camera, then come home to the boat and put my observations and feelings into words. Having done that, if I thought I'd captured something more than a journal entry, I'd go back and take the pictures that filled out the story. But it doesn't work out. We don't go back. And often it's a week or a month or even more before a story idea congeals. Looking at photos we've taken will put me more often than not on the track of a story.

For slide shows, or for telling a relative or friend about your trip, photos are a big help. But the act of taking them changes the experience, and everyone involved should be aware of this.

VIDEOS

I'm prejudiced. People pointing their camcorders at me or my surroundings irritate me profoundly. I'm even more irritated if I have to listen to the commentary of the taper. I can see faces frozen in boredom as the tape is played for relatives, the glazed, trapped eyes of desperation.

I know, because I've been there. A friend with whom we shared events made a video of Trinidad's carnival. From six hours of tapes, he and I discarded 4¾ hours. He made me a copy which I took home on a visit to my son, his wife, and their two children. We set aside an evening. Everyone perched or squatted in front of the TV. "We're going to see something of Nanna and Grandad's trip!" I sensed great expectations, which unfortunately soon turned to glazed eyes and frozen faces. At the end I realized that the full story should have run no more than a minute and a half.

They say that home is where they have to watch your videos. So when my son offered to buy me a camcorder with the condition that I send tapes home on a regular basis, I demurred. It would have been too much of an investment in disappointment.

We do have a VCR and a library of over 70 movies, which we swap with other VCR-equipped cruisers. We enjoy watching movies. Unfortunately our first VCR broke, and after a futile attempt to have it repaired, we bought a new one. Now the TV doesn't work, and I'm taking this as a karmic statement on the appropriateness of watching TV when you're supposedly having your Very Own Adventure.

Which reminds me of a typical scene aboard SEA FOAM. We were sailing to a perfect breeze through the magical islands of northern Tonga. Fluffy cloudsheep rambled lazily westward. The sky, unsullied by haze, was a rich, royal blue. Palm trees stood in protective ranks behind beaches of golden sand.

"Nancy, come on up here. It doesn't get any better than this."

After three such prompts of gradually increasing insistence, she stuck her head out of the companionway and looked around.

"Nice," she said. "I'm reading a terrific book." With that she disappeared below for the rest of the afternoon. After six years, even Paradise can be taken for granted.

MUSIC

We have a stereo tape player, and go through spells of using it constantly versus not using it at all. I have a Yamaha synthesizer (keyboard). From the time I got it for my 60th birthday, a gift from Nancy and the children, until we came to the Rio Dulce (about seven years), I used it about a dozen times. Since coming to the Rio a year and a half ago and teaming up with Bill Clark, a Southern California trumpet player, I've played more often, maybe a gig a month. About once a week I get it out and refresh my memory of tunes I used to play as a professional. Here on the river we're occasionally paid a fee. Usually we play for drinks and dinner. Sometimes with the drink-and-dinner gig comes a credit at that restaurant. If I didn't find it fun to play again I'd hang up my glove.

In 1974-5, in Russell, New Zealand, a small town on North Island with a population of maybe 5,000, I played four or five gigs. The band included a sax player, a guitarist, a drummer, and me. The drummer was the postmaster and the town's only barber. He was married to a Maori woman who'd borne him a dozen hungry mouths. This man worked so hard to keep his kids in shoes that he was always exhausted, sometimes falling asleep during the tune and requiring a nudge to get him to stop drumming, many measures after the ending. Three of the gigs paid ten dollars. One, for the Oysterman's Convention, paid all the oysters I could eat. Given the income-generating possibilities of performing in foreign countries, I'd have to list this under 'recreation'.

The best thing about playing was as an entry into local society. Normally yachties weren't invited into the homes of locals. Nancy and I were. As for playing here on the Rio Dulce, aside from the fun of making music, the greatest benefit is the friends we've made. But isn't that also the greatest benefit of cruising?

Any tale involving music has to include Christina and Brad, a couple who cruised Belize and the Rio Dulce in AVENTURA, their MacGregor 22. "And in my suitcase I shall put a guitar, a mandolin, and a trombone." Christina played guitar and sang. During one of my gigs at a waterfront restaurant called Hollymar's they sat in. When they left they gave us their address in Sarteneja, Northern Belize, saying, "Come visit."

Nearly a year later we decided to explore Chetumal Bay and remembered their invitation. Our welcome in Sarteneja could not have been warmer. Our friends lived in a tree house (very Mosquito Coastish) and entertained us there. We had a music evening that included Brad's employer, a talented amateur guitarist. Then Brad and Christina and a young guest, Jacob, joined us in AVENTURA to cruise the rest of the bay. We were three generations, no gaps.

Any shared interest might have brought us together. This time it happened to be music. We have friends who are avid mushroomers, and they are constantly running into soulmates. Remember the man in *Trustee from the Toolroom* by Nevil Shute? A model train enthusiast, he was always being helped along on his quest by fellow railroaders. A passionate hobby is a key admitting you to a world less accessible to others. I don't know much about horse people, but I'll bet they're everywhere. We've made friends simply by sailing with a cat. And in a gathering where all else fails, one has only to bring up computers. . .

NAVIGATION

So it's his thing, but you can take an interest, can't you? Learn to use the sextant, work out the problems? Nancy finds it most satisfying to mark our daily progress on the chart.

You're not interested in navigation? My only suggestion is that you take some opportunity to be a participant rather than a passenger. Do you go along with 'his' adventure, or do you make it your adventure, too? Why not learn all you can about sailing, how to best use the wind? Why not learn about weather, fronts, barometers? How about your getting a ham radio license? Your purpose, of course, is not to challenge, but to share.

COOKING

Nancy loves to cook, and after her first few queasy days she takes pleasure in providing gourmet meals at sea. Craig was our baker, keeping us supplied with cakes, biscuits, and bread. Not long after we cast off, Nancy began to keep notes, the beginnings of her cookbook. For her, the process has been at least as important as the product. Which is good, because 20 years later she's still at it.

FISHING

Our sons were the fishermen on our Pacific cruise. On RED SHOES I am. We trail a boat line at sea, and the few times we've hooked a fish I just pull it in, hand over hand. I'm in it for food, not sport. Some boats, however, use a rod and reel, and the fisher person actually plays the fish. (Unfortunately the added time in playing the fish increases the chance of a shark biting off half your prize.) We know several boats on which the woman does all the fishing.

SHELL COLLECTING

This obviously isn't an activity for a passage, but it can be an objective when you reach an anchorage. On our Pacific cruise, Nancy and Craig were shell collectors. Now we feel differently about killing the live animal merely to own its shell. Collecting dead shells is far less interesting, as good specimens are almost impossible to find. In our nearly nine years aboard RED SHOES, Nancy has kept three live shells. In our seven years aboard SEA FOAM we kept well over three hundred. Pillage, pure and simple. Our attitude then was, there are millions of shells, our small intrusion won't affect the balance. When we returned to the States and saw all the shells displayed in stores, however, we knew we'd been part of some serious exploitation.

Should one collect live shells? We abstain out of guilt for our previous excess. Very selective shell collecting shouldn't be taboo. We still hunt shells, and will often bring one up to the boat to inspect before returning it to the exact spot where we found it. Believe it or not, it's almost as satisfying. And if you're into nature photography, you can take a picture of your find.

How would you feel about a birder who insisted on displaying the stuffed carcasses of hundreds of rare specimens? And what's your position on butterflies?

SEWING

Nancy keeps a sewing machine on board, and we give as much space to material as we do to food. Well, almost. I complain, after which I usually get a new shirt. Nancy has saved us money by making all our courtesy flags. After not touching the sewing machine for six months, she recently completed a new sail cover, which was a big job, and is currently recovering our cockpit cushions. So I log these events and shut up about her fabric collection.

Needlepoint projects can keep some people amused for hours. Nancy worked on a crewel bell pull for years. Laurie, a friend, also worked for years on something called a Tifaefae, a bedspread made using appliqué. Nancy suggested a crochet project, but decided against knitting: "It's wool, and you usually have the work on your lap. You never see anyone

Nancy with hand crank sewing machine. *Sea Foam*'s spacious saloon provided plenty of room for Nancy to produce clothes.

knitting in the tropics." With any of these projects, one should set aside funds against a need for reading glasses.

When we commissioned RED SHOES, Nancy got several sizes of sketch pads, oil paints, water colors, pastels, and brushes. In nine years she's never touched them. At first this bothered me. As time went on, however, I realized that whether or not she ever used them, their presence exists as a possibility, and the comfort that this gives her is worth the space.

John Samson of ferro-cement boat fame insisted that people who cruise for protracted periods need a project. In the South Pacific in the 70's, he and his wife, Pat, were working on a cruising guide. As far as I know it was never published, but working on it fulfilled its own purpose. For most people a succession of visits to other countries becomes tiresome after a time. Samson's is a thought worthy of consideration.

WM, you asked what to do on a small boat, pointing out that what you'd miss most are the active sports you like. Because the opportunity for these on a passage are nil, I've used this space to suggest distractions. But don't lose heart. Bear in mind that reaching anchorage will once more open up opportunities for aerobic endeavors.

Are you reassured at least a little? I hope so.

CHAPTER **50**

Cruising Then, Now, and Tomorrow

Dear Herb: Because your cruising covers over two decades, I'd like your thoughts on how it has changed, and the direction in which you think it's headed. Write philosophically, if you must.

Seeker Of Truth

Dear SOT: I Kant. You've thrown me a ball with too much Spinoza on it. Just for fun, however, imagine a philosophical cruise that sends Alfred north. Buoyed up by the existential ideas of the French conservative, Sartre the Tory, Alfred dinghies ashore in search of the meditative balm of the wind Russelling in the Socratrees. He uses his oars like a Greek god (see Thor row.) His crew is his old Jewish buddy, Sid Arthur.

Frankly, the answer to your question is no secret. At the risk of putting Descartes before the horse, one might say "I cruise, therefore I am." In fact, the truth is the reverse: who I am determines how I cruise. We change as we learn, however, and technology is one of our many teachers. So let's take a look at where ocean cruising is coming from, where it is now, and where it might be going in the future.

All who are familiar with Joshua Slocum's voyaging admire the man, his spirit, his persistence, and his endurance. I don't know anyone who wants to model their cruising style on his. Dodge Morgan single-handed around the world in a million dollar custom yacht built by the Hood yard in Marblehead, Massachusetts, expressly for Morgan's circumnavigation. Redundancy was carried to an extreme only a wealthy man could afford, and much of the space of his 60-foot yacht was given to backups. AMERICAN PROMISE was a special purpose yacht that served Morgan well, but soon after his circumnavigation he gave it to the U.S. Naval Academy. I don't know anyone who wants to model their cruising style on that, either.

Among present day voyagers, Lin and Larry Pardey best represent the concept of 'sail simple'. They began that way in SERAFFYN because they had little money. Except for the fact that we had a marine engine and a marine toilet, Nancy and I voyaged equally simply during the seven years we cruised in SEA FOAM. The Pardeys, however, with funds no longer a primary concern, continue in their second boat, TALEISIN, to sail simple, whereas Nancy and I have put aboard RED SHOES all the modern aids and conveniences we could sensibly afford. To the degree that our plans are governed by this stuff, we are in bondage. I tell myself that we are still self-sufficient, but that must be qualified to 'reasonably' self-sufficient. In fact, I can think of two instances where our cruising plans were amended because one or another 'essential' item was not working. The great majority of North American and European cruisers equip their boats as we have. Modern devices have a way of insinuating themselves into our lives. Lin Pardey is an exceptional woman in that she embraces the idea of cruising simply, but many women would never have been tempted to try cruising in the first place, had it not been for propane stoves, refrigeration, and flush toilets. "You mean I have to do it in a bucket? You gotta be kidding."

But before women rise up and shout, "Don't blame us, you Macho Conceited Poop," let's include us men lusting for GPS, radar, electronic charts, interfacing, computers aboard, weatherfax machines, and fancy radios. Both sexes are caught up in the possibilities (enjoyment seasoned with frustration) of advancing technology.

In my opinion, we are right to be wary of techno-slavery. But think about it: we're all in bondage to essentials. What's fascinating is how quickly an item can slide from the 'extra' to the 'essential' column. The fact is, a truly essential item is one that will cripple you if you don't have it. Let's see, are proper charts essential? We on one occasion proceeded without them. On a cutter or sloop, is a torn mainsail essential? We've lowered ours because it was torn, and sailed on. Is an engine essential? We sailed hundreds of miles with a non-functioning transmission. Is a marine toilet essential? We have, on occasion, gone the bucket route until I was able to fix or rebuild the head.

Is a rudder essential? Ha! How about a mast? The other concept of essentiality is, "I won't leave port without it." I took that position with our malfunctioning SSB radio when we were trying to leave for Brazil. It was hurricane season and I wanted to have weather information, even though on SEA FOAM we sailed 50,000 Pacific Ocean miles without it. I took the same position when our wind generator was damaged and I refused to set out across the Pacific until it was repaired. Aboard RED SHOES we have many things that depend on the electrical system. In an emergency, running lights are the only items that are truly essential. All others are necessary only because we've become used to and attached to them.

In my book *Blown Away*, I devoted a whole chapter to folks who cruised with toys that ruled their cruising lives, and now I'm one of them.

I can talk with authority out of both sides of my face. Given the fact that accessories taint the very fundamental precepts—the search for basics, the Thoreauvian concept—that attracted so many cruisers in times past, does this corrupt the cruising experience?

Yes.

And no.

Yes, accessories do corrupt the experience in that at least some of your life in port will be spent fixing or maintaining them. And those you can't fix yourself will have to be sent somewhere other than where you are to be repaired. If the device breaks in a remote anchorage, you'll have to do without it till you get to a port. There you can send for parts, or send the item back to the manufacturer, or to the closest service center. Do you have to wait there for the parts? Not if you don't want to—you can have them sent on to the next port, or the next, where you pick them up at your convenience. This, however, will probably involve paying duty on the received items, even though they're being returned to you.

We've pointed out that today's cruisers are opting for larger and larger yachts, with a corresponding increase in and dependence on electrically or hydraulically powered gear. I feel strongly that beginning cruisers should be aware of this when they choose a boat. It's one thing to limp into a Caribbean port to deal with importing parts and effecting repairs. It'd be a different scene in the Red Sea. You need to consider carefully where you are going to cruise, and pay careful attention to the degree of self-sufficiency you can accomplish.

I'm reminded of a friend in an Island Packet who insisted on having his radar working. He was in Georgetown, the Exumas, in the Bahamas, where the charges that the government heaps on imported parts and/or repaired gear are unconscionable. My friend was wealthy, but even he winced as the grand total crept toward two thousand dollars. The moral? If your radar malfunctions in the Bahamas, do without! Ninety percent of the 300 boats there never had it in the first place. The problem, of course, is that you have this piece of gear, it cost a lot of money to put it aboard, and it should work! In the case of my friend with the malfunctioning radar, however, it would have been cheaper for him to fly home and have a chat with his analyst.

On the subject of modern equipment, one final thought: dependency begets anxiety. Each increase in self-sufficiency dispels anxiety and creates confidence. Cruisers who intend to have all the modern stuff aboard would do well to test themselves: we will make this leg, this passage, without using 'X'. It could be a game, and a most valuable one for peace of mind. I'm forever grateful for our seven years aboard basically equipped SEA FOAM. They made us appreciate tenfold the wonderful aids and, yes, luxuries we've been able to have aboard RED SHOES. Better yet, they remind us that we can do without them and still enjoy our cruise.

Besides the proliferation of sophisticated gear, the other big change is in the growing number of people who are world cruising. A friend just wrote me that in 1996, the number of cruising yachts in the Marquesas at the same time reached three hundred. When we were there in 1973, the total number of visiting yachts was less than two dozen.

The change this brings to the cruising experience is marked and fundamental. Put yourself in a Marquesan's shoes (a figure of speech—they rarely wear them). Twenty years ago, in many anchorages in French Polynesia, a visitor was a rare event, and one to be celebrated. The paradigmatic welcome involved canoes, often paddled by beautiful, topless, island women, coming alongside laden with gifts of fruit. It was as much fun for the Marquesans to break their routine with a welcoming party as it was for the visiting crewmembers.

But now, our barefoot islander looks up and sees another dozen yachts sail into the anchorage, and he shrugs. No longer a novelty, yachts provoke at best a ho-hum reaction, perhaps an acquisitive one (sell them something), or even a more antagonistic "Oh no, not another one." The once quiet lagoon thrums with auxilliary engines charging batteries, with generators rumbling, with outboard-powered dinghies snarling as cruisers race around arranging inter-yacht cocktail parties. Yachts are no longer individual, but are considered by locals as a group, much like a tour bus.

From the unusual to the commonplace to the intrusive, pure numbers have made a tremendous difference in the way yachts are received in over-run locations. I remember people saying to us in the 70's, "You should have seen Papeete 20 years ago, it was much better then." We couldn't turn back the clock, but what it used to be in the past didn't spoil our visit. Sure, we received an extravagant welcome when we were the first yacht to visit an island in months or years, and we also found it deflating to be visitor number 371 and be greeted with yawns or, worse yet, sighs. But we could still find remote places that yachts seldom visited. We could have all to ourselves an azure anchorage off a golden beach. Because these experiences were not always easy to come by, they were more to be treasured.

The future? Without a war, or a plague, or a world-wide economic disaster, the number of people out cruising is going to continue to increase. Longing for things to be as they were will only lead to disappointment.

The most satisfied cruisers we've met are those who don't insist on their experiences living up to their expectations, but who instead are open minded, who enjoy what's there and are creative in seeking their own adventures.

People are constantly reinventing cruising. For those who are setting out for the first time, all will be new. We wish you in particular the courage to explore or not, to load up with accessories or not, and to design your own cruising life style or adopt someone else's. But as you agonize over your choices, remember what it comes down to in the end—a set of sails drawing well, a destination that stirs your imagination, and a fullness of spirit that comes from living your dream.

Red Shoes sailing under cruising spinnaker.

BIBLIOGRAPHY

Adler, Mike. *The Box Book*. Kenyon Inc., Clinton, CT.

Ashley, Clifford W. *Ashley Book of Knots*. Doubleday, New York, NY. 1944.

Beilan, Michael H., M.D. *Your Offshore Doctor, 2nd edition*. Sheridan House, Dobbs Ferry, NY. 1996.

Berkow, Robert, M.D., ed. *Merck Manual, 15th edition*. Merck Publishing Group, NJ. 1992.

Bowditch, Nathaniel. *Bowditch American Practical Navigator*. U.S. Navy Hydrographic Office, Washington, D.C. 1968.

Calder, Nigel. *Boatowner's Mechanical and Electrical Manual*. International Marine, Camden, ME. 1990.

Calder, Nigel. *Marine Diesel Engines: Maintenance, Troubleshooting and Repair, 2nd edition*. International Marine, Camden, ME. 1991.

Calder, Nigel. *Refrigeration for Pleasure Boats*. International Marine, Camden, ME. 1991.

Coles, K. Adlard. *Heavy Weather Sailing*. Adlard Coles Nautical, London, and International Marine, Camden, ME. 1992.

Dana, Richard Henry. *Two Years Before the Mast*. New American Library, New York, NY. 1964.

Darwin, Charles. *Voyage of the Beagle*. Doubleday, New York, NY. 1962.

Eastman, Peter F., M.D. *Advanced First Aid Afloat, 4th edition*. Cornell Maritime Press, Centreville, MD. 1995.

Heyerdahl, Thor. *Fatu Hiva*. Buccaneer Books, Cuthogue, N.Y.

Heyerdahl, Thor. *Kon Tiki*. Pocket Books, New York, NY. 1950.

Hiscock, Eric. *Cruising Under Sail*. Adlard Coles Nautical, London, and International Marine, Camden, ME. 1985.

Hitz-Holman, Betsy. *Sitting Duck*. Seven Seas Press, Newport, RI. 1983.

Howard, Jim. *Handbook of Offshore Cruising*. Sheridan House, Dobbs Ferry, NY. 1994.

Huck, Michael V., Jr. *Lightning and Boats: A Manual of Safety and Prevention*. Seaworth Publications, Brookfield, WI. 1993.

Hydrographer of the Navy. *Ocean Passages for the World*. British Admiralty, Hydrographic Office, Somerset, England

Jerome, Jerome K. *Three Men in a Boat*. Bristol and London 1889.

Keenan, J.J. *Breaking Out of Beginner's Spanish*. University of Texas Press, Austin, TX.

Kollman, R.R. *Do-It-Yourself Boat Refrigeration*. Kollman Marine, Ft. Lauderdale, FL.

Maloney, Elbert S. *Chapman's Piloting, 61st edition*. Hearst Marine, New York, NY. 1993.

Mason, Charles, ed. *The Best of SAIL Trim*. Adlard Coles Nautical, London, and Sheridan House, Dobbs Ferry, NY. 1975.

Michener, James. *Caribbean*. Ballantine, New York, NY. 1989.

Mowat, Farley. *The Boat Who Wouldn't Float*. Doubleday, New York, NY. 1970.

Nordhoff, Charles. *Mutiny on the Bounty*. Little, Brown and Company, Boston, MA. 1940.

Pardey, Lin and Larry. *Storm Tactics Handbook: Modern Methods of Heaving-To for Survival in Extreme Conditions*. Paradise Cay Publications, Middletown, CA. 1995.

Payson, Herb. *Blown Away*. Sheridan House, Dobbs Ferry, NY. 1995.

Payson, Herb. *You Can't Blow Home Again*. Hearst Marine, NY. 1984.

Porter, Eliot, photographer, Eisley, Loren, text, and Brower, Kenneth, ed. *Galápagos, The Flow of Wilderness*. Sierra Club. San Francisco, CA. 1967.

Smead, David and Ishihara, Ruth. *Living on 12 Volts with Ample Power*. Rides Pub. Co. Seattle, WA. 1990.

Staton-Bevan, Tony. *Osmosis and Glassfibre Yacht Construction, 2nd edition*. Adlard Coles Nautical, London, and Sheridan House, NY. 1995.

Textor, Ken, ed. *The New Book of SAIL Trim*. Sheridan House, NY. 1995.

Toss, Brion. *Chapman's Knots*. Hearst Marine, New York, NY. 1990.

Van Loan, Derek. *The Chinese Sailing Rig: Designing and Building Your Own*. Paradise Cay Publications, Middletown, CA. 1993.

Van Sant, Bruce. *The Gentleman's Guide to Passages South, 5th edition*. Cruisers Guide Publications. Clearwater, FL. 1995.

Webb, Barbara and Manton, Michael. *The Yachtsman's Ten Language Dictionary*. Adlard Coles Nautical, London, and Sheridan House, Dobbs Ferry, NY. 1995.

Werner, David. *Where There Is No Doctor*. The Hesperian Foundation, Palo Alto, CA.

Index

More Books for the Cruising Sailor

Handbook of Offshore Cruising
by Jim Howard

". . . addresses an incredible number of the most important and basic issues. . . . One of the most thorough primers to come along in quite some time." *Cruising World*

Safety Preparations for Cruising
by Jeremy R. Hood

A book that comprehensively covers the safety aspects of every facet of cruising. Topics include the structural integrity of the vessel and its potential for breakdowns, basic skills, dangerous situations and more.

The Great Cruising Cookbook
by John C. Payne

Over 350 recipes collected from the author's travels around the world. Special attention is given to the unique needs of cruising sailors, including rough weather foods, worldwide provisioning and a professional approach to galley equipment.

Tamata and the Alliance
Bernard Moitessier
Translated by William Rodarmor

Moitessier became famous for his daring sailing exploits, often done solo. This fascinating memoir spans the time from Moitessier's magic childhood in Indochina to the months before his death in June 1994. A memorable story of an exciting life.

Blown Away
by Herb Payson

Herb and Nancy Payson and their large brood of teenage children cruise the Pacific for six and a half years. "A realistic portrait of an adventurous, enterprising family, with enough sailing lore to satisfy most bluewater buffs." *Publishers Weekly*

By Way of the Wind
by Jim Moore

The adventure begins when Jim Moore announces to his bride of two months that they will build a boat and sail to the South Pacific. "The best sailboat cruising book to come out in a long time." *Washington Post*

Sheridan House
America's Favorite Sailing Books